# How to Do Christian Ethics

# How to Do Christian Ethics

*Living the Grammar of Christian Life Every Day*

## Brian Brock, Nadine Hamilton, and Daniel R. Patterson

LONDON • NEW YORK • OXFORD • NEW DELHI • SYDNEY

T&T CLARK

Bloomsbury Publishing Plc, 50 Bedford Square, London, WC1B 3DP, UK
Bloomsbury Publishing Inc, 1385 Broadway, New York, NY 10018, USA
Bloomsbury Publishing Ireland, 29 Earlsfort Terrace, Dublin 2, D02 AY28, Ireland

BLOOMSBURY, T&T CLARK and the T&T Clark logo are trademarks of Bloomsbury Publishing Plc

First published in Great Britain in 2025 by T&T Clark

Copyright © Brian Brock, Nadine Hamilton, and Daniel R. Patterson, 2025

Brian Brock, Nadine Hamilton, and Daniel R. Patterson have asserted their right under the Copyright, Designs and Patents Act, 1988, to be identified as Editor of this work.

For legal purposes the Acknowledgments on p. vii constitute an extension of this copyright page.

Cover design: Gita Kowlessur
Cover Image: Blue Galatea (For Fear of the Ox) © Clive Head

All rights reserved. No part of this publication may be: i) reproduced or transmitted in any form, electronic or mechanical, including photocopying, recording or by means of any information storage or retrieval system without prior permission in writing from the publishers; or ii) used or reproduced in any way for the training, development or operation of artificial intelligence (AI) technologies, including generative AI technologies. The rights holders expressly reserve this publication from the text and data mining exception as per Article 4(3) of the Digital Single Market Directive (EU) 2019/790.

Bloomsbury Publishing Plc does not have any control over, or responsibility for, any third-party websites referred to or in this book. All internet addresses given in this book were correct at the time of going to press. The author and publisher regret any inconvenience caused if addresses have changed or sites have ceased to exist, but can accept no responsibility for any such changes.

A catalogue record for this book is available from the British Library.
Library of Congress Cataloging-in-Publication Data
Names: Brock, Brian, 1970- editor. | Hamilton, Nadine, editor. | Patterson, Daniel R., editor.
Title: How to do Christian ethics : living the grammar of Christian life every day / Brian Brock, Nadine Hamilton, and Daniel R. Patterson.
Description: London : T&T Clark, 2025. | Includes bibliographical references and index. | Summary: "Discover how pressing contemporary moral issues can be approached and discussed in a distinct and coherently theological fashion. This book displays a more direct approach that has the distinct advantage of being approachable, dramatic, and contemporary. Each chapter approaches its subject matter by demonstrating how the sources of Christian moral reasoning-Scripture and church doctrine-can be imaginatively brought to bear on contemporary moral perplexities. This mode of teaching shows in tangible ways how the Christian gospel does in fact reveal our moral world in clear and penetrating ways"- Provided by publisher.
Identifiers: LCCN 2024052154 (print) | LCCN 2024052155 (ebook) | ISBN 9780567717504 (paperback) | ISBN 9780567717511 (hardback) | ISBN 9780567717528 (epub) | ISBN 9780567717535 (ebook)
Subjects: LCSH: Christian ethics.
Classification: LCC BJ1251 .H79 2025 (print) | LCC BJ1251 (ebook) | DDC 241--dc23/eng/20250213
LC record available at https://lccn.loc.gov/2024052154
LC ebook record available at https://lccn.loc.gov/2024052155

ISBN HB: 978-0-5677-1751-1
PB: 978-0-5677-1750-4
ePDF: 978-0-5677-1753-5
ePUB: 978-0-5677-1752-8

Typeset by Deanta Global Publishing Services, Chennai, India
Printed and bound in Great Britain

For product safety related questions contact productsafety@bloomsbury.com.

To find out more about our authors and books visit www.bloomsbury.com and sign up for our newsletters.

# CONTENTS

*Acknowledgments* vii
*List of Contributors* viii

Introduction  *Brian Brock, Nadine Hamilton, and Daniel R. Patterson*  1

1  Christ, Culpability, and Social Deprivation  *Michael Banner*  13

2  Garbage: An Invitation to Face Our Creaturely State  *Brian Brock*  33

3  In Our Image and Likeness: Theological Ethics and Artificial Intelligence  *Ad de Bruijne*  57

4  The Trunk of the Cross Is the Tree of Life: The Frailty of the Risen Christ and Theology of Disability  *Nadine Hamilton*  75

5  Who Cares? A Response of Christian Ethics to Shortages of Care  *Stefan Heuser*  99

6  The Spirit and Surveillance: Examining Forms of Knowledge, Power, and Discernment in the Church  *Emily Beth Hill*  119

7  "What Will We Eat?" Or "What We Will Drink?": Meat Consumption and the Messianic Contours of "The Peaceable Kingdom"  *Marco Hofheinz*  141

8  The Politics of Truth-Telling in the "Post-Truth" Age of "Fake News" *Michael R. Laffin* 165

9  Cancel Culture: Mobilizing Christian Ethics at the Scene of Judgment *Daniel R. Patterson* 185

10  Family as Mystery: Theological Ethics beyond Polarization *Petruschka Schaafsma* 207

11  The Grammar of Christian Ethics in Human Rights *Christine Schliesser* 227

12  Preserved in God's History: On the Ethics of Dying with Some Regard to the Discussion about Assisted Suicide *Hans G. Ulrich* 245

13  What Belongs to Whom? Property and Sustainability in Theological Light *Cornelis van der Kooi* 263

14  Stress or Vocation: Ethics and/in Work *Edward van 't Slot* 283

15  The "Risk of Faith" and the Desire for Safety in a Security Society *Pieter Vos* 301

*Index* 317

# ACKNOWLEDGMENTS

This volume has been under construction for well over a decade, not for a lack of commitment among the contributors nor our commitment to the vision of the project as a whole. The editorial board and contributors are therefore collectively grateful to see this book finally come to print.

The current makeup of the editorial board looks very different to the original instigators of the project. Of particular note, Bernd Wannenwetsch was instrumental in providing overall shape to the project, while Michael Laffin kept the project on track for some years, editing some essays and communicating with prospective contributors. We remain grateful that Michael has given us permission to keep his wonderful essay on the nature of truth in a "post-truth" social context in the volume. For their respective contributions, and that of many others, we remain genuinely grateful.

Finally, we would like to thank Anna Turton and her team at T&T Clark Bloomsbury for seeing the potential of this volume and being flexible and demonstrating unending patience as we sought to get this project over the finish line.

Brian Brock, Nadine Hamilton, and Daniel R. Patterson

# CONTRIBUTORS

**Michael Banner** is Dean and Fellow at Trinity College, University of Cambridge, UK. He has extensive experience at the intersection of ethics and policymaking. His publications include *Britain's Slavery Debt: Reparations Now!* (2024) and *The Ethics of Everyday Life* (2014).

**Brian Brock** is Professor of Moral and Practical Theology at the University of Aberdeen, UK. He has published widely on scripture in Christian ethics, technology, and theology of disability. A selection of his publications includes *Wondrously Wounded* (2020), *Christian Ethics in a Technological Age* (2010), and *Singing the Ethos of God* (2007).

**Ad de Bruijne** is Professor of Ethics and Spirituality at the Theological University in Utrecht, the Netherlands. He has published a range of articles and chapters in the areas of public theology, gender and sexuality, and hermeneutics. He is the author of *Verbonden voor het leven* (2022).

**Nadine Hamilton** is Assistant Professor of Systematic Theology/Dogmatics at Friedrich-Alexander University Erlangen-Nurnberg, Germany. She is co-editor of *Bonhoeffer and Christology* (2024) and has published articles on the theology of Dietrich Bonhoeffer, Christology, the problem of evil, suffering, and the significance of scripture for Christian faith.

**Stefan Heuser** is Professor for Systematic Theology/Ethics and Head of the Institute of Protestant Theology and Religious Education at the Technical University, Braunschweig, Germany. He has published on social, political, medical, technical, and educational ethics. His publications include the forthcoming volumes: "How Metaphors

Shape Biotechnology" (2024, edited together with Stefan Dübel), "Von der Krise zur Kritik" (2024, edited together with Marco Hofheinz) and "Zusammenwirken von natürlicher und künstlicher Intelligenz" (2024, edited together with Otto Richter).

**Emily Beth Hill** is Assistant Director of Theological Formation at InterVarsity Christian Fellowship, USA. Her research interests include economics, surveillance, and the impact of cultural systems on worship in the church. She recently published *Marketing and Christian Proclamation in Theological Perspective* (2021).

**Marco Hofheinz** is Professor of Systematic Theology/Ethics at Leibniz University, Hannover, Germany. His primary research areas are political ethics, especially peace ethics, biomedical ethics, and the history of ethics in Reformed Protestantism. His publications include *Die Kunst des Zusammenlebens* (2022) and *Christus Peregrinus* (2022).

**Michael Richard Laffin** is an independent scholar from the United States. He is the author of *The Promise of Martin Luther's Political Theology* (2016) and has published articles relating to the themes of freedom, agency, and conscience.

**Daniel R. Patterson** is Dean of Theology and Lecturer in Systematic Theology at Saint Trivelius Institute in Sofia, Bulgaria, and Adjunct Lecturer at Sheridan Institute of Higher Education in Perth, Australia. His main area of research is at the intersection of gender theory and theology. His publications include *Reforming a Theology of Gender* (2022).

**Petruschka Schaafsma** is Professor of Theological Ethics at the Protestant Theological University, the Netherlands. Her recent research focuses on the meaning of family, givenness, and dependence as mystery (*Family and Christian Ethics*, 2023). She is project leader of the Moral Compass Project (*The Transcendent Character of the Good*, 2022).

**Christine Schliesser** is Senior Lecturer in Systematic Theology at Zurich University; Director of Studies at the "Center for Faith & Culture" at Fribourg University, Switzerland; and Research Fellow at Stellenbosch University, South Africa. She has published widely on the theology and ethics of Dietrich Bonhoeffer, Public Theology, and peace and reconciliation. She is co-editor of the book series *Religion Matters* (2023) and author of *On the Significance of Religion for the SDGs* (2023).

**Hans G. Ulrich** is Professor Emeritus at Fachbereich Theologie Universität, Erlangen, Germany. His publications include *Transfigured Not Conformed: Christian Ethics in a Hermeneutic Key* (2022) and *Wie Geschöpfe leben: Konturen evangelischer Ethik* (2005).

**Cornelis van der Kooi** is Professor Emeritus of Systematic Theology at Vrije Universiteit Amsterdam, the Netherlands and Distinguished Lecturer at EETI/Erasmus University Rotterdam, the Netherlands. He is co-editor of *Theology, Morality and Adam Smith* (2022) and is the author of *This Incredibly Benevolent Force* (2018).

**Edward van 't Slot** is Professor of Spiritual and Vocational Formation, Protestant Theological University, the Netherlands. His publications include *Zondig dapper: Bonhoeffer over christelijk handelen* (2019) and *Negativism of Revelation? Bonhoeffer and Barth on Faith and Actualism* (2015).

**Pieter Vos** is Professor of Ethics and Military Chaplaincy Studies at Protestant Theological University, Utrecht, the Netherlands, and director of the International Reformed Theological Institute. He is author of *Longing for the Good Life: Virtue Ethics after Protestantism* (2020) and co-editor of *The Law of God: Exploring God and Civilization* (2014), *Liturgy and Ethics: New Contributions from Reformed Perspectives* (2018), and *The Calling of the Church in Times of Polarization* (2023).

# Introduction

## *Brian Brock, Nadine Hamilton, and Daniel R. Patterson*

*Happy are those whose way is blameless
who walk in the law of the Lord.*
PSALM 119:1[1]

## A New Way

There are some in the field often called "religious ethics" who have wondered aloud in recent years about whether the discipline has reached its end. As an academic field, there may be something to this judgment. When we pick up older Christian ethics volumes, they often seem dated, quaint even, and bearing the marks of sedimented tradition. Against this backdrop, this book gathers a group of theologians who still believe the Christian gospel has the power to reveal new and ethically productive ways of living in our ever-changing contemporary world, and in a way that we believe will both stand the test of time and be accessible to those just entering the field for the first time.

One of the main reasons the field of Christian ethics often feels so dated is that many of its practitioners place great emphasis on learning ethical theories. While the authors of this volume all agree that learning those theories has great value in offering distinctions

---

[1] NRSV (Updated Edition).

and viewpoints that are important for thinking well about ethical questions, we also agree that teaching theories is a disastrous place to begin with those who are new to the field. Rather, the central strategy of this volume is to dive right in, that is, to simply model what it looks like to do Christian ethics in a manner that invites readers to begin to try on the moves and ideas on offer. Just as an apprentice plumber learns their craft on the work site, so too does the Christian ethicist learn the craft one question, and one investigation at a time.

The chapters in this volume should be understood as one such worksite. By entering it with attentive ears and eyes, the ethics student will be inducted into a widely untapped, yet historically vibrant and rich, ethical tradition that, in some broad sense, all the authors of this volume share. While it may be tempting to plunder single essays for the ethical resources and conclusions they propose, the volume is not intended for that kind of use. It is intended instead to be explored as a single conversation, one that is most fruitfully entered by being studied as a lively to-and-fro as these master-workers explore what the Christian faith means in specific domains of contemporary life. They are therefore best studied together to grasp the continuities between approaches. This amounts to learning ethics *on the way*, as in fact we always do. This is the distinctive mode of reasoning this book is attempting to teach. We can never step out of the lives we are already living to learn the thing called Christian ethics.

These chapters therefore present a sustained and rigorous intellectual training exercise in the grammar of Christian moral reasoning, not as training in a set of conceptual ideas or tools—we do not offer information or theory. We aim instead to help readers become proficient in its ways—its ways of reasoning and the paths of living that are intrinsically associated with it.

## An Old Way

This approach to ethical inquiry, which is relatively unknown in English-speaking contexts, is rooted in Protestant Christian thought from continental Europe, particularly Germany and Holland. Only recently has this tradition begun to influence Christian ethics further afield spurred on in part by the surge in interest specifically in the theological and philosophical writings and life of Dietrich Bonhoeffer, but also of people like Martin Luther, Søren Kierkegaard, Hannah Arendt, Jacques Ellul, and Walter Benjamin. These figures, among others, form a shared "canon" allowing access to the intergenerational conversation with scripture and Church dogmatic tradition that is Christian theology. Theological thinking has from the beginning asked about how Christians should live and engage in a range of pressing ethical matters. The authors of this volume will often reference this historical tradition as a way of finding their bearings in relation to scripture, the long-held claims of Christian faith, and the moral priorities often in view among Christians of different eras who faced very different moral problems.

This volume is an offering to the global church out of a local context. We are all too aware that in a globalizing world, amid an increasingly diversifying Christianity, some of the most vibrant expressions of faith and rapidly growing churches are often found outside the English-speaking West. We take that as good news. But we also believe that it would be premature to write off the "old world," where Christianity was so influential over a whole cultural space, as having run its course, having spent its energies, and declining into tired old age. In many respects this is true, a reality that leads many to despair. The group of thinkers who have contributed to this volume, for the most part, work at the margin of the European theological establishment, but still firmly believe that the wisdom gathered among European Christians can still contribute something important—however minor—to the thinking of an increasingly global ecumenical church. This book is the first attempt to present European theologians as contextual thinkers, and as such, is an invitation to learn well from Christians thinking about their local context. It therefore serves to provoke Christians in other parts of the world to share their own ways of drawing on the deposit of faith in their own local contexts, with the pressing ethical questions and demands that face them, which are very likely to resonate with Christians in other parts of the world.

One of the central shared beliefs of the authors of this volume is a conviction that the Christian gospel reveals our moral world in clear and penetrating ways. While this might seem like a rather obvious claim, a superficial survey of many forms of Christian ethics will quickly reveal a real hesitancy about this power of the gospel. One is far more likely to find arguments that end with enjoining readers to act prudently, develop their virtues, or perhaps, alternatively, offer a ringing proposal that Christians can only hold a single position in a moral debate. The picture begins to look a bit different among ethicists who genuinely believe Christian ethics concerns living out the belief that the gospel is God's power for salvation (Rom. 1:16). Living confidently in this truth has dramatic implications for our heavenly future, of course, but this final end is often assumed to have limited ethical import for the issues we confront in our daily lives. The authors of this volume, in contrast, are united in the affirmation that the gospel is God's power for salvation, and that this affirmation has equally dramatic implications for the present as the future. This is a gospel that matters for Christians who desire to learn how to walk in the way of the Lord today. The goal of this volume is to display how the distinct light of the gospel of Jesus Christ, as savior and judge of all things, markedly repositions the moral life of contemporary Christians in fresh and exciting ways—ways to be learned and handed on to others.

Another notable feature of this ethical tradition is an interest in seriously reckoning with the ways that power shapes the context of action. The authors of this volume share the sensibility that becoming attuned to power dynamics is, in important respects, more significant and primary than the analytic impulse to "get concepts straight." As post-Christian power centers and cultural influencers have grown in cultural power, experienced as they are through a ubiquitous kaleidoscope of rapidly changing technologies and evolving social structures, many Christians and church congregations have been left in a state of confusion about how to speak about individual moral matters. It is important to note this disorientation, first as a reminder that the essence of Christian life is not to change the world, but to witness to the good news of Jesus Christ. An important part of witnessing, we contend, is to begin to grasp the distinctive inner logic of Christian thought that has been handed down through the centuries to help us reflect on such problems. Christian ethics can only be fruitfully constructive and exhortative after having been shaken by these forces, a salutary shock that is also a useful reminder of the importance of critically analyzing the ideological context of Christian witness and the power dynamics that are at play shaping the field in which any Christian witness must take place.

Cultural critique plays a foregrounded role in this Christian ethical tradition, expressing a profound frustration and disillusionment with the contemporary church's ability to recognize and address endemic structural sins and social evils in our world. Many Christians today are reeling from the sexual scandals, abuses of power, and blatant hypocrisy that they see in well-known and previously respected Christian leaders and organizations. One of the advantages of seeing investigations of church history as part of Christian ethics is the realism it injects into our theological procedure.

European history over the past 500 years has seen regular debasements of the Christian gospel by Christians, while at the same time being a tradition which seems to have regularly funded prophetic voices who bore witness to the truth, sometimes under the most personally taxing circumstances. Think of Martin Luther in the sixteenth century who observed abuses within the Catholic Church; or Søren Kierkegaard in the nineteenth century who railed against a Christianity coopted for political or social ends, being driven by media cultures and accommodationist cultural elites. Consider the more recent, well-known, and multiple-claimed life of Dietrich Bonhoeffer, who (along with some of his teachers, most famously, Karl Barth) watched aghast as Christians and church leaders stood silent or were complicit in Hitler's evil policy that led to the Second World War and the Shoah. Each of these figures was forced to discern what they should do in a context that was fundamentally deformed by the powerful cultural forces at work, the context in which Christian deliberation was to be done. Working out one's place in the world was of first importance. Despite living in vastly different political and religious contexts, the task before Luther, Kierkegaard, Bonhoeffer, and others was the same: to mobilize theology and ethics by reimagining it on the way, beginning with the critical task of teasing apart the strands of real-world confusion, and only having done so, venturing to discern what it meant in such a context to walk in the way of the Lord.

In this regard, Bonhoeffer's profound gift to the church is an ethical life that he figured out *on the way*. "With God," Bonhoeffer states in his commentary on Psalm 119, "one does not just mark time but one walks along a path. God knows the entire way; we only know the next step and the final goal."[2] What is dangerous about importing fixed ethical truths or maxims from a past age is that it can render us vulnerable to an ethics of abstraction. We are *acting* like Christians without awareness of the power centers and cultural influencers that have shaped our minds and hearts. The costly lesson we learn from the likes of Luther, Kierkegaard, and Bonhoeffer is that *we should not confuse acting like a Christian with walking in the way of the Lord.* This way is offered to us in scripture, which Bonhoeffer rightly saw not as a catalogue of ethical concepts, but as words handed down that point to a living God's works which are "new every morning."[3]

## The Way of Listening Before Speaking

In this volume the work of learning how to do ethics is a matter of learning how to make sense of the world in which we live as we confess that God is still at work, having promised not to abandon it to its sin and despair. Ethics so understood cannot be a onetime task but one that is continually reassessed and considered by believers as they walk along the way. Readers ought to take note in each chapter of how the author initially pulls apart the threads of our cultural context as it relates to their topic. Each author has very intentionally thought about the questions they pose, the assumptions that are widely shared in our time but which they refuse to assume, and the tones of voice they choose to employ. You might be surprised to find our authors drawing on figures some church members consider "out of bounds" because of what they are understood to represent or believe. Brian Brock, for example, draws on the atheist philosopher Slavoj Žižek in his chapter "Garbage," and Michael R. Laffin engages the Jewish philosopher Jacques Derrida in his treatment of "Fake News," while Daniel R. Patterson draws on the influential queer philosopher Judith Butler in addressing "Cancel Culture." None of these interlocutors are Christian, and

---

[2]Dietrich Bonhoeffer, "Meditation on Psalm 119, 1939–1940," in *Theological Education Underground: 1937–1940, Dietrich Bonhoeffer Works* 15, ed. Dirk Schultz, trans. Victoria J. Barnett (Minneapolis: Fortress Press, 2012), 504.
[3]Lam. 3:22-23.

in some cases are positively anti-Christian, but each is taken to have said something genuinely penetrating about the truth of the contemporary situation. As Balaam's donkey was able to see the spiritual reality to which the prophet was blind (Num. 22:21-34), so too Christians might sometimes hear great ethical insights from the voices of their supposed opponents. The authors of this volume attempt to model how listening well to all sorts of contemporary voices—in conversation with the words left to us in scripture by our ancient predecessors in the faith—often catalyzes crucial ethical insights for those seeking to apprehend the contemporary moment as we seek to follow the way Jesus Christ is making through our world.

In Rom. 12:1-2 the Apostle Paul presents the scriptural grounding for Christian ethics that proceeds as we have suggested. Here Paul speaks of the task of Christian thought as the active pursuit of an understanding of the difference the gospel makes when seen against the "patterns of the world" of any era. Patterns of the world have the power to enforce paradigms of perception, and very often what we think is the right thing to do because it just "looks right." The lesson Paul learned when Jesus rewrote all that he knew made him keen to provoke his readers to pay the closest attention to the distinctive claim of the patterns that rule the way of life characteristic of any time and place, since these so deeply shape how moral issues will appear. Each chapter in this volume may be fruitfully read as challenging the particular patterns that have become dominant in our particular times and places. Placing these patterns alongside the promise of the good news of Jesus Christ will, we anticipate, reveal the invaluable difference made by a hermeneutic of the gospel for walking in the way of the Lord today.

## Walking in the Way

Learning to walk in the way of the Lord at first glance appears to be a double task of learning *how* to walk and then learning the *way* to walk. A toddler learns to walk before she learns how to navigate the uneven path to the sandpit in the backyard. In contrast to this approach—learn then apply—our conviction is that the double task is one and the same: we learn to walk on the way. A toddler does not learn to walk conceptually before applying the knowledge to the real world. She learns to walk as a person living in time and in place. She must learn to walk in the sand or the snow around her place, or perhaps outside others' homes. Similarly, learning to do Christian ethics is a thinking exercise that falls entirely within time. If we think of the Christian life as a matter of learning to perceive and follow the way of the Lord, we can call the learning a necessary one of grasping *the grammar of Christian life*. Ethics is for all Christians and is something that is learned as they live. Such an approach is encouraging because it also entails the corollary that we are never too old to invest in learning this grammar better.

Christian ethics was never an academic specialty in the sense we have come to know it in the modern university. If Christian ethics is the sequestered domain of trained ethicists who are primarily concerned with treating especially tricky or complex topics, this would be disempowering for most Christians. This problematic view reflects how Christian ethics has been traditionally taught in modern university, college, and seminary settings. Students here are expected to learn a variety of moral theories (utilitarian, deontological, teleological, contextual, etc.) before applying them to a series of major topics like abortion and euthanasia. The assumption is that, once students have their formal ethical models in hand, they have been given the tools necessary to navigate any particular topic and to arrive at the answer/s which they can then apply by acting. They also then possess the knowledge base to convince others to do the same. Under the sway of such a view, Christian ethics has become an academic discipline reserved for those with specialized preparation. Christian ethics has been turned into expert knowledge.

Every Christian must live the Christian life, however. In this life, questions about how best to live crop up all the time, and in the most unexpected and mundane places. The Christian life is something that is lived by everyone, and navigated in a welter of moments: some ordinary and apparently insignificant and others complex, convoluted, and seemingly irresolvable. By learning to do Christian ethics as a matter of grasping the animating grammar of Christian life, believers are equipped to walk in the way of the Lord, whether the matters at stake seem to be ethically significant or insignificant. The "seem to" here is important, for what we often think is insignificant is the crux of the matter of Christian witness in a given domain, while, conversely, some of the "big questions" of our time evaporate when subjected to careful critical theological interrogation.

Such are the reasons why we have not organized this volume around "hot" ethical topics. Instead, we began by selecting a wide variety of domains in which Christians must live out their faith, doing so with the intent of raising questions about the animating logic of the Christian faith. This approach allows each author (and the reader) to focus attention in a more concentrated way on what theological resources exist within the Christian faith, and which should be brought forward to address the ethical issue at hand. Not unlike the emphasis that has been called situation ethics, we hold that the Christian life can only be and is always lived out in concrete circumstances. Departing from situation ethics, however, we affirm that one of the key tests of fidelity to the gospel is that our lives exhibit a coherent witness across the many domains in which we live it out. In this we seek to live a life that expresses a single grammar of Christian life. This is why the authors of this volume are united in the belief that Christians must always engage afresh with theological ideas held by past Christians in all aspects of human life. To walk with those who preceded us always means engaging anew with the grammatical unity that made believers of very different ages and places appear recognizable to one another as fellow travelers on the way of the one true God.

## The Way Forward

The form of this volume is intentionally shaped by these presuppositions. Its fifteen short chapters can be understood as a reflection of one under-appreciated practice in the Reformation era, specifically of theologians writing letters. The ethics of the Reformation is in large part contained in letters, in which particularly pressing personal and theological matters can often hardly be distinguished. Letters were used to provide support and persuade the reader about the significance of a particular ethical question, while the writers themselves realized that their personally addressed letters could be read by others, and even be found in the wrong hands and published to smear the writer. Letters were personal, yet powerful forms of communication.

In the early stages of the planning of this volume, the authors and editors considered writing each chapter as a letter to the churches, rather than in the form they now appear, as short essays. We judged that, in the end, the genre of the letter would be unnecessarily burdensome and less communicative than we hoped to be, such as making it awkward to reference our sources or point to further reading. What we hope we have retained from this early idea is the goal of making each essay deliberately short and gripping, with each addressing a single topic that is socially pressing even if not an obvious candidate for Christian ethical inquiry by a practicing theologian.

The brevity of the chapters allows for quicker reading and extended analysis of *how* the author is arriving at understanding and *how* the gospel sheds its own light on it. This analysis is open to be cross-examined with other essays allowing the reader to build confidence and proficiency in the use of the common and unifying gospel grammar in the volume. This also means that there is no single place to begin reading, though in order to grasp the unifying grammar of the volume we do suggest that the most will be gained by reading each essay in the light cast from others preceding it in the volume.

Each chapter has three basic components, though these may be tackled in various ways by each author. One component is that of critical analysis. Here the author will dive deep into the question at hand, revealing the complexities that bear on how it is understood within the current moment. A second component is an appeal to theological sources—biblical and doctrinal sources—that shed theological light on the complex components drawn out in the critical analysis. A third component is a constructive movement, with authors returning to the original problematic in order to show how the theological sources adduced offer Christians today newfound moral clarity on the ethical questions under discussion.

The goal of this volume is not to provide a compendium of definitive ethical "answers" or to "solve" ethical problems once and for all. For this reason, we have decided not to offer short overviews of each chapter in the introduction as is customary. This further reflects our desire to draw the reader into the grammar of Christian life as it emerges in its different facets when seen in the context of the various topics with which each chapter is concerned. Given the state of the university today and the conventions of

Christian ethics, driven as they are by starting with teaching ethical methods, we feel sure that many readers will be unsettled by our refusal to set out the method of this volume more than we have done in this introduction. Our shared conviction as editors and as authors, however, is that a genuine desire to learn how to do Christian ethics—and more importantly, to be ethically formed—can be fruitfully met if readers are prepared to patiently explore this volume as a single, multifaceted exploration of the difference the gospel makes in the world.

This volume, then, offers a cluster of worked examples of ethical thinking as it has developed among twenty-first-century European protestant thinkers. We believe the coherence of this tradition remains promising for those who wish to learn to walk in the way of the Lord today.

# 1

# Christ, Culpability, and Social Deprivation[1]

## Michael Banner

### Introduction

In this chapter I ask a question as to whether social deprivation should be allowed as a mitigating factor in assessing culpability and punishment for criminal offences. In some ways this will seem quite a small and perhaps even a rather technical question—and assessing the current practice of the English courts in this regard certainly relies on our attending fairly carefully to how the courts do indeed operate in this regard. But as we explore what can seem to be a minor issue, we will find ourselves attending to questions which go to the very heart of what it is to be human and what it is for us to have responsibility for our actions. In what sense are we free? In what sense are our paths through life chosen rather than being matters of, in a manner of speaking, fate or destiny? What I contend is that Christianity's way of asking and answering

---

[1] This chapter is based on the Charles Gore Lecture I gave at Westminster Abbey in March, 2019. I am grateful for the discussion which occurred, and in particular for the immensely useful discussion before, during, and after the lecture with my Cambridge colleague, Professor Sir Anthony Bottoms, who is as generous as he is distinguished.

these questions will turn us away from the harshness which typifies so many contemporary penal regimes toward practices of true liberation.

## Christ on a Cold Stone

The image known to art historians as "Christ on a cold stone" achieved huge popularity especially across northern Europe in the early fifteenth century, so much so that it is this image (whether in wood or in stone or painted), not Christ on the cross, which is the typical production of the period according to Mâle.[2] In these images Christ is shown just before his crucifixion—in some versions,[3] a skull by his left foot indicates that Christ is indeed at Golgotha "which means the place of a skull" (Mt. 27:33)—stripped of his cloak, crowned with thorns, marked with the wounds of his flagellation, and seated on a stone. And it is a cold stone, in the sense that it is a place without consolation or comfort. The focus of these images is not exactly Christ's physical suffering, which is for this moment suspended, but rather his psychological pain or anguish as he awaits his crucifixion. Christ appears withdrawn, utterly abandoned, and alone, in deep thought and dejection.

But images labeled "Christ on a cold stone" are by no means all the same, and the particular version of the image I have referenced, draws our attention especially to something I have not yet mentioned, that Christ's life ends as a prisoner. A heavy and tightly woven crown of thorns binds his head, while his hands and feet are bound by a sinuous rope. By his right foot, and attached to his feet, is a small board, topped with five or six spikes, a so-called "trip block," a device designed to knock backward and forward between a prisoner's feet or ankles, further adding to their suffering as they struggled to the gallows. But the device is now idle since Christ is going nowhere. Christ is bound, and bound to die.

---

[2]E. Mâle, *Religious Art from the Twelfth to the Eighteenth Century* (Princeton: Princeton University Press, 1982), 113.
[3]Such as the famous image of 1443 in the Hôtel-Dieu de Beaune in France.

The popularity of this image-type tells us that its "consumers" found it, with its multiple "resonances,"[4] highly affective. One might then speculate, as does the great art historian Emile Mâle, that the image's popularity was not merely as a representation of a single imagined moment in the passion narrative but more, as he puts it, as its "summing up."[5] Through this image one accessed not just one moment of that narrative, but captured something of the whole. Indeed, in the figure of Christ as a prisoner, we are referred not only to the meaning of his passion, but to something essential to the meaning of his life, for it is as a prisoner that Christ most truly represents the humanity which he takes on and takes up in his incarnation. Our humanity is not one of glorious liberty and freedom, for we are all, each and every one, tightly bound by the histories, circumstances, needs, desires, and longings which shape our destinies. Thus, as a bound and dejected prisoner, Christ ends his earthly life visibly sharing in the human condition which he has taken on: a prisoner for the sake of prisoners. On the cold stone, Christ mourns the human condition, our lonely and abject bondage in sin, which he here represents, and for which he suffers.

It is on account of this bondage that *the* problem for Christian ethical life, thought, and practice, the problem which distinguished it fundamentally from the ethical life, thought, and practice of the classical or pagan world, was the problem of the will. In the classical world, the problem of ethics, of right action, was chiefly conceived as a problem of knowledge. Pagans typically worried about knowing what was the right thing to do; but Christians worried about whether, knowing what to do, they would do it. And they didn't worry a bit, they worried a lot. Or at least, they worried a lot if they had learned their theology from Augustine and not from Britain's first known theologian, and heretic, Pelagius.

For Pelagius the challenge of the human will might be likened to the challenge of training a puppy to be a good pet—with time and perseverance you should have a perfectly house trained and thoroughly reliable companion. But for Augustine, the challenge of training the unruly human will was more like taking a young wolf

---

[4]Gabriele Finaldi, "Christ on the Cold Stone, about 1500," in *The Image of Christ*, ed. G. Finaldi (London, 2000), 120.
[5]Mâle, *Religious Art*, 115.

into your house; you would always be wondering, even as it lay quietly in its basket, whether it might at any moment revert to its wolfish ways. As Woody Allen has it in another context, "The lion and the calf shall lie down together, but the calf won't get much sleep."[6]

It was Augustine's view of human nature which informed the work of that great architect of the Christian world of the Middle Ages, St. Benedict. His rule established the monastery as a school of virtue, just as a pagan philosopher might have established such a school, but with the crucial and distinctly odd feature of the monastic school, that, like the Hotel California, you can check in but you can never leave. The monastic school was one which had no graduation ceremony, because the will that it sought to govern was always and ever bound by the ties of sin represented by those sinuous ropes which constrain Christ as he sits on the cold stone.

Augustine's attitude to Pelagius, and his complaint against him, is contained in his observation that the Pelagians heap "cruel praise on human nature":[7] "praise" because Pelagius would not allow that human nature was the deeply wounded thing which Augustine held it to be, and "cruel" because Pelagius's praise of human nature led him to the stern moralism which such a favorable appraisal naturally invited. If human nature deserves praise, and if human nature is not bound in sin, as Augustine thought, then our faults and failings can and should be judged more severely. We really can and should have done better, as school reports used to say. But so Augustine argued: Pelagius's praise of human nature was wrong and, thus, cruel.[8] [9]

---

[6]Woody Allen, "The Scrolls," *The New Republic*, August 31, 1974. https://newrepublic.com/article/113899/scrolls-woody-allen.
[7]Augustine, *On Marriage and Concupiscence*, II. 9.
[8]For his part, Pelagius was famously disgusted by Augustine's plea in the *Confessions*, directed to God: Lord "thou commandest continence; give what Thou commandest, and command what thou wilt." As Augustine tells it, when Pelagius heard this line, he very nearly came to blows with the Bishop who quoted it (*On the Gift of Perseverance*, 20, 53). For if Augustine heard "cruel praise" in Pelagius's teaching about the human capacity to do good, Pelagius, the stern and demanding ascetic and confessor, heard in Augustine a lack of moral backbone, and an invitation to lazy excuses for a failure to keep God's clear commandments.
[9]It is sometimes said that Pelagius didn't believe in grace, but that is not quite right. He certainly didn't deny it; indeed, he talked about it quite a lot. But as Augustine

Christ on the cold stone, bound, helpless, and alone, expresses the human condition as conceived by Augustine. Here on the cold stone, the prisoner who became a prisoner for the sake of prisoners, most fully encapsulates and reveals what it is to be human. He is bound—and the trip block, though currently idle, is the token of the full measure of his plight, for even were he to try to stand, his own efforts would be frustrated and punished. Christ on a cold stone is an anthropology wrapped up in a statue, and its popularity in the fifteenth century witnesses the triumph of Augustine over Pelagius, in official teaching and popular piety.

## Mitigation, Culpability, and Social Deprivation

Turning from the medieval to the modern world, and from a particular prisoner to prisoners in general, I want to ask whether the Augustinian perspective on the bondage of the will governs our attitudes and policies here and now. Is our criminal justice system Augustinian or Pelagian? Do we or do we not reckon with the affliction and disablement of the human will which Augustine diagnoses and which is represented to us in that statue?

I propose to get at this big question by answering a more specific and smaller one, which I think will nonetheless get us to the heart of the matter: the question as to whether social deprivation should function as a mitigating factor in relation to the sentencing of offenders.

---

very clearly and quickly discerned, Pelagius and his followers meant by grace (i) our nature as we have it (the very nature which Adam had), (ii) divine enlightenment by means of the law and Christian teaching, and (iii) the remission of our sins by Christ by means of baptism. But as Augustine insisted: "Neither knowledge of the divine Law, nor our nature, nor the remission of sins alone constitute Grace: but it is given to us by our Lord Jesus Christ, so that, by it, the Law may be accomplished, nature delivered, and sin vanquished" (*Grace and Free Will*, 14, 27). They had then, very different ideas of grace: for Pelagius, grace is, if you like, a term for the wholesome conditions in which we begin the moral life; for Augustine it is a fourth thing, the current ministrations of God to that wounded condition, or thus a vital addition to that condition, whereby our nature, knowledge, and wills are enabled to do the good.

Those of you who don't feel inclined to shout out an answer may be thinking, quite reasonably in my view, that it would be sensible to ask what is the case before you declare your mind on what should be the case. So let us ask that question: Is social deprivation a mitigating factor in law?

The Criminal Justice Act of 2003[10] holds that the guiding principle of sentencing should be the proportionality of the sentence to the seriousness of the offence. And the seriousness of any offence is defined as having two elements (s.143 [1]): the harm it causes and the offender's culpability.

Now plainly the social deprivation of the offender does not touch the harm caused by the offence—grievous bodily harm is grievous bodily harm, racial abuse is racial abuse, and so on, whether the offender attended Eton or a less-well-funded establishment. But does social deprivation have a bearing on culpability, as the law sees it?

The Sentencing Guidelines Council has issued guidance on this element in establishing the seriousness of an offence, and allows that culpability may be reduced depending on whether the offender "intends to cause harm, is reckless about causing it, has knowledge of the risks, or is negligent."[11] These guidelines construe culpability, in other words, as a scale running from deliberately intended to negligently allowed, and to such a scale, social deprivation is plainly irrelevant. A socially deprived individual intends to damage the car, is reckless about damaging the car, is negligent in regard to the car, or whatever it may be. The offender being socially deprived does not, as such, affect culpability so conceived.

This, however, is not the end of the story. For the Criminal Justice Act also provides (s. 166) that nothing in preceding sections "prevents a court from mitigating an offender's sentence by taking into account any such matters as in the opinion of the court, are relevant in mitigation of sentence."[12] So even after the court has reflected on and determined the seriousness of the offence, there

---

[10]For details and discussion, see A. Ashworth, *Sentencing and Criminal Justice* (Cambridge, 2015), 113.
[11]Sentencing Guidelines Council, *Overarching Principles: Seriousness – Guideline* (London, 2004).
[12]Thus allowing in principle that culpability may be mitigated, as commonsense moral intuitions suggest, other than by lack of intention alone.

is a second moment in the process of sentencing when mitigation, so-called "personal mitigation," may bear on a sentence at which moment social deprivation may yet get a look in. Indeed "pleas in mitigation," which may contribute to a sentencer's reflections on personal mitigation, tend to assume that social deprivation really does count at this point.[13]

But does it? In seeking to understand practice and thinking around personal mitigation in general, Jacobson and Hough undertook an empirical study which had two elements: first, an analysis of 132 actual cases involving sentences being passed on 162 defendants; and second, interviews with practicing sentencers in which their views were elicited by questions and by exploration of certain scenarios. I can't, in the context of this chapter, provide you with the details of their study but only with a sense of its flavor and conclusions. And this is just that in practice, sentencers do not allow social deprivation to mitigate a sentence.[14]

---

[13]Personal mitigation, as Jacobson and Hough put it, refers "to mitigation that relates to the background or circumstances of the offender rather than the facts of the offence" (J. Jacobson and M. Hough, *Mitigation: The Role of Personal Factors in Sentencing* [London: Prison Reform Trust, 2007]). And since the Sentence Guidelines Council has offered no very directive guidance on what may count in personal mitigation, judges have considerable discretion. Note: they have issued guidance on sentencing "Youth Offenders," which allows for disrupted childhood, but not for social deprivation as such, as a mitigating factor.

[14]In the analysis of the actual cases, Jacobson and Hough categorized the 254 mentions of mitigating circumstances in judges' accounts of their sentencing into 46 different mitigating factors. Suffice to say that the factor Jacobson and Hough labeled "difficult/deprived background" did not score highly, whereas for example, "good character" was allowed to mitigate in twenty-one cases, youth in nineteen cases, and "can/is addressing drug problems" in fourteen, "difficult/deprived background" got only three mentions. Only 3 out of 254. When it came to interviews and scenarios, the researchers found the same relatively low weight accorded to social deprivation as in the actual cases. When the forty interviewees were asked, "what kinds of personal mitigation most frequently influence the sentences that you pass?" "difficult/deprived background" got four mentions as against eleven mentions of good character and fifteen for "can/is addressing drug problems." And in the scenarios used during the interviews, judges were given three imagined cases each with a set of accompanying potential mitigating factors (thirteen in all) and were asked to score these factors as to whether they made a big impact (such as shifting a custodial to a noncustodial sentence, or halving sentence length), some impact or minimal or no impact.

Let me give a single example where the researchers put to the experienced sentencers different scenarios, in one of which, an imagined defendant, 22 years old, with several previous convictions for shoplifting, pleads guilty to a charge of burglary, the victim being a 76-year-old woman who was alone in her house at the time. One possible mitigating factor is that the defendant is "functionally illiterate (mother discouraged school attendance)" and has "never had a regular job." Another is that he had "physically and emotionally abusive parents" and spent his "childhood mainly in care." Now these two factors, if not equating with social deprivation as such, may reasonably be taken to be associated with it.

So how weighty did the sentencers consider these two factors to be? All you need to know is that the two factors I mentioned came bottom of the list of 13: 13th and 11th.[15] Between the forty or so respondents there was some variation, but no one sentencer thought a physically and emotionally abused childhood, spent mostly in care, should have a big impact in mitigating a sentence, and only one would allow the impact of being functionally illiterate as a result of being discouraged from attending school by a mother. The broad consensus among the sentencers was that these two factors should have minimal or no impact, rather than some.[16]

Looking at their study as a whole, Jacobson and Hough ask, "what is the relationship between mitigation and disadvantage?" and answer that "The evidence from our research is that there are manifold contradictions in this relationship."[17] The only contradiction I can see is that "defense" advocates routinely assume that sentencers *are* swayed by accounts of their clients' social deprivation, whereas the evidence from the surveys of actual decisions made and of the responses given to the scenarios is quite simply that "sentencers appear to be somewhat immune to accounts of disadvantage."[18]

---

[15] Factors which the sentencers said would have a big impact scored 4 points, those which would have some impact 2, and minimal or no impact scored 0. The two factors identified had average scores of 0.9 and 0.6.
[16] Twenty-four and nineteen respondents, respectively, for each of the factors saying minimal or no impact; six and ten saying some.
[17] Jacobson and Hough, *Mitigation*, 42.
[18] Ibid. There is, of course, some contrary evidence in other surveys, which I should mention.

So the position seems to be that while s.166 of the Criminal Justice Act allows, in principle, that social deprivation (along with anything else the court deem relevant) may mitigate a sentence, in practice it doesn't. But should it?

In the standard and influential text *Sentencing and Criminal Justice*, Andrew Ashworth identifies the issue, rehearses some of the arguments, but comes to no very clear or definite conclusion.[19] In his jointly authored work with Von Hirsch, *Proportionate Sentencing: Exploring the Principles*, however, there is a more extended and conclusive discussion, in which the authors conclude that social disadvantage should mitigate a sentence, but as a matter of compassion, not as reducing culpability.[20]

Their reasoning for saying that it should count I find unexceptional. Social disadvantage, so Von Hirsch and Ashworth argue, alters the "stakes" which individuals have in keeping the law; thus to take a very obvious point, depending on what you can or can't easily afford to buy, theft is more or less tempting. Similarly, depending on your social standing, the social sanction of gaining a conviction will seem more or less. Those with very little may also have very little to lose. As Ashworth and Von Hirsch put it, "the deprived offender is truly in a more troubled situation, one in which the temptations to offend become harder to resist."[21]

But this circumstance, so they say, though it deserves compassion, does not warrant the view that the disadvantaged are less culpable if they do offend. Why? "To make a case that an offender is less culpable for his crime would seem to require that almost anyone in his situation would find it extraordinarily difficult to desist—that compliance would be a matter of heroism or something akin to that."[22] But they note that "many individuals in deprived neighbourhoods remain law-abiding." In other words, "more self-disciplined persons will still be able to comply, and it is only the

---

[19] Ashworth, *Sentencing and Criminal Justice* (Cambridge: Cambridge University Press, 2005).
[20] A. Von Hirsch and A. Ashworth, *Proportionate Sentencing: Exploring the Principles* (Oxford: Oxford University Press, 2005).
[21] Ibid., 68.
[22] Ibid.

more 'susceptible' ones who may not"²³ and thus, as they see it, the offenders deserve compassion but can't be considered less culpable. I think this may be a bit of a muddle, though one which might be thought not to matter much in practice. If a court hands me down a noncustodial rather than a custodial sentence, I am probably not too concerned whether they did so on grounds of compassion or on the basis of my reduced culpability. Either way I may be grateful. I suggest, however, that it is worth getting the issue straight for the reason that Von Hirsch and Ashworth's disinclination to recognize the case for allowing diminished culpability involves a failure to understand the nature of the connections between social deprivation and crime, and thus risks perpetuating what I take to be a mistaken attitude to offending.

Remember Von Hirsch and Ashworth's claim: "To make a case that a[n] [socially deprived] offender is less culpable for his crime would seem to require that almost anyone in his situation would find it extraordinarily difficult to desist—that compliance would be a matter of heroism or something akin to that."[24]

I fear that Von Hirsch and Ashworth may have been somewhat mislead by what other researchers have called a "criminological puzzle," or even the paradox of social deprivation and crime, which is that "Although most persistent offenders come from disadvantaged backgrounds, most people from disadvantaged backgrounds do not become persistent offenders."[25] To put it another way, if you visit a prison you will find that the prison is full of the socially deprived, but you would be wrong to assume that the socially deprived are generally criminals.

Now plainly, as these same researchers suggest, what must be needed to solve this puzzle "is a better understanding of the *mechanisms* through which social disadvantage is implicated in the development of persistent offending."[26] And what they propose is that among the socially disadvantaged, those who offend have what the researchers call (a) a "high crime propensity" and (b) a

---

[23]Ibid.
[24]Ibid.
[25]See especially, P.-O.H. Wikström and K. Treiber, "Social Disadvantage and Crime: A Criminological Puzzle," *American Behavioral Scientist* 60, no. 10 (2016): 1232–59.
[26]Ibid., 1233.

higher "exposure" to criminogenic context. Now crime propensity is a matter, they suggest, of morality (or lack of it) and the ability to exercise self-control, and exposure is a matter of being in "contexts . . . conducive to engagement in acts of crime (i.e. those in which rules of law are loosely applied and/or weakly enforced."[27]

I think this research is very compelling, and there are nuances to it which I can't explore here. But since, as the researchers themselves suggest, possessing a high crime propensity and being more often exposed to criminogenic contexts is itself a function of social deprivation, we can safely conclude as follows: that although it is misleading to say that social deprivation is a cause of crime (just in the sense that the vast majority of the socially deprived are not criminals), it is true to say that social deprivation is a cause of the causes of crime.

So, to go back to Von Hirsch and Ashworth, in shying away from allowing that social deprivation may reduce culpability, they seem to have been impressed by the fact that the socially deprived generally don't offend. But within that group, if we identify subpopulations more narrowly, the figures look very different. According to data published by the Cabinet Office in 2002, 65 percent of boys with a convicted father will themselves go on to offend.[28] To take another set of figures: a child in care in this country is fifteen times more likely to be criminalized in any one year than one their peers not in care. Furthermore, 70 percent of those who offend while in care "have been taken into care because of acute family stress, family dysfunction, parental illness/disability or absence."[29] And a further 14 percent of those who offend while in care were taken into care "primarily because of abuse or neglect," giving us a total of 84 percent of those who offend while in care coming from such distressed circumstances.

Such numbers deserve careful examination, investigation, and analysis, but on the face of it they surely allow us to hold just what Von Hirsch and Ashworth require we should hold if

---

[27]Ibid., 1236.
[28]Social Exclusion Unit, *Reducing Re-Offending by Ex-Prisoners* (London: Cabinet Office, 2002), cited in Bernardo's Report, "On the Outside: Identifying and Supporting Children with a Parent in Prison" (2014), 5.
[29]Howard League for Penal Reform, "Ending the Criminalisation of Children in Residential Care: Briefing One" (2017), unnumbered pages.

social deprivation is to count as a mitigating factor, which is that in certain circumstances of deprivation it really is the truly exceptional individual who doesn't offend. If 65 percent of boys with a convicted father go on to offend, compliance for such boys is plainly a minority achievement, and I doubt very much that heroism constitutes a good explanation of an individual's avoiding a conviction. In the way of things, it may be something altogether more banal such as pure and simple moral luck—things fell out in such a way that the occasions and opportunities which might have led them to offend just did not come their way. (There was no "exposure" as the researchers would put it.) But it is hard to see that the fact that a few young men don't offend should prevent our holding that those who do are less culpable.

I suspect that what we are hitting up against here is a legacy of the Enlightenment which makes us disinclined to entertain the thought that we in general, and some in particular, are "bound to sin," to borrow the title of an important book which explores this theme[30]—disinclined, that is, to entertain the anthropology of Augustine, which reckons with the bondage of the will, and its implications for the criminal justice system. Were we to do so, we would have to accept that there are criminal acts which are fully and unequivocally intended, and yet for which the actor may lack culpability just in the sense that though their choices may be theirs and may be wrong, their pattern of choosing is itself, and very importantly, not of their choosing.

If the Enlightenment's refusal of the bondage of the will is one factor in our thinking, another and much more recent one is a matter of current fashion in criminology, where some find a turn against a "political economy" approach to crime, which would seek to understand social deviance in its widest historical and social setting, in favor of what has been labeled "realism." Realism here indicates an impatience with trying to fathom the deep origins of criminality, and a preference for simply identifying those levers (such as changes in patterns of policing, an increase in prison terms, or whatever) which might effect a reduction in crime.[31]

---

[30]A. McFadyen, *Bound to Sin* (Cambridge: Cambridge University Press, 2000).
[31]I here simply repeat the argument of Robert Reiner, "Political Economy, Crime and Criminal Justice," in *The Oxford Handbook of Criminology*, 3rd ed., ed. A. Liebling,

Whether it is current fashion, or the legacy of the Enlightenment, which prevents our acknowledging the lesser culpability of socially deprived offenders, these blocks to a proper appreciation of our social conditions need to be overcome. We need, I suggest, to accept that we have created a society in which individuals receive as a woeful birthright, a criminal destiny. Of course, the story of most criminality could be told as a story in which individuals take individual decisions which bring them face to face with the courts; but those stories are themselves part of larger histories in which individuals learn patterns of perception, judgment, and behavior such that their later decisions and conduct look more determined than merely chosen. This is not to deny choice, but it is to say with Ricoeur that sin sometimes lies behind an action, more than actually in it.

I want to make a distinction here between fate and destiny, suggesting that criminality, though not a matter of fate, is often a matter of destiny. We can think of fate as what befalls us whatever we do, no matter what we do. Thought of like that, fate pursues us in spite of the choices we make against it – thus Oedipus is a victim of fate, in the sense that no matter his twists and turns, he ends up unwittingly marrying his mother. We might think of destiny differently, not as an external force determining our histories, but as an internal one, written in our nature so to speak, not in the stars. So, when we follow our destinies, unlike Oedipus, we willingly and knowingly intend our crimes, rather than committing them unwittingly. Thus, if we allow, as we should, that the human will can been sequestered, colonized, and coopted by social dynamics which determine our choosing, we may say that in some cases criminality is best thought of as a destiny and not as a simple, innocent, or uncomplicated choice.[32] (Though to describe my fraudulent completion of a tax return in these terms would undoubtedly be a matter of dishonest melodrama.)

---

S. Maruna and L. McAra (Oxford, 2017), 116–37. Of course, as Reiner warns, we should beware a false opposition here—one might seek to identify and support all legitimate means of reducing crime, while thinking that failure to consider the wider background and context will only result in "liddism," as he terms it: the attempt to put a lid on behavior while ignoring the deeper social malaise to which it may point.
[32] See McFadyen, *Bound to Sin*, 133ff.

## On Being Practical (as Opposed to Being Religious)

A friend of mine, taking questions after a lecture, faced a very cross questioner, who, as is often the way with these things, didn't ask a question but made a statement, the statement being that the lecturer had been unfair to Aristotle. To which my friend replied that it had never been his intention to be fair to Aristotle.

Someone may say I have not been practical. But then, it was not exactly my intention to be practical. But let me say two things about that.

First, nothing I have said is meant to suggest that regular findings of moral or legal culpability don't have their place and even their own validity. It is to say, however, that they have their limits, and that they have to be placed in a wider, more adequate, perspective of moral reflection. I am not proposing that we close the courts tomorrow. But I am saying that we should look behind the regular judgments which the courts make and the assumptions on which they operate, to consider deeper questions of anthropology which naturally enough are not the immediate concern of courts. I have picked up a thread of thought about culpability specifically in relation to the matter of mitigation of sentencing, but I am further suggesting, of course, that were we to keep pulling on this thread, we might unravel quite a bit of the tapestry of the criminal justice system (and in particular the system's commitment to punishment). For once we reckon with the fact of the bondage of the will as I have termed it (the fact that there are criminal destinies which may explain criminal choices), we would surely look at the whole system with different eyes, finding it, I would suggest, insensitive to the plight of those who are bound to sin.

Of course, an objector might also go on to say that the most impractical element of my impractical musings, is just that I have been religious in a secular age. What is the intellectual currency of that image of Christ on the cold stone from which I started, and the anthropology which it presupposes, when such a starting point is one which secular political thought eschews?

I would insist, however, that the anthropology I commend, with its particular conception of the travails of human agency, can commend itself to reflective secular thought. There is something slightly odd, to say the least, in the latter-day triumph of Pelagius's thinking, consisting as it does of the cruel praise heaped on human nature when that nature's moral affliction is denied. Pelagius's great moment came, of course not in the fifth century when Augustine opposed him root and branch, but with the Renaissance and the Enlightenment, with those moments in intellectual life and thought which had as their Christian counterpoints, Martin Luther (on the bondage of the will) and Jonathan Edwards (on freewill and original sin). His time in the sun came when thinkers such as Joseph Priestly (eighteenth-century scientist and Unitarian) could confidently announce that "Whatever was the beginning of this world, the end will be glorious and paradisiacal, beyond what our imaginations can conceive.... Men will make their situation in this world abundantly more easy and comfortable; they will probably prolong their existence in it, and will grow daily more happy."[33]

But here is the deep irony: that it was not Luther or Edwards who most tellingly announced the death knell on the sunny Pelagian optimism regarding human nature of the Renaissance and the Enlightenment, but that greatest of Enlightenment thinkers, Immanuel Kant himself, the man who both achieved the Enlightenment's greatest feats of thought and intellect, while at the same time drawing boundaries around the Enlightenment's most vaunting ambition and optimism. In relation to human nature, Kant, in effect, declares himself for Luther, stating in *Religion Within the Boundaries of Mere Reason*, that human beings are born in bondage to radical evil, and can only be liberated by a divine grace, the existence of which cannot be known to theoretical reason.[34]

And if this isn't enough to disconcert any latter-day Pelagians, we might add that any happy Enlightenment thoughts about human nature run into the roadblock not only of Kant, but of the nineteenth century in which Marx, Nietzsche, Darwin, and Freud, those great masters of suspicion, paint a picture, in their different ways, of human action as darkly determined. Augustine won the

---

[33]Cited by Bernard M.G. Reardon, *Kant as Philosophical Theologian* (London: Macmillan, 1988).
[34]Immanuel Kant, *Religion Within the Boundaries of Mere Reason* (New York: Harper and Brothers, 1993).

war once in the fifth century, and he won it again in the eighteenth and again in the nineteenth—even if it still remains for him to win the peace in our day.

# Unbind Him!

Preaching in his cathedral church in Hippo around 418, Augustine turns to the gospel for the day, that wondrous and beautiful story of the raising of the only son of the widow of Nain, from Luke 7.[35]

There are three occasions in the gospels in which Christ raises the dead says Augustine, but each in different locations. In the case of the son of the widow of Nain, Christ meets the burial party at the town wall as he approaches and they are leaving, for the son was due to be buried, as Jews (Christ included) were, "without a city wall." And it is there that he raises the son and returns him to his mother, halfway between house and tomb. However Jairus's daughter (Jairus being the leader of the synagogue who comes begging at Jesus's feet to plead for his sick daughter, only for word to reach them that his daughter is dead, and for Jesus to press on regardless) was raised inside the four walls of her parents' house.[36] The third resurrectee, Lazarus, was however, raised from the tomb itself, where he had lain for four days and "stinketh," as the Authorized Version so memorably has it.[37]

Now says Augustine, these three dead people, in their different locations, represent "three sorts of sinners whom Christ is raising even now."[38] We might think of them as those who are a bit dead in sin, very dead in sin, or very very dead in sin. Jairus's daughter, still in her house, is like "people who have sin inside their hearts, but don't yet have it in actual deed":[39] they have not actually carried it out. The widow's son, at the gates, is like someone who moves from "consenting to the wicked thought," to "put[ting] it into practice": someone who has carried it out, just as the son of the widow was

---

[35] Lk. 7:11-15.
[36] Mk 5:22-24 and 35-43.
[37] Jn 11:11-44.
[38] Augustine, *Sermon 98*, 5.
[39] Ibid.

carried out to the walls of the town. And what of the one who is four days dead and stinketh? He is like one who is very very dead in sin, "who has added habit to sinful action such that it becomes addiction."[40] The sorry state of the latter is shown by the fact, says Augustine, that while Jesus raises the other two with a simple and gentle word, he raises Lazarus with a great shout: "Lazarus! Come out!" After all, he has to speak loudly enough to wake the very very dead.

This sermon reprises Augustine's anthropology, the anthropology of Christ on the cold stone—for if it is Lazarus who emerges bound, and is most manifestly bound to sin, all three of the dead are dead, dead in sin, and bound together in sin and death.

But as if this exegetical tour de force were not enough, Augustine has another move up his sleeve. Ever the attentive and close reader of the text, Augustine reminds us that though Jesus summoned Lazarus from the tomb, he emerges still with "his hands and feet bound with strips of cloth, and his face wrapped in a cloth."[41] So it is that Christ addresses an instruction to the bystanders: "unbind him and let him go." This, he says, "is the office he gave to the disciples." There is a need "for the person who has come back to life to be unbound, absolved, and allowed to walk free."[42]

I have looked in this chapter at one small detail of the criminal justice system, but I end by suggesting that the detail I have looked at provides a perspective on the whole. Our criminal justice system is Pelagian—it doesn't seem to reckon with the fact of criminal destinies. It doesn't reckon with the fact that many are bound in sin. And if we followed the offender from court to prison, we would too often find a system which is more likely to bind the offender further than it is to help in fashioning new and better destinies. Indeed, and even worse to say, if we were to follow offenders beyond the prison gate, after they are released, we would find practices and attitudes which leave their bindings firmly in place.

If the command "unbind him" is to have the force it deserves, we will perhaps need to go back to that sublime image of Christ on a cold stone and learn what it has to teach us. That image invites us

---

[40]Ibid, 98, 6.
[41]Jn 11:44.
[42]Augustine, *Sermon 98*, 6.

to see ourselves and other selves in Christ the prisoner. He is bound as we all are bound, and bound for our common sakes. And is it his being bound for our sakes which is the force of the command to the disciples to unbind Lazarus, the one who is deep in the death of sins? Augustine remarks at the beginning of his sermon, "Not all . . . have the wherewithal to see those who are dead in heart rise again; to see that, you need to have already risen in the heart yourself."[43] Or as Augustine would say, in effect, when he implored magistrates to show leniency toward convicted criminals: I a sinner, plead before you a sinner, for the sake of sinners.

# Bibliography

Ashworth, Andrew. *Sentencing and Criminal Justice*. Cambridge: Cambridge University Press, 2005.

Augustine. *On Grace and Free Will*, vol. 5 of *A Select Library of the Nicene and Post-Nicene Fathers of the Christian Church: Saint Augustine: Anti-Pelagian Writings*, translated by Peter Holmes. New York: The Christian Literature Company, 1887.

Augustine. *On Marriage and Concupiscence*, vol. 5 of *A Select Library of the Nicene and Post-Nicene Fathers of the Christian Church: Saint Augustine: Anti-Pelagian Writings*, translated by Peter Holmes. New York: The Christian Literature Company, 1887.

Augustine. *On the Gift of Perseverance*, vol. 5 of *A Select Library of the Nicene and Post-Nicene Fathers of the Christian Church: Saint Augustine: Anti-Pelagian Writings*, translated by Robert Ernest Wallis. New York: The Christian Literature Company, 1887.

Augustine. *Sermons*, vol. 4 of *The Works of Saint Augustine: A Translation for the 21st Century*, translated by E. Hill. New York: New City Press, 1992.

Augustine. *The Confessions,* translated by Maria Boulding. New York: New City Press, 1997.

Finaldi, Gabriele. "Christ on the Cold Stone, about 1500." In *The Image of Christ*, edited by Gabriele Finaldi. London: National Gallery London, 2000.

Jacobson, Jessica and Mike Hough. *Mitigation: The Role of Personal Factors in Sentencing*. London: Prison Reform Trust, 2007.

---

[43]Ibid., 98, 1.

Kant, Immanuel. *Religion Within the Boundaries of Mere Reason Alone*, translated by Theodore Greene. New York: Harper and Brothers, 1993.

Mâle, Emile. *Religious Art from the Twelfth to the Eighteenth Century*. Princeton: Princeton University Press, 1982.

McFadyen, Alistair. *Bound to Sin: Abuse, Holocaust and the Christian Doctrine of Sin*. Cambridge: Cambridge University Press, 2000.

# 2

# Garbage

# An Invitation to Face Our Creaturely State

*Brian Brock*

## Introduction

What does a theologian have to do with garbage? Like air, garbage is ubiquitous, but unlike air, we work very hard to hide it. To look directly at it is thus to try to expose ourselves as modern human beings. The creator of a website entitled "365 Days of Trash: One man's attempt to throw nothing 'away' for a year . . . and beyond" describes his rationale in usefully diagnostic terms:

> The idea for this project came about six months ago as I was throwing something away in the garbage. It occurred to me that I was doing nothing more than that. I was making it go away, not dealing with it, not accounting for it, simply removing it from my sight. When you think of it in simple terms like that, it's really quite insane. I came to the realization that if we were all accountable for our waste, if we couldn't simply make it disappear, we'd have to deal with some pretty ugly truths about

the way we live. And in so doing, it would cause us to start making better decisions about what we buy, where we buy, and what's left over when we are done with that purchase.[1]

By suggesting we journey down the stream of garbage we produce, I hope to display the "trashiness" of our relationships with other creatures that is good neither for us nor them, and how in Christian worship, especially the Lord's Supper, we are offered a way of escape.

Today ecological champions often stoke worries about the human footprint in the natural world by figures who in effect take on the mantle of prophet and judge of conscience once held by religion. Yet geological records indicate that environmental catastrophes are not the exception but the rule on this planet, observes Slavoj Žižek:

> The ultimate paradox here is that today's excessive catastrophism (the mantra that "the end of the world is near") is itself a defense mechanism, a way of obfuscating the real dangers, of not taking them seriously. This is why the only appropriate reply to an ecologist trying to convince us of the impending threat is that the true target of his desperate plea is *his own non-belief*. Consequently, our answer to him should be something like, "Don't worry, the catastrophe will come for sure!—the impossible is already happening all around us; but watch patiently, don't succumb to hasty extrapolations, don't indulge in the properly perverse pleasure of thinking 'This is it! The dreaded moment has arrived!'" In ecology, this apocalyptic fascination takes many diverse forms: global warming will drown us all in a couple of decades; biogenesis will mean the end of human ethics and responsibility; the bees will soon die out and global starvation will follow . . . Take all these threats seriously, yes, but don't be seduced by them or wallow in the false sense of guilt and justice that they invite ("We offended Mother Earth, so are getting what we deserve!"). Instead, keep a cool head and . . . "watch".[2]

Žižek is exposing why investigations of the ethics of waste-production that proceed only out of fear of the environmental

---

[1] Cited in Shannon O'Lear, *Environmental Politics: Scale and Power* (Cambridge: Cambridge University Press, 2010), 117.
[2] Slavoj Žižek, *The Year of Dreaming Dangerously* (London: Verso, 2012), 132.

apocalypse are in reality only stabilizing the status quo, in which minor ameliorative hopes dominate. And he also highlights how stories of the origins of our world and its final ends continue to constitute the moral horizons of secular modernity framing the moral exhortations that make sense within it. Garbage provokes us to think theologically, and genuinely theologically, precisely because it seems impossible to think outside the protologies and eschatologies of modern secular rationality. These, I hope to show, differ in significant ways from traditional Christian narratives.

## Trash, Care, and Perception

Our world is one shaped by the techniques of marketing, packaging, virtuality, disposability, and the iron law that economies must expand. Precisely in this world, I would like to meditate on the biblical protology, the story of the Garden of Eden. The story of Eden is a heuristic, an alternative perception of creation to that offered in modern secular rationality. This is a tale unencumbered by some of our more problematic conceptual polarities, like nature/culture or consumer/producer, or even useful/garbage.

In that story humans are depicted as created by God from the earth and set in a garden that was ordered and beautiful and sufficient for all their needs along with the other plant and animal species of the world. It was all this before humans began to act, and they contributed nothing to their emergence, nor their emplacement in this fertile and hospitable part of creation. The first of the two creation narratives depicts God as telling humans that their job in this Eden is to "till and to keep it," and, strikingly, in the second account the very creation of humans is depicted as being for the purposes of this tilling and keeping—God having created streams to water the plants, and humans to tend them.[3] For the writers of ancient Israel to depict the beginnings of human life in this way was

---

[3] "The Lord God took the man and put him in the garden of Eden to till it and keep it" (Gen. 2:15).

> In Hebrew "to till" is literally "to serve". Even in his relationship with the soil, mankind must maintain his humility. The use of the verb paves the way for the condemnation of the "destroyers of the earth" (Rev. 11:18), those guilty of ecological depredation. Not only will man rule over nature by obeying its laws (F. Bacon), but he will do so for the good of creation itself, so that it may fulfil

not a nostalgic projection but an expression of hope that humans were capable of living rightly in the created world. To envision humans as set right with the natural world by pointing to their gardening activity is to invite fallen humans to attend to forms God has and is giving to creaturely beings, with patience and hope, and over time. Human work ordered by care is grounded in taking an interest in the other, not for the purposes of their use value for us, but because the very form of that other body calls forth care from us, a care that extends across the nonhuman, the human, and even the suprahuman realms.

The primeval history also insists that humans have been cast out of this garden. Having suggested the importance of attentiveness amid a world, it at the same time tells us that we must do so in a world that no longer celebrates this engaged yet non-self-referential gardener-like caring.

It is hard to dispute Žižek's core claim that we are moving toward a trash-filled future and that we must stop hiding from this reality by learning to love the world, *this* world, as it is. But is Žižek right to conclude, further, that in order to love the world we must become more comfortable living our lives and finding our pleasures entirely on the side of culture, and to give up our nostalgic and impossible notions of "pristine nature"? Nature, he says, is already adulterated, there is no longer any "unspoiled" territory—if we are going to love the world as it is, we must become *more* detached, go deeper into the severing from nature that has led us already to have altered so much of the material world. If our ecological thinking is based on the idea of protecting the wild and unspoiled we will be forever in a rearguard and losing battle to prove that this or that aspect of the material world is unspoiled enough to be worth saving. Why protest wind farms in a landscape already dotted with houses and power lines? Why resist human genetic modification or nano-enhancement of a species that is quite different from its predecessors in being sodden with

---

its "vocation" to glorify the Creator. The cultivated garden will be like a song of praise to the God of order and of life, the God of peace.

Henri Blocher, *In the Beginning: The Opening Chapters of Genesis* (Downers Grove: InterVarsity Press, 1984), 120.

antibiotics and studded already with prostheses for its teeth and eyes?

When Christians refer to the cosmos as "creation" they locate their deliberations within the affirmation that the fantastic diversity and fertility of the physical world precedes all human willing, and therefore that all human willing is able to do is to discover and use materiality in a manner that recognizes and responds responsibly to its given form. We can make plastic only because oil has certain atomic properties. We can produce cloned sheep because we have figured out how to alter one small portion of the complex nature of biological life. But we cannot create plastic or sheep from nothing, certainly not from absolutely nothing as the Christian doctrine affirms of the Creator God. The Christian tradition has unpacked this last insight to suggest a basic rule for all human relations to, and possession of, material things: properly speaking, only God can be said to own the world, human ownership is therefore only a name for the right to use, a right that is always subject to abrogation in the face of manifest injustice of any given property or use regime. This right, however, also makes a claim when understood as a call for responsive human work. The Hebrew concepts for tilling and keeping indicate a form of appropriating the earth, so that ownership is not simply "there" but needs to be ratified. Christian ethics is the work of asking how we contemporaries are ratifying (or not) the goodness that characterizes a creation God called good—and sufficient to fulfill the needs of all creatures.

## Disposability, Commodity, and Trash

The contents of the contemporary landfill are born in our perceiving the material world in a specific way. The Styrofoam cup, for instance, is designed to be thrown away as soon as it is used. This is what makes it attractive as a manufactured, packaged, and marketed item. It offers itself to us as an object for which we will not have to care. It will serve us once and be thrown away. In the Styrofoam cup we discern that a core objective of modern capitalism has been to break down the tendency of humans to care in any enduring way for the material things of this world. The technical term for this process is commodification, the commodity being one of the core conceptual innovations of capitalism—the object designed to be discarded and then replaced in order to keep the waterwheels of commerce turning. There is an aesthetic here too: like the modern hotel room, the whiteness and promise of sterility the Styrofoam cup holds out is the guilty pleasure of claiming something that has been touched by no one else by "dirtying" it with our physical presence and then discarding it.[4]

Consider the transformation of an apple into a commodity. From time immemorial humans have picked, eaten, thrown away parts of the fruit, and later expelled the waste of digestion.[5] Where human population densities have been high, these waste products might have pooled to become smelly, threaten groundwater supplies or attract various creatures who live off these wastes. Through these

---

[4]Michel Serres, *Malfeasance: Appropriation Through Pollution?* (Stanford: Stanford University Press, 2011), chap. 1. "Convenience—brief 'vacations,' easier work, and freedom from attention, care and responsibility—joined cleanliness as a selling point for a wide variety of products. . . . Spotlessness and ease, once attainable only with servants—if at all—could now be achieved by buying things and throwing things away. With Kleenex, you could always have a clean handkerchief." Susan Strasser, *Waste and Want: A Social History of Trash* (New York: Metropolitan Books, 1999), 187.

[5]According to the *Oxford English Dictionary*, "waste" is the oldest term used in relation to our theme, and is derived from the Latin "vastus." In line with this derivation, its earliest usages (thirteenth century) designate lands that humans found to be unproductive: deserts, mountains, the ocean expanses. Over time a minor definition, designating uselessness in general, has become the major usage, and hence the connection with excrement. "Rubbish" was the next term to appear (fourteenth century), and though its etymological origins are obscure, it came by way of building sites, where it was applied to leftovers of building projects or useless parts of ruined buildings. Again, a minor definition has in modern usage become the dominant one, in this case indicating worthless writing of various stripes. "Garbage" emerges in the fifteenth century from the kitchen, and originally designated offal, and later general refuse or filth. Again, it came to be applied in the modern period to literary matter considered foul, and again the origins of the term are obscure. The origins of the term "trash" are likewise obscure though it arose only in the sixteenth century in handwork and agricultural contexts, denoting broken or torn off bits or cuttings in the first case, and in the second the leftover chaff from sugarcane after it has been pressed. Again, we find that in the modern period it had been used to describe writing considered worthless, and by the nineteenth century in North America even to people considered to be disreputable (as it still is today). "Junk" is a nautical term, used in the fifteenth century but becoming widespread in the seventeenth, which initially denoted old or inferior rope, and then a lump or chunk of something, such as a lump of salt meat or a specific part of a sperm whale's inner anatomy. It is remarkable how much the state of the art etymologies leave unexplained.

processes the wastes of the original apple would be reabsorbed into the earth by the working of living beings. In short, you don't need a landfill for these types of waste. We could even say that this kind of waste is ontologically superior to all other trash. Theologically speaking, waste might even be considered exemplary in its humble obedience to the divine Word—as a creature content to play its indispensable servant's role in the lives of many other creatures.

We can, however, attempt to disrupt these processes, or at least create the illusion that the apple has risen at least partially above its nature as future waste. To transform an apple into a commodity demands it be rendered nice to look at, interchangeable with equivalent commodities, and marketable. To make an apple, or let's say four apples, into a commodity, four very uniform and visually stereotypical apples are placed on a Styrofoam undertray and wrapped in transparent plastic. Then add a label, preferably one which betrays as little of the origins of the "product" as legally permitted (so as to make it saleable in the maximum number of legal jurisdictions). While this new object, the apple-as-commodity, can be handled differently than the old box of apples, sorted by machines, for instance, or thrown into a bag for home delivery after having been clicked online, it also generates something new beyond the wastes which have always attended apple eating. This something new is "trash"—whatever is left over from the apple mixed with several kinds of plastic which had been destined, from the very beginning, to be discarded. This garbage is very different in constitution from simple waste.

What makes the apple-as-commodity attractive? Its plastic wrapping makes loose spheres easier to stack and market, but more importantly, like the Styrofoam cup, its marketability rests on its power to remove the apple from the nexus of life. Apples-as-commodities promise to be clean right down to the microscopic level. For us cleanliness is no longer just being visually dirt-free, but is now defined as the absence of life: as sterility. The imperatives of the commodity—to be uniform, visually attractive, and interchangeable—are intertwined with the desire that this thing we buy and eat be germ-free: totally disconnected from the rest of the organic world. The COVID-19 pandemic has been a stark reminder of how powerfully our fear of germs shapes all the institutions of the modern globalized world. In sum, observes Greg Kennedy: "Packaging individualizes food, stealing it away from the grand natural nexus and locking it safely in its own monadic container. The commodification of food privatizes it economically, socially and . . . ontologically."[6]

## Caring for Creatures in a Creaturely Manner

The commodity and the concept of germs express a modern desire to opt out of the webs of reciprocal relations that are constitutive of the created realm. What makes the commodity attractive to us is its promise to release us from care. The disposable cup is one that we will not have to wash or attend to in any way after use. The apple-as-commodity will not have to be selected out of a heap, nor washed, nor any blemishes or "bad spots" be cut out—it will wait patiently and inertly at our disposal (at least, we are guaranteed on the package, until the "sell by" date). At the same time, the ways we once might have related to apples, by smelling them, for instance, are replaced with more abstract means of assessment: How much do they cost? What essential vitamins or threatening calories do they contain? This abstract mode of relation somehow, yet again, increases consumption by demanding more transportation, as is plainly visible in the fact that commodified apples turn out to be cheaper coming from Spain than from Somerset. (We are suspicious that this has to do with how much the labor in Spain is paid, but we try not to think about that, along with facts such as the United States devoting almost as much energy to packaging food as to growing it.[7]) What is certain is that now, in addition to the packaging that we at least incipiently throw away the very minute we buy a commodified apple, we have also consumed a far higher portion of petrochemicals than we would have if we had access to the local apple, warts and all.

This observation reveals that it is the *image* of an apple that we are in fact buying when we buy them in commoditized form,

---

[6]Greg Kennedy, *An Ontology of Trash: The Disposable and Its Problematic Nature* (Albany: State University of New York Press, 2007), 69.
[7]Ibid., 75. Also, Tim Land and Michael Haeasman, *Food Wars: The Global Battle for Mouths, Minds and Markets* (London: Earthscan, 2004), chap. 6.

and it is the leap from local places into the realm of the ideal that is so characteristic of and universal in modern capitalism. Phenomenologically and theologically speaking, the term "food" designates living organisms destined to die by being ingested by other organisms in order for the latter to live. It is clearly possible to acknowledge or resist acknowledging this reality in the ways we eat, by, for instance, passing all that will be eaten through sterilizing and isolating procedures. This form of life comes with obvious costs, measurable in fossil fuel use and garbage production. Yet, because we are inhabitants of a world that trains us as consumers, we don't really *see* any real alternatives. Is there a more caring and attentive way to proceed as mortal beings who must eat? Understanding that there are germs in the world, and they can make us sick, we still face the question of how the challenges they present might be met, only one of which is to try to sterilize all our food.

Psychologically, we do feel mildly heroic as we recycle for having braved the sticky and germy biological substances that stubbornly adhere to the very packaging that promised to protect us from such mess. More importantly, the primary satisfaction of sorting recycling is the relief of having put things in a place from which we can be sure that they will be taken away forever by someone else, a classic atonement mechanism.

Historically speaking, industrialized recycling programs developed as sophisticated psychological screens designed to hide this nest of problems. As the inventors of the idea and logo of recycling realized (the packaging industry itself) without a publicly recognizable idea of recycling, consumers could not be weaned from age old habits of rationing consumption or reusing products.[8]

---

[8]We tend to think, for example, that recycling is an environmentally responsible thing to do. Most would recognize the recycling logo, but few would suspect that it was developed by the packaging industry. Indeed, "the Container Corporation of America commissioned the design a few months after the first Earth Day [in 1970] to advertise its reprocessed products and left the logo in the public domain for others to adopt." H. Rogers, *Gone Tomorrow: The Hidden Life of Garbage* (New York: New Press, 2005), 171. Manufacturers, in this way, were at the forefront of shaping public perception of this new concept of recycling and played a critical role in promoting recycling over reducing consumption or reusing products. Now, we rarely question the process once we have put materials into the recycling bin. Yet even by the mid-1990s: ". . . recycling did not minimize the creation of discards. Instead, this back-end refuse management strategy left wasteful mass production and consumption

As recycling has developed in modern capitalist economies, garbage must be viewed as a commodity or resource to be mined, once again deferring the root question mark raised by the trash produced in consumer societies. For instance, when we *sort* recycling, are we in this process learning to *value* creatures, to be *reconnected* with creation?

Ironically, within the logic of capitalism recycling inevitably generates a market and so a demand for garbage, whether as raw material for manufacturing or for energy extraction.[9] Garbage brokers are very explicit that their interests are first in profit and only secondarily in reducing the volume of garbage going into landfills.[10] Recycling thus fits neatly within another subroutine of modern capitalism, the idea of planned obsolescence. Car manufacturers paved the way on this front, understanding that if they kept making cars that would work for decades, they would dry up their own markets. Consumers needed to be taught that taking care of things is futile. You might as well use things hard because they are designed to be used up and thrown "away" and "someone" can be counted on to remove them to a place from which they can never return. Recycling, it seems, is a practice that teaches us to see what we once considered worthless to be financially valuable, tradable—but which does nothing to draw us into care for any creaturely entities.

---

unaltered and even encouraged. People started believing that their trash was now benign." O'Lear, *Environmental Politics: Scale and Power*, 122, citing Rogers, *Gone Tomorrow*, 176–7.

[9]Lars Haltbrekken, the chairman of Norway's oldest environmental group, observes that in a hierarchy of environmental goals, producing less garbage should be at the top, while generating energy from garbage should be at the bottom. "The problem is that our lowest priority conflicts with our highest one," he said. "So now we import waste from Leeds and other places." John Tagliabue, "City that Learns How to Put Garbage to Use Finds it Doesn't Have Enough," *International Herald Tribune*, May 2, 2013.

[10]Nate Morris, the founder of Rubicon, a now multimillion-dollar international trash brokerage, is irritated that the pro-business political right in the United States is disinterested in environmentalism. "I feel it should be our issue. . . . The main driver of environmental change should not be government or N.G.O.s—it should be the market." David Zax, "Dividing and conquering the trash," *New York Times*, October 25, 2014, BU1.

## The Producer-Consumer Binary as Trash-Producing

One of the main conceptual distinctions undergirding these developments is the producer-consumer polarity, despite the reality that much of our lives does not fit this schema. Do we "produce" a meal when we cook? Does the farmer "produce" crops? Do we "consume" education by attending class? Despite the oddness of putting everything we do under one of these two labels, contemporary public discourse, shaped as it is by economic rationality, continually forces us into a conceptual grid that obscures the patterns of energy exchange that link human beings to the world, and human beings to each other. Consumers are people who have been taught that the "consumer goods" that populate our lives are on a unidirectional trajectory; they came from a mine or a field, were processed, consumed, and will be thrown away, with a small portion of the best effluvium skimmed off for recycling. What is missing in this account, observes Wendell Berry, is any language to articulate how things return to the life cycle. This hermeneutic of the material world also does not confine itself to commodities. "Along with its glittering 'consumer goods,' the modern city produces an equally characteristic outpouring of garbage and pollution—just as it produces and/or collects unemployed, unemployable, and otherwise wasted people."[11]

Berry takes us onto perilous ground with this perhaps incautiously worded description of people as wasted. Yet as anti-sweatshop activists remind us, there are direct links between our taste for "throwaway fashion" and exploitative labor practices that treat people as expendable.[12] Theologically speaking, the poor are indeed unwilling avatars of garbage in Western industrialized societies—disposable, not worth investing in, and not worth re-integrating into the social space of the consuming majority. From

---

[11] Wendell Berry, *The Unsettling of America: Culture and Agriculture* (San Francisco: Sierra Book Club, 1977), 137.
[12] Jack Wright, "The Real Price of Your Throwaway Fast Fashion: Chile's Environment Ministers Demand the West Stops 39,000 tons of Unsold Clothing Being Illegally Dumped in the Atacama Desert," *MailOnline*, January 26, 2022, 8:57. O'Lear, *Environmental Politics*, 143.

this vantage point it is obvious why glittering hubs of global travel and finance like Mumbai are surrounded by slums in which people live by collecting and even sorting trash. In such social orders and through the medium of trash the poor get to join the rich as hostages of global market fluctuations. Those whose sole income is derived from collecting recyclables are the ones most directly affected by the commoditization of trash and its discovery as an "untapped resource" by the business entrepreneurs of the West.[13] It would not be too farfetched to say that in the modern global metropolis, trash ought to be read within the biblical imagery of the "gleanings" that Israel was to leave for the poor—a loophole and accidental social safety net that "the market" cannot but covet.

Like consumer waste itself, the lives of the poor are another aspect of what must be "wasted" in order to achieve the comfort to which the masses aspire.[14] The language of "wasted people" also evokes the hygiene hysteria which gripped the Western world during the nineteenth century, engendering toxic eugenic movements on both sides of the Atlantic. However, the "contagious" ones have been defined (whether poor, disabled or Hispanic; Jew or gypsy), the logic of germ-avoidance and hygiene as a necessary part of protecting the health of bodies clearly remains attractive to global citizens for very deep-seated reasons. The material habits in which globalized living trains us not only produces trash and isolates us from the created world but also isolates us from human relationships.

## Feasting, Fasting, and Sacrifice

They also demand our celebration. In his "Capitalism as Religion" Walter Benjamin provocatively observes that, in capitalist societies,

---

[13]Katherine Boo, *Behind the Beautiful Forevers: Life, Death and Hope in a Mumbai Slum* (London: Portobello Books, 2013). David Gelles, "As Oil Sinks, So Does Recycling," *International New York Times*, October 13–14, 2016, B10, 12. For the larger trajectories that impinge on this market-recycling relationship see Frank Trentmann, *The Empire of Things: How We Became a World of Consumers, from the Fifteenth Century to the Twenty-First* (London: Allen Lane, 2016), chap. 15, esp. 638–40.
[14]William Stringfellow, *My People Is the Enemy: An Autobiographical Polemic* (Eugene: Wipf and Stock, 1964), 29–30.

"There is no day that is not a feast day, in the terrible sense that all its sacred pomp is unfolded before us; each day commands the utter fealty of each worshipper."[15] In the West at least, feasting has been traditionally understood as a celebration that allows humans to identify with and celebrate the bounty and fertility of the world. Its celebrants understand themselves as both beneficiaries and participants in the liveliness of the world. But such feasting only makes sense in contrast with the normal state of affairs, in which the needs of the body are met within a regime of scarcity and toil. The meaning of the feast is constituted in its being an exception to the normal course of events. It renders the labor of base survival meaningful by interrupting it to focus its celebrants on the fertility which underlies and must sustain their normal labor in leaner times. Feasts remind humans that they depend on the processes of the natural world to satisfy their need as finite mortals, and here any wastage or excess is an unavoidable aspect of a bounded celebration of plentitude in general. But the consumer society produces excess as a matter of course. There is always more than we can ever consume: "individual or collective waste as a symbolic act of expenditure, as a festive ritual and an exalted form of socialization," writes Jean Baudrillard, must thus be distinguished "from its gloomy, bureaucratic caricature in our societies, where wasteful consumption has become a daily obligation, a forced and often unconscious institution like indirect taxation, a cool participation in the constraints of the economic order."[16]

---

[15]Walter Benjamin, "Capitalism as Religion," in *Selected Writings, vol. 1, 1913–1926*, 288.

> From the earliest customs of nations it seems to come to us as a warning that in accepting what nature so bountifully provides we should eschew the gesture of greed. . . . Has society, through hardship and greed, degenerated to an extent where it can now only plunder the gifts of nature, wrenching fruit from the trees still unripe in order to be able to sell at a good price, having to empty every dish, simply in order to fill it up? If it has, then the earth will grow poor and the land bear poor harvests.

Walter Benjamin, "One Way Street" (Einbahnstrasse) in *One Way Street and Other Writings*, trans. J.A. Underwood and intro. Amit Chaudhuri (London: Penguin, 2009), 63–4.

[16]Jean Baudrillard, *The Consumer Society: Myths and Structures* (London: Sage, 1998), 47.

This modern institutionalization of the unending feast comes at a great cost. First, continual consumption turns a celebration entered willingly into something like an exhausting force-feeding. Second, in a genuine feast the celebrants are joined with and tangibly appreciate the life-force of the natural world. The joy that attends feasts can only be turned into a masquerade if it does not punctuate more routine times of fasting or need. Third, a feast is as much about convivial fellowship as it is about eating, and drinking— eating *together* is intrinsic to it. This is why, fourth, a tight linkage developed in Western Christianity between sacrifice and feasting. The condition of the joy of the feast is gratitude to God. Gratitude without joy is as contradictory as feasting without the sacrifice of offering.[17]

The rituals of conspicuous consumption and the dumping and pulping of so-called "excess" commodities are institutionalized forms of venting the excessive productivity that overspills the demands of the continual mandatory feasting that is modern capitalism. But such rituals do not link us in any sort of sympathy with the created world in the way the feast does. Nor do they call forth joy, since in continuous secular feasting the fecundity of creation as appropriated by human work is experienced as an overwhelming threat met by trying to destroy and hide what has been excessively gathered. Like recycling, then, such rituals of destruction sustain a status quo that jealously guards and inflames our "consumptive eye" for which, as Locke so influentially put it, all things are a waste or less than useful until they are converted into things which can be bought, sold, and consumed. Can we escape our entrapment in this hermeneutic of liberal capitalism in which we are so hermetically sealed?

## Christian Ritual and the Renewal of Perception

Christian worship is anchored in a highly developed ritual in which the offering, feasting, and eating that consumer culture denies is offered in a weekly rhythm to the worshipper. The Christian

---

[17] Kennedy, *An Ontology of Trash*, 14.

insistence on a day of rest organized around a Eucharistic rite offers an alternative way of living in creation to modern consumers. The faithful bring the fruits of their labor, offer them to God, and receive them back in the form of a feast celebrating them as a work of God. A path is opened here leading back toward a mode of integrative perceiving the world, and so a transformative inversion of perception. This formulation draws on Martin Luther's linkage of the Eucharist with the estrangement of humans from the material world depicted in the biblical account of the Fall. At the beginning of the biblical story, we find an account of the origins of human estrangement from the material world encapsulated in the false promise of the serpent: "Your eyes will be opened, and you will be like God, knowing good and evil" (Gen. 3:5). Thus, concludes Luther, certain types of knowledge must be understood as blinding us to theologically essential realities. As sinners we "would rather see what is fine and pretty and well formed," a mousetrap that dulls our minds. "But Christ came to teach these eyes to see and to take away the blindness, in order that we should not make this distinction between young and old, beautiful and ugly, and so on."[18] To perceive creation *as* creation demands the reversal of the "opened eyes" the first human beings coveted. Modern Christians have been deeply formed by the Enlighteners' quest for true perception through extracting eternal essences through disembodying perception. For Luther, in contrast, the renewal of perception comes via a practice. For Luther the Lord's Supper is the primal liturgical form in which the goodness of all God's works can be learned, the point at which Jesus Christ's power to open eyes and ears (Mk. 7:34-35) is promised to humans.

Luther develops this claim by way of a reference to the logic of the Passover sacrifice. As Israel was commanded annually to recall and so appropriate their divine liberation from temporal death in their offering of the first fruits of their labor to God, so too in the celebration of the Lord's Supper are Christians offered a refreshed

---

[18]"Rather all are equal, wise man or simpleton, sage or fool, man or woman; it is enough that he is a man with our flesh and blood, a body common to all. For such perception one must have a fine, acute, and well-trained mind." Martin Luther, "Sermon on the Man Born Blind, John 9:1-38," *Luther's Works* 51 (March 17, 1518): 38–9.

view of the divine working on which their lives and salvation rest.[19] It is a "sure and infallible rule" that God makes Godself manifest to humans, "by some definite and visible form that is . . . within the scope of the five senses."[20] The externality and tangibility of the divine presence through creatures is therefore both the condition of faith and God's chosen mode of calling humans to responsibility, of clothing specific creatures in the divine promise and claim.

Because the divine works of care are so mulitiplicitous, however, human beings are tempted to complacency about God's care in both the material and ritual worlds. "[W]e cannot sufficiently marvel at [the Lord's Supper] and contemplate it in eternity. And yet, when we hear about it, we clods . . . yawn about it and say: 'Oh, is this the first time you have ever seen a rotten apple drop from a tree?'"[21] The Eucharistic feast discloses by showing us what it means for creatures to be clothed in the divine word, so rendering the material world articulate, Luther insists. Luther's explication of how Eucharistic observance loosens the voice of a sterile and inert material world is especially interesting given the problem of the hermetic nature of capitalist consumption.

## Doxological Perception and Our Re-Education as Creatures

As they celebrate God's works in the worship service, the doxological perception fostered in the communion feast allows humans to discover fertility and new life in all its forms as modalities of divine care. In his interpretation of Gen. 6:22, God's command to Noah to provision the Ark before the flood, Luther finds scripture to raise a question: Why did God make Noah provision the Ark for the animals? God could have fed Noah as he fed Elijah and other biblical saints, directly from heaven. God did not do this because, "God governs the things He has created in such a way that He

---

[19]Martin Luther, "Psalm 111," *Luther's Works* 13, American Edition, ed. Jaroslav Pelikan (St Louis: Concordia, 1956) 373.
[20]Martin Luther, *Lectures on Genesis: Chapters 15–20. Luther's Works* 3. American Edition, ed. Jaroslav Pelikan (St Louis: Concordia, 1968), 122.
[21]Luther, "Psalm 111," 373.

allows them to function with their distinctive activities," Luther proposes.

> God makes use of definite means and tones down His miracles in such a manner that He makes use of the service of nature and of natural means.... And He demands from us too that we do not waste the products of nature (for that would be tempting God), but that we use with thanksgiving the means He has provided and offered.

God told Noah to do the work of collecting food and building the ark from trees so that Noah would "make use of the means provided by wood or trees, in order that human effort might have this course, as it were, on which to train itself."[22]

Noah is confronted not only by institutionalized sin and violence but by imminent ecological disaster. The ark is depicted as the first divinely given replacement for Eden, a space in which humans and animals can live amid the inhospitable regions of the world. Because he is listening to God, the adamic figure of Noah is able to hear God's direction to build this ark of safety, and to go out from it to serve those who will live in it by gathering food for them. In Noah, Luther thus suggests, we see a depiction of a walking with God characterized by an ever deepening appreciation of the created world explored out of a primary interest to remain in God's story. To be trained in appreciating creation is here displayed as an engagement with it by beings who seek to know it as God's gift, and therefore as the medium of our communion with God and other creatures.[23]

When humans are recalled to celebrate the sheer materiality of divine care, willing, joyful, and grateful attention is fostered for the ways in which God, through the immanent processes of the created world, donates or "invests in" human life. Luther's view reveals the capitalist understanding of all goods as essentially, if

---

[22]Luther, comment on Gen. 6:22, *Luther's Works* 2, American Edition, ed. Jaroslav Pelikan (St Louis: Concordia, 1960) 76-7.
[23]It is an insight recently recovered by Norman Wirzba, *The Paradise of God: Renewing Religion in an Ecological Age* (Oxford: Oxford University Press, 2003), 33-4.

not yet actualized garbage, as a modality of refusing this gratitude. Even in the icon of fecundity, fruit, those who seek the pleasures of commodities can in the end only find blemishes, offensively limited pleasures, and the banality of the "fact" which does not convey any "meaning." If garbage as I have described it is at its root the effluvium of a disordering mode of perceiving material things, then the reordering on offer in Christian worship is precisely what is needed if we are to live lives less "trashy" as a whole and produce less garbage. This is why Christians can both admit that recycling is entrapped in the deadening and trashing epicycles of the consumerist economy and still engage in it, seeking to be transformed by facing their own refuse.

The question is what, precisely, we do when as Christians we recycle. My suggestion is that, theologically speaking, the act of sorting our own effluvium is, for Christians as it was for Noah, a tactile education about the contours of our own concrete complicity in the fallen human resistance to worshipfully acknowledging the proximity of God's creative and sustaining works. When we bend down to our garbage, we face a report card on our performance of the one human vocation to be joyful recipients of God's works. There will be repentance called forth here as we discover our complicity in broken and avaricious ways of screening the plentitude of the creation as from God. But because this is the judgment of Jesus Christ, with it comes a hope and anticipation for the emergence of something different, better, more accepting of the inter-reliance constitutive of our creaturely nature.

Given the potent practical and ethical import of such a renewed perception, it is no surprise that the beachhead of alternative rationality that is opened up in Christian worship is envied by the gods committed to fostering consumptive perception. The early twentieth century also saw crusades to replace the common communion cup in Christian worship by individual "hygienic" and often disposable communion cups. The early advocates for abandoning the age old practice of sharing a communion cup put their case in terms that display the encroachment of modern consumptive capitalism into the heart of the church's self-understanding: "The old lady, pure in mind and body, sips from the cup which has just left the lips of one physically impure . . . [while] the old lady's pure and healthy child takes the cup from the unfortunate child of heredity, the offspring of physical impurity."²⁴ While such a communion might still interrupt the 24/7 feasting of consumer societies, it does nothing to draw worshippers into relations with the created world (being sterile, at least in aspiration), and it actively discourages proximity with the underclass and the genetically impure, who are labelled even in the body of Christ to be carriers of threat. The penetration of this logic into middle-class American and British Protestantism explicitly embraced and preached the cleanliness that can be maintained through eugenics.²⁵ And as those who fought the rise of disposable communion cups feared, their use in churches changed the character of Christian worship itself by dissolving the experience of worship as a collective feast. The new construction of communion is best understood as the parallel and simultaneous consumption of commoditized elements. This logic destroys Christian gathering as church because worshippers consider themselves no more mutually constitutive of one another than any other accidental gathering, such as an audience of moviegoers. A feast that had once simultaneously invited the worshipper to reconnect to the superabundance of creation and the Creator (without creating any garbage at all), was thus reabsorbed by the laws of consumer society, by way of a promise to escape the human curse and vocation to labor. Thus are

---

[24]Quotation from M.O. Terry, a doctor in Utica, New York, whose paper entitled "The Poisoned Chalice" was read out to the Oneida County Homeopathic Society in 1887. In Daniel Sack, *Whitebread Protestants: Food and Religion in American Culture* (New York: St. Martin's Press, 2000), 36. The sentiment remains common in American churches.

[The inventor of the prepackaged communion set, Jim] Johnson touts the hermetic seal as a way to prevent foreign substances, such as warfare chemicals that may be present during a religious service on a battlefield, from contaminating the communion host and wine. The seal also helps prevent possible transmission of disease by people sharing a common cup or loaf of bread. That's one of the things that sold Rev. Huford Norwood of the Maryland Avenue church on the idea. "When they put their hands on the tray to take communion, they may not be clean," he said, explaining that he learned of the cups at a recent national convention of Baptist ministers. "I think this is much more sanitary."

Tara Gruzen, "Communion In A Cup Has Its Converts, Naysayers," *The Chicago Tribune*, April 19, 1996, http://articles.chicagotribune.com/1996-04-19/news/9604190345_1_common-cup-communion-grape-juice.
[25]Amy Laura Hall, *Conceiving Parenthood: American Protestantism and the Spirit of Reproduction* (Grand Rapids: Eerdmans, 2008), chap. 3.

Christians shrink-wrapped in their isolation from one another and the created world.

## Garbage as Mirror and Open Door

While worship is not a talisman that can magically open our eyes to the created world, if Christians today can find their way to take the rites of Christian worship seriously as well as re-engage the Eden account with a little sympathy, they might begin to rediscover the care that reengages us bodily and intellectually in the whole range of creaturely relationships. Only as we find in garbage an invitation to step toward living as the mortals we are, as Kennedy nicely puts it, can we "give up the ill-fitting mantle of a lord and god; we can resume our natural place of service."[26]

Though a philosopher, in the end Kennedy manages to articulate the crucial theological point: insofar as garbage presents us with a problem, it is ultimately an inflection of our sinful temptation to float godlike above materiality and relationships.[27] We better learn again what it might mean in practice to embrace our reality as limited beings who must find a way of working and caring for the world in which its superabundance can be celebrated together in a non-destructive and non-anthropocentric manner. Cornell West rejoices in the fact that Christian celebration might be a bit smellier and more uncomfortable than our sanitized and isolated contemporary world. The gospel might smell and feel differently than the togetherness of the world, but it gets us "dancing and laughing, rapping and exposing the hypocrisy of a soulless and sanitized civilization."[28]

Facing our trash allows us to raise questions about environmental ethics without the bondage and heaviness that comes with the law of fear of environmental apocalypse highlighted by Žižek. Christ

---

[26]Kennedy, *An Ontology of Trash*, 185.
[27]Dietrich Bonhoeffer, *Creation and Fall: A Theological Exposition of Genesis 1–3*, *Dietrich Bonhoeffer Works* 3, ed. John de Gruchy, trans. Douglas Stephen Bax (Minneapolis: Fortress Press, 1996), 115–20.
[28]Cornel West, with David Ritz, *Brother West: Living and Loving Out Loud: A Memoir* (New York: Hay House, 2009), 5.

frees human beings into creatively responding to God's works in the world by releasing us from the crushing guilt that accompanies honestly facing the size of the environmental predicament. Faithful practices of consumption and waste management will flow from joyful gratitude for the plenitude of creation. This would mean to not see trash as a mirror, but as a material locale to listen for the call and claim of our creator and redeemer.

Freed into gratitude for the beauty and diversity of the creaturely realm, Christians are liberated to think differently and critically about the mechanics of waste processing, its place in relating us to other human beings, and the institutional structures that support our ways of living. Christians are free to choose between better and worse activities, and to redirect the prodigious forces of technology and commerce toward more faithful ends. The practical task is to become more attentive as to which practices the church should denounce as indefensible offenses against God's good creation and our human and animal neighbors.[29]

These are problematics that we not only need theologians to discuss, but ones which even city planners, economists and waste managers might well also learn to see anew. Such a rediscovery may well lead Christians to pay more attention to the ways in which work and feasting, immanent and transcendent economies have been fleshed out in practice in the cultures of the West. Here we can turn to studies like the brilliant anthropological treatment of a nineteenth-century Greek island done by Juliet Boulay, who described how its inhabitants understood their worship as very directly giving them a deep appreciation for the land, its seasons, and the need for them to care for it. For instance, they considered the year's agricultural toil to find its fullest expression in being prepared as loaves of bread to be offered to the priest in the context of the worship service, who would in turn represent God's returning their toil in the form of a Eucharist to be consumed.[30] This Greek rite displays the forgotten and crucial insight of the patristic church that the offertory and Eucharist are intrinsically linked because in

---

[29] J. Marques Rollison, *A New Reading of Jacques Ellul: Presence and Communication in the Postmodern World* (Lanham: Lexington Books, 2020), 160.

[30] Juliet du Boulay, *Life and Liturgy in a Greek Orthodox Village* (Limni: Denise Harvey, 2009), chap. 5.

the offering the participants are giving themselves to God through their gifts laid on the altar.[31] Here, as elsewhere in the clearing that we call pre- and early modern Christendom, the relation of human life to the energy cycles of the created world was understood as intertwining with human rhythms in which work and rest, heaven and earth, the domestic and the agricultural were knitted together in the celebration of the Eucharist in ways which quite obviously generated closer attention to what it means to care for and tend the earth as something through which God sustains human life. I would suggest it behooves us to think much harder about those forms of life, which were sustained and elaborated through social institutions very different from ours, which produced no garbage at all.

## Bibliography

Baudrillard, Jean. *The Consumer Society: Myths and Structures*. London: Sage, 1998.

Benjamin, Walter. "Capitalism as Religion." In *Selected Writings, Volume 1: 1913–1926*, edited by M. Bullock and M. W. Jennings, 288–91. Cambridge, MA: Harvard University Press, 1996.

Benjamin, Walter. "One Way Street" (Einbahnstrasse). In *One Way Street and Other Writings*, translated by J. A. Underwood, 66–142. London: Penguin, 2009.

Berry, Wendell. *The Unsettling of America: Culture and Agriculture*. San Francisco: Sierra Book Club, 1977.

Blocher, Henri. *In the Beginning: The Opening Chapters of Genesis*. Downers Grove: InterVarsity Press, 1984.

Bonhoeffer, Dietrich. *Creation and Fall: A Theological Exposition of Genesis 1–3*, Dietrich Bonhoeffer Works 3, edited by John de Gruchy, translated by Douglas Stephen Bax. Minneapolis: Fortress Press, 1996.

Boo, Katherine. *Behind the Beautiful Forevers: Life, Death and Hope in a Mumbai Slum*. London: Portobello Books, 2013.

Dix, Dom Gregory. *The Shape of the Liturgy*. London: Continuum, 2005.

---

[31] Bernd Wannenwetsch, "Eucharist and the Ethics of Self-Giving," in *Liturgy and Ethics: New Contributions from Reformed Perspectives*, ed. Pieter Vos (Leiden: Brill, 2018), 131–48. Dom Gregory Dix, *The Shape of the Liturgy* (London: Continuum, 2005), 116–22.

Du Boulay, Juliet. *Life and Liturgy in a Greek Orthodox Village*. Limni: Denise Harvey, 2009.
Hall, Amy Laura. *Conceiving Parenthood: American Protestantism and the Spirit of Reproduction*. Grand Rapids: Eerdmans, 2008.
Kennedy, Greg. *An Ontology of Trash: The Disposable and Its Problematic Nature*. Albany: State University of New York Press, 2007.
Land, Tim and Michael Haeasman. *Food Wars: The Global Battle for Mouths, Minds and Markets*. London: Earthscan, 2004.
Luther, Martin. *Lectures on Genesis: Chapters 15–20*. Luther's Works 3. *American Edition*, edited by Jaroslav Pelikan. St Louis: Concordia, 1961.
Luther, Martin. "Psalm 111." In *First Lectures on the Psalms: Psalms II: Psalms 76–126*. Luther's Works 11. American Edition, edited by Hilton C. Oswald, 371–83. St Louis: Concordia, 1976.
Luther, Martin. "Sermon on the Man Born Blind, John 9:1-38." In Luther's Works 51. American Edition, edited by Hilton C. Oswald. St Louis: Concordia, 1976.
Marques Rollison, J. *A New Reading of Jacques Ellul: Presence and Communication in the Postmodern World*. Lanham: Lexington Books, 2020.
O'Lear, Shannon. *Environmental Politics: Scale and Power*. Cambridge: Cambridge University Press, 2010.
Rogers, Heather. *Gone Tomorrow: The Hidden Life of Garbage*. New York: New Press, 2005.
Sack, Daniel. *Whitebread Protestants: Food and Religion in American Culture*. New York: St. Martin's Press, 2000.
Serres, Michel. *Malfeasance: Appropriation Through Pollution?* translated by Anne-Marie Feedberg-Dibon. Stanford: Stanford University Press, 2011.
Strasser, Susan. *Waste and Want: A Social History of Trash*. New York: Metropolitan Books, 1999.
Stringfellow, William. *My People is the Enemy: An Autobiographical Polemic*. Eugene: Wipf and Stock, 1964.
Trentmann, Frank. *The Empire of Things: How We Became a World of Consumers, from the Fifteenth Century to the Twenty-First*. London: Allen Lane, 2016.
Wannenwetsch, Bernd. "Eucharist and the Ethics of Self-Giving." In *Liturgy and Ethics: New Contributions from Reformed Perspectives*, edited by Pieter Vos, 131–48. Leiden: Brill, 2018.
West, Cornel and David Ritz. *Brother West: Living and Loving Out Loud: A Memoir*. New York: Hay House, 2009.
Wirzba, Norman. *The Paradise of God: Renewing Religion in an Ecological Age*. Oxford: Oxford University Press, 2003.
Žižek, Slavoj. *The Year of Dreaming Dangerously*. London: Verso, 2012.

# 3

# In Our Image and Likeness

# Theological Ethics and Artificial Intelligence

*Ad de Bruijne*

## Introduction

In spring 2022, Dutch police tried to solve a cold case with deepfake technology. Self-learning artificial intelligence brought thirteen-year-old Seder Soares back to life in a virtual setting. Surrounded by his real-world relatives, he appealed to the public. Is this AI-driven blending of virtual and physical reality (and of past and present) ethically justified? Deepfake can be used for good purposes or bad. On one hand, Alzheimer's patients could be enabled to communicate with deceased former relatives they still remember, while on the other hand, celebrities have been ruined because deepfakes exposed them performing in porn movies. This chapter aims to develop a theological-ethical grammar to address ethical challenges concerning AI.

AI is developing very quickly raising profound and urgent ethical questions. Consequently, ethical reflection on AI has exploded in recent years.[1] Many respond with enthusiasm and optimism. Many others, among them prominent public figures such as Henry Kissinger, Stephen Hawking, and Elon Musk, warn of unprecedented risks.

However, Christian ethics is lagging behind. In 2019, leading evangelical theologians published a statement on AI that follows the paradigm of 1 Timothy 4.[2] AI constitutes a good gift of creation that can be used for either good or ill. The statement lists important criteria for good use and identifies derailments. Yet, the challenges run deeper. Recent philosophies of technology question the underlying paradigm of such statements which suppose that technology is a means for human disposal, neatly distinguished from humans themselves.[3] These philosophies claim humans and technology to be inevitably interconnected and even mutual actors. Such analyses illustrate that ethical reflection needs to delve deeper into the character of contemporary technology. It is also the case that theological ethics should offer more than guidelines and boundaries. It possesses a unique grammar that could result in a unique description and interpretation of AI. I distill this grammar from Augustine, Dietrich Bonhoeffer, and Oliver O'Donovan. First, I offer an impression of current ethical reflection on AI. Then I

---

[1]Markus D. Dubber, Frank Pasquale, and Sunit Das, eds., *The Oxford Handbook of Ethics of AI* (Oxford: Oxford University Press, 2020), 34; Mark Coeckelbergh, *AI Ethics* (Cambridge: MIT Press, 2020); Keith Frankish and William M. Ramsey, *The Cambridge Handbook of Artificial Intelligence* (Cambridge: Cambridge University Press, 2014); Henry A. Kissinger, Eric Schmidt, and Daniel Huttenlocher, *The Age of AI* (London: John Murray, 2021); S. Matthew Liao, ed., *Ethics of Artificial Intelligence* (Oxford: Oxford University Press, 2020); Patrick Lin, Keith Abney, and Ryan Jenkins, eds., *Robot Ethics 2.0* (New York: Oxford University Press, 2017); Stuart Russel and Peter Norvig, eds., *Artificial Intelligence* (Hoboken: Pearson Education Limited, 2021.); Stephen J. Thompson, ed., *Machine Law, Ethics, and Morality* (Hershey: IGI Global, 2021).

[2]"Artificial Intelligence: An Evangelical Statement of Principles" (Nashville: The Ethics & Religious Liberty Commission of the Southern Baptist Convention, 2019), https://erlc.com/resource-library/statements/artificial-intelligence-an-evangelical-statement-of-principles/.

[3]Peter-Paul Verbeek, *Moralizing Technology: Understanding and Designing the Morality of Things* (Chicago: University of Chicago Press, 2011); Luciano Floridi, *The Onlife Manifesto: Being Human in a Hyperconnected Era* (Heidelberg: Springer, 2014).

develop a theological-ethical grammar. I conclude by applying this grammar to some ethical challenges.

## AI as an Ethical Challenge

The rise of AI since the Second World War is part of the fourth industrial revolution. After the stages of mechanization (1), electricity and mass communication (2), and digitization (3), the final industrialization stage integrates the output of these earlier phases, brings automation, and connects mechanical and organic realities. AI means that a mechanical entity can perform tasks that actually belong to the human brain, such as logical reasoning, choosing, learning, and problem solving. Existing AI includes three types: Good Old Fashioned AI (GOFAI), machine learning, and deep learning. In GOFAI, algorithms, a kind of recipe in symbolic language, prescribe step-by-step how AI should move from a given input to a desired output. In machine learning, algorithms prompt AI itself to learn. In deep learning, this is no longer done via a step-by-step recipe but through a neural network structure, resembling the neuronal structure of the human brain. This causes a rich pattern of interaction consisting of several layers, as in the brain itself. What happens in the intermediate layers between input and output is so complicated and operates so fast that it partially eludes human understanding. Deep learning AI appears autonomous and creative. The famous victory over humans in the board game "Go" in 2017 originated in deep learning AI, as does ChatGPT, a program that has summoned much public attention since 2022 because of its ability to replace humans in writing well-informed and creatively about all kinds of subjects.

AI is now an integral part of our existence. It plays a role in translation software and apps that convert speech into writing, in facial recognition at the border and for security purposes. AI determines the ranking of sites on Google, monitors our preferences and needs, and responds with targeted advertising offers. AI carries out preselection for job applications, mortgage decisions, fraud prevention, and organ transplants. AI improves medical diagnostics and operations, and predicts weather phenomena and earthquakes. AI connects people through social media. AI chats, dates, tweets, debates, plays chess, mows the lawn, ignites lights on movement, filters email, gives route advice, dances, plays sport, paints, or composes music in any style, and acts as a receptionist.

Existing AI already contains major ethical challenges. Governments and courts judge people through AI, which has led to ethnic and social profiling. Self-driving cars or autonomous weapons systems can malfunction and harm people. In such cases, who, then, is responsible? People enjoy social, sexual, or caring relationships with AI. Is this healthy? AI invades our bodies. Electronic brain implants correct impaired vision, hearing and speaking, the effects of Parkinson's disease, paralysis, depression, epilepsy, and perhaps, one day, dementia. AI can neutralize negative emotions and awaken positive feelings of happiness. It can enlarge human tolerance and physical, cognitive, and even spiritual capabilities. AI is increasingly adopting more human tasks. Should we fear mass unemployment or look forward to a leisure paradise with guaranteed incomes? AI tracks us using facial recognition and other traceable features. It can rather accurately identify whether someone is gay or straight. Might AI encroach on our freedom, privacy, or identity? Might we allow AI to increase, as it does, inequality between nations, races, and classes, and to provide multinationals with more power than governments? Some expect AI to prolong our lives or even abrogate death. The person born human in 2022 will perhaps die as a cyborg beyond 2122.[4]

Confronted with these manifold challenges, current ethical reflection predominantly searches for the solution by equipping AI itself with a moral compass. But such an ambition comes with enormous complications. People have contradicting ethical opinions. Whose ethics should become AI ethics? There are many competing basic ethical theories and methods that exist. Which ethics should be programmed into AI? It appears to a certain extent that only deontology and consequentialism fit the one-dimensional symbolic world of algorithms. The mere inclusion of a "no harm principle" could serve to prevent some malicious intentions, including when there are consequences for a client of AI, and for other stakeholders. A tax authority wants to detect as many fraudsters as possible. But the AI to be developed for this purpose must also respect the

---

[4]Katleen Gabriels and Ann Dooms, *Van melkweg tot moraal* (Gent: Academia Press, 2020).

interests of diverse citizens with a variety of life circumstances on its radar.

However, most ethicists today agree that, in a human context, these two ethical theories are insufficient for many of the ethical challenges. Some, therefore, also try to convert virtue ethics and teleology into symbolic language. But this proves complicated. Moreover, even if all basic ethical theories are able to be converted into AI applications, questions would remain as to their hierarchical order. Some propose to solve this question pragmatically by combining them all into a mathematical matrix. Others, however, depart from all the effort of such "top-down" programming. "Deep learning," they claim, requires a "bottom-up" approach. AI itself is much better at observing how people make decisions and what is in peoples' interests and could learn ethics by itself. They refer to neurobiology and recent learning theories which have shown that the human brain itself has acquired ethical sense during a long evolutionary process. AI could do the same, it is suggested, albeit much faster and without the burden of humanity's dark animal past. It would start "from scratch," with some expecting AI to develop even better morals than humans. However, neurobiology has also revealed that ethical decisions are not made primarily cognitively but intuitively and affectively. Humans have learned to feel what is right and wrong. But AI cannot feel.

At least, not yet. The forms of AI discussed above count as "weak" or "near term" AI. Many thinkers and professional scientists claim that "long term" or "strong" AI is imminent, usually called Artificial General Intelligence (AGI). Where AI is capable of just a single intellectual task within a single domain, AGI would possess the entirety of human mental abilities, including emotion, intuition, and moral sense. And it would operate in a variety of domains. Whether AGI will emerge is controversial, but it would make ethical challenges even greater. Soon the mental capabilities of AI would surpass those of humans. Without human interference, it could set and achieve goals by itself. With the ability to bypass humans, AI would be able to create better versions of itself. Humans would lose control. This possible unique dominance of AGI is called singularity.

Some parallel technological developments further increase the challenges around AI and AGI. For instance, the internet is growing into a network that connects everything to everything.

In this "internet of things," smart devices communicate among themselves without human mediation. Combined with AI's invasion of our bodies, this "internet of things" could conceivably develop into an "internet of bodies." People would become part of an interconnected "ecosystem" that combines the physical, material, and virtual worlds. Their thoughts and actions could be controlled remotely. In addition, a lot of money and energy goes into creating "artificial life." Combined with such developments, many believe AGI brings a new leap in human evolution or even a new species that surpasses humans. Theocentrism and anthropocentrism are giving way to data-centrism. Transhumanist and posthumanist ideals fascinate many, and some of those who are concerned about such developments tend toward embracing transhumanism. If humans are not to be surpassed, many believe they must physically connect with AI and AGI. Those who refute this new Nietzschean humanity would end up as subhuman creatures amid cyborgs. If you cannot beat them, join them.

More than AI, AGI raises the ethical question of whether we can go along with such developments. AGI also underlines an already heavily debated question in contemporary AI-ethics, namely, whether we should grant AI consciousness and personality. If so, AI would also deserve moral and legal rights. Many support such an idea. Others see a qualitative difference between a living neural network in the brain and its silicon-made simulations. Granting AI rights would devalue humans, but some judge that disrespecting simulations of humanity would also be harmful for real humans. For example, the EU wants to grant AI "electronic personality" with matching rights.

# Describing and Evaluating AI with a Theological-Ethical Grammar

Alasdair McIntyre has shown voluntarism to be a core problem of modernity and modern ethics.[5] Neither nature nor created

---

[5]Alasdair MacIntyre, *After Virtue* (Notre Dame: University of Notre Dame Press, 2007).

order guides the direction of human effort. In addition, decisions about good and evil are no longer rooted in a given reality with a predetermined meaning, but in the human will. Basic ethical theories become competing contingent tools for dealing with phenomena that have no meaning in themselves. In this, modernity is reacting partly to traditional visions of reality understood as unchanging nature or static creation. Oliver O'Donovan has improved this tradition with a more biblical focus on history and eschatological transformation in Christ.[6]

This should bring the question of the meaning of reality back to the ethical agenda, not just by referring to nature or creation but as Dietrich Bonhoeffer does.[7] Ultimate reality is God's work in Christ who encompasses the beginning, history, and the end. This ultimate reality sheds true light on all the penultimate realities of our lives with which we are ethically concerned. Concerning AI, it offers at least three unique insights.

## Inheritance and Decay

According to Bonhoeffer, this Christological reality has deeply affected Western history with the consequence that in many ethically qualified realities we now witness both its inheritance and its decline. Bonhoeffer reflects explicitly on technology, with accents that resemble other mid-twentieth-century thinkers about technology such as Jacques Ellul and Martin Heidegger.[8] Of course, technology belongs to every period in history, but influenced by the gospel its development reached unparalleled speed and heights in the Christian West. Creation became desacralized and, made in God's image, humankind dared to subject the powers of creation. This was accompanied and followed, however, by its counterpart of unparalleled decay, especially in post-Christian times. Especially

---

[6] Oliver O'Donovan, *Resurrection and Moral Order* (Leicester: Apollos, 1994); Oliver O'Donovan, *Self, World, and Time* (Grand Rapids: Eerdmans, 2013).
[7] Dietrich Bonhoeffer, *Ethics, Bonhoeffer Works* 6, ed. Clifford Green, trans. Reinhard Krauss, Charles West, and Douglas W. Scott (Minneapolis: Fortress Press, 2005).
[8] Jacques Ellul, *The Technological Society* (New York: Vintage Books, 1964); Martin Heidegger, *The Question Concerning Technology* (New York: HarperCollins Publishers, 2013).

in technology does Bonhoeffer recognize "a rare repetition of the Fall." Humankind wants to be like God and denies the given reality of God's work. This unleashes forces humans can no longer control. Instead of being controlled, technology turns against and controls its creator. Later, O'Donovan applies this Bonhoefferian scenario to AI. God once created a free creature similar to himself. Now humans, too, want to make creatures in their own image and likeness. But where God could handle this risk of freedom, for them self-destruction looms. It is telling that the atheist storyteller Ian McEwan has derived the title of his 2019 novel about AI, *Machines like Me,* from Genesis 1. Moreover, the main character is a robot called Adam.

Bonhoeffer developed these thoughts about technology when AI or AGI did not yet exist. This helps us realize that the distinction between the two eras is more relative than present debates suggest. Even if AGI was not achieved, the mechanism of self-deification has already characterized post-Christian technology. AI already fits Bonhoeffer's grammar more explicitly than ever before.

This suggests the abovementioned common paradigm of "good use" versus "bad use" of created entities, derived from 1 Timothy 4, to be insufficient for interpreting AI. Paul does not engage in this unique post-Christian tendency, of which he could not yet be aware. He responds to the Hellenistic undervaluation of the material world. Perhaps Romans 1 would be more helpful as it uncovers mechanisms of decay in a culture that has fallen from its former heights. AI is not to be seen simply as a part of good creation that can be used rightly or wrongly. The challenge is much more radical: Could this phenomenon, despite the accompanying underlying post-Christian ambitions, still fit the ways of the Lord?

# Evil Powers and Temporary Peace: A Second Unique Insight from a Theological-Ethical Grammar

Bonhoeffer's reference to the Fall reminds us of the reality of evil powers. A theological grammar will remind late moderns of the fact that humans, searching for the good life, are in fact not independent, autonomous, and free actors but inevitably interconnected with transhuman powers that are both good and evil.⁹ When the quest for the good concerns the unique new reality of AI, this insight receives extra relevance, since deep learning AI and AGI have proved to be beyond direct human control. Technology here has become an actor in itself within a framework of interconnectedness that also includes humans. This insight is not specifically theological but has been a dominant emphasis in the works of contemporary philosophers of technology, such as Bruno Latour, Luciano Floridi, and Peter-Paul Verbeek. In precisely this respect they see a qualitative transition between former instrumental and present-day interconnective technologies.

From creation onward, relative freedom for creatures has been the gateway that allows evil powers entry into created reality. They cannot create anything themselves but are parasitic on given realities. That is why evil, disease, and disaster always have both natural causes and demonic instigators. It also explains why humans can employ means from reality to counteract and fight such forces. However, now deep learning AI and AGI imply a new—this time nonhuman—version of relative freedom, at least from direct human control. This human deficit expands the playing field for transhuman evil powers, while it becomes difficult for humans to fight their influences by employing created reality themselves. A kind of black hole seems to develop in humanity's dealing with reality that escapes the possibility of human counteraction. Evil powers (demons), in turn, will still have no problem in seeing through the natural processes involved and, as always, will be able to manipulate them. After the Fall, only the human being Jesus Christ could handle such semi-independent created realities. His very reign, after all, created some of the conditions within which human creative potential could develop. Yet, there are unpredictable consequences for a culture that abandons him and opens the door to evil powers. For this reason, the Christian philosopher Egbert Schuurman rightly links late modern Western technological development to the biblical symbol of Babel.¹⁰

That symbol reminds us of Augustine's doctrine of the two cities: the city of God, centered on his worship, and the anti-city of

---

⁹Sander Griffioen, *Kracht ten goede* (Utrecht: KokBoekencentrum, 2022).
¹⁰Egbert Schuurman, *Faith and Hope in Technology* (Toronto: Clements, 2003).

humanity, with a shared love of demons.[11] Since Genesis 4, apart from the Christian period in Western history, the highest cultural and technological developments have always occurred in Babel-like contexts. All the more telling is the intriguing mixing of Babel and fallen Jerusalem in the Book of Revelation. This suggests that Babel-like tendencies should be expected in unprecedented forms, especially in post-Christian cultures like the West.

However, according to Augustine, citizens of the city of God will find no other dwelling place than Babel during history. And despite its harmful ultimate direction, even Babel will be granted periodic temporary blessings and peace. Despite their very contradictory ultimate loves, both Christians and others will be able to recognize these as good and find each other in shared commitments for the time being. In line with the New Testament, living in Babel implies acknowledging both moments of cultural abstinence and moments of engagement and above all the discerning wisdom to distinguish between these. Times of suffering, perhaps even being treated as subhuman creatures, and periods of flourishing will relieve each other until the end of history. With this awareness, Christians could and should navigate the developing "age of AI" too.

Returning to Bonhoeffer, it is intriguing that, at first, he tended toward a negative evaluation of late modern technology but later reconsidered his position. Fundamentally, he claims, only one ultimate reality of God exists in the incarnate, crucified, and resurrected Christ. However, this ultimate reality manifests itself within the penultimate realities of this world. At the same time, it judges, reconciles, and therefore bears these realities. Thus, in all ambivalence, these can still function as the pathway that prepares the world for Christ's future. This vision leads to a stance of being antithetical yet bearing responsibility at the same time. In this manner, the reality of AI, and even AGI, cannot escape Christ and could become preparatory for the ultimate eschatological reality and thus a stage for sanctification. The contemporary theological ethicist Brent Waters has made a comparable shift. In an initial study, he warned against the posthumanist dynamics around AI and advocated cultural retreat.[12] Some years later, however, he

---

[11] Augustine, *The City of God* (Cambridge: Cambridge University Press, 1998).
[12] Brent Waters, *From Human to Posthuman* (Aldershot: Ashgate, 2005).

considered this to be no longer an option. Like all technology, AI has become too intertwined with our existence for that kind of response. Appealing to God's providence, he now expects periodic livable-in oases, even in a possible desert of harmful developments. That is why Christians must continue to participate and employ ad hoc adjustments from a Christian perspective on humanity and reality.[13]

Christians should not pretend to be able to take such technological developments into their own hands once more and direct them to God's purposes. Yet, unexpected fruits and temporary countermovements could result from their commitment to temporary peace, even for a post-Christian and transhumanist Babel. Neither utopia nor dystopia fits the reality of AI as it appears in the light of this theological-ethical grammar of God's work in Christ.

## Eschatological Creativity and Penultimate Order

A theological-ethical grammar confirms elements of truth in the transhumanist flavor around AI, but theologians differ on that point. Some applaud transhumanist ambitions, for example, connecting these with the classical concept of *theosis* (divinization).[14] God and humanity are growing toward each other in a historical process wherein humans are "created cocreators" who help shape that future. Traditionally, Christians have expected a radical eschatological transformation, of which these recent developments remind us. Some even consider the possibility that AGI might have a soul, since they see the soul as a function of the brain and not a unique substance. It is constituted by a relationship to God that could perhaps also be a possibility for future AI. Others object, since, according to the Bible, the soul lives on even without a body and therefore has to be different from what is implied in neural

---

[13]Brent Waters, *Christian Moral Theology in the Emerging Technoculture* (London: Routledge, 2014).
[14]Russell C. Bjork, "Christianity Allows for the Possibility of Artificial Intelligence," in *Artificial Intelligence: Opposing Viewpoints*, ed. Noah Berlatsky (Detroit: Greenhaven, 2011); Ted Peters, "Theologians Testing Transhumanism," in *Theology and Science* 13, no. 2 (2015): 130–49 (also see the volume's other contributions).

structures. They warn against the disembodied and anti-relational tenor of AI that renders humans into narcissistic individual minds within self-created virtual bodies.[15]

We should recognize at least that transhumanist ambitions are distorted fragments of a Christian inheritance. God's reality in Christ will ultimately appear as a new creation, unimaginably elevated above now-existing natural and creational boundaries to which we have become accustomed. God's works consist not only of the actualization of existing potentialities but are often surprisingly new. Both spiritually and physically humans will indeed transform to hitherto unsurpassed levels. In principle, therefore, we should not automatically refute forms of interconnectedness between humans and technology that head toward transcending what until now has been considered normal.

However, granting this in a theological-ethical light, the risk proves to be a premature grasping at an Enlightenment or Anabaptist type of eschaton. Hypothetical experimental anticipations of coming transformations should remain recognizable from the order of this world. Here, I refer to the biblical notion of "impurity."[16] Acknowledging many interpretative complications, I would claim this is at least partly related to the given order in creation and history. When God created in the beginning, he distinguished between light and dark, earth and heaven, human and animal, and man and woman. Each creature's nature required human acknowledgment and respect (as exemplified in Adam's name-giving in Genesis 2). The distinction between clean and unclean teaches this lesson. From New Testament and intercultural perspectives, we realize in hindsight that specific manifestations of impurity will have been culturally colored or dispensationally temporary. God's created order also encompasses historical and eschatological dimensions. Our inability, however, to repeat the specific biblical instances today does not abrogate the principle itself. Now, the creation story, while acknowledging their similarity, distinguishes between humans and "earthly matter." Moreover, Paul's eschatological perspective in 1 Corinthians 15 does not abolish but further reinforces this distinction.

---

[15] Alvin Plantinga, "Christianity Suggests Limits to Artificial Intelligence," in *Artificial Intelligence: Opposing Viewpoints*, ed. Noah Berlatsky (Detroit: Greenhaven, 2011).
[16] Mary Douglas, *Leviticus as Literature* (Oxford: Oxford University Press, 2000).

AI, on the contrary, tends to humanize matter and materialize the human. Granted the inevitability of interconnectedness we should always try, in one way or another, to respect this distinction. It is telling that many people respond to anthropomorphic machines or outrageous interfaces between matter and body with the same disgust as our ancestors did with former expressions of impurity. Disrespect for the order of the present dispensation would render AI impure.

Bonhoeffer has substantiated this necessary connection between the ultimate and the penultimate in yet another way. In a more dynamic and relational way, his concept of mandates covers the same entities that others describe as "estate," "ordinance," "sphere," or "practice." By this is meant particular fields or dimensions in reality such as family, care, economy, friendship, education, culture, science, technology, politics, warfare, and professions. The development of AI and AGI should not completely transcend these or harm or even contradict their specific character as created realities.

# Addressing Some Ethical Challenges

## Human-centered

We should relativize the current concentration on programming ethics into AI itself. Instead, ethical deliberation should remain something human. Ethics constitutes a human response to God and his work in Christ. Its core is a heart-to-heart relationship with God and fellow humans. Also, the various basic ethical theories will receive their harmony and fitting moments for application not from a mathematical matrix but from relational responsibility at specific moments and in specific contexts. Moral deliberation is not a digital recipe but the result of spiritual, philosophical, emotional, intuitive, and intersubjective human wisdom. Not surprisingly, the concept of an ethical matrix was first proposed by theological ethicists.[17] The comprehensive narrative of God's action traditionally leaves room for aspects of all the basic classical ethical theories. They do

---

[17]Patrick Nullens, Michener, *The Matrix of Christian Ethics: Integrating Philosophy and Moral Theology in a Postmodern Context* (Colorado Springs: Paternoster, 2010).

not constitute tools with which people should morally address a meaningless reality at will. They are contingently mobilized in the moment people respond to God's action in the face of God.

Furthermore, the proposed alternative, namely, trusting the self-learning moral capacity of AI, is naive. In a Babel-like culture, AI would thereby most likely acquire morals that often and ultimately serve evil. Therefore, the European Union has rightly advocated human-centered AI. Perhaps obvious and universal binary choices could be additionally supported by algorithms that are able to reason deontologically or from a consequentialist perspective, and even recognize what fits generally accepted virtues or purposes. Also, the digital potential of some more refined classical ethical theories, such as probabilism and tutiorism, has been pointed out. These do not seek the absolute right choice but the most probable or the safest. However, such digital "voices" should never replace humans but only interact with them and maintain a subordinate position.

## Respecting Spheres

Human ethical deliberation, perhaps interconnected with contributions from AI, would be wise to concentrate on AI's relation to the various spheres and practices within which it is employed or that will be affected by it. For example, in spheres such as friendship or care relationships AI could easily displace their unique characteristics. The use of AI would be acceptable as long as it, instead, respects and furthers these. Again, this would also be possible within a paradigm of interconnectedness, which means that, in the face of societal relational poverty, deploying care-robots will not be necessarily shameful or bad. As long as interhuman relationality convincingly remains the meaningful context, they could represent a temporary good.

Global power structures, originating in the use of AI by mega-sized companies, can easily contradict smaller circles of authority and responsibility. Deliberation about what respects the spheres at stake should involve representatives of all participants and stakeholders. This will slow down the pace of development, but it is precisely that blind pace of technological progress that signals some problematic autonomous dynamics around technology in general and AI in particular.

## Just War

The relative loss of control by humans in certain domains indicates that some developments have been derailed for some time. As today's ecological crisis confirms, this analysis characterizes post-Christian technological developments in other ways. Perhaps we should conclude in hindsight, that, like the atomic bomb, autonomous weapons and even completely self-driving cars should never have been developed at all. At a minimum, the traditional ethical doctrine of just war stands in unbearable contradiction to autonomous weapons. That doctrine, in fact, presupposes a relational connection to the enemy as fellow human and fellow sinner under God's judgment. As Augustine claims, deciding to kill someone is by definition unjustified, when not embedded in sorrow, pity, and even neighborly love. Autonomous weapons fall short of this foundational conviction. Either a new theological theory of just war is required, or Christians should increasingly abstain from AI-driven warfare.

## AGI

Even though AGI has not yet been realized, it is entirely conceivable that the development of AGI should be deemed to be unclean in itself. Though materializing human capabilities and thus enhancing them are characteristic of all technology and could also include intellectual capabilities, unifying these into new forms of presumed consciousness in nonhuman embodiments is unacceptable. It betrays an idiosyncratic pursuit of a post-Christian eschaton and contradicts the order of the present age. Once developed, however, Christians would inevitably have to interact with them. Then it would become all the more important to uphold in every way the distinction between human and tech, including when dealing with both of the then-existing versions of "consciousness."

## Rights

In line with this, AI should not become entitled to any rights. However, the already present anthropomorphisms do necessitate codes of conduct. The way we treat anthropomorphic machines will have formational effects on individuals and societies. Therefore, it is indirectly morally laden at the very least. At the same time, contrary to commercial habits and popular sensationalization and eagerness, AI—for example virtual assistants, health care robots, therapeutic robots, and robot-weapons—should in principle not receive anthropomorphic designs and traits, or, at least, as limited as possible. And no longer should real and direct (nonhuman-mediated) relationality between humans and AI be suggested. Prevailing tendencies, therefore, deserve backlash.

## Enhancements

As argued above, a theological grammar leaves some room for what transcends the existing order. That includes virtual realities and invasive interfaces. Moreover, the distinction between restoring and enhancing effects is thereby not always clear and viable. Some interfaces seem to be just extensions of long-standing accepted and traditional improvements of the body in the form of earrings, nose rings, cosmetics, strength exercises, memory training, growth hormones, or food supplements.

At the same time, according to Colossians 3, the future order is hidden. At most, an incipient hint to some dimensions that we do know, not disengaging from the present order, would be acceptable. People can greatly increase their muscle strength or memory through training and still not contradict their present existence and their lives with others. In a comparable manner, interfaces must also remain recognizable from the existing order. The same applies to virtual worlds. Disembodied interactions, meetings, friendships, and living environments require a convincing embedding in their original embodied source realities. While open to tendencies that develop and mutually connect the physical, material, and virtual, these distinctions, as such, should not become blurred and our sense of their specific character should not be erased. As long as we recognize the virtual as virtual and the physical as physical, combining both could be useful and acceptable. However, as soon as they unrecognizably intermingle in our experience, we have entered dangerous terrain.

## Conclusion

Returning to the example of the crime-solving deepfake with which I opened this chapter, I arrive at a balanced conclusion. Considering this scenario within the traditional model of technology as creational instrument, there would not be a problem. Although many deepfakes cause harm, this one serves a good purpose. However, a theological-ethical grammar uncovers the surrounding post-Christian and transhumanist cultural meanings of such phenomena. They fit an increasing tendency to relativize given reality and display a post-Christian eschatology. Yet, living as those in Babel we cannot escape participation, and so by looking forward to still unimaginable renewals of creational existence, we can suspect affinities with that future. Virtual realities, summoned by surprisingly new—and at first sight mysterious—means, indicate that there is more reality than we are used to. Under certain conditions these can be entered and connected to more common realities. These conditions include respect for given realities such as the irreversibility of death and the reality of loss within a mourning family. Besides, it must be made clear that virtual reality is of a different kind and should not spoil human experience and recognition of the physical and material worlds.

## Bibliography

Augustine. *The City of God Against the Pagans*. Cambridge: Cambridge University Press, 1998.

Bjork, Russel C. "Christianity Allows for the Possibility of Artificial Intelligence." In *Artificial Intelligence: Opposing Viewpoints*, edited by Noah Berlatsky, 30–41. Detroit: Greenhaven, 2011.

Bonhoeffer, Dietrich. *Ethics, Bonhoeffer Works 6*, edited by Clifford Green, translated by Reinhard Krauss, Charles West, and Douglas W. Scott. Minneapolis: Fortress Press, 2005.

Coeckelbergh, Mark. *AI Ethics*. Cambridge: MIT Press, 2020.

Dooms, Ann and Katleen Gabriels. *Van melkweg tot moraal; wetenschap en verwondering*. Gent: Academia Press, 2020.

Douglas, Mary. *Leviticus as Literature*. Oxford: Oxford University Press, 2000.

Dubber, Markus D., Frank Pasquale, and Sunit Das, eds. *The Oxford Handbook of Ethics of AI*. Oxford: Oxford University Press, 2020.

Ellul, Jacques. *The Technological Society*. New York: Vintage Books, 1964.
Floridi, Luciano. *The Onlife Manifesto. Being Human in a Hyperconnected Era*. Heidelberg: Springer, 2014.
Frankish, Keith and William M. Ramsey. *The Cambridge Handbook of Artificial Intelligence*. Cambridge: Cambridge University Press, 2014.
Griffioen, Sander. *Kracht ten goede: een filosofie van de tijd*. Utrecht: KokBoekencentrum, 2022.
Heidegger, Martin. *The Question Concerning Technology, and Other Essays*. New York: HarperCollins, 2013.
Kissinger, Henry A., Eric Schmidt, and Daniel Huttenlocher, eds. *The Age of AI: And Our Human Future*. London: John Murray, 2021.
Liao, Matthew, ed. *Ethics of Artificial Intelligence*. Oxford: Oxford University Press, 2020.
Lin, Patrick, Keith Abney, and Ryan Jenkins, eds. *Robot Ethics 2.0: From Autonomous Cars to Artificial Intelligence*. New York: Oxford University Press, 2017.
MacIntyre, Alasdair C. *After Virtue: A Study in Moral Theory*. 3rd ed. Notre Dame: University of Notre Dame Press, 2007.
Nullens, Patrick and Ronald T. Michener. *The Matrix of Christian Ethics: Integrating Philosophy and Moral Theology in a Postmodern Context*. Colorado Springs: Paternoster, 2010.
O'Donovan, Oliver. *Resurrection and Moral Order: An Outline for Evangelical Ethics*. 2nd ed. Leicester: Apollos, 1994.
O'Donovan, Oliver. *Self, World, and Time*. Grand Rapids: Eerdmans, 2013.
Peters, Ted. "Theologians Testing Transhumanism." *Theology and Science* 13, no. 2 (2015): 130–49.
Plantinga, Harry. "Christianity Suggests Limits to Artificial Intelligence." In *Artificial Intelligence: Opposing Viewpoints*, edited by Noah Berlatsky, 42–8. Detroit: Greenhaven, 2011.
Russel, Stuart J. and Peter Norvig, eds. *Artificial Intelligence: A Modern Approach*. 4th ed. Hoboken: Pearson Education Limited, 2021.
Schuurman, Egbert. *Faith and Hope in Technology*. Toronto: Clements, 2003.
Thompson, Steven John, ed. *Machine Law, Ethics, and Morality in the Age of Artificial Intelligence*. Hershey: IGI Global, 2021.
Verbeek, Peter-Paul. *Moralizing Technology: Understanding and Designing the Morality of Things*. Chicago: University of Chicago Press, 2011.
Waters, Brent. *Christian Moral Theology in the Emerging Technoculture: From Posthuman Back to Human*. London: Routledge, 2014.
Waters, Brent. *From Human to Posthuman: Christian Theology and Technology in a Postmodern World*. Aldershot: Ashgate, 2005.

# 4

# The Trunk of the Cross Is the Tree of Life

# The Frailty of the Risen Christ and Theology of Disability

*Nadine Hamilton*

## The Modern "Ought"

No other group challenges our modern self-understanding more than people with disabilities. They expose, as Stanley Hauerwas rightly points out, the pretentiousness of our modern humanism in plain sight.[1] This humanism entails that we take care of them as soon as they are among us; that we try to integrate them into our society, even if this often seems only marginally possible. At the same time, however, this same humanism tries to prevent such human beings from existing in the first place because they are viewed as

---

[1] Stanley Hauerwas, "Timeful Friends: Living with the Handicapped," *Journal of Religion, Disability and Health* 8, no. 3–4 (2008): 14.

incapable of achieving full humanity.² For we, as modern people, assume that it is the nature of being human to be autonomous and self-determined.

However, looking at these human beings, for whom our humanism demands that we let them participate in our society but who cannot participate equally because of their seemingly obvious deficits, it becomes clear at the same time that the categories and norms on which our current self-understanding is based must be questioned. Perhaps we have managed to convince ourselves that our modern Western society has become more open and hospitable to these people by making virtually every public building accessible without barriers and by trying to make the lives of people with disabilities more livable by being slightly less inconvenient. But this turns out to be just another illusion of our humanism: namely, the illusion that "interpersonal change is less important than infrastructural improvement."³ For it is, as Brian Brock correctly points out, these human beings in whom "reality tears through the paper-thin beliefs about human life that are characteristic of modernity."⁴ Their very existence calls into question the foundations of modernity and challenges us to critically evaluate our conception of ourselves.

We, modern people, understand our being primarily in the categories of self-determination and autonomy. The context for this perception is an understanding of "wholesome," "healthy," and "strong" that defines the image of what it means to be human. Western cultures, in particular, based on values and assumptions of modernity, relate these concepts to intellect and reason. "Normal" is the person who can choose his or her life in a self-determined way. This understanding of human being emerges from an idea that has its origin in the conception of human being as an independent and thereby isolated subject that originated in the Enlightenment. Starting with Kant's transcendental turn, from which metaphysics and with it the orientation toward a reality of a higher order loses its importance, the self-conscious subject replaces the reflexive decipher of reality. The nature of this self-conscious subject consists

---

²Cf. Ibid.
³Brian Brock, *Wondrously Wounded* (Waco: Baylor University Press, 2019), 1.
⁴Ibid., xvi.

primarily in using its reason and thus in leading a rational life.[5] Its activity of reason is its distinguishing feature. Freedom, autonomy, and self-determination have their original place in the consciousness of the subject.

However, if this modern norm describes the "ought" of the human being, it abstracts from the concrete existence of the individual human being; it proceeds without regard to individual conditions and realities of life; rather, it sets certain standards which it does not reflect upon itself. Accordingly, the ambivalence of the modern answer to the question of human being arises directly from the answer given by and with Kant and from the subsequent modern self-understanding of human being. The "normal being" of the human being is based on the positing of the human being's ability to reason and its resulting rational life. Autonomy, freedom, and self-determination are among the central guiding concepts of Western modernity. They are not only at the center of the historical changes in thought, social and legal history during the development of the modern era, as Martin Laube points out, but also serve as identity-forming key categories of the self-understanding of modern Western societies, their political-institutional constitutions as well as their cultural lifestyle. All ethical ideals and values of modern society are oriented toward these guiding categories.[6]

These modern values and assumptions provide the meaning of the category "disabled" insofar as they exaggerate and overstate the fundamental values of autonomy,[7] freedom, and self-determination. In the liberal democratic understanding of modern times, this can easily lead to an absolutization of the independent and thereby isolated subject.[8] Self-imposed immaturity due to lack of

---

[5]Cf. Wolfgang Schoberth, *Einführung in die theologische Anthropologie* (Darmstadt: Wissenschaftliche Buchgesellschaft, 2006), 46. Cf. Immanuel Kant, "Anthropology from a Pragmatic Point of View" [1798], in *Anthropology, History, and Education. The Cambridge Edition of the Works of Immanuel Kant*, ed. Robert B. Louden and Günter Zöller (Cambridge: Cambridge University Press, 2007).
[6]Cf. Martin Laube, "Die Dialektik der Freiheit. Systematisch-theologische Perspektiven," in *Freiheit* (Themen der Theologie Bd. 7), ed. Martin Laube (Tübingen: Mohr Siebeck, 2014), 119.
[7]Cf. John Swinton, "Who Is the God We Worship? Theologies of Disability; Challenges and New Possibilites," *International Journal of Practical Theology*, no. 14 (2011): 279. Cf. also Hauerwas, "Timeful Friends," 14.
[8]Cf. Schoberth, *Anthropologie*, 143.

enlightenment becomes a serious moral reproach.[9] From this point of view, the modern perception of "disability" appears, as John Swinton clearly shows, "radically reframed."[10] If an understanding of "normal" is that human beings are autonomous and free masters of their own lives, then all those who can only be so to a limited extent or with assistance are not normal. This leads to a causal decoupling of disability and impairment: For if being impaired once meant having a disability, this connection is broken; now, one can be impaired, but it does not necessarily follow that one is disabled. Rather, as the Union of the Physically Impaired Against Segregation (UPIAS) points out, someone is disabled when the social circumstances in which one finds oneself oppress or exclude that person from meaningful participation in the social and political system.[11] Thus disability in this sense, as Swinton shows referring to disability studies,[12] is "as much a social issue as it is a biological one."[13] If in contemporary Western societies we find the answer to disability primarily in medical treatment and rehabilitation,[14] this alone reproduces the distinction between "normal"/"abled" and "non-normal"/"disabled." Ultimately, it is not about the human being, but about its value for society.[15] However, this cannot be supported from a Christian perspective.

---

[9]Cf. Immanuel Kant, "An Answer to the Question: What is Enlightenment?" [1784], *Practical Philosophy. The Cambridge Edition of the Works of Immanuel Kant*, ed. Mary J. Gregor (Cambridge: Cambridge University Press, 1999), 11–22.
[10]Swinton, "Who," 279.
[11]Cf. UPIAS, *Fundamental Principles of Disability* (London: Union of the Physically Impaired Against Segregation, 1976), 3: "In our view, it is society which disables physically impaired people. Disability is something imposed on top of our impairments, by the way we are unnecessarily isolated and excluded from full participation in society. Disabled people are therefore an oppressed group in society."
[12]Cf. Gary L. Albrecht, Katherine D. Seelman, and Michael Bury, eds., *Handbook of Disability Studies* (Thousand Oaks: Sage Publications, 2001).
[13]Swinton, "Who," 278.
[14]Cf. Topher Endress, Hannah Waite, and Land Julie Marie, "Enacting a Theology of Disability: Framing Swinton," in *Disciples and Friends: Investigations in Disability, Dementia, and Mental Health*, ed. Armand Léon van Ommen and Brian R. Brock (Waco: Baylor University Press, 2022), 14.
[15]Cf. differently: "There is no worthless life before God, because God holds life itself to be valuable." Dietrich Bonhoeffer, *Ethics*, *Bonhoeffer's Works 6* (Minneapolis: Fortress Press, 2005), 193.

The present contribution, therefore, seeks a different angle as it wants to ask what constitutes creation and what constitutes being human according to Christian understanding and how this understanding can contribute to a change in the social and political perception of people with disabilities.

## The "Athens" and "Jerusalem" Models

Theologically, an objection to this worldview must begin where the perception of life is fixed in terms of what it makes of itself and what others make of it. If the value of a human being is measured in terms of his or her contribution to society, then not only the underlying categories of this society must be called into question, but also, in theological terms, the fundamental conception of creation and of human beings.[16] By tying the meaning of life and the dignity of human beings to their capacity for autonomy and self-determination, the vulnerable and weak human being is necessarily marginalized, as are those times and situations in the lives of *all human beings*, abled or not, in which they are weak, vulnerable, and in need of help. However, this conception presupposes human beings as autonomous subjects which they are not in biblical terms.

The Christian theological conception of what it means to be a human being must offer a contrast to the dominant societal conception. Dietrich Ritschl brings this point to the fore succinctly in his comparison of the "Athenian model" and "Jerusalem model" of human beings. Ritschl describes the "Athenian human being" as the "old Greek ideal, which saw in the 'normal' human being a young, balanced and happy human being, equally strong in the academy and on the sports field,"[17] as the basis of our present-day image of humankind. We educate our children according to this model: they should develop themselves to the maximum in their gifts and find their best own possible way in any situation. Ritschl also finds the influence of this model in the Christian church. In contrast, however, he emphasizes: "whatever one can justify as a

---

[16]Cf. Hauerwas, "Timeful Friends," 14.
[17]Dietrich Ritschl, *Zur Logik der Theologie. Kurze Darstellung der Zusammenhänge theologischer Grundgedanken* (München: Chr. Kaiser, 1984), 86ff.

generalization of the various images of human being: this is not the understanding of the biblical scriptures."[18]

In the "Athenian" image of human being, the sick, the weak, and the vulnerable have no place; at best, they appear as human beings in a deficient manner.[19] The ideal human is "competitive, can maximally self-actualize and optimally adapt to the situation in which he finds himself."[20] In the "Jerusalem" model, on the other hand, as Ritschl calls it, "the sick and broken human being, the suffering and unactualized, is the beloved, the true human being, the bearer of human dignity."[21] Ritschl sees this tension running throughout the Bible: it begins with the election of Israel, a small stiff-necked, insignificant people, through the prophets to the Servant of God, who has neither prestige nor beauty. All the way to the New Testament, God's power is present in human beings who are insignificant and sick. In the Crucified this power is completed, then the persecuted Early Church takes center stage. "Not that happiness, strength, and equilibrium were not known in the Old Testament; or in the New, good marriages, just governments, and sound states. But as a 'norm' none of this is central,"[22] Ritschl points out.

The "Jerusalem model" of human being therefore differs from the "Athenian model" mainly in one important respect: it is obviously not suitable as an abstract model of humanity, from which it would be apparent what "real" humanity should be like. And this could be seen as a genuine weakness of the Jerusalem model in contrast to the Athenian—for who would not wish their children "the fullest and most self-fulfilling development, and their neurotic and unfree acquaintances a maximum self-realization"?[23] And precisely in this, it offers a counter-proposal for a different outline of the understanding of human being. It resists any normative ideal. Accordingly, its significance lies in the fact that it fundamentally

---

[18]Ibid.
[19]Cf. Schoberth, *Anthropologie*, 145.
[20]Dietrich Ritschl, "Die Erfahrung der Wahrheit," in *Ökumene, Medizin, Ethik. Gesammelte Aufsätze*, ed. Dietrich Ritschl (München: Chr. Kaiser, 1986), 160.
[21]Ibid.
[22]Dietrich Ritschl, *Zur Logik der Theologie. Kurze Darstellung der Zusammenhänge theologischer Grundgedanken* (München: Chr. Kaiser, 1984), 87.
[23]Ibid.

rejects the orientation of human being to any specific, static norm. Thus it "corrects" the Athenian model in two ways, as Wolfgang Schoberth aptly points out:

> On the one hand, the religious exaltation of social and economic success is vehemently rejected, as if God were the ally of the strong and the victors . . . On the other hand, the "Athenian model" is shaken in its apparent self-evidence: does it really represent the desirable shape of being human if it represses the other side of life?[24]

Ritschl makes clear: *Christianity cannot be about establishing a "norm" of being human. Instead, it requires a revision of established categories. If "impairment" and "weakness" are social categories, the Christian task is to question and reformulate these categories.* The answer to the reality of the frailty and weakness of human life cannot be its relegation to the margins of society. Rather, the need for social change and radical political action for justice, inclusion, and full citizenship rights for human beings with disabilities is at hand. This way of thinking has become known as the social model of disability. It must work through the tension of the crucified Jesus Christ and the Greek hero. The problem, as Ritschl rightly points out, "lies in the theologically unresolved relationship between 'normal' human beings, as both demanded and sought to be offered by our environment, and the 'new' human being of whom the biblical scriptures know of."[25]

The present contribution wants to start here and ask what constitutes creation and what constitutes being human according to Christian understanding. Subsequently, from there, it is necessary to ask further how this understanding can contribute to a change in the social and political perception of people with disabilities. In doing so, it follows the direction that Stanley Hauerwas has been proposing for many years, beginning with a Christian understanding of what it means to be human, which starts from Jesus Christ, and from there developing proposals for change in political and social

---

[24]Schoberth, *Anthropologie*, 146.
[25]Ritschl, *Logik*, 87–8.

action.[26] To this end, reflections aimed at participation and political change are correct and important. Equally, such considerations can be supported by a Christian understanding of the human being from its creaturely nature. For a theology of disability that wants to change the ingrained patterns and categories of our modern thinking, it seems to me that it is precisely an approach via ontology from which a revision of these categories and patterns must start. Whereas in Hauerwas's work an ontological approach to the topic is repeatedly mentioned marginally,[27] my desire is to bring it to the front and center for more explicit consideration. This can only be done within the framework of a preliminary sketch. It becomes clear that a restructuring of the understanding of reality is necessary. This refers to the entire view of reality, a task that cannot be solved tomorrow or the next day, but must necessarily start in this dimension. This contribution therefore aims at a change of the existing order.[28] Not, however, by abandoning liberal politics and democratic society, but by evaluating and, if necessary, readjusting the categories on which they are based and which we use so naturally.

The approach presented here for a revision of the understanding of human being, therefore, begins at the only place where the human being and its nature can be understood theologically: in Jesus Christ, the incarnate, crucified and risen one. From him alone, the one who is the new, true human being, can one speak in Christian terms of the human being and the entire reality of creation. The emphasis is particularly on the cross and the resurrection: only from these is an adequate understanding of the reality of the fallen and reconciled creation possible. Accordingly, the thesis of the present contribution can be phrased in the following way: Starting with the crucified and risen Jesus Christ,

---

[26]Cf. for example Jennie Weiss Block, *Copious Hosting: A Theology of Access for People with Disabilities* (New York and London: Continuum, 2000).
[27]Cf. Hauerwas, "Timeful Friends," 16.
[28]This is Swinton's criticism of Hauerwas that his approach does not come to any real political change. But the changes Hauerwas thinks are necessary, and if I'm looking at this correctly, go deep into our understanding as modern human beings and take time to enforce and implement. Cf. Swinton, "Who," 298–9. Swinton's criticism is also directed at Hans Reinders, *The Future of the Disabled in Liberal Society: An Ethical Analysis* (Notre Dame: University of Notre Dame Press, 2000).

the nature of creation and of the creature is revealed in their frailty, which constitutes the nature of the creature as well as the whole creation. The prevailing categories of "whole," "healthy," and "strong" do not exist in Christian terms.[29] Rather, the nature of the creature and creation shows itself in this brokenness, which is to be understood from Christ, and which receives its permanence only in the life-grounding relationship of the creature to its Creator—a relationship which proves to be dependent on the Creator and fellow creatures. The perfection of the creature is to be found in this Christocentric view of creation as Christ-reality in exactly this dependence and dependency. On this basis the competing understanding of the human being as an autonomous and self-determined subject and the understanding of political structures are to be questioned. Accordingly, the task is to revise and readjust the taken for granted categories of being human. The response to the fragility and weakness of human life must not be to marginalize these people. Rather, what is needed is social change and radical political measures for justice, integration, and full civil rights for people with disabilities, and not only in society, but also in the church. From a theological perspective, the desire for these changes is rooted in the model of the crucified Christ as opposed to the Greek hero.[30]

Using the thought of Dietrich Bonhoeffer, I will briefly outline what is to be understood by a reality in Christ and in what context such an understanding of reality has consequences for a Christian understanding of the human being. Based on this, I will conclude with a brief outline of the extent to which this understanding of reality, including that of the human being, must change our current social value systems and assumptions.

---

[29]Swinton rightly points out: "... to divide up human beings is a category mistake which assumes the imaginative analogy to be empirically true" (Swinton, "Who," 301).
[30]Cf. Ritschl, *Logik*, 87–8.

## The Trunk of the Cross Is the Tree of Life

The goal of Dietrich Bonhoeffer's theological efforts, in short, lies ultimately in an understanding of reality as reality in Christ.[31] He is concerned with the ultimate, the one true reality that carries "into the reality of God's revelation in Jesus Christ from which it comes."[32] Accordingly, Bonhoeffer sees "the subject matter of a Christian ethic [in] God's reality revealed in Christ becoming real among God's creatures, just as the subject matter of doctrinal theology is the truth of God's reality revealed in Christ."[33] Yet, how is reality in Christ to be understood theologically? Bonhoeffer himself tried to outline this in different ways and in different forms, but he did not elaborate it systematically. Thus, starting from and with Bonhoeffer, the task is to further elaborate his idea of the one reality in Christ. This is no small task, but it is an important one. Only from an adequate understanding of this reality, which according to Bonhoeffer comes from Christ as well as aims toward him, can appropriate ethical consequences be derived for a change in current social and political values and assumptions, on the one hand, for the understanding of creation itself, and on the other hand, for that of human beings in this creation.[34]

Numerous theological approaches to disability have found various ways to answer the question of how Jesus Christ changes one's perspective on disability and people with disabilities and thus also on creation itself. Nancy Eiesland points to the disabled risen Christ, from which she develops a hermeneutic that begins with the experience of human disability, through which one gains a deeper understanding of God.[35] For her, the cross and the resurrection are the focus of a theology of disability. I would like to continue in this direction. Unlike Eiesland, however, I do not understand the cross

---

[31]In my reading, this goal does not only emerge in his later writings, but already guides his early writings, sometimes more obviously, sometimes more implicitly. I would therefore say that the issue of comprehending the reality of Christ has always driven Bonhoeffer's theology.
[32]Bonhoeffer, *Ethics*, 49.
[33]Ibid.
[34]Cf. my forthcoming book on a Christological ontology.
[35]Cf. Nancy Eiesland, *The Disabled God, Toward a Liberatory Theology of Disability* (Nashville: Abington Press, 1994). Cf. Swinton, "Who," 284.

and the resurrection merely as hermeneutical reading instructions; rather, with Bonhoeffer, they are the form by which the shape of creation is to be described in its nature.[36]

Bonhoeffer reads the creation accounts from the "end," that is, he does not read them from the incarnation alone, but also and above all from the cross and resurrection. He reads them from the perspective of the whole history of Jesus Christ.[37] Jesus Christ is not only the moral model for an ethic that includes the excluded. He is the one from whom and from whose life and death we can recognize what creation is and, specifically, who we human beings are. In this connection between the event of creation and the event of the cross/resurrection, something becomes clear that should not be underestimated for a theology of disability: Bonhoeffer equates the tree of life from paradise with the trunk of the cross. *The trunk of the cross is the tree of life*: "The trunk of the cross becomes the wood of life, and now in the midst of the world, on the accursed ground itself, life is raised up anew. In the center of the world, from the wood of the cross, the fountain of life springs up."[38]

By understanding the cross as the tree of life, Bonhoeffer changes how one views the reality of creation. This has far-reaching consequences for an understanding of the whole reality: The nature of creation does not lie in a perfect original state of whatever kind,

---

[36]It is not only in his *Ethics* that Bonhoeffer gives clues to his understanding of the reality that is grounded in and aimed toward Jesus Christ. This is evident in his Genesis lectures which were published as *Creation and Fall*, which he announces as a "theological exposition" (Cf. Bonhoeffer, *Creation*, 22). Accordingly, the preface operates like a hermeneutical "reading instruction" of the Scriptures, which emphasizes the necessity to read these creation stories from a Christological perspective. However, though he expounds these Christian "reading instructions" for the whole reality of creation, he does this without "Christianizing" the creation stories, that is, reading Christ into these Old Testament texts. Rather, it is essential to him to preserve these texts in their uniqueness and otherness and to take their otherness seriously. At the same time, however, he sees the reference to the new in Christ already contained in them. To what extent can this be helpful for a theology of disability?
[37]Cf. Bonhoeffer, *Creation*, 22.
[38]Ibid., 146.

that is, in a healed, healthy, and "abled" state. Rather, the nature of creation is revealed in the trunk of the cross. Bonhoeffer continues:

> What a strange paradise is this hill of Golgotha, this cross, this blood, this broken body. What a strange tree of life, this trunk on which the very God had to suffer and die. Yet it is the very kingdom of life and of the resurrection, which by grace God grants us again. It is the gate of imperishable hope now opened, the gate of waiting and of patience. The tree of life, the cross of Christ, the center of God's world that is fallen but upheld and preserved—that is what the end of the story about paradise is for us.[39]

The nature of creation, if we follow Bonhoeffer, is therefore not in a perfect original state. Creation is not an ideal world, or as we like to stylize it, as "normal," but broken and constantly threatened. In its fallen nature, the brittleness that results from being thrown upon itself becomes vivid. Similarly, the nature of Jesus does not lie in perfection, as is too often attributed to him. It lies in a conception exactly opposite to the one that Christian tradition too often suggests. Ritschl's reference to the Athenian model, which has obviously found its way into Christian theology, becomes vivid here: Jesus Christ is also conceived as a modern autonomous superman, who is in control of his life at all times and at the same time still saves the world—one man pitted against the whole vile world, like an action movie hero.[40] This conception becomes the model for a perfect human being and thus the "Christian" ideal toward which one strives. And this distorted conception of the true human being, Jesus Christ, results in a distorted perception of the whole creation. For if creation is perceived as perfect in itself and complete in its

---

[39]Ibid.
[40]Julie Hopkins, "Sind Christologie und Feminismus unvereinbar? Zur Debatte zwischen Daphne Hampson und Rosemary Radford Ruether," in *Vom Verlangen nach Heilwerden. Christologie in feministisch-theologischer Sicht*, ed. Doris Strahm, Regula Strobel (Fribourg/Luzern: Edition Exodus, 1991), 206. See also, Stanley Hauerwas, "Suffering the Retarded: Should we prevent Retardation," in *Suffering Presence: Theological Reflections on Medicine, the Mentally Handicapped, and the Church*, ed. Stanley Hauerwas (Notre Dame: University of Notre Dame Press, 1996), 104.

primal nature, then perfection is an inherent potential in creation itself, apart even from God, which only needs to be fulfilled, and those who strive the most are able to develop this potential more.

Yet, the broken and redemptive nature of creation is biblically evident (Rom. 8:18ff.). To Bonhoeffer, this brokenness and frailty of creation is vivid in the cross, in this disabled, pain-wracked, and deeply broken body, which carries the frailty of all human beings, but which in this frailty in the light of the resurrection is its consummation. In his completion through the resurrection by the life-giving and completing Spirit, he *retains these stigmata that are a tactile expression of his essential brokenness.*[41] These stigmata are part of his consummated being. They have not simply disappeared, not even for the resurrected Jesus Christ. Accordingly, medieval iconography can equate the trunk of the cross with the tree of life. Thus, when Nancy Eiesland speaks of the resurrected Jesus as disabled,[42] this highlights an important point: even and especially that the resurrected body of Jesus Christ is and remains a marked body. His stigmata testify to his frailty. His "being more able" than before is not, as Swinton suggests,[43] due to a perfection removed from creation, but precisely because of these stigmata and the story of frailty associated with them. He did not simply overcome this frailty, in the sense of leaving it behind. This frailty is an essential feature of the resurrected part of his being. In this he is more than abled. This "new" human being is healed, not in the sense that he would be without any flaw or impairment; *his being healed lies in the realization of his nature, which happens to be the consummation of the (hi-)story between creator and creature/creation.*

If an understanding of the human being is to be gained precisely from this understanding of Jesus Christ based on the cross and the resurrection, it is correspondingly important for an understanding of the human being, as this frailty is part of creaturely being. If this "new" human being is the true one in his frailty, then according to Christian understanding there is no "perfect" human in the sense

---

[41]This is illustrated, for example, in the case of the unbelieving Thomas, who recognizes his master only after he has seen and felt the wounds (Jn 20:24-30).
[42]Cf. Eiesland, *Disabled God*, 98.
[43]Cf. Swinton, "Who," 284. Swinton no longer sees the risen Christ in this brokenness, but stresses his perfection, his being "more abled."

of wholesome, healthy, and strong. Rather, this frailty of the Risen One, which completes his being, invites us to think anew about the prevailing categories of an understanding of being human.

## "Wondrously Wounded"

What does this contribute to a theology of disability? If Bonhoeffer recognizes the nature of creation in God's saving action for this creation, which is embodied in Jesus Christ as a person, then this has far-reaching consequences for an understanding of creation in general. Creation is not to be understood as paradise, and its consummation not as a return to this paradise.[44] Rather, it is to be perceived in its true creatureliness, and that is, in its frailty, still awaiting its future (Rom. 8:20-22). What has already been applied to Jesus Christ above applies analogously here: the "paradise" that we imagine as perfect was never perfect, nor does it have its consummation in any kind of perfection. *The "paradise" of primordial creation does not lie in any form of essential perfection, but in the disposition of creation to a story, to being in relationship with its Creator.*

The nature of creation is thus to be found in this story. God creates this world in order to stand in a relationship, and thus in a (his-)story, with it. Creation is in its nature aligned with its Creator. The ancient doctrine of Christ as the mediator of creation emphasizes this very aspect. The nature of creation lies in the three

---

[44]Jürgen Moltmann points out that this conception of paradise as very good and perfect goes back to the formation of Christian dogmatics in the realm of Greek thought. Paradise is perfection already laid out in the beginning; redemption in this conception is nothing else than restoration of the perfect, original creation. The history between creation and redemption is then nothing else than history of the fall; it cannot bring anything new, it can only bring deterioration. Cf. Mircea Eliade's description of the "myth of the eternal return" in the history of religion. Mircea Eliade, *The Myth of the Eternal Return: Cosmos and History* (Princeton: Princeton University Press, 2018). Moltmann, on the other hand, points out, "Biblically, historical faith in salvation determines faith in creation and, insofar as redemption determines historical faith in salvation, eschatology also determines the experience of history and faith in creation." Jürgen Moltmann, "Creation as an Open System," in *Future of Creation. Gesammelte Aufsätze*, ed. Jürgen Moltmann (München: Chr. Kaiser, 1977), 125.

Trinitarian hypostases: The Creator creates and sustains creation through the eternal Logos in the Spirit (cf. Col. 1:16); in the incarnation of the eternal Logos (Jn 1:14), the nature of creation is to be understood, starting from Jesus Christ, as a relational event of the Creator with the creation. Jesus Christ is the relationship of the Creator to the creature made person. But as Colossians 1:16 and Bonhoeffer's identification of the tree of life with the trunk of the cross make clear, it is not a conception of the ideal Jesus Christ that is to be projected back onto creation,[45] but rather the nature of this creation is to be recognized from the broken and risen Christ.

Creation has its nature in the frailty of the crucified and risen One, a frailty that even after the resurrection is part of this glorified body. It is a visible sign of his nature, which lies in his story, in his relationship with the Creator.[46] In this frailty of Jesus Christ the true nature of creation is revealed, as Bonhoeffer writes, because here in this abiding frailty the hope of redemption has become person. As Brian Brock's book title *Wondrously Wounded* makes clear, the nature of Jesus Christ can thus be pointedly (and poetically) summed up in the following manner: *penultimately[47] being vulnerable and wounded is, wondrously, part of the nature of Jesus Christ. Our humanity, however, is fed by this wondrously wounded nature of Jesus Christ, "the entanglement of blessing and suffering."*[48]

## The Frailty of the Image of God and Creation in the Likeness of God

What, one may ask, does this understanding now contribute to an understanding of every human being in the present? This frail and risen Jesus Christ is, according to Bonhoeffer, the one image of God in whom all things are created, through him, and toward him (Col. 1:15-17). The image of the God of all human beings from Gen. 1:26

---

[45]Cf. to the alleged ideality of Jesus Christ also Schoberth, *Anthropologie*, 24–6.
[46]Cf. therefore my forthcoming book on a Christological ontology with Mohr Siebeck (Tübingen).
[47]Cf. Bonhoeffer's distinction between "ultimate and penultimate things." Bonhoeffer, *Ethics*, 146–70.
[48]Brock, *Wondrously Wounded*, xv. (My emphasis.)

is to be interpreted accordingly: likeness in this understanding is not to be found in an intrinsic quality of the human being (as it has often been interpreted, for example as intellect or freedom), but instead in an intrinsic openness to the Creator, to one's fellow creature and to oneself.[49] Bonhoeffer correspondingly interprets the likeness of the creature with its Creator as *analogia relationis*.[50] The nature of human being consists in its relatedness to the Creator, from which its openness to the other human beings is made possible.[51] This ability to relate constitutes one's whole being as a creature, and being a creature can only be realized in this relationship.[52]

The likeness of human beings to the image of God thus does not lie in any kind of perfection, but in a being that is based on relationship. The nature lies in Christ, the personified relationship between creator and creature. In him the nature of human being, which after the rupture in its relationship with God cannot recognize itself as a creature, is "redescribed and reinterpreted."[53] Hence, the nature of the human being lies not in autonomy, freedom or its contribution to a particular society in which it happens to live, but instead in its inherent being, which is designed for relationship.[54]

Bonhoeffer demonstrates what effect a violation of the life-giving relationship with the Creator has on the human being and its nature: Adam and Eve hide from their Creator, and when the Creator nevertheless calls on them to admit what they have done, they not only reject the blame, but even more so, they accuse each other and finally the Creator himself.[55] From the former

---

[49]Cf. Bonhoeffer, *Creation*, 60–7.
[50]Cf. Ibid., 65. Bonhoeffer understands accordingly creative freedom as dependent freedom, cf. Ibid., 64.
[51]Cf. Sarah Melcher, "Genesis and Exodus," in *The Bible and Disability: A Commentary*, ed. Sarah Melcher, Mikeal Parsons, and Amos Yong (London: SCM Press, 2018), 33, cites Walter Brueggemann, *Theology of the Old Testament: Testimony, Dispute, Advocacy* (Minneapolis: Fortress, 1997), 453–4.
[52]Cf. Bonhoeffer's interpretation of the fallen human being as a "*sicut deus*" (Bonhoeffer, *Creation*, 111–14).
[53]Cf. John Swinton, *Becoming Friends of Time: Disability, Timefulness, and Gentle Discipleship* (Waco: Baylor University Press, 2016), 186.
[54]Cf. Thomas Reynolds, *Vulnerable Communion: A Theology of Disability and Hospitality* (Grand Rapids: Brazos Press, 2008), 14.
[55]Cf. Bonhoeffer, *Creation*, 127–30.

"two becoming one"[56] follows "breaking apart [Entzweiung],"[57] and "dividedness."[58] If Adam and Eve were an "undivided unity of giving"[59] according to their creaturely being, now the other becomes recognizable to them only as a "limit" of their own being. The other becomes the boundary of one's own self-realization, whereas before, the other encompassed the reality of the unfolding of one's own relational being.

For the reflections on a theology of disability presented here, it should be noted, based on Bonhoeffer, that in Christian terms the nature of the human being does not lie in an autonomous understanding of freedom or in an intact body with a minimum degree of intelligence, as frequently suggested by political-democratic discourses. In Christian terms, the nature of human being lies in Jesus Christ, in whose being related to God a relationship to our fellow creature is opened. In the new human being this relationship is confirmed by God in its open frailty. This frailty, however, is a permanent part of creaturely being.[60] According to Bonhoeffer, the nature of human being is to be grasped in the fact that it is founded in dependence, namely in a being which is dependent on the other. Freedom in this sense is neither autonomy nor freedom *from* something; on the contrary, it is freedom *for* God and the fellow creature. For in the language of the Bible, freedom is not something that people have for themselves, but something they have for others.[61] This constitutes the similarity between the image of God on earth and the Creator in heaven.[62] However, by transgressing God's command not to eat from the Tree of Knowledge, Adam and Eve invert this nature of the creature. In Bonhoeffer's description, Adam and Eve lose their nature, they can no longer perceive themselves as creatures, they are no longer addressable as such. They are, as

---

[56] Ibid., 97.
[57] Ibid., 122.
[58] Ibid.
[59] Ibid.
[60] Cf. Bernd Wannenwetsch, "'My Strength Is Made Perfect in Weakness': Bonhoeffer and the War over Disabled Life," in *Disability in the Christian Tradition: A Reader*, ed. Brian Brock and John Swinton (Grand Rapids: Eerdmans, 2012), 361.
[61] Cf. Bonhoeffer, *Creation*, 62.
[62] Cf. The afterword by the editors in ibid., 162.

Bonhoeffer emphasizes, "sicut deus."[63] Their transgression of the commandment is in this context, as Bonhoeffer makes bluntly clear, "not merely a moral lapse but the destruction of creation by the creature."[64] Bonhoeffer even draws a conclusion from this for the whole creation:

> The extent of the fall is such that it affects the whole created world. From now on that world has been robbed of its creatureliness and drops blindly into infinite space, like a meteor that has torn itself away from the core to which it once belonged. It is of this fallen-falling world that we must now speak.[65]

## Redefining the Categories

Bonhoeffer's interpretation provides a fundamental insight for a theology of disability: The nature of human being *is just not perfect*, that is, perfect in and for itself. The human being receives its perfection in its being a creature only through its relationship to God and to the other creature. In Bonhoeffer's words, "it is in this *dependence on the other that their creatureliness consists*."[66] Dependence and being dependent on the other constitute the nature of human being.[67] This intrinsic dependence of human being is its perfection as a creature of God. In Christ this relationship to the other creature is only (again) possible. The importance of community, which other theologians such as Hans Ulrich and Thomas Reynolds have already pointed out,[68] is an ontological condition of being human, based on Bonhoeffer.

This, of course, changes the entire approach to the subject of theology and disability. If the nature of human being is not found in being autonomous, free, and self-determined, that is, if reason and

---

[63]Ibid., 111–14.
[64]Ibid., 120.
[65]Ibid.
[66]Ibid., 64.
[67]Cf. Hauerwas, "Timeful Friends," 14.
[68]Cf. Hans Ulrich, "Bodily Life as Creaturely Life: The Ethical Coexistence of Human Beings with Disabilities and its Fulfillment," *Journal of Religion, Disability and Health*, no. 15 (2011): 42–56, and Reynolds, *Vulnerable Communion*.

intellect do not constitute its nature, but rather a dependence on the Creator and fellow creature that gives a person its nature, then the entire structure of norms on which the modern understanding of human being and, based on this, on which society is built, is called into question. The categories of autonomy, freedom, and self-determination appear in this light as a distortion of the actual nature of human being; they appear as self-empowerment of the creature over creation and, finally, also the Creator. As a result, values which are seen as foundation to humanism as well as liberal democracy prove to be unsustainable for these very traditions themselves. For in every effort to attain equality and participation, they solidify the power imbalance that their conception of human nature prescribes. With Brock:

> What is clear is that nothing can happen until the patronizing certainty that "we" are the ones bearing the duty to include "them" is fundamentally destabilized—including for those who, feeling themselves outsiders, desperately want to join the "us."[69]

From a Christian point of view, *dependence and limitation cannot be understood as impairment.* Rather, the modern idea of the autonomous, self-determined human being is based on the hubris that only the lonely hero can fulfill their true destiny. In contrast to our modern need for autonomy and individuality, there is an ontic dependency that constitutes our whole being. This frailty, which is shown in the risen Jesus Christ[70] in and by his stigmata, characterizes our whole being—"wondrously wounded." From a realization of the new human being, every standardized ideal of the human being finally becomes invalid. The categories on which our secular liberal democracy is often based: "healthy" and "strong" do not exist in Christian terms.

But what are the consequences that can and must be drawn from such a realization? If the modern categories of the Enlightenment, on which our liberal, democratic societies are founded, are based on false basic assumptions, then these basic assumptions must be revised. This does not imply a rejection of liberal politics and

---

[69]Brock, *Wondrously Wounded*, 201.
[70]This frailty is pinpointed in Jesus Christ's cry for the father in Mt. 27:46.

democracy, as Swinton fears.[71] That is not the point of such criticism. Rather, the basic understanding of how such systems can function must itself be put to the test with a revised understanding of human being. Hans Reinders also points this out.[72] Brock's statement from the beginning of this section also shows this necessity. In many ways, it is evident that liberal society has neither the practical nor the moral capacity, nor indeed the desire, to protect human beings with disabilities and ensure their future. In contrast, the goals and assumptions of modernity shape people in ways that limit, if not entirely,[73] the desire to accept and care for human beings with socially significant differences. Thus, a revision of existing categories and values is necessarily pending.

The category "normal," and based on it "abled," must be rethought on the basis of an understanding of human beings for whom dependence is to be recognized as a central characteristic of being human. Freedom and self-determination are not absolute; they are possible only in dependence on other human beings. They are conditional. Relationships necessarily presuppose such an understanding: placing oneself in dependence on someone else. This is where a revised understanding of democracy must start. Christian theology can show how these concepts can be rethought. In this way, a rethinking of political concepts and political action can be achieved, which admittedly does not take effect immediately, but has far-reaching ethical consequences. Of course, this is an epochal task that cannot be solved in the next few days. It is also obvious that the existing systems can at the same time "serve as a positive force for good if they are properly engaged," as Swinton points out.[74] Knowing the provisionality of all secular systems,[75] they can also "provide a legal framework which can at least act as a brake on the excess of liberal thinking."[76] At the same time, however, it is necessary to work on the perception of the basic assumptions. Christian communities that start from an understanding of their

---

[71] Swinton, "Who," 299.
[72] Cf. Reinders, *Future*.
[73] Cf. Ibid., 14–15.
[74] Swinton, "Who," 299.
[75] Cf. Bonhoeffer's distinction of "ultimate and penultimate things," in Bonhoeffer, *Ethics*, 146–70.
[76] Swinton, "Who," 299.

nature in Christ necessarily challenge hegemonic social structures.[77] The church has the task to constantly recall this dependent nature of human being and to challenge the state to change its basic assumptions according to this nature.[78] A concept of democracy must be developed that can think and implement non-autonomy and dependence. Dependency and frailty have to be considered as the basic orientation of this new value and world order.

## Bibliography

Albrecht, Gary L., Katherine D. Seelman, and Michael Bury, eds. *Handbook of Disability Studies*. Thousand Oaks: Sage Publications, 2001.

Bonhoeffer, Dietrich. *Ethics, Bonhoeffer Works 6*, edited by Clifford Green, translated by Reinhard Krauss, Charles West, and Douglas W. Scott. Minneapolis: Fortress Press, 2005.

Brock, Brian. *Wondrously Wounded*. Waco: Baylor University Press, 2019.

Brueggemann, Walter. *Theology of the Old Testament: Testimony, Dispute, Advocacy*. Minneapolis: Fortress, 1997.

Eiesland, Nancy. *The Disabled God: Toward a Liberatory Theology of Disability*. Nashville: Abington Press, 1994.

Eliade, Mircea. *The Myth of the Eternal Return: Cosmos and History*. Princeton: Princeton University Press, 2018.

Endress, Topher, Hannah Waite, and Julie Marie Land. "Enacting a Theology of Disability: Framing Swinton." In *Disciples and Friends: Investigations in Disability, Dementia, and Mental Health*, edited by Armand Léon van Ommen and Brian Brock, 11–30. Waco: Baylor University Press, 2022.

Hauerwas, Stanley. "Suffering the Retarded: Should we prevent Retardation." In *Suffering Presence: Theological Reflections on Medicine, the Mentally Handicapped, and the Church*, edited by Stanley Hauerwas, 87–104. Notre Dame: University of Notre Dame Press, 1986.

Hauerwas, Stanley. "Timeful Friends: Living with the Handicapped." *Journal of Religion, Disability and Health* 8, no. 3–4 (2008): 11–25.

---

[77]Endress, Waite, and Land, "Enacting," 19.
[78]Cf. John Swinton and Harriet Moat, *Practical Theology and Qualitative Research*, 2nd ed. (London: SCM Press, 2016), 26.

Hopkins, Julie. "Sind Christologie und Feminismus unvereinbar? Zur Debatte zwischen Daphne Hampson und Rosemary Radford Ruether." In *Vom Verlangen nach Heilwerden. Christologie in feministisch-theologischer Sicht*, edited by Doris Strahm and Regula Strobel, 194–206. Fribourg/Luzern: Edition Exodus, 1991.

Kant, Immanuel. "An Answer to the Question: What is Enlightenment?" [1784]. In *Practical Philosophy. The Cambridge Edition of the Works of Immanuel Kant*, edited by Mary J. Gregor, 11–22. Cambridge: Cambridge University Press, 1999.

Kant, Immanuel. "Anthropology from a Pragmatic Point of view" [1798]. In *Anthropology, History, and Education. The Cambridge Edition of the Works of Immanuel Kant*, edited by Robert B Louden and Günter Zöller, 227–9. Cambridge: Cambridge University Press, 2007.

Laube, Martin. "Die Dialektik der Freiheit. Systematisch-theologische Perspektiven." In *Freiheit. Themen der Theologie Bd. 7*, edited by Martin Laube, 119–91. Tübingen: Mohr Siebeck, 2014.

Melcher, Sarah. "Genesis and Exodus." In *The Bible and Disability*, edited by Sarah Melcher, Mikeal C. Parsons, and Amos Yong, 29–56. London: SCM Press, 2018.

Moltmann, Jürgen. "Creation as an Open System." In *Future of Creation*, edited by Jürgen Moltmann, 123–39. München: Chr. Kaiser, 1977.

Reinders, Hans. *The Future of the Disabled in Liberal Society: An Ethical Analysis*. Notre Dame: University of Notre Dame Press, 2000.

Reynolds, Thomas. *Vulnerable Communion: A Theology of Disability and Hospitality*. Grand Rapids: Brazos Press, 2008.

Ritschl, Dietrich. "Die Erfahrung der Wahrheit." In *Ökumene, Medizin, Ethik. Gesammelte Aufsätze*, edited by Dietrich Ritschl, 147–66. München: Chr. Kaiser, 1986.

Ritschl, Dietrich. *Zur Logik der Theologie. Kurze Darstellung der Zusammenhänge theologischer Grundgedanken*. München: Chr. Kaiser, 1984.

Schoberth, Wolfgang. *Einführung in die theologische Anthropologie*. Darmstadt: Wissenschaftliche Buchgesellschaft, 2006.

Shakespeare, Tom, ed. *The Disability Reader: Social Scientific Perspectives*. London: Continuum, 1998.

Swinton, John. *Becoming Friends of Time: Disability, Timefulness, and Gentle Discipleship*. Waco: Baylor University Press, 2016.

Swinton, John. "Who is the God We Worship? Theologies of Disability; Challenges and New Possibilities." *International Journal of Practical Theology*, no. 14 (2011): 273–307.

Swinton, John and Harriet Moat. *Practical Theology and Qualitative Research*. 2nd ed. London: SCM Press, 2016.

Ulrich, Hans. "Bodily Life as Creaturely Life: The Ethical Coexistence of Human Beings with Disabilities and its Fulfillment." *Journal of Religion, Disability and Health*, no. 15 (2011): 42–56.

UPIAS. *Fundamental Principles of Disability*. London: Union of the Physically Impaired Against Segregation, 1976.

Wannenwetsch, Bernd. "'My Strength is Made Perfect in Weakness': Bonhoeffer and the War over Disabled Life." In *Disability in the Christian Tradition: A Reader*, edited by Brian Brock and John Swinton, 353–90. Grand Rapids: Eerdmans, 2012.

Weiss Block, Jennie. *Copious Hosting: A Theology of Access for People with Disabilities*. New York: Continuum, 2000.

# 5

# Who Cares? A Response of Christian Ethics to Shortages of Care

*Stefan Heuser*

## Introduction

One of the most pressing social issues of aging, individualized, functionally differentiated, deinstitutionalized capitalist societies today is to cope with the growing need of care. The question "Who cares?" has gained enormous relevance both in the field of professional health care (e.g., regarding nursing shortages) and in the lifeworldly fields of care that promote capabilities and well-being (e.g., childcare, education and teaching, domestic work, personal assistance, or care for elderly persons). This question also concerns all forms of care or welfare work of churches from the level of parish communities to the level of church-sponsored health care companies which currently struggle to find their specific place and identity in secularized societies and their economized health care systems. The question "Who cares?" therefore touches upon the core of Christian ethics in two ways: First, it requires further clarification on the social tasks of Christians; and, second, it calls for a deeper understanding of the theological grammar of caring practices.

In the following, I will first comment on the central aspects and reasons for caring shortages in the lifeworld of modern societies. Second, I will sketch exemplary social and political responses to lifeworldly shortages of care. Finally, I will outline the theological grammar of caring and its significance for the contribution of Christian ethics to the recovery of care.

## Shortages of Care in the Modern Lifeworld

In the sector of health care, countries worldwide face severe nursing shortages.[1] These shortages of professional nursing staff are due to various factors, but mainly to demographic changes, low recruitment rates, high turnover rates, low economic esteem, stress, low job satisfaction, and emotional or physical abuse in nursing professions.[2] As a result, the number of people in need of long-term care is rising, and with them the number of caring relatives who need support, while the number of professional nurses, of nursing assistants, and of voluntary helpers is stagnating or even decreasing.[3] So far national action plans, work intensification and rationalization, technological assistance systems, or international labor migration do not sufficiently compensate for this shortage, and they generate their own severe ethical problems.[4]

These nursing shortages go hand in hand with a "crisis of care" in many fields of the lifeworld.[5] Besides discourses on the importance

---

[1] Britta Zander et al., "The State of Nursing in the European Union," *Eurohealth*, no. 22 (2016): 3–6.
[2] Halter Mary et al., "The Determinants and Consequences of Adult Nursing Staff Turnover: A Systematic Review of Systematic Reviews," *BMC Health Services Research*, no. 17 (2017): 824.
[3] World Health Organization, *Global Strategy on Human Resources for Health: Workforce 2030* (Consultation paper, 2015).
[4] Piotr Żuk, Paweł Żuk, and Justyna Lisiewicz-Jakubaszko, "Labour Migration of Doctors and Nurses and the Impact on the Quality of Health Care in Eastern European Countries: The Case of Poland," *The Economic and Labour Relations Review*, no. 30 (2019): 307–20; Ursula Apitzsch and Marianne Schmidbaur, ed., *Care und Migration: Die Ent-Sorgung Menschlicher Reproduktionsarbeit Entlang von Geschlechter- und Armutsgrenzen* (Opladen: Budrich, 2010).
[5] Brigitte Aulenbacher and Maria Dammayr, eds., *Für sich und andere Sorgen. Krise und Zukunft von Care in der modernen Gesellschaft* (Weinheim: Beltz Juventa,

of caring in nursing,[6] and on staff shortages among care workers and social practitioners,[7] much attention has been directed to the huge field of unpaid, often "invisible" and widely unnoticed lifeworldly care work which has been thematized mainly from economic and gender perspectives.[8] There is an extensive "care-economy" that helps to maintain societal functions, but remains politically and economically neglected.[9] Single mothers, children from socially disadvantaged families, socially excluded or marginalized people, caregiving relatives, people and their relatives whose jobs require high flexibility and irregular working hours, precariously employed workers, or socially isolated elderly people may to various degrees experience what it means not to be sufficiently supported, assisted, and cared for, and lack sufficient time or capacity for self-care.

These are only some examples of a long list of people who may somehow get along in life, but who, due to disabling, adverse, or less supportive factors in their environment, struggle to achieve what they themselves would call a "good" life.[10] Intense social empirical research in the past decades based on standard indicators of the quality of life and of well-being has provided evidence for care deficits in various fields of life.[11]

The reasons for this care "crisis," and for the decline of social structures in which care is practiced, can be found in long-term

---

2014).
[6]Margareta Karlsson and Sandra Pennbrant, "Ideas of Caring in Nursing Practice," *Nursing Philosophy* 21, no. 4 (2020): e12325.
[7]Kathleen Galvin and Les Todres, *Caring and Well-Being: A Lifeworld Approach* (London: Routledge, 2014).
[8]Almut Schnerring and Sascha Verlan, *Equal Care: Über Fürsorge und Gesellschaft* (Berlin: Verbrecher Verlag, 2020); Brigitte Aulenbacher, Birgit Riegraf, and Hildegard Theobald, "Sorge und Sorgearbeit – Neuvermessungen eines traditionsreichen Forschungsfeldes," in *Sorge: Arbeit, Verhältnisse, Regime. Soziale Welt, Sonderband 20*, ed. Brigitte Aulenbacher, Birgit Riegraf, and Hildegard Theobald (Baden-Baden: Nomos, 2014), 5–20.
[9]Mascha Madörin, "Care-Ökonomie: eine Herausforderung für die Wirtschaftswissenschaften," in *Gender and Economics, Feministische Kritik der politischen Ökonomie*, ed. Christine Bauhardt and Gülay Çağlar (Wiesbaden: VS Verlag für Sozialwissenschaften, 2010), 81–104.
[10]Amartya Sen, *Inequality Re-examined* (Oxford: Oxford University Press, 1992); Amartya Sen, "Capability and Well-being," in *The Quality of Life*, ed. Martha C. Nussbaum and Amartya Sen (Oxford: Clarendon Press, 1993), 30–53.
[11]Aulenbacher and Dammayr, *Für sich und andere sorgen*.

transformation processes of modern societies.[12] Many factors of this transformation have been identified by sociology, such as functional differentiation, de-traditionalization, de-institutionalization, economization of formerly public service tasks, cuts in social services, individualization, urbanization, globalization, and digitalization.[13]

For a deep understanding of such transformation processes, one may refer to Jürgen Habermas's account of modernization. In response to Max Weber's theory of modernity, Habermas describes modernization as a "rationalization" of the lifeworld which gradually erodes communicative action and thus the specific form of communication by which social integration and solidarity are achieved.[14] According to Habermas, the communicative rationality of the lifeworld is gradually colonized by the functional imperatives of systemic mechanisms (e.g., by the exchange rationality and the mobility imperatives of the market). The pressure that system integration exerts on the lifeworld leads to an erosion of social structures and of lifeworldly bonds which previously promoted caring interactions.

The question "who cares?" is hence simultaneously acute in health care, in professional and paid forms of social care, and in all informal fields of care, of support and of assistance in daily life. Despite the intensity and sometimes intimacy of caring activities, caring is not only a "private" but also a "public" issue of enormous social relevance. While the culture of domestic care and family-based support for people in need of long-term care in their home environment remains a strong factor in care, demographic, economic, and cultural factors tend to erode social structures in

---

[12]Birgit Riegraf, "Care, Care-Arbeit und Geschlecht: gesellschaftliche Veränderungen und theoretische Auseinandersetzungen," in *Handbuch Interdisziplinäre Geschlechterforschung. Geschlecht und Gesellschaft Bd. 65*, ed. Beate Kortendiek, Birgit Riegraf, and Katja Sabisch (Wiesbaden: Springer, 2017): 1–10.
[13]Claudia Steckelberg, Barbara Thiessen, and Vera Taube eds., *Wandel der Arbeitsgesellschaft. Soziale Arbeit in Zeiten von Globalisierung, Digitalisierung und Prekarisierung* (Opladen: Budrich, 2020); Ulrich Beck and Elisabeth Beck-Gernsheim, *Riskante Freiheiten: Gesellschaftliche Individualisierungsprozesse in der Moderne* (Frankfurt a. M: Suhrkamp, 1994).
[14]Jürgen Habermas, "Theory of Communicative Action," in *Lifeworld and System: A Critique of Functionalist Reason*, trans. Thomas A. McCarthy (Boston: Beacon Press, 1987), 196.

which care work and social interactions are being performed or promoted.

In this situation, the question is how to preserve, regain, or develop social institutions in which professional and voluntary care work are performed, and where societal integration is realized.

## Political and Social Responses to the Crisis of Care

Two types of responses to this crisis of care can be distinguished: Type 1 focuses on changes to the legal, political, and economic conditions to improve the framework under which care activities may flourish. Type 2 addresses the problem of the dissolution of common social worlds and practices by fostering or organizing communities.

### Type 1

In order to improve both social determinants of human development and individual substantive freedom, social activists and social scientists often demand a higher political and economic recognition of caring-activities, ranging from political redistribution measures and changes in economic or social arrangements to person-centered empowering interventions.[15] Above all, the factor of "time" has been identified as central to supporting care work in socially accelerated societies,[16] be it through a politically mediated rise of economic equity between unpaid care work and paid labor,[17] be it through a new "politics of time" which valorizes the specific time and presence required by caring activities, or be it through a transformation of capitalist modes of production in the course of

---

[15] Mara A. Yerkes, Jana Javornik, and Anna Kurowska eds., *Social Policy and the Capability Approach: Concepts, Measurements and Application* (Bristol: Policy Press, 2019).
[16] Hartmut Rosa, *Social Acceleration: A New Theory of Modernity*, trans. Jonathan Trejo-Mathys (New York: Columbia University Press, 2013).
[17] Nancy Fraser, "After the Family Wage: Gender Equity and the Welfare State," *Political Theory* 4 (1994): 591–618.

a "care revolution."[18] During and after the COVID-19 pandemic, care work also became a topic of political initiatives such as "Care Mainstreaming" which seeks to promote the political debate based on new ways of organizing care work and including the concerns of caregivers and care receivers in all aspects of political decision-making.[19]

## Type 2

Alongside such approaches, ethicists have taken up the communitarian critique of liberalism's individualism[20] and have developed conceptions of community organizing.[21] The main idea of caring communities is to coordinate the cooperation between citizens, organizations of civil society, institutions of the state, and professional service providers in the maintenance or formation of social spaces in order to meet the social, cultural, and economic needs of a local population.[22] Some concepts explicitly exclude government support for ideological reasons.[23] Caring communities can be organized as networks, neighborhoods, and cooperatives, and they increasingly use online communication and internet

---

[18] Valerie Bryson, *Gender and the Politics of Time: Feminist Theory and Contemporary Debates* (Bristol: Bristol University Press, 2007); Gabriele Winker, *Care Revolution. Schritte in eine solidarische Gesellschaft* (Bielefeld: transcript, 2015).
[19] Barabara Thiessen, et al., *Clean Up Time! Redesigning Care after Corona* (Care-macht-mehr.com, 2020).
[20] Alasdair MacIntyre, *After Virtue* (Notre Dame: University of Notre Dame Press, 1981); Michael J. Sandel, *Liberalism and the Limits of Justice* (Cambridge: Cambridge University Press, 1998).
[21] Karin Jurczyk et al., "Caring Communities: Häusliche Versorgung gemeinschaftlich unterstützen," *Blätter der Wohlfahrtspflege* 167, no. 1 (2020): 3–6; Luke Bretherton, *Resurrecting Democracy: Faith, Citizenship and the Politics of a Common Life* (Cambridge: Cambridge University Press, 2015); Luke Bretherton, *Christ and the Common Life: Political Theology and the Case for Democracy* (Grand Rapids: Eerdmans, 2019).
[22] Institut für Sozialarbeit und Sozialpädagogik e. V., ed., *ISS im Dialog: Sorgende Gemeinschaften – vom Leitbild zu Handlungsansätzen*, expert talk 16th December 2013 (Frankfurt am Main: ISS-Aktuell, 03/2014).
[23] Riegraf, "Care, Care-Arbeit und Geschlecht."

platforms.[24] Following the idea of subsidiary solidarity, they understand themselves as small societies in which people take care of others on account of mutual trust and of reciprocal responsibility in order to supplement the caring activities of families and of the welfare state.[25]

Although the idea of caring communities can be regarded as a timely and ingenious response to today's caring shortages, it gives cause for various points of criticism:

1. Insofar as the motivation of volunteers to join or remain in caring communities rests on the mutuality and reciprocity of services, those care receivers who cannot offer care may be excluded. It is open to question whether caring communities as network organizations tend to create high-level conditions that exclude the most vulnerable from participation: people in social isolation, people who feel ashamed to enter a network in which they expose their neediness, people who themselves have nothing to contribute to the network and would only be receivers of care, or elderly people without sufficient skills in online communication.

2. It is open to question whether we have invested enough effort in stopping the erosion of caring contexts by improving the economic, social, and political conditions under which social integration and solidarity might flourish in the lifeworld. It is structurally important and subject to political decisions to reduce the systemic pressures that weigh upon the lifeworld. People need to be empowered to take care of others simply by better material presuppositions, working conditions, more opportunities for relieving and sharing burdens, professional outreach work,

---

[24]Zentrum für Zivilgesellschaftliche Entwicklung (ZZE), *Begleitung der Pilot-Anwendungen im Projekt SoNaTe – Soziale Nachbarschaft und Technik* (2019).
[25]Thomas Klie, "Caring Community – leitbildfähiger Begriff für eine generationenübergreifende Sorgekultur?" in *ISS im Dialog: Sorgende Gemeinschaften – vom Leitbild zu Handlungsansätzen*, ed. Institut für Sozialarbeit und Sozialpädagogik e. V., expert talk 16th December 2013, (Frankfurt am Main: ISS-Aktuell, 03/2014), 10–23.

structures of care visits, and simply being granted more time to care for themselves, and for others.

3. Efforts in the organization of new forms of common life must answer the question whether enough effort has been invested in maintaining the existing social structures of care, such as families, neighborhoods, social spaces, social services, diaconal work in the parish, support centers, and low-threshold services of case- and care-management.

Insofar as caring communities are organized around a common interest, namely, to give and receive care, and uphold this goal by behavioral expectations directed to the reciprocity of care, they may help to coordinate mutual and symmetrical care, but are prone to fail to include those who need care but have nothing to give in return. Caring communities hence suffer from the same processes that lead to the erosion of care in the lifeworld, namely, that people relate to others predominantly in terms of reciprocal interests, but lack experience of care as an *ethos* which sustains their own lives and on which they can embark for the sake of others.

It has often been noted that the rate of volunteers has grown continually over the last decades, but that the number of those who commit themselves on a long-term basis or in executive positions has been decreasing at the same time.[26] While volunteering has become a project for many, caring has remained a contested life form. Is it at all possible to transform a life form into a project in order to find more people who care?

One of the most interesting suggestions to transform care into a form of organized civic action is to make it part of the overarching societal trend of autonomy. As motivation research has shown, volunteers may have a bundle of functionally diverse, both cognitively and emotionally shaped motifs.[27] These comprise

---

[26] Julia Simonson et.al., *Freiwilliges Engagement in Deutschland. Zentrale Ergebnisse der 5. Deutschen Freiwilligensurveys (FWS 2019)* (Berlin: Bundesministerium für Familie, Senioren, Frauen und Jugend, 2021); Julia Simonson, "Freiwilliges Engagement in Deutschland," in *Der Deutsche Freiwilligensurvey 2014* (Berlin: Bundesministerium für Familie, Senioren, Frauen und Jugend, 2016).
[27] E. Gil Clary et al., "Understanding and Assessing the Motivations of Volunteers: A Functional Approach," *Journal of Personality and Social Psychology*, no. 74 (1998): 516–30.

a wide range of both altruism and egoism, with an emphasis on values, enriched experience, meaning, and justice.[28] One of the most important values in all these motivational items, however, is *autonomy*: volunteers are attracted by the chance to perform autonomously and to support autonomy in the lives of others.[29]

Does care work comply with this motivation? According to Frits de Lange, the inner telos of care relationships is to restore or guarantee the autonomy of the care-receiver, and to avoid a lasting dependency on the caregiver.[30] De Lange claims that the "undeniable asymmetry of the care relationship is an essential, but temporal moment in its dynamics."[31] But what if these asymmetries are permanent, and autonomy cannot be achieved or restored? The equal and inalienable autonomy of all human beings is a transcendental idea that must be distinguished from the capacity to self-determine independent action. The first is an idea that should basically regulate all human relationships, the latter is one possible "telos" of care, but not the "inner telos" of all caring actions.

If we look at the phenomenon of care from the viewpoint of constitutive asymmetries between caregivers and care receivers, we find that caring is a practice that not only entails what somebody *does*, but *in what* he or she *participates*, and *who* he or she *becomes* for someone else, and for him- or herself in the process of caring. To take up caring practices entails participating in a life form, and even sometimes fully entering it, as casual or spontaneous as the specific action might eventually be. Such a "life form," in the sense of the later Wittgenstein, is the specific cultural and social shape of a general life process in which speaking and acting intertwine and help us get along in situations in which we inevitably find ourselves

---

[28]Elisabeth Kals, Isabel T. Strubel, and Stefan T. Güntert, "Gemeinsinn und Solidarität: Motivation und Wirkung von Freiwilligenarbeit," *Bibliothek Forschung und Praxis*, no. 45 (2021): 14–25.
[29]Stefan T. Güntert, "Selbstbestimmung in der Freiwilligenarbeit," in *Psychologie der Freiwilligenarbeit: Motivation, Gestaltung und Organisation*, ed. Theo Wehner and Stefan T. Güntert (Berlin: Springer, 2015), 77–93.
[30]Frits de Lange, "Restoring autonomy: Symmetry and asymmetry in care relationships," *Nederduitse Gereformeerde Teologiese Tydskrif* 1, no. 52 (2011): 61–8.
[31]Ibid., 68.

in the course of human life.³² To participate in this life form is not primarily a matter of decision or option, but an experience that happens to somebody in the course of his or her life. Caring is part of the *conditio humana* (human condition) in general, but specifically belongs to human beings as a form of life, as an ethos that is embedded in the ordinary, daily life, to which we actively relate whenever we find ourselves called to care, or to be cared for.³³

This is why caring can only to some extent be voluntarily or professionally organized when traditional structures and life forms of care erode. In life forms like these, people experience that receiving and giving care belongs to them, and to their social life, and they pragmatically learn to practice care in its diverse dimensions. The erosion of care as a life form, for which we can draw on Habermas's theory of rationalization of the modern and late modern lifeworld and on the empirical findings as mentioned above, concerns simultaneously the language and activities of care. Hence, it is difficult to restore caring as a life form where people have lost or never learned the "language game" of care. The problem of care deficits is rooted in care illiteracy, and this cannot be solved by socio-technological means or convincing arguments alone. This also applies to morally persuasive regulative ideas such as that of a transcendental symmetry of all human beings which are unlikely to orientate caring practices, or to motivate membership in caring communities.

Care must already to some extent belong to the life form of those who are called to care, and it is this contingency and lack of disposability of care that needs to be accounted for when it comes to organizing or maintaining caring practices or communities. Who cares, then? This is less a matter of a decision to start a care project somewhere in one's own biography, but a calling to practice a life form that people inhabit or become drawn into.

If we follow Joan Tronto's reconstruction of the caring act from "caring about," "care taking," and "care giving" to "care

---

[32]Ludwig Wittgenstein, *Philosophical Investigation*, trans. G.E.M. Anscombe (Oxford: Blackwell, 1958).
[33]Sandra Laugier, *Politics of the Ordinary: Care, Ethics and Forms of Life* (Leuven: Peeters, 2020).

receiving,"[34] we find a process in which somebody comes to see the need of the other simultaneously with the care that he or she can give and follows this invitation to act. According to Tronto, it is characteristic for caring that one does not choose somebody else as an object of care, but that one finds oneself to be called into the reality of care that occurs for both the caregiver and the care-receiver to be experienced, received, and shared.

Caring retains this moral grammar of a life form, even if people only spontaneously or casually participate in it. It can only to some extent be made the subject of an "organization" of people who pursue a self-defined common goal, but it belongs to the social reality of "institutions" that can be defined as established and often codified social formations that answer to given tasks that any society needs for its reproduction.[35]

This, however, adds some hope to our discussion of care, and to solutions of the care crisis. According to protestant theologian Ernst Wolf, "institutions" are social forms of existence which bear a theological promise, namely that they not only realize what lies within *human* skills or scope but are life forms in which people are called to encounter *God's own care*, and witness to it practically.[36] After taking a life form perspective on caring, I will therefore now analyze the moral grammar of care a bit further, and switch to a theological perspective on caring as "institution" or as "mandate," as Dietrich Bonhoeffer has named it with reference to the mandatory and evitable character of given social tasks.[37]

---

[34]Joan C. Tronto, *Moral boundaries: A Political Argument for an Ethic of Care* (New York: Routledge, 1993), 108.
[35]Anthony Giddens, *The Constitution of Society: Outline of the Theory of Structuration* (Cambridge: Polity Press, 1984).
[36]Ernst Wolf, *Sozialethik, Theologische Grundfragen*, ed. Theodor Strohm (Göttingen: UTB, 1988), 173.
[37]Dietrich Bonhoeffer, *Ethics, Dietrich Bonhoeffer Works 6*, ed. Clifford Green, trans. Reinhard Krauss, Charles West, and Douglas W. Scott (Minneapolis: Fortress Press, 2005), 66–9; 388f.

## The Theological Grammar of Care

In order to proceed to the theological dimension of care, philosopher Paul Ricoeur's analysis of the process of being called into care may serve as an instructive starting point. Ricoeur draws on the parable of the good Samaritan (Lk. 10:30-37) to unfold a dialectics of "the socius and the neighbor."[38] He argues that people usually encounter each other in various social functions but can any time be drawn into the relationship of being "neighbors." This relationship is characterized by a transition from a social role to a personal, immediate encounter during which someone makes himself present and available for the other, thereby establishing a "hypersociological mutuality."[39] For Ricoeur, the sociological category of the "Socius" and the theological category of the "Neighbor" are two ways through which the "movement of charity behind which stands the Son of Man" may reach people.[40] The organization of social functions can only prepare for charity, it cannot yield or replace it. For Ricoeur, different modes of social organization can both block and pave the way for the step from socially mediated to immediate relationships, yet it cannot guarantee that somebody lets himself be called to encounter the other as neighbor and become a medium of charity. This charity is primordial to any encounter between the social partners in the sense that their encounter is fitted with the promise that they already belong to each other as neighbors—a reality that they are called to embark on and explore in their interaction. The caregiver may discover himself as neighbor of the care-receiver and vice versa, and by doing so, both find themselves in an economy of care which neither of them produces, but which seizes them to become real for these specific human beings.

Following Ricoeur, the ethical sense of structures and contexts of care is not only to formally supply people, but to institutionalize personal encounters in which people discover and communicate the charity that is entrusted to them. Ricoeur refers to Mt. 25:31-42,

---

[38]Paul Ricoeur, "The Socius and the Neighbor," in *History and Truth*, ed. Paul Ricoeur, trans. Charles A. Kelbley (Evanston: Northwestern University Press, 1965), 98–109.
[39]Ibid., 100.
[40]Ibid., 108.

however, to make clear that this ultimate meaning of institutions or social life forms such as care remains hidden to human beings in the course of history: "No one can evaluate the personal benefits produced by institutions; charity is not necessarily present wherever it is exhibited; it is also hidden in the humble, abstract services provided by post offices and social security officials; quite often it is the hidden meaning of the social realm."[41] For Ricoeur, we do not have the power to perform the eschatological judgment of whether we have been bearers of this charity for others, or not: "Thus, as long as the sociological veil has not fallen, we remain within history, that is, within the debate of the *socius* and the neighbor, without knowing whether charity is here or there."[42]

What might be added to Ricoeur's reconstruction of the dialectics of *socius* and neighbor is that the movement of charity is not just a hidden power that now and then grasps people and turns them into its instruments, but that becoming a neighbor is a life form that can be regarded as commanded and instituted, as the Jesus of Luke 10 says: "Go and do likewise" (Lk. 10:37). To care for somebody then bears the theological promise that by doing so, one does not only answer to the need of the other, but also to God's will for humanity as it has been revealed in Jesus Christ. Caring is not only open to become a personal encounter with the other but also to become an instrument of God's care for his creatures. By entering this life form, one may expect, discover and dwell in God's presence in Christ.

In this sense, caring as a practice may follow the theological grammar of the good works as Martin Luther has framed them, as works which God performs through human beings.[43] The act of caring then can not only be regarded as paying tribute to the idea of a better world, or to human moral excellence, but as witnessing to God's care. The task of Christians, then, is not only to call for more or better care, but primarily to let oneself be drawn into the life form of caring that is accompanied and sustained by God's own care and by his promise, and witness to God's care through caring for others.

---

[41] Ibid., 109.
[42] Ibid.
[43] Martin Luther, "Treatise on Good Works," in *The Christian in Society 1*, Luther's Works 44, ed. James Atkinson (Philadelphia: Fortress Press, 1966), 21–114.

This witness implies that all caring bears a theological promise: albeit being permanently prone to paternalism and to the abuse of power, caring is open to participate in God's care. Whenever somebody cares for somebody else, he or she enters a life form in which God has promised to let himself be encountered. Through caring, human beings may participate in "*Christ becoming real among God's creatures*," as Dietrich Bonhoeffer puts it.[44] Through the practices of care, people are invited to experience how the reality of God and the reality of the world meet in Christ, and to explore how God's care for humankind becomes real in the world. Hence, we may theologically spell out caring as an exemplary activity that is open to "*participating in the reality of God and the world in Jesus Christ today*, and doing so in such a way that I never experience the reality of God without the reality of the world, nor the reality of the world without the reality of God."[45]

Bonhoeffer calls life forms in which people can discover that their world is related to Christ and is subject to God's transformative work "mandates."[46] If we, unlike Bonhoeffer himself but true to his line of thought, interpret caring as "mandate," it can be regarded as an exemplary place for encountering, realizing, and witnessing to God's salvific care in the midst of the world:

> We speak of divine mandates rather than divine orders, because thereby their character as divinely imposed tasks [*Auftrag*], as opposed to determinate forms of being, becomes clearer. In the world God wills work, marriage, government, and church, and God wills all these, each in its own way, through Christ, toward Christ, and in Christ. God has placed human beings under all these mandates, not only each individual under one or the other, but all people under all four. There can be no retreat, therefore, from a "worldly" into a "spiritual realm." The practice of the Christian life can be learned only under these four mandates of God.[47]

This does not mean that extraordinarily perfect or selfless caring activities may be declared to be good works in the sense that they

---

[44]Bonhoeffer, *Ethics*, 49. (Emphasis original.)
[45]Ibid., 55.
[46]Ibid., 68.
[47]Ibid., 69.

participate in the economy of God's care for his creatures. As Ricoeur has rightly emphasized, this judgment has to be left to God. It is important to note that the concept of "mandates" does not serve to theologically inflate given social structures or practices. Theology's task is not to theologically affirm or legitimize life forms such as caring, but to witness to the promise that is associated with them as places for the exploration of God's advent in this world. Hence, also the talk of "good works" does not refer to an objective but to an eschatological reality.

The mandate of care and its social institutions can be regarded as specific, exemplary places in which people may encounter God's will and action in their everyday lives. The practices of care can witness to God's care whenever human beings let themselves be interrupted in their ordinary course of carelessness, let their eyes be opened for what is necessary to be done, and serve their neighbor, thereby following God's call to care for those in need. The inner "telos" of caring, then, is not "autonomy" but God's charity as it is revealed in Christ.

Against the backdrop of this theological grammar of care, we would rather shift our concentration from the organization of caring networks to the social institutions of human life in which direct care is practiced. This means to give priority to the maintenance, recovery, and empowerment of given social institutions as life forms in which people experience that they are being cared for and learn to take care of others. These life forms are not just a part of a welfare mix among others, but can be unique places in which people may become who they are through the life they share with others, and through the practices of care.

The organization of networks, communities, or social relations can, however, complement or compensate such basic social life forms and the goods that people may experience and explore through the practices that are assigned to them. This is especially necessary where social life forms, such as families, fail to be places of care. To institutionalize care then means to create or sustain structures which orbit around the direct, personal work of care; structures which enable people to participate in the life form of care, to turn toward each other in care. At the same time, abuse and violence in families as well as the neglect of children (e.g., during the COVID-19 pandemic) call for direct interventions that do not disregard responding to the need for care of children, single parents, or elderly persons.

As German theologian Hans Joachim Iwand said in regard to the situation of postwar refugees in Germany: "The personal, human act of love is the basis for all organized help."[48] The organization of care, then, has to answer the question about which message, gifts, resources, competences, support, and structures people need to participate in care, to receive care, or to be able to perceive the need of others, to take care of them, and to hand on to them what is necessary for their well-being. We therefore need to shift our concentration from organizing networks of caring relations to institutionalizing direct care as a mandate in which people find the freedom, the time, the means, the resources, and the gifts to care for others, as a witness to God's care for all of humanity.

## Bibliography

Apitzsch, Ursula and Marianne Schmidbaur, eds. *Care und Migration: Die Ent-Sorgung menschlicher Reproduktionsarbeit entlang von Geschlechter- und Armutsgrenzen*. Opladen: Budrich, 2010.

Aulenbacher, Brigitte and Maria Dammayr, eds. *Für sich und andere sorgen. Krise und Zukunft von Care in der modernen Gesellschaft*. Weinheim: Beltz Juventa, 2014.

Aulenbacher, Brigitte, Birgit Riegraf, and Hildegard Theobald. "Sorge und Sorgearbeit –Neuvermessungen eines traditionsreichen Forschungsfeldes." In *Sorge: Arbeit, Verhältnisse, Regime. Soziale Welt, Sonderband 20*, 5–20. Baden-Baden: Nomos, 2014.

Beck, Ulrich and Elisabeth Beck-Gernsheim. *Riskante Freiheiten: Gesellschaftliche Individualisierungsprozesse in der Moderne*. Frankfurt a. M: Suhrkamp, 1994.

Bonhoeffer, Dietrich. *Ethics, Dietrich Bonhoeffer Works 6*, edited by Clifford Green, translated by Reinhard Krauss, Charles West, and Douglas W. Scott. Minneapolis: Fortress Press, 2005.

Bretherton, Luke. *Christ and the Common Life: Political Theology and the Case for Democracy*. Grand Rapids: Eerdmans, 2019.

Bretherton, Luke. *Resurrecting Democracy: Faith, Citizenship and the Politics of a Common Life*. Cambridge: Cambridge University Press, 2015.

---

[48]Hans Joachim Iwand, "Zur religiösen Lage der Flüchtlinge (1949)," in *Frieden mit dem Osten. Texte 1933–1959*, ed. Gerard C. den Hertog (München: Chr. Kaiser), 28. (My translation).

Bryson, Valerie. *Gender and the Politics of Time: Feminist Theory and Contemporary Debates.* Bristol: Bristol University Press, 2007.
Clary, E. Gil, Mark Snyder, Robert D. Ridge, John Copeland, Arthur A. Stukas, Julie Haugen, and Peter Miene. "Understanding and Assessing the Motivations of Volunteers: A Functional Approach." *Journal of Personality and Social Psychology*, no. 74 (1998): 516–30.
Fraser, Nancy. "After the Family Wage: Gender Equity and the Welfare State." *Political Theory*, no. 4 (1994): 591–618.
Galvin, Kathleen and Les Todres. *Caring and Well-Being: A Lifeworld Approach.* London: Routledge, 2014.
Giddens, Anthony. *The Constitution of Society: Outline of the Theory of Structuration.* Cambridge: Polity Press, 1984.
Güntert, Stefan T. "Selbstbestimmung in der Freiwilligenarbeit." In *Psychologie der Freiwilligenarbeit: Motivation, Gestaltung und Organisation*, edited by Theo Wehner and Stefan T. Güntert, 77–93. Berlin: Springer, 2015.
Habermas, Jürgen. *Theory of Communicative Action, Volume Two: Lifeworld and System: A Critique of Functionalist Reason*, translated by Thomas A. McCarthy. Boston: Beacon Press, 1987.
Halter, Mary, Olga Boiko, Ferruccio Pelone, Carole Beighton, Ruth Harris, Julia Gale, Stephen Gourlay, and Vari Drennan. "The Determinants and Consequences of Adult Nursing Staff Turnover: A Systematic Review of Systematic Reviews." *BMC Health Services Research*, no. 17 (2017).
Iwand, Hans Joachim. "Zur religiösen Lage der Flüchtlinge" (1949). In *Frieden mit dem Osten. Texte (1933–1959)*, edited by Gerard C. den Hertog, 25–32. München: Chr. Kaiser, 1988.
Jurczyk, Karin, Maria S. Rerrich, and Barbara Thiessen. "Caring Communities: Häusliche Versorgung gemeinschaftlich unterstützen." *Blätter der Wohlfahrtspflege*, no. 167 (2020): 3–6.
Kals, Elisabeth, Isabel T. Strubel, and Stefan T Güntert. "Gemeinsinn und Solidarität: Motivation und Wirkung von Freiwilligenarbeit." *Bibliothek Forschung und Praxis*, no. 45 (2021): 14–25.
Karlsson, Margareta and Sandra Pennbrant. "Ideas of Caring in Nursing Practice." *Nursing Philosophy* 21, no. 4 (2020): e12325.
Lange, Frits de. "Restoring Autonomy: Symmetry and Asymmetry in Care Relationships." *Nederduitse Gereformeerde Teologiese Tydskrif* 1, no. 52 (2011): 61–8.
Laugier, Sandra. *Politics of the Ordinary: Care, Ethics and Forms of Life.* Leuven: Peeters, 2020.
Luther, Martin. "Treatise on Good Works." In *The Christian in Society 1. Luther's Works* 44, *American Edition*, edited by James Atkinson, 21–114. Philadelphia: Fortress Press, 1966.

MacIntyre, Alasdair. *After Virtue*. Notre Dame: University of Notre Dame Press, 1981.
Madörin, Mascha. "Care-Ökonomie: eine Herausforderung für die Wirtschaftswissenschaften." In *Gender and Economics: Feministische Kritik der politischen Ökonomie*, edited by Christine Bauhardt and Gülay Çağlar, 81–104. Wiesbaden: VS Verlag für Sozialwissenschaften, 2010.
Nussbaum, Martha C. *Creating Capabilities*. Cambridge, MA: Harvard University Press, 2011.
Ricoeur, Paul. "The Socius and the Neighbor." In *History and Truth*, edited by Paul Ricoeur, translated by Charles A. Kelbley, 98–109. Evanston: Northwestern University Press, 1998.
Riegraf Birgit. "Care, Care-Arbeit und Geschlecht: gesellschaftliche Veränderungen und theoretische Auseinandersetzungen." In *Handbuch Interdisziplinäre Geschlechterforschung*, edited by Beate Kortendiek, Birgit Riegraf, and Katja Sabisch, 763–72. Wiesbaden: Springer, 2017.
Rosa, Hartmut. *Social Acceleration: A New Theory of Modernity*, translated by Jonathan Trejo-Mathys. New York: Columbia University Press, 2013.
Sandel, Michael J. *Liberalism and the Limits of Justice*. Cambridge: Cambridge University Press, 1998.
Schnerring, Almut and Sascha Verlan. *Equal Care: Über Fürsorge und Gesellschaft*. Berlin: Verbrecher Verlag, 2020.
Sen, Amartya. "Capability and Well-being." In *The Quality of Life*, edited by Martha C. Nussbaum and Amartya Sen, 30–53. Oxford: Clarendon Press, 1993.
Sen, Amartya. *Inequality Re-examined*. Oxford: Oxford University Press, 1992.
Steckelberg, Claudia, Barbara Thiessen, and Vera Taube, eds. *Wandel der Arbeitsgesellschaft. Soziale Arbeit in Zeiten von Globalisierung, Digitalisierung und Prekarisierung*. Opladen, Berlin, Toronto: Budrich, 2020.
Tronto, Joan C. *Moral Boundaries: A Political Argument for an Ethic of Care*. New York: Routledge, 1993.
Winker, Gabriele. *Care Revolution: Schritte in eine solidarische Gesellschaft*. Bielefeld: transcript Verl, 2015.
Wittgenstein, Ludwig. *Philosophical Investigation*, translated by G.E.M. Anscombe. Oxford: Blackwell, 1958.
Wolf, Ernst. *Sozialethik. Theologische Grundfragen*. Göttingen: Vandenhoeck and Ruprecht, 1988.

Yerkes, Mara A., Jana Javornik, and Anna Kurowska. *Social Policy and the Capability Approach: Concepts, Measurements and Application.* Bristol: Policy Press, 2019.

Zander, Britta, Linda H. Aiken, Reinhard Busse, Anne Marie Rafferty, Walter Sermeus, and Luk Bruyneel. "The State of Nursing in the European Union." *Eurohealth*, no. 22 (2016): 3–6.

Żuk, Piotr, Paweł Żuk, and Justyna Lisiewicz-Jakubaszko. "Labour Migration of Doctors and Nurses and the Impact on the Quality of Health Care in Eastern European Countries: The Case of Poland." *The Economic and Labour Relations Review*, no. 30 (2019): 307–20.

# 6

# The Spirit and Surveillance

# Examining Forms of Knowledge, Power, and Discernment in the Church

*Emily Beth Hill*

## Introduction

A television commercial from technology company IBM begins, "Dear Tech. . ." The commercial is a letter to its own industry articulating a foundational belief of contemporary society: "We have a pretty good relationship, you've done a lot of good for the world . . . but I feel like you have the potential to do so much more." We tend to view technology as a tool that humans can use toward good ends. The commercial goes on to champion tech that enables diverse organizations, women's rights, human rights, and "tech that helps people understand each other."[1]

---

[1] IBM, "Dear Tech: An Open Letter to the Industry," iSpot.tv, accessed January 25, 2024, https://www.ispot.tv/ad/Ijcp/ibm-dear-tech-an-open-letter-to-the-industry.

Is technology only or always a mere tool to achieve good human goals? Can technology solve challenges we face? Or does this message and belief disguise realities that can deform our culture, organizations, and even the church?

As Western lawmakers debate how to regulate technology companies and artificial intelligence (AI), they often articulate concerns about the use of social scoring by authoritarian governments. Social scoring is the idea that governments can use AI to "rank people's trustworthiness and punish them for undesirable behaviors."[2] But Melissa Heikkilä reports that such a system is far from actualized. Heikkilä contends that lawmakers should spend less energy on a dystopian myth and look closer to home where algorithms are already in use by companies and organizations to make decisions about human beings on a regular basis.[3]

Lawmakers' concerns about authoritarian mass surveillance are captured well by George Orwell's novel *Nineteen Eighty-Four*. Yet today's surveillance culture is more accurately represented by the corporate surveillance depicted in recent novels like *Feed* by M.T. Anderson and *Zed* by Joanna Kavenna, or the documentary *The Social Network*. Writer Rebecca Solnit has argued that not even George Orwell could have foreseen our current circumstances. She writes, "In many ways, we are not living in the world of Orwell's *Nineteen Eighty-Four*, but we certainly have a gang of Big Brothers watching us now."[4]

This watching occurs at the intersection of governance, security, and marketing, and it depends on our own participation via user-generated data.[5] As we've become accustomed to being watched, we also participate in the watching whether by holding jobs that

---

[2]Melissa Heikkilä, "The AI Myth Western Lawmakers Get Wrong," *MIT Technology Review*, November 29, 2022, https://www.technologyreview.com/2022/11/29/1063777/the-ai-myth-western-lawmakers-get-wrong/.
[3]Ibid.
[4]Rebecca Solnit, "A Planet in Peril and Our Embrace of Big Brother: George Orwell would have been Shocked," *The Guardian*, June 24, 2022, https://www.theguardian.com/commentisfree/2022/jun/24/big-brother-george-orwell-climate-change-surveillance.
[5]David Lyon, "Big Data Surveillance," *Surveillance Studies Centre*, May 18, 2022, https://www.surveillance-studies.ca/sites/sscqueens.org/files/bds_report_eng-2022-05-17.pdf.

use surveillance, using doorbell cameras, or simply browsing social media profiles.[6] We are not watching and collecting personal data for no specific reason, but with a particular, systematized intention: for the purposes of "control, entitlement, management, influence or protection."[7] While watching can appear innocuous, fun, necessary for our safety, and beneficial to some, it has significant consequences on the "opportunities, life-chances and choices" of others based on how we "collect, store, classify and analyse those data."[8] These systems are not mere tools.

In this chapter I will first outline some of the ways churches participate in this culture of surveillance. Second, I will begin to develop a brief theology of big data that draws attention to conflicts in the knowledge and power generated by surveillance, and the knowledge and power at work in the church. Finally, I will argue that as a result of their reliance on technology to know and communicate with the congregation, churches have lost their capacity for spiritual discernment. The implications of this will suggest a radical reorganization of the church today.

## Surveillance Culture and the Church's Complicity

The shift and expansion in surveillance is driven by computer technology—specifically, big data and the attendant capability for using algorithms and machine learning. Big data refers to "high-volume, high-velocity and high-variety information," used primarily to generate actionable insights.[9] This data is derived from social networks, mobile devices, online and offline tracking such as web cookies and shopper loyalty cards, wearable devices like

---

[6]David Lyon, *The Culture of Surveillance: Watching as a Way of Life* (Medford: Polity Press, 2018), 2, 4.
[7]Jason Pridmore and David Lyon, "Marketing as Surveillance: Assembling Consumers as Brands," in *Inside Marketing: Practices, Ideologies, Devices*, ed. Detlev Zwick and Julien Cayla (Oxford: Oxford University Press, 2012), 281.
[8]Lyon, *The Culture of Surveillance*, 4–5.
[9]Kirstie Ball, Maria Laura Di Domenico, and Daniel Nunan, "Big Data Surveillance and the Body Subject," *Body and Society* 18, no. 2 (2016): 60.

FitBits, and other smart devices like the Nest thermostat. While big data refers to the quantity of data, more importantly it refers to the "ubiquity of data, the completeness of coverage over our entire lives."[10] In its omnipresence, big data-fueled surveillance is the spirit of our society.

People are trained to opt in and participate in the surveillance of their own lives for various reasons, including convenience and customization. Stores and mobile apps often pitch this to us in the form of personalization. For example, Twitter repeatedly prompts users to turn on "personalized ads" so that one only sees ads relevant to their Twitter activity, activity offline, and their "inferred identity."[11]

While citizens opt in for one reason, this is driven and disciplined by the business model itself which prioritizes the power of those who hold the data. In the past, companies collected data in order to improve their products and therefore the value generated for customers, but now collecting data is the business model itself: to "create patterns and reveal trends" that can be sold to other organizations who want to use that data to influence, control, or shape behavior.[12] By turning on personalized ads, Twitter then collects data from your device and sells a behavioral profile to those interested in advertising or knowing more about someone with your "inferred identity." The now commonsense rationale for using any number of data-driven tools is to better know the people you are trying to reach or communicate with, in order to tailor more effective, influential communication to them.

Among many concerns that could be articulated about surveillance, it is important to note that the power generated by surveillance is not evenly distributed. As data profiles of human beings are generated and sold, they privilege some and are disproportionately used against those on the margins of society. The data gathered can be used to discriminate against people that the algorithms deem risky—including those in poverty and people of certain genders, races, and ethnicities. The algorithms perpetuate

---

[10] Ibid., 65.
[11] Twitter Settings, accessed September 6, 2022, https://twitter.com/settings/off_twitter_activity.
[12] Lyon, "Big Data Surveillance," 1.

inequality and stigmatization, and prevent the poor from accessing housing and government benefits.[13] They can also enable predatory targeting of services such as payday loans for those already ripe for exploitation.[14]

Gillian Tett reveals that just as individuals are willing to barter and give up their own personal data in order to get free, customized, or more convenient services, institutions such as universities, hospitals, and churches are happy to give up their data—which includes that of their constituents—in order to get free services provided by data analytics companies.[15] As institutions trade their data for services to help know and communicate better with their people, they contribute to a massive imbalance in knowledge and power in society when firms utilize this data to predict and control human behavior.

It is not surprising that the spirit of surveillance has become the spirit of many churches and religious organizations, though arguably without recognizing that they are engaged in surveillance. The scale at which churches participate varies significantly, but at any level, our culture of surveillance dictates "the kind of social relations we imagine to be possible."[16] The church is not exempt from having her imagination shaped by this culture.

Here I'll provide three examples of how churches utilize big data and surveillance with the consistent aim of knowing people in order to engage and communicate well with members to meet their goals. First, churches participate in big data surveillance by utilizing tools like Facebook, Instagram, Google, or YouTube. At one level, simply having a Facebook page is to participate in the system. More pointedly, targeted advertisements on Facebook or Google employ data profiles generated by surveillance in order to identify and communicate with people a church thinks would be interested in their products or services. A variety of firms offer churches expertise

---

[13]Karen Hao, "The Coming War on the Hidden Algorithms That Trap People in Poverty," *MIT Technology Review*, December 4, 2020, https://www.technologyreview.com/2020/12/04/1013068/algorithms-create-a-poverty-trap-lawyers-fight-back/.
[14]Eric Stoddart, *The Common Gaze: Surveillance and the Common Good* (London: SCM Press, 2021), 11, 35.
[15]Gillian Tett, *Anthro-Vision: A New Way to See Business and Life* (New York: Simon and Schuster, 2021), 165.
[16]Stoddart, *The Common Gaze*, 11.

in maximizing free Google ads available to nonprofits and running social media campaigns to advertise their programs and services.[17]

Second, churches utilize big data surveillance with their church management software. There are a number of companies that provide these services—two examples are PushPay and Gloo. PushPay argues their "tools and technology helps your church know, and grow your church body."[18] In a free e-book on "The Data Revolution" they matter-of-factly point out how "data is the new oil" that churches must "collect, refine, and use."[19] By collecting this data churches can track attendance, giving, and serving to know and communicate with members via customized emails, individual messages, or push notifications.[20] All of this aims to "encourage spiritual maturity and generosity in your congregation."[21] Gloo offers churches the ability to "extend the Church's capacity to reach, know and move every person it serves."[22] They do this by integrating multiple data sources to connect with those who do not normally go to church, and to work with your congregation to "serve a range of needs ranging from spiritual development, relationships, health, vocation, prayer, financial training and more."[23]

Finally, churches may participate in digital surveillance through the use of their own mobile apps or partnering with apps from other organizations. For example, one prominent mega church has their own app which according to their privacy policy does not sell user

---

[17]ChurchMarketing.is is one example of a church marketing service that offers consulting to help churches take advantage of these Google grants. They also offer social media management and Facebook advertising management. "ChurchMarketing.Is," ChurchMarketing.is, accessed February 22, 2022, https://churchmarketing.is/.

[18]Pushpay, "7 Ways Your Church Can Reach More People," accessed September 6, 2022, https://engage.pushpay.com/7waystoreachmore-ebook/.

[19]Pushpay, "The Data Revolution and the Future of Giving for Churches," accessed September 6, 2022, https://grow.pushpay.com/lp-ebook-data-revolution.html?_ga=2.126714893.1408271196.1657050378-946233963.1657050377&_gac=1.213650918.1657050521.CjwKCAjwwo-WBhAMEiwAV4dybQl-s_Z5SKpnM FZU6dSRAG0HBOuAGoDMk_a2Dw7XyhWnICiE8c_BTxoCb68QAvD_BwE.

[20]Pushpay, "Church Communications," accessed September 6, 2022, https://pushpay.com/solutions/church-communications.

[21]Pushpay, "The Data Revolution and the Future of Giving for Churches," 4.

[22]Gloo, "About Us," accessed September 6, 2022, https://www.gloo.us/about-us.

[23]Ibid.

information but utilizes data generated to communicate personally, help you grow spiritually, and enable staff to work better.[24] Pray.com is an app that offers free services to churches to share prayer requests and receive tithes, but tracks and sells personal data entered as prayer requests to third parties, and matches their data with information provided by data brokers.[25]

In all these examples, the church is employing available technology toward apparently good goals. Naming these activities as surveillance goes some way in bringing to light the ethical questions we might want to consider. Graham Sewell and James Barker articulate that when considering surveillance within organizations leaders are often trying to navigate the tension between coercion and care. "Coercive" tactics of leaders are seen as intrusive acts of power to keep people in line, while "caring" tactics may be seen as those designed to look out for the best interests of everyone.[26] However, they demonstrate that there are many paradoxical instances where surveillance can be experienced as both coercive and caring.[27] While the church desires to care for its members and to reach, disciple, and increase the spiritual maturity of its members, we should recognize the logic of contemporary surveillance as an intent to systematize information in categories to influence people for the goals of the organization. This trajectory tends toward control and teaches human beings to rely on their own power.

---

[24]Crossroads Church, "Privacy Policy," accessed September 9, 2022, https://www.crossroads.net/privacypolicy/.
[25]Emily Baker White, "Nothing Sacred: These Apps Reserve the Right to Sell Your Prayers," *Buzzfeed News*, January 25, 2022, https://www.buzzfeednews.com/article/emilybakerwhite/apps-selling-your-prayers.
[26]Graham Sewell and James R. Barker, "Coercion vs. Care: Using Irony to Make Sense of Organizational Surveillance," *Academy of Management Review* 31, no. 4 (2006): 935.
[27]Ibid.

# A Brief Theology of Big Data: Personalization and the Word of God *Pro Me*

I have briefly outlined the ways in which churches in a surveillance culture rely on the power of surveillance to know and communicate with those in the body of Christ. In the process, we are accumulating and relying on human power for the pastoral task. How might we begin to think theologically about the use of this knowledge and power for communication? Is there an alternative? In this section I will introduce Martin Luther's *pro me* ("for me") theology to help us think about how we communicate in the church. This will reveal that the knowledge and power generated by surveillance are not only at odds with the knowledge and power in the church, but they are unnecessary—and idols disguised as tools for good. This will suggest that to live in the grammar of the gospel we must abandon our attempts at control and expect all good and everything we need to come from God.

## Luther's *Pro Me* Theology

Luther continually emphasizes the use of pronouns in his reading of scripture, and those pronouns play a crucial role in his theology. For example, in the *Large Catechism*, after explaining what the sacrament is, Luther clarifies who receives such benefits: "It is the one who believes what the words say and what they give, for they are not spoken or preached to stone and wood but to those who hear them, those to whom he says, 'Take and eat' etc." Those who receive the benefit of the sacraments are those who respond in faith to the words that his body has been "given FOR YOU" and "shed FOR YOU."[28] The significance of the pronouns is rooted in Luther's theology of the Word, his Christology, and his understanding of the gospel.

---

[28] Martin Luther, "The Large Catechism," in *The Book of Concord: The Confessions of the Evangelical Lutheran Church*, ed. Robert Kolb, Timothy J. Wengert, and Charles P. Arand (Minneapolis: Fortress Press, 2000), 470.

For Luther, God creates, sustains, and redeems human beings through his powerful, effective Word. As human beings we are surrounded by words we hear, receive, and can respond to. Our ultimate existence and freedom depend on whether we respond to the word of the law that encourages us to create and redeem ourselves through our own power or if we respond to the promise of the gospel in which we come to trust in God's rescue and action on our behalf, and in God's provision and care for us.

For Luther, to respond to the word of the gospel is not to assent to a list of facts about Christ's life and teaching, but to believe that everything Christ did was *for us,* on our behalf. Luther's *Theses Concerning Faith and Law* articulate this well. He writes in thesis 18, "[T]rue faith says, 'I certainly believe that the Son of God suffered and arose, but he did this all for me, for my sins, of that I am certain.'" Acquired faith looks at Christ's work and says, "That is nothing to me" while in thesis 22, "True faith with arms outstretched joyfully embraces the Son of God given for it and says, 'He is my beloved and I am his.'"[29] Thus, in thesis 24 Luther summarizes: "Accordingly, that 'for me' or 'for us,' if it is believed, creates that true faith and distinguishes it from all other faith, which merely hears the things done."[30] Belief or understanding of the historical facts is meaningless if one cannot believe that what Christ said and did is true "for you."

I will briefly outline three components of Luther's *pro me* theology which begins with the fact that Christ is *for us.* This can be seen clearly in his *Lectures on Galatians 1535.* Luther calls the "true and correct definition of Christ" the one "who gave Himself for our sins."[31] "Learn this definition carefully," Luther encourages. "Especially practice this pronoun 'our' in such a way that this syllable, once believed, may swallow up and absorb all your sins, that is, that you may be certain that Christ has taken away not only the sins of some men but your sins and those of the whole world."[32] Christ is, by definition, in his being and action *for us.*

---

[29]Martin Luther, "Theses Concerning Faith and Law," in *Luther's Works* 34, ed. Lewis W. Spitz (Philadelphia: Muhlenberg, 1960), 110.
[30]Ibid., 111.
[31]Martin Luther, "Lectures on Galatians 1535," in *Luther's Works* 26, ed. Jaroslav Pelikan (Saint Louis: Concordia, 1963), 39.
[32]Ibid., 38.

Not only is Christ himself *for us*, but he continually communicates himself for us. While Christ's atoning work was real and effective in itself, Luther often exclaims that "a hundred thousand Christs might have been crucified without avail if men remained ignorant of the use of His Passion."[33] Christ's death and resurrection really achieved satisfaction for sins, but it is distributed through the preaching of the gospel and the sacraments by which Christ himself continually communicates with human beings and proclaims the promise of the gospel.[34]

If Christ is for us and communicates this to us, it follows for Luther that humans must accept the benefits of Christ "for us" personally. This is the second aspect of Luther's *pro me* theology. Luther insists that it is easy to believe that Christ died for others one might perceive worthier but much more difficult to "believe from your heart that Christ was given for *your* many great sins."[35] Therefore, "These words, OUR, US, FOR US, must be written in letters of gold. He who does not believe this is not a Christian."[36]

To modern ears this may sound like an individualized, subjective appropriation of the gospel. But it is not subjective, even as it is personal. Christ's own *promeity* grounds Luther's *pro me* theology and distinguishes it from later applications beginning with Immanuel Kant. For Kant, the *pro me* became associated with subjective knowledge and "whether or not I wish to accept the existence of a supreme being."[37] But for Luther, there is no question of subjectively choosing whether God exists and how to relate to God, but only the objective reality that Christ is *for us*.

God is really for us and God communicates it, but the question is: Will I accept this is true "for me?" Hans Joachim Iwand writes

---

[33]Ian D. Kingston Siggins, *Martin Luther's Doctrine of Christ* (New Haven: Yale University Press, 1970), 110.
[34]Jeffrey G. Silcock, "Luther on the Holy Spirit and His Use of God's Word," in *The Oxford Handbook of Martin Luther's Theology*, ed. Robert Kolb, Irene Dingel, and Lubomir Batka (Oxford: Oxford University Press, 2014), 296.
[35]Luther, "Lectures on Galatians 1535," 26:34.
[36]Martin Luther, "Lectures on Isaiah 40-66," in *Luther's Works* 17, ed. Hilton Oswald (Saint Louis: Concordia, 1972), 221.
[37]Hans Joachim Iwand, *Hans Joachim Iwand on Church and Society*, ed. Benjamin Haupt, Michael Basse, Gerard den Hertog, and Christian Neddens, trans. Christian Einertson (London: T&T Clark, 2023), 140.

that the "I" who is addressed by the word that Christ is *pro me* is the "'I' of God's election that, hidden and determined in the story of Jesus Christ, expects to be taken hold of by me and made into the center of my self in faith."[38] To accept in the gospel that God is *pro me* is not to find a way to leverage oneself out of existential chaos and create ethical certainty but to confess one's incorporation into God's story. It is this personal acceptance that opens up true knowledge of God and creates the ultimate faith in God as the grounds of human life and identity. This "daring confidence"[39] in God opens us up to acknowledge and trust God in all areas of our lives.

If Christ is for us, and human beings must believe Christ is for us to receive the benefits, then the third component of Luther's *pro me* theology follows: the church must preach Christ "for you" and "for me." In *The Freedom of a Christian,* Luther emphasizes, "Christ [ought] to be preached to the end that faith in him may be established that he may not only be Christ, but be Christ for you and me, and that what is said of him may be effectual in us."[40] Christ has established the preaching office and the task of the preacher is to proclaim the promise in Word and sacrament, the primary means the Spirit uses to communicate Christ to us.[41] It is this preaching that draws us to Christ and creates trust in the gospel, and this is the preaching that Luther urges for the church.

Such preaching for Luther must focus on "why Christ came, what he brought and bestowed, and what benefit it is to us to accept him."[42] Luther writes,

> For the preaching of the gospel is nothing else than Christ coming to us, or we being brought to him. When you see how he works, however, and how he helps everyone to whom he comes or who is brought to him, then rest assured that faith is accomplishing

---

[38]Ibid., 141.
[39]Martin Luther, "Preface to the Epistle of St. Paul to the Romans," in *Luther's Works* 35, ed. Jaroslav Pelikan (Saint Louis: Concordia, 1955), 370.
[40]Martin Luther, "The Freedom of a Christian," in *Luther's Works* 31, ed. Harold J. Grimm (Philadelphia: Muhlenberg, 1957), 357.
[41]Silcock, "Luther on the Holy Spirit and His Use of God's Word," 297.
[42]Luther, "The Freedom of a Christian," 31:357.

this in you and that he is offering your soul exactly the same sort of help and favor through the gospel.[43]

To believe in the promise of the gospel and be reborn is not an other-worldly reality, but to trust God's goodness and provision in the midst of our concrete experiences. Luther illuminates this in his commentary on the creed in the *Small Catechism*. On the meaning of the first article of the Apostles' Creed he writes:

> I believe that God has created *me* together with all that exists. God has given *me* and still preserves my body and soul: eyes, ears, and all limbs and senses; reason and all mental faculties. In addition, God daily and abundantly provides shoes and clothing, food and drink, house and farm, spouse and children, fields, livestock, and all property—along with all the necessities and nourishment for this body and life. God protects *me* against all danger and shields and preserves *me* from all evil. And all this is done out of pure, fatherly, and divine goodness and mercy, without any merit or worthiness of mine at all.[44]

If the task of the preacher is to proclaim Christ for us in the midst of concrete circumstances, do they need surveillance and big data to help know the circumstances of those they are preaching to? After all, Gloo offers their services to churches because they hear from pastors that it's "more difficult than ever to truly know how our people are doing."[45] I now want to outline several contrasts between the promise of the gospel proclaimed for us, and the knowledge and power accumulated through surveillance.

---

[43]Martin Luther, "A Brief Instruction on What to Look for and Expect in the Gospels," in *Luther's Works* 35, ed. Jaroslav Pelikan, Hilton C. Oswald, and Helmut T. Lehmann (Philadelphia: Fortress Press, 1999), 121.
[44]Martin Luther, "The Small Catechism," in *The Book of Concord: The Confessions of the Evangelical Lutheran Church*, ed. Robert Kolb, Timothy J. Wengert, and Charles P. Arand (Minneapolis: Fortress Press, 2000), 354–5. (My emphasis.)
[45]Gloo, "About Us."

## "Observation without Witness" and the God Who Sees

Shoshana Zuboff calls the knowledge generated by surveillance capitalism "radically indifferent" and "observation without witness."[46] By this she means that as companies and organizations collect data distanced from actual human beings and their experiences, they are able to interpret it for their own objectives. Yet, they do not actually know how that data accords with the personal, lived experience of those they are surveilling. As Ball et al. write, "For those who surveil, the impulse is to surface and capture lived interiority to denote truth, authenticity and value within the surveillance dispositif . . . But at times this may not coincide with an individual's lived, embodied identity and their sense of morality, and this is how the contestation arises."[47] Thus, surveillors remain blind to the actual lives of those they watch.

While technologists often refer to creating a "God's eye view" through technology,[48] attention to God's action in scripture reveals God's knowing is characterized by relational connection and mutual concern, in contrast to the surveillance of big data that seems more akin to the accounting records of Egyptian slaveholders. God is intimately, emotionally involved with the lives of God's people; God hears, sees, responds. God knows them by name. God's knowledge is not only *not indifferent*, but shows a particular concern for the poor, marginalized, and oppressed.[49] This is the knowledge, presence, and sight that the people of God experience, trust, and praise—and this is the kind of knowledge we ought to practice among ourselves.

Not only is the knowledge gathered apart from personal relationship and care antithetical to the body of Christ, Luther emphasizes that the Word that proclaims God for us comes from the

---

[46]Shoshana Zuboff, *The Age of Surveillance Capitalism: The Fight for a Human Future at the New Frontier of Power* (New York: PublicAffairs, 2020), 377.
[47]Ball et al., "Big Data Surveillance and the Body Subject," 74.
[48]Zuboff, *The Age of Surveillance Capitalism*, 418–19.
[49]In *The Common Gaze* Eric Stoddart argues for an ethic of surveillance and data gathering based on God's preferential option for the poor. *The Common Gaze: Surveillance and the Common Good.*

outside, as something that people did not know they needed but do in fact need. In Gal. 1:4, Paul announces that Christ "gave Himself for our sins to set us free from the present evil age" (NRSVUE). This reveals that not only has Christ given himself for us, but that human beings are sinners. Luther writes that without this disclosure "we are indifferent, and we regard sin as something trivial, a mere nothing." Therefore, "we should note here the infinite greatness of the price paid for it. Then it will be evident that its power is so great that it could not be removed by any means except that the Son of God be given for it."[50] This emphasizes that true knowledge of human beings comes from God through the Spirit.

Even as surveillance techniques of knowing grow ever more sophisticated in their approximation of human beings, they can never know what only God knows and can communicate. Technology can never see or discern the real needs of people. Thus, the claim of big data researchers—that through their work "the Truth will be present in everything. You'll know everything about yourself and your loved ones"[51]—is not only impossible but also deceived.

## Human Power and God's Verbum Efficax

The power that fuels individualized communication via big data surveillance is also at odds with the powerful, effective Word of God. To walk with Luther in the grammar of the gospel, we need to note that he understands the gospel as a proclamation of God's promise. Oswald Bayer details that Luther's understanding of God's promises found in scripture are performative statements, they "[constitute] a reality; it does not affirm something as if it exists already, but presents it for the first time."[52] The *promissio* (promise) is for Luther a particular type of speech, the *Verbum efficax* (effective

---

[50]Luther, "Lectures on Galatians 1535," 26:33.
[51]Joseph Turow, *The Aisles Have Eyes: How Retailers Track Your Shopping, Strip Your Privacy, and Define Your Power* (New Haven: Yale University Press, 2017), 221.
[52]Oswald Bayer, *Martin Luther's Theology: A Contemporary Interpretation* (Grand Rapids: Eerdmans, 2008), 51.

word)—"that which establishes communication, which frees one and gives one confidence: an effective, accomplishing Word."[53]

Therefore, the power of the gospel proclamation rests not with a charismatic preacher, or knowledge gained through surveillance, but on the *Verbum efficax*. "For the word of God is living and active, and sharper than any two-edged sword, piercing until it divides soul from spirit, joints from marrow; it is able to judge the thoughts and intentions of the heart" (Heb. 4:12, NRSVUE). Christ is really *present for us* and communicates *himself for us* personally, through the Spirit. God's word accomplishes what it says—it creates faith and sets people free.

To proclaim the news that God has forgiven our sins for Christ's sake is not abstract, esoteric, or only applicable to a future situation. It is the pronouncement of a new reality and a new identity where God gives life as a gift and relieves human beings of all efforts to create and sustain themselves. The promise sets people free in the midst of daily life. Preaching must make the benefits of Christ's life, death, and resurrection come to life in a way that breaks through and makes a difference to the life of the listeners. A preacher must bring Christ *pro nobis* into present realities of family life, work, finances, and friendships. Here the pastoral task of understanding the lives of a congregation is certainly relevant, but as the previous discussion indicates, it should be seen as partial and relationally, lovingly discerned.

## Spiritual Discernment in the Body of Christ

That the gospel comes via an external word reveals that surveillance cannot provide true knowledge and that human beings are sinners who resist God. Luther emphasizes that it is impossible for human beings to want God to be God, and that our sin is our own attempt to be God.[54] Given this, it is very difficult for us to accept that we are included among those for whom Christ died—that Christ died

---

[53]Ibid., 53.
[54]Iwand, *Hans Joachim Iwand*, 144.

for *our* sins not just those in the world who seem more worthy or who we think need it more. God's own effective Word must come to us to create faith that our sins are forgiven and we can trust God to provide for us. Without this revelation and the gift of faith, people cannot know what we need or desire, and therefore cannot generate our own knowledge or work of salvation.

This also forestalls the possibility of any ethical knowledge on our own. Here we encounter another contrast between Luther's articulation of the *pro me* and Kant's interpretation that also speaks to the church's use of surveillance to make decisions and communicate in the body. Under Kant, the subjective appropriation of the *pro me* is an attempt to secure our own knowledge; for Luther, this is impossible. Since we cannot want Christ on our own, our righteousness and therefore ethical knowledge exists in Christ alone. Iwand writes, "[we] must give up [our] ethical presumption in order to live in a foreign righteousness."[55]

That our certainty is rooted in Christ *pro nobis* (for us) reminds us that even as we are assuredly a new creation, the "Christ-life" by which we live is outside ourselves. "The Gospel commands us to look not at our own good deeds or perfection but at God Himself as He promises, and at Christ Himself, the Mediator."[56] Luther continues:

> Here I cannot have any doubts, unless I want to deny God altogether. And this is the reason why our theology is certain: it snatches us away from ourselves and places us outside ourselves, so that we do not depend on our own strength, conscience, experience, person, or works but depend on that which is outside ourselves, that is, on the promise and truth of God, which cannot deceive.[57]

This suggests that the church's attempt to generate knowledge and power via surveillance tools is an attempt to be like God,

---

[55]Ibid.
[56]Luther, "Lectures on Galatians 1535," 26:387.
[57]Ibid.

an attempt to discern and make decisions on our own terms. As Luther's famous definition of a god reminds us,

> A "god" is the term for that to which we are to look for all good and in which we are to find refuge in all need. Therefore, to have a god is nothing else than to trust and believe that one with your whole heart . . . Anything on which your heart relies and depends, I say, that is really your God.[58]

Thus in accepting Christ's life given "for us" the church is freed to let God sustain the church and lay down its own attempts at knowledge and power.

This analysis has revealed that surveillance is an idol, an invading evil spirit that has distorted our knowledge of human beings in the body of Christ. As we have turned to this idol, we have become deaf and blind (Ps. 135:15-18), losing our ability for spiritual discernment.

By looking at Paul's discussion of spiritual gifts and the body of Christ in 1 Corinthians 12, we can see some important contrasts with the discernment generated by big data. This contrast is significant not just in the means of discernment, but in the type of organization likely generated. I have mentioned the radically indifferent knowledge generated by surveillance, but now need to highlight another dominant paradigm of surveillance: to sort and filter human beings into predetermined categories. The use of data to know and communicate with people entails grouping people into like categories to discern trends among those groups and communicate to them based on these trends. This necessarily involves prioritizing people deemed most valuable to the leaders, whether in terms of finances, volunteer status, or marketing target. The intention is to communicate in a way that is likely to get each group to respond as desired for the needs of the organization.

With this in mind, let us turn to some key points from 1 Corinthians 12. First, in verses 4-11 we read of the gifts of the Spirit present in the body and Paul repeats that these are from the same Spirit, and are activated by the Spirit. Further, when moving on to verses 14-26 about the different parts of the body, we read that it

---

[58]Luther, "The Large Catechism," 386.

is God through the Spirit who organizes the body. Not only does each part of the body matter, but "God arranged the members in the body, each one of them, as he chose" (v18). Therefore, while big data offers leaders ways to organize and communicate with their congregation, we see that this action is reserved for the Spirit.

We also see that human beings tend to approach the body with predetermined goals and categories while God prioritizes those who the culture would not predict—those who seem to be "weaker" or "inferior members." As Brian Brock writes, Paul suggests that to discern gifts in the body we must begin "by becoming more aware of the codes of decency and honor that are inevitably present in every social grouping."[59] The Spirit reveals gifts in ways that subvert any predetermined categories and socially constructed realities human beings might bring to decision-making. Brock writes, "Paul wants believers to be wholly invested in learning to pick up the crackling energy of the *charismata*. The receptivity required for discernment is only acquired, however, when the codes of social superiority and inferiority learned in the world are revealed as false social constructions."[60] Therefore, to discern the gifts of the body—to hear how the Spirit is communicating personally to us and our community—is to expect the Spirit to work in places we cannot determine ahead of time, in ways distanced data gathering cannot.

Granted, many leaders intentionally and sincerely seek the Spirit to develop their goals. However, in relying on the tools of surveillance we drive out the Spirit and disfigure the body of Christ. Renewed capacity to discern the Spirit among concrete human beings will be more reflective of God's unique attention to the poor and marginalized in our midst rather than participating in systems that increase the inequality of knowledge and power in society and disadvantage and exploit those on the margins.

---

[59] Brian Brock, *Wondrously Wounded: Theology, Disability, and the Body of Christ* (Waco: Baylor University Press, 2019), 215.
[60] Ibid., 216.

## Conclusion

Sociologist Felicia Wu Song describes that one effect of our reliance on digital technology is that we begin to reify others, turning them into objects such that the "the complex dance of social interaction is halted and made more transactional."[61] She is concerned that "[W]e may be 'losing a taste for' . . . the amazing fruit that can be borne out of a social landscape where human presence is unmediated and our social horizons are bounded enough to discover the depths of who we are in ourselves."[62] As our lives together are mediated by technology, we lose the ability to participate in and grow through messy, inefficient relationships of attention and care.

In this chapter I have brought to light our culture of surveillance, and that its modes of knowledge, power, and relationship have become the spirit of the church. What appears to be a tool for good is an idol in disguise, intent on driving out the Holy Spirit and crippling our spiritual discernment. In this context, the dominant motivation for the church and other organizations to use these tools is to better know and communicate with their congregations. Whether one deems these techniques coercive or caring, I have shown that even as the church is tasked to proclaim the promise of the gospel *for you* and *for me*, it does not need the tools offered by big data and surveillance because the personalization of the word is achieved through the Spirit, God's own loving, attentive knowledge, and God's own *Verbum efficax*.

Discernment, unity, and growth in the body is based not on effective communication as determined by management techniques, but occurs as we hear and respond to God's own effective word. It occurs as we receive the gifts and communication of the Spirit through the lives of others, as we suffer with those who suffer, and rejoice with those who rejoice (1 Cor. 12:26). Rather than blindly relying on surveillance, we can learn to see and hear those in our churches and communities, and how the Spirit reveals the gifts and needs of people in a diverse body. As we grow in our trust of God's

---

[61] Felicia Wu Song, *Restless Devices: Recovering Personhood, Presence, and Place in the Digital Age* (Downers Grove: IVP Academic, 2021), 80.
[62] Ibid., 88.

provision and care, and our attention to the Spirit's direction, we can communicate according to how God is at work among us.

Therefore, rather than jumping to use social media and other technologies that are part of our culture of surveillance in order to help disciple our congregations, the church needs to *be discipled* about big data and surveillance. Christ's *promeity* reveals our own desire to be God and our reliance on human power and surveillance as idolatry. Revived trust in God and attunement to the Spirit in the gathered body is likely to lead to a significant rearrangement of the body so that the church witnesses to the reality of God's relational love and care in a culture striving for power and control. Only in accepting Christ's life "for us" can we be freed from our sins and able to embody the transformed social relationships the gospel generates.

## Bibliography

Ball, Kirstie, Maria, Laura Di Domenico, and Daniel Nunan. "Big Data Surveillance and the Body Subject." *Body and Society* 18, no. 2 (2016): 58–81. DOI: 10.1177/1357034X15624973.

Bayer, Oswald. *Martin Luther's Theology: A Contemporary Interpretation*. Grand Rapids: Eerdmans, 2008.

Brock, Brian. *Wondrously Wounded: Theology, Disability, and the Body of Christ*. Waco: Baylor University Press, 2019.

ChurchMarketing.Is. "ChurchMarketing.is." Accessed February 2022. https://churchmarketing.is/.

Crossroads Church. "Privacy Policy." Accessed September 2022. https://www.crossroads.net/privacypolicy/.

Gloo. "About Us." Accessed September 2022. https://www.gloo.us/about-us.

Hao, Karen. "The Coming War on the Hidden Algorithms That Trap People in Poverty." *MIT Technology Review,* December 4, 2020. https://www.technologyreview.com/2020/12/04/1013068/algorithms-create-a-poverty-trap-lawyers-fight-back/.

Heikkilä, Melissa. "The AI Myth Western Lawmakers Get Wrong." *MIT Technology Review*, November 29, 2022. https://www.technologyreview.com/2022/11/29/1063777/the-ai-myth-western-lawmakers-get-wrong/.

IBM. "Dear Tech: An Open Letter to the Industry." iSpot.tv. Accessed January 2024. https://www.ispot.tv/ad/Ijcp/ibm-dear-tech-an-open-letter-to-the-industry.

Iwand, Hans Joachim. *Hans Joachim Iwand on Church and Society*, edited by Benjamin Haupt, Michael Basse, Gerard den Hertog, and Christian Neddens, translated by Christian Einertson. London: T&T Clark, 2023.

Luther, Martin. *Luther's Works*, edited by Jaroslav Pelikan and Helmut T. Lehman. *American Edition*. 55 vols. Philadelphia: Fortress, and St. Louis: Concordia, 1955.

Luther, Martin. "The Large Catechism." In *The Book of Concord: The Confessions of the Evangelical Lutheran Church*, edited by Robert Kolb, Timothy J. Wengert, and Charles P. Arand, 379–480. Minneapolis: Fortress Press, 2000.

Luther, Martin. "The Small Catechism." In *The Book of Concord: The Confessions of the Evangelical Lutheran Church*, edited by Robert Kolb, Timothy J. Wengert, and Charles P. Arand. Minneapolis: Fortress Press, 2000.

Lyon, David. *The Culture of Surveillance: Watching as a Way of Life*. Medford: Polity Press, 2018.

Pridmore, Jason and David Lyon. "Marketing as Surveillance: Assembling Consumers as Brands." In *Inside Marketing: Practices, Ideologies, Devices*, edited by Detlev Zwick and Julien Cayla, 115–36. Oxford: Oxford University Press, 2012.

Pushpay. "Church Communications." Accessed September 2022. https://pushpay.com/solutions/church-communications.

Pushpay. "7 Ways Your Church Can Reach More People." Accessed September 2022. https://engage.pushpay.com/7waystoreachmore-ebook/.

Pushpay. "The Data Revolution and the Future of Giving for Churches." Accessed September 2022. https://grow.pushpay.com/lp-ebook-data-revolution.html?_ga=2.126714893.1408271196.1657050378-946233963.1657050377&_gac=1.213650918.1657050521.CjwKCAjwwo-WBhAMEiwAV4dybQl-s_Z5SKpnMFZU6dSRAG0HBOuAGoDMk_a2Dw7XyhWnICiE8c_BTxoCb68QAvD_BwE

Sewell, Graham and James R. Barker. "Coercion vs. Care: Using Irony to Make Sense of Organizational Surveillance." *Academy of Management Review* 31, no. 4 (2006): 934–61.

Siggins, Ian D. Kingston. *Martin Luther's Doctrine of Christ*. New Haven: Yale University Press, 1970.

Silcock, Jeffrey G. "Luther on the Holy Spirit and His Use of God's Word." In *The Oxford Handbook of Martin Luther's Theology*, edited by Robert Kolb, Irene Dingel, and Lubomir Batka, 294–309. Oxford: Oxford University Press, 2014.

Solnit, Rebecca. "A Planet in Peril and our Embrace of Big Brother: George Orwell Would have been Shocked." *The Guardian*, June 24, 2022.

Song, Felicia Wu. *Restless Devices: Recovering Personhood, Presence, and Place in the Digital Age.* Downers Grove: IVP Academic, 2021.

Stoddart, Eric. *The Common Gaze: Surveillance and the Common Good.* London: SCM Press, 2021.

Tett, Gillian. *Anthro-Vision: A New Way to See Business and Life.* New York: Simon and Schuster, 2021.

Turow, Joseph. *The Aisles Have Eyes: How Retailers Track Your Shopping, Strip Your Privacy, and Define Your Power.* New Haven: Yale University Press, 2017.

Twitter, "Twitter Settings." Accessed September 2022. https://twitter.com/settings/off_twitter_activity.

White, Emily Baker. "Nothing Sacred: These Apps Reserve the Right to Sell Your Prayers." *Buzzfeed News*, January 25, 2022. https://www.buzzfeednews.com/article/emilyb.

Zuboff, Shoshana. *The Age of Surveillance Capitalism: The Fight for a Human Future at the New Frontier of Power.* New York: Public Affairs, 2020.

# 7

# "What Will We Eat?" Or "What We Will Drink?"

# Meat Consumption and the Messianic Contours of "The Peaceable Kingdom"

*Marco Hofheinz*

## The Initial Question and "Animal Turn" as Observational Starting Point

Currently, it would seem that animals, quite literally, are on everyone's lips. In the meantime, a real "animal turn" is not only a talking matter in the field of animal ethics.[1] When Pope Francis spoke in "Laudato Si" of a "despotic" and "misguided anthropocentrism," which disregards the intrinsic value of animals and the priority

---

[1] Cf. Heike Baranzke, "Auf der Suche nach dem Humanum in Ansehung des 'animal turn' – die ethische Perspektive," in *Der Mensch, ein Tier? Das Tier, ein Mensch?* ed. Peter Heuser and Johannes Weinzirl (Würzburg: Königshausen and Neumann, 2017), 127–42.

of their existence over their usefulness, he was preaching to the converted. The "animal turn" is apparent in the "broad consensus on the moral status of animals, which grants them not merely an instrumental value, but rather an inherent or intrinsic value."[2] The "animal turn" has been expressed in various ways in daily life outside academic discourse in the following ways:

1. Although we love animals as food, they are nevertheless not "on everyone's lips." Presently, veganism and vegetarianism are being increasingly discussed and practiced.[3] Even the meat industry has vegetarian and vegan sausages on offer. According to the German Vegetarian Association (Vebu), 900,000 Germans abstain from eating any animal products. They are thus classified as vegans and make up about 1.1 percent of the population. Long considered as eccentric, they are quickly becoming widely accepted. In 2015, the Allensbach Institute found that 7.8 million Germans claim to be vegetarians. Additionally, an increasing number of people would consider following a meat-free diet, either occasionally or completely.[4]

2. A shift in paradigms has also occurred in the sport of fishing: "Many anglers don't fish for food, but only for fun. The question is raised: What do fish feel? And how should humans treat animals?"[5] Fishing trophies are now no longer preserved pike heads on varnished wooden boards, but rather photos of large, photogenic fish, occasionally taken

---

[2] Eve-Marie Engels, "Art. Tier V. Ethisch," *Religion in Geschichte und Gegenwart 8*, no. 4 (2005): 406–8.
[4] Ibid., 406.
[3] For discussion comparing opposing views see Bernhard H.F. Taureck, "Plädoyer für einen Veganen Humanismus. Was ist und was sein soll," *fiph. Forschungsinstitut für Philosophie Hannover 29*, no. 4 (2017): 27–34; Clemens Wustmans, "Veganer essen ihre Freunde nicht? Anfragen an den Absolutheitsanspruch der Motive veganer Ernährung," *Ethik und Gesellschaft*, no. 2 (2016), https://doi.org/10.18156/eug-2-2016-art-7.
[4] Jenny Hoch, "Die fröhlichen Veganer," *Süddeutsche Zeitung Magazin*, no. 111 (May 16, 2016): 51.
[5] Christoph Cadenbach, "Das Recht des Stärkeren," *Süddeutsche Zeitung Magazin*, no. 28 (July 13, 2018): 9.

by a drone.⁶ Of course, there remains a problem: the catch is in the hook so to speak: namely the one in the fish's mouth. The fish bite the hooks, which then pierce their flesh.

3. British theologian David Clough placed the animal question at the center of his two-volume *Systematic Theology* thereby taking an "animal turn" of his own.⁷ Significantly, *On Animals* is the title of the work, which claims to do nothing less than to develop a new understanding of human and nonhuman creatures in the fields of dogmatics and ethics, namely in the tradition of Karl Barth, under the headings of creation, reconciliation, and redemption.

This so-called "animal turn" poses the question for Christians, whether it is permissible to kill animals for consumption. The following question will be discussed: Should Christians keep to a vegetarian or vegan diet?

## Perception from a Theological Perspective: Creation as an Eschatological Confession

The outlined initial question is one of perception. Ethical discernment begins with perception.⁸ Problems, situations, and behavior patterns are not simply entities in the sense of objective circumstances. We perceive them as we do because of who we are. In his *Nichomachean Ethics* Aristotle pointed out: "The decision lies in the perception."⁹

---

⁶Cf. Ibid., 14.
⁷David L. Clough, *On Animals. Volume 1: Systematic Theology* (London: T&T Clark, 2012); and *On Animals. Volume 2: Theological Ethics* (London: T&T Clark, 2018).
⁸Cf. Bernd Wannenwetsch, "The Fourfold Pattern of Christian Moral Reasoning according to the New Testament," in *Scripture's Doctrine and Theology's Bible: How the New Testament Shapes Christian Dogmatics*, ed. M. Bockmuehl and A.J. Torrance (Grand Rapids: Eerdmans, 2008), 180–5; Marco Hofheinz, "Wahrnehmen – Urteilen – Prüfen. Explorative Annäherung an eine 'selbstdarstellende' theologische Identitäts- und Gemeindeethik," in *Was ist Theologische Ethik? Grundbestimmungen und Grundvorstellungen*, ed. M. Held and M. Roth (Berlin: de Gruyter, 2018), 69–71.
⁹Aristotle, *Nicomachean Ethics*, trans. Terence Irwin (Indianapolis: Hackett, 1985), 1109b, 23.

Martha Nussbaum aptly notes: "Moral knowledge ... is not simply intellectual grasp of propositions; it is not even simply intellectual grasp of particular facts; it is perception."[10]
Bearing this in mind, ethical discernment will not directly ask for the explanation of values, norms, and principles that precede actions, but should rather take into account aesthetic and verbal communicative conditions of the development and reflection of ethos. Ethical discernment must not simply begin with direct appeals and demands, but with the perception of reality.

The proprium of Christian theology and theological ethics is accordingly found on the level of this specific perception of the world.[11] That is, the world is perceived from the perspective of the Christian faith in which the world is disclosed as God's creation and at the same time the human being as a created being. Therefore, theology is concerned with the perception of creation. In the light of biblical testimony, one must specify and add: "The present form of this world is passing away" (1 Cor. 7:31; NRSV). In Rom. 8:18-23, Paul speaks of the groaning of the entire present creation (*pasa hä ktisis*), including the suffering creatures.[12]

Creation, in other words is an eschatological notion: "To say that creation is an eschatological notion is to say that the universe is part of the drama that is not of its own making. That is, creation is a part of a story Christians learn through being initiated into a community that has learned to live appropriately to that story."[13]

---

[10]Martha C. Nussbaum, "Finely Aware and Richly Responsible: Moral Attention and the Moral Task of Literature," *Journal of Philosophy* 82 (1985): 521.
[11]Emphasized by Stanley Hauerwas:

> Christian ethics ... is not first of all concerned with "Thou shalt" or "Thou shalt not." Its first task is to help us rightly envision the world. ... In other words, the enterprise of Christian ethics primarily helps us to see. We can only act within the world we can envision, and we can envision the world rightly only as we are trained to see.

*The Peaceable Kingdom: A Primer in Christian Ethics* (Notre Dame: Notre Dame Press, 1986), 29.
[12]Cf. Erich Grässer, "Das Seufzen der Kreatur (Röm 8:19-22). Auf der Suche nach einer 'biblischen Tierschutzethik'," in *Jahrbuch für Biblische Theologie 5: Schöpfung und Neuschöpfung* (Neukirchen-Vluyn: Neukirchener, 1990), 93–117.
[13]Stanley Hauerwas, *In Good Company: The Church as Polis* (Notre Dame: Notre Dame Press, 1995), 195.

Hans Ulrich puts the eschatological perspective of faith, which is linked to the passing away of the old form, more specifically:

> The indeterminate world will disappear. It is the place of an infinite, endless, undetermined waiting for an advent. It fails to recognize, in its blindness, that the advent of God's actions has already been realized in his Messiah. And God's story continues to break the indeterminacies of this world age. In its witness the testimony of the church exposes them as indeterminacies. According to Romans 12, it is God's renewal of our minds that most visibly displays this transition into a different logic or paradigm. The freedom of an ethics that follows the apocalyptic-messianic contours of God's story comes from beyond the logic of liberty and limits; it does so because it has been initiated and completed with the given determinacy of God's own story.[14]

The perspective from which the initial question shall be discussed is thereby defined. The question in the Sermon on the Mount, "What will we eat?" or "What will we drink?" (Mt. 6:31), which in the following shall be freely applied to our question, should be understood as an eschatological question. It is a matter of presenting a view on the question of nutrition and vegetarianism "that is not one that can be for everyone; rather, it is the perspective that a particular people called to be the church must embody in their relationship to other animals, given that Christians live in God's space and time."[15]

# Perception of Animals in the Light of Biblical Testimony

Testimony in scripture is abundant and varied where the perception of animals is concerned.[16] They are not merely secondary

---

[14]Hans G. Ulrich, "The Messianic Contours of Evangelical Ethics," in *The Freedom of a Christian Ethicist: The Future of a Reformation Legacy*, ed. Brian Brock and Michael G. Mawson (London: T&T Clark, 2016), 15–26.
[15]Hauerwas, *In Good Company*, 196.
[16]Cf. Bernd Janowski, "Auch die Tiere gehören zum Gottesbund. Gott, Mensch und Tier im alten Israel," in *Die Zukunft der Tiere – Theologische, ethische und*

phenomena. The doves report the receding flood to Noah in his ark, the "cage to preserve biodiversity" (Gen. 8:8-12); Balaam's mule sees the angel with his drawn sword (Num. 22:27); ravens provide Elijah with bread and meat at God's behest (1 Kgs 17:4, 6); ox and donkeys are symbols of God's faithfulness (Isa. 1:3); the birds of the sky testify to a carefree life (Mt. 6:26) and sparrows to divine providence (Mt. 10:29, 31). In the manner of legends, the Bible ascribes almost divine qualities to animals: They proclaim the glory of God (Isa. 43:20; Ps. 148:7-12).

It is interesting to note that animal welfare regulations also appear in the Bible: The threshing ox must not be muzzled (Deut. 25:4); game have a part in the Sabbath year (Lev. 25:7), and animals take part in the Sabbath, according to the ten commandments (Exod. 20:10; Deut. 5:14); the mother bird must not be taken from the nest (Deut. 22:6) and one must help the enemy's donkey that has collapsed beneath its burden (Exod. 23:5). Righteous human beings are said to be aware of their animals' needs (*näfäsch [soul]*; Prov. 12:10). The intrinsic value of all living things is stressed in the book of Job when God's first answer out of the storm refers to the ostrich that God has endowed with neither wisdom nor understanding (Job 39:17), but that still lives under God's sovereignty.

When Jesus began his ministry and was tempted in the desert, he "was with the wild beasts; and the angels ministered to him" (Mk 1:13). Regarding the coming of God's kingdom and the resurrection, snakes and scorpions cease to instill fear (Lk. 10:19; Mk 16:18). What does this enigmatic verse mean? Here we find the motif of the eschatological restoration of paradisiacal animal peace, known from Isa. 1:6-9 and 65:25: "Mark here alludes to the restoration of conditions in paradise before the fall."[17] Jesus's coming is accompanied by the new creation. He brings the kingdom of the Messiah in which peace will reign even among the wild beasts.

The most relevant example is without doubt the story of Genesis 1–11, at least as far as its impact on this matter is concerned.

---

*naturwissenschaftliche Perspektiven*, ed. B. Janowski and P. Riede (Stuttgart: Calwer, 1999), 31–60.

[17] So cautiously C. Clifton Black and Mark Abingdon, *Abingdon New Testament Commentaries: Mark* (Nashville: Abingdon, 2011), 62. So also Wilfried Eckey, *Das Markusevangelium. Orientierung am Weg Jesu* (Neukirchen-Vluyn: Neukirchener, 1998), 64.

According to the creation narrative from the priestly source,[18] a "pre-Flood narrative" (Jürgen Ebach), humankind and the beasts of the earth are both formed on the sixth day of creation. Admittedly, only humankind is made in God's image (Gen. 1:27) and assigned with the *dominium terrae* (Gen. 1:26-28),[19] the command to rule over the earth, which includes all living creatures. This provision finds resonance in the second creation story, according to which the man names the animals (Gen. 2:15).[20]

However, even the notorious *dominium terrae* must not be interpreted as humankind replacing God as owner and ruler with unlimited[21] powers.[22] Although the semantic of the Hebrew verb "to reign" (*radah*) is still disputed, with controversy[23] ranging from "tread down" to "take care of" (depending on whether it derives from the Arabic *rada*: tread, tread down, or the Akkadian *redu*: to lead), scholars are in agreement that privileged humankind reigns as God's representative and not as a rival, much less the new owner.[24]

---

[18]Concerning the priestly source cf. Jürgen Ebach, "Ende des Feindes oder Ende der Feindschaft? Der Tierfrieden bei Jesaja und Virgil," in *Ursprung und Ziel. Erinnerte Zukunft und erhoffte Vergangenheit. Biblische Exegesen, Reflexionen, Geschichten* (Neukirchen-Vluyn: Neukirchener, 1986), 16–47.

[19]Cf. Bernd Janowski, "Die lebendige Statue Gottes. Zur Anthropologie der priesterlichen Urgeschichte," in *Die Welt als Schöpfung. Beiträge zur Theologie des Alten Testaments vol. 4*, ed. B. Janowski (Neukirchen-Vluyn: Neukirchener, 2008), 140–71.

[20]Cf. Lukas Ohly, *Ethische Begriffe in biblischer Perspektive* (Tübingen: Narr Francke Attempto), 257–62.

[21]Concerning the self-limitation of creation cf. Marco Hofheinz, *Gezeugt, nicht gemacht. In-vitro-Fertilisation in theologischer Perspektive* (Münster: LIT, 2008), 81–106.

[22]Cf. Ute Neumann-Gorsolke, *Herrschen in den Grenzen der Schöpfung. Ein Beitrag zur alttestamentlichen Anthropologie am Beispiel von Psalm 8, Genesis 1 und verwandter Texte* (Neukirchen-Vluyn: Neukirchener, 2004), 136–315.

[23]For further discourse cf. Holger Delkurt, "Schöpfung – Aspekte der exegetischen Diskussion," *Zeitschrift für Pädagogik und Theologie* 55, no. 3 (2003): 236–53; Bernd Janowski, "Herrschaft über die Tiere. Gen 1:26–28 und die Semantik des *rdh*," in *Die rettende Gerechtigkeit. Beiträge zur Theologie des Alten Testaments vol. 2*, ed. B. Janowski (Neukirchen-Vluyn: Neukirchener, 1999), 33–48; Udo Rütersworden, *Dominium terrae. Studien zur Genese einer alttestamentlichen Vorstellung* (Berlin: de Gruyter, 1993); Manfred Weippert, "Tier und Mensch in einer menschenarmen Welt. Zum sog. Dominium terrae in Gen 1," in *Ebenbild Gottes – Herrscher über die Welt*, ed. Hans-Peter Mathys (Neukirchen-Vluyn: Neukirchener, 1998), 35–55.

[24]Weippert mentions "a kind of indirect rule" (Weippert, "Tier und Mensch," 44).

With regard to animals, humankind is first placed in a vegetarian form and way of life. At creation both humankind and beasts are intended to live off the plants and fruit of the earth (Gen. 1:29f.). However, in the so-called "Noachide commandments" (Gen. 9:1-13), which explicitly imbed the animals in Noah's covenant (Gen. 9:10),[25] the eating of meat is a matter of course (Gen. 9:3), but the consuming of blood remains forbidden: "Only you shall not eat flesh with its life, that is, its blood" (Gen. 9:4; NRSV). In revisiting the Eden narrative (Gen. 2:7; creation of man as a living being), the account of the Flood (Gen. 7:15) emphasizes that animals share in the breath of life (*näfasch haja*). God places man in the garden so that he may "till it and keep it" (Gen. 2:15; NRSV). The fulfillment of this assignment is by no means a matter of counter-existence but rather of coexistence with the animals as created beings.[26]

## The Vision from Isaiah 11 as a Vegetarian/Vegan Imperative?

The vision of a peaceable animal kingdom portrayed in Isa. 11:1-10 is of particular significance for a messianic outline for (animal) ethics.[27] This is a graphic description of an animal kingdom, which also includes humans:

> The wolf shall live with the lamb, the leopard shall lie down with the kid, the calf and the lion and the fatling together, and a little child shall lead them. The cow and the bear shall graze, their young shall lie down together; and the lion shall eat straw like the ox. The nursing child shall play over the hole of the asp,

---

[25]Concerning the role of animals in the covenant cf. Christian Link, *Schöpfung, Ein theologischer Entwurf im Gegenüber von Naturwissenschaft und Ökologie* (Neukirchen-Vluyn: Neukirchener, 2012), 89–96.
[26]Cf. Alexandra Grund, "Mitgeschöpflichkeit," *Religionsunterricht an höheren Schulen* 44, no. 6 (2002): 332–8.
[27]Cf. For an introduction see Janowski, "Auch die Tiere gehören zum Gottesbund," 45–9. For more detail: Bernd Janowski, "Der Wolf und das Lamm. Zum eschatologischen Tierfrieden in Jes 11:6-9," in *Der nahe und der ferne Gott. Beiträge zur Theologie des Alten Testaments* vol. 5, ed. B. Janowski (Neukirchen-Vluyn: Neukirchener, 2014), 55–70.

and the weaned child shall put its hand on the adder's den. (Isa. 11:6-8; NRSV)

The peaceable animal kingdom, which is described as a coexistence of deadly enemies, characterizes the rule of the eschatological redeemer. What is fascinating about this vision is the counterfactual emphasis. The primeval vegetarianism, as pictured in the creation narrative from the priestly source, is joined by an eschatological one. This kind of vegetarianism points toward a time in which eating and being eaten will cease. Could it not be precisely in this deictic function related to the coming kingdom of God that the special valence of a vegetarian diet lies? In this prophetic vision, the eschatological time of salvation is contrasted with the present in order to motivate people to act in a contrary manner. This intention becomes clear when Isaiah 11 is compared with Virgil's 4th eclogue:[28] Both Virgil and Isaiah are hoping for peace among animals and name lions and snakes as representatives. However, Virgil does not predict peace, but the extinction of these animals. The eclogue does not want to confront the present with anything that points beyond it, but seeks rather to legitimize it and the status quo, that is, to celebrate Emperor Augustus and his *pax Romana* (Roman Peace). Isaiah 11 is different: peace is realized here "not in the eradication of the adverse, but in its conversion to no longer be adverse."[29]

If, however, an eschatological peace is at stake, then the question of anticipation in the "here and now" is raised. Stanley Hauerwas states with reference to Isaiah 11:

> [T]he Christian commitment to the protection of life is an eschatological commitment. Our concern to protect and enhance life is a sign of our confidence that in fact we live in a new age in which it is possible to see the other as God's creation. We do not value life as an end in itself—there is much worth dying for—rather all life is valued, even the lives of our enemies, because God has valued them. The risk of so valuing life can only be

---

[28]For more see Ebach, "Ende des Feindes oder Ende der Feindschaft? Der Tierfrieden bei Jesaja und Virgil," 75–89.
[29]Ibid., 80.

taken on the basis of the resurrection of Jesus as God's decisive eschatological act. For through Jesus' resurrection we see God's peace as a present reality. Though we continue to live in a time when the world does not dwell in peace, when the wolf cannot dwell with the lamb and a child cannot play over the hole of the asp, we believe nonetheless that peace has been made possible by the resurrection. Through this crucified but resurrected savior we see that God offers to all the possibility of living in peace by the power of forgiveness.[30]

Nevertheless, there are irrefutable dangers lurking in an approach that understands veganism as anticipation of the kingdom of God. The classic Lutheran objection states that law and gospel are reversed. More specifically, anyone who derives an imperative for veganism from Isa. 11:6-9 ("The Peaceable Kingdom") threatens to make the gospel of promise the law of one's own preconceived convictions. However, it is not the ability of eschatological visions to provide an orientation that should be disputed, but, rather, their direct implementation in norms of conduct. All too often this is associated with a devaluation of relative improvements in the treatment of animals, which then appear to be only insignificant changes, though relative improvements can be a powerful witness for the kingdom of God, or rather God's vision for the peaceable kingdom, especially in their temporary nature. Isaiah 11 would thus not be a direct call to action ("stop eating animals entirely"), but could easily be interpreted as molding ethos and guidance. In other words: Isaiah 11 as a vision of complete absence of violence in eating and drinking remains a vision for the end times in the sense of God's intervention in his final advent. We are therefore talking about an eschatological picture of completion.

The motivating and orienting force of these visions should not be underestimated, even if it is not possible to directly translate them into norms of conduct: "without vision the people perish" (Prov. 29:18).[31] Max Horkheimer spoke of the "longing for perfect

---

[30]Hauerwas, *The Peaceable Kingdom*, 88ff.
[31]Cf. Max Horkheimer, "Die Sehnsucht nach dem ganz Anderen. Ein Gespräch mit Helmut Gumnior (1970)," in *Max Horkheimer Gesammelte Schriften vol. 7* (Frankfurt: Fischer Verlag, 1985), 388: "Politics, which, be it highly unreflected,

justice."[32] The *extra nos* (outside of us) of the messianic future concerning our history must be mentioned: "He/she who hopes can act."[33] It is furthermore necessary to translate this *extra nos* of the messianic future into an appropriate form of human conduct: a translation that neither replaces nor anticipates God's action in the end-time, but rather joins in with it, for this action can and will after all manifest itself in the worldly impact of the eschatological vision of the "Peaceable Kingdom."

## What about Non-Christians? Vegetarianism as a Plausible Option?

Stanley Hauerwas has aptly pointed out: "Christian vegetarianism might be understood as a witness to the world that God's creation is not meant to be at war with itself. Such a witness does not entail romantic conceptions of nature and/or our fallen creation but is an eschatological act, signifying that our lives are not captured by the old order."[34] At the same time Hauerwas clearly emphasizes the implicit limitations of his ethical remarks by marking the Christian perspective of perception.

> For just as we believe that Christians are not called to be non-violent because non-violence is a strategy to free the world from war, but because as Christians we cannot conceive of living other than non-violently in a world of war, so it may also be true that Christians are called to live non-violently toward animals in a world of meat-eaters. Thus, the perspective that we have

---

does not retain theology in itself, but remains, as skillful as it may be, ultimately business."
[32]Ibid., 393: "This [longing for perfect justice] can never be fulfilled in secular history; for even if a better society were to replace the present social disorder, the misery of the past would not be redeemed and the distress of the surrounding nature would not be removed."
[33]Johannes Rau, *Wer hofft, kann handeln. Gott und die Welt ins Gespräch bringen*, ed. Matthias Schreiber (Holzgerlingen: Hänssler, 2006).
[34]Hauerwas, *In Good Company*, 196ff.

presented that leads us toward vegetarianism is not one that can be for everyone.³⁵

Hauerwas emphasizes that the particular scope of his statements raises the question of what this means for non-Christians.³⁶ From a universalistic perspective, for example, an analogy to peace ethics was sought and a vegetarian way of life was placed alongside radical pacifism as a minority agenda.

> Vegetarian and vegan lifestyles must remain a minority agenda. Nevertheless, minorities who are particularly committed to an aspect of good living and who testify to this through their lives are important for society. For they bear witness to something which they believe with all their hearts and which concerns every human being. Through their lifestyle, which in this one aspect clearly stands out from the majority, they are living reminders that the majority should not make their lives too easy.³⁷

With Michael Rosenberger,³⁸ the following arguments can be cited to justify the postulated minority status: from a comprehensive economic-ecological and/or systemic point of view (i.e., not only one of individual animal ethics) this would lead to the following:³⁹

1. *Organic farming would be robbed of its foundations:*
   Organic farming cannot cultivate a field without the natural fertilizer from the manure of its livestock. A circular economy needs the interplay of soil and animals: The animals feed on what grows on the soil of the ecological farm, and their manure serves as fertilizer, which again returns the essential substances to the soil.⁴⁰

---

³⁵Ibid., 196.
³⁶The universal range of application is to be distinguished from the particular. Cf. Gerhard Sauter, *Gateway to Dogmatics: Reasoning Theologically for the Life of the Church* (Grand Rapids: Eerdmans, 2003), 175–8.
³⁷Michael Rosenberger, "Sich nähren wie ein Pelikan? Tierethische Überlegungen zur menschlichen Ernährung," *Loccumer Pelikan* 2 (2016): 71.
³⁸For an in-depth approach cf. Michael Rosenberg, *Der Traum zwischen Mensch und Tier. Eine christliche Tierethik* (Munich: Kösel, 2015).
³⁹A vegan lifestyle would exacerbate the listed problems or even add further problems.
⁴⁰Rosenberger, "Sich nähren wie ein Pelikan?" 70.

2. *Large areas of arable land would remain barren:*
   From a global perspective, 69 percent of all arable agricultural soil is not suitable for growing food for humans, but for cultivating feed for livestock. Think of alpine pastures and areas on steep slopes, wet meadows, and other soils that cannot be cultivated. If these were left unmanaged, a considerable loss of food for human consumption would result.[41]
3. *The failure to farm pastures would entail an enormous loss of biodiversity:*
   Extensively used pastures and hay meadows contribute highly to the diversity of species and biotopes. In Europe about 30 percent of the almost 200 different types of habitat to be conserved can only be preserved by extensive animal husbandry, which together account for half of all areas worthy of protection.[42]
4. *Extensive livestock farming, which also increases soil fertility and is a key factor in sustainable agriculture, would cease:*
   While overgrazing leads to erosion, under-grazing leads in the short term to scrubland and in the long term to forestation. Yet the most fertile soils in the world are those that have been grazed extensively for a long period of time.[43]
5. *The hunting of animals would be called into question:*
   Animals that are hunted have few natural predators and often reproduce so quickly that even without human feeding endanger tree populations, even in close proximity to nature reserves. Hunting regulates livestock if it is practiced properly in accordance with hunting rules.[44]
6. *Fishing would likewise be called into question:*
   More than 70 percent of the earth's surface is water, most of which is in the ocean. The ocean stores a large part of the solar energy that reaches the earth. However, on land,

---

[41] Ibid.
[42] Ibid., 71.
[43] Ibid.
[44] Ibid.

this storage takes place (in addition to thermal storage) primarily in animals, but not so much in plants. Although the world's oceans are currently hopelessly overfished, can we really do without fishing if we want to feed humanity?[45]

A categorical rejection of animal husbandry and slaughter can be ruled out based on this universalistic approach for the (six) abovementioned reasons according to current scientific knowledge. "A complete renunciation of meat and fish consumption would pose unsolvable problems for human nutrition, and to abstain completely from using animals would massively reduce the biodiversity of the planet."[46] Yet at the same time the way in which the livestock industry currently operates should be challenged since the majority of livestock farming is not extensive, the majority of agriculture is not organic, and the majority of fishing is far from sustainable.

Rosenberg, who gives the listed arguments, rejects a fundamental vegetarianism or even veganism, but demands the virtue of moderation from those who continue to eat meat, according to the measure of health, ecological, and social compatibility as well as to the measure of animal welfare.[47] According to him, a reasonable amount of meat consumption means enjoying less meat more! This would include a partial renunciation[48] of meat: It is possible to go without! That which should be put into practice also develops the ability to enjoy and savor what we consume.

One may understand this virtuous ethical plea as a kind of "minima moralia," applying also to Christians. For in fact the following might apply:

> Good reasons can be given for abstaining from certain products, such as meat from mass livestock farming: he who learns to abstain testifies that God is enough for a life of fullness. Those who can do without expose the logic of "more and more" as deception and practice self-discipline, which in turn produces

---

[45]Ibid.
[46]Cf. Ibid.
[47]Cf. Ibid., 71ff.
[48]Cf. Ruben Zimmermann, "Von der Schönheit des Verzichts. Eine Ethik der Freiwilligkeit und Flexibilität kann die Welt verändern," *Zeitzeichen* 19, no. 8 (2018): 47–9.

character. Living simply makes it possible for others, including future generations, to be able to live at all. Moderation is not a recipe for world improvement. Those who restrict themselves in their eating habits are open to the reality of God wanting to work in this world through his children. Those who choose their food more carefully—and in my opinion this means seasonally, regionally, ecologically sensitively—acknowledge that when it comes to food, the logic of efficiency is not everything.[49]

## Conclusion: A Reconciled Diversity

Such an argumentation does not in itself invalidate a vegetarian way of life, but can certainly be appreciated in the sense of the ecumenical paradigm of a "reconciled diversity" (Harding Meyer). Karl Barth, for example, has already remarked on the necessity of protest by vegetarians:

> Yet it is not only understandable but necessary that the affirmation of this whole possibility should always have been accompanied by a radical protest against it. It may well be objected against a vegetarianism which presses in this direction that it represents a wanton anticipation of what is described by Isaiah 11 and Romans 8 as existence in the new aeon for which we hope. It may also be true that it aggravates by reason of its inevitable inconsistencies, its sentimentality and its fanaticism. But for all its weaknesses we must be careful not to put ourselves in the wrong in face of it by our own thoughtlessness and hardness of heart.[50]

The dignity of theologically motivated vegetarianism or veganism is based on the reference to the coming kingdom of God, to his Advent, which overcomes all hostility, including that between humankind and animal. Furthermore, a vegetarianism or veganism that does

---

[49]Christoph Raedel, "Mahlzeit! Nachhaltiger Genuss aus christlich-ethischer-Perspektive," *Transparent* 20, no. 6 (2017): 6.
[50]Karl Barth, *Church Dogmatics* III/4, *Doctrine of Creation*, ed. Geoffrey W. Bromiley and Thomas F. Torrance (Edinburgh: T&T Clark, 1961), 355ff.

not share or reject this theological perspective is nevertheless appreciated as a "problem indication" against mass animal killing or mass animal husbandry and is additionally an admonition and a warning against an unbridled consumption of meat. However, a vegetarian or even vegan way of life should not be made obligatory for all Christians: "Abstaining from meat can be an expression of a Christian hope as a symbolic realization of the promised eschatological peace. However, it remains bound to the provisional nature, fragility and ambiguity of all earthly actions and can therefore not be made obligatory as a necessary element of Christian life."[51]

In view of the vegetarian way of life of Christians, I would deem it necessary to consider whether it should be located[52] in the context of supererogatory or over-compulsory actions.[53] It should be noted that, from a theological perspective, the supererogatory character depends strictly on the context of the reference to the coming of the kingdom of God, that is, its Advent. If it detaches itself, it loses its unique dignity. Therefore, it is less about actions of choice than about actions of duty, indeed about actions beyond duty. For Protestants the term *opus supererogatorium* (supererogatory work) certainly sounds like indulgences and ideas of merit, since supererogatory

---

[51]Bernd Oberdorfer, "'. . . ein jegliches nach seiner Art.' Tiere in der Schöpfung: Theologische Perspektiven," in *Von armen Schweinen und bunten Vögeln. Tierethik im kulturgeschichtlichen Kontext*, Ethik – Text – Kultur vol. 10, ed. Stephanie Waldow (Paderborn: Wilhelm Fink, 2015), 70.
[52]Cf. Marco Hofheinz, "Whose Gift? Which Love? Das story-Konzept als Typ narrativer theologischer Ethik in der transplantationsmedizinisch-ethischen Debatte zur Lebendspende von Organen," in *"Die Moral von der Geschicht . . ." Ethik und Erzählung in Medizin und Pflege*, ed. M. Coors and M. Hofheinz (Leipzig: Evangelische Verlagsanstalt, 2016), 184; Dietmar Mieth<sc>, </sc>"Narrative Ethik als in der literarischen Fiktion als Ermöglichung von 'ethischen Modellen'," in *Die Moral von der Geschicht*, ed. M. Coors and M. Hofheinz (Leipzig: Evangelische Verlagsanstalt, 2016), 102ff.
[53]This is also asserted by Dieter Witschen, *Mehr als die Pflicht. Studien zu supererogatorischen Handlungen und ethischen Idealen*, Studien zur Theologischen Ethik vol. 114 (Freiburg i.Ue. / Freiburg i.Br.: Universitätsverlag / Herder Verlag, 2006), 143–56. Witschen names the following characteristics for *opera supererogata*: they go "beyond basic moral demands" (ibid., 17), bring "serious personal disadvantages with them or demand unusual effort" (ibid., 19), are "carried out voluntarily" (ibid., 20), can be "grounded in a personal ideal" (ibid., 20) and are "ascribed an exemplary character" (ibid., 21).

actions in the period of the Reformation and in the confessional age became an object of controversial theology.⁵⁴ As an object of the doctrine of sanctification, however, the term does not have to contradict the *sola gratia*; at least not if God is understood as the subject of sanctification.

It is important that the doctrine of the *opera supererogata* (supererogatory works) follows the grammar of sanctification.⁵⁵ Calvin developed this in a groundbreaking way.⁵⁶ According to Calvin, there is a "double grace"⁵⁷ (*duplica gratia*) of God: God justifies and sanctifies; indeed, "the Lord justifies his own by grace, and at the same time, through the sanctification of his Spirit, conforms them to true righteousness."⁵⁸ The human being is not justified initially in order to supplement this action of God in sanctification by human action. No, God acts as subject in a twofold way on humankind. Justification and sanctification are complementarily linked. While justification deals with the total aspect of *transitus* (transition) through the granting of grace, sanctification deals with the partial aspect of *progressus* (progress). Through sanctification, God renews through his Spirit a new life in good works so that the human being can progress by allowing God's sanctifying action in him to be valid. The more human beings are renewed (*renovatio*), the more Calvin can speak of growth and development with regard to them. Calvin does not want to conceal human imperfection but rather show the purposefulness of the Christian life:

> But no man in this earthly dungeon of the body has strength enough to hurry along his course with real joy; indeed, most suffer from such weakness that they only make modest progress

---

⁵⁴Cf. Also Johannes von Lüpke, *Wege der Weisheit. Studien zu Lessings Theologiekritik, Göttinger Theologische Arbeiten 41* (Göttingen: Vandenhoeck & Ruprecht, 1989), 138–42.
⁵⁵Cf. Hans G. Ulrich, *Wie Geschöpfe leben. Konturen evangelischer Ethik, Ethik im Theologischen Diskurs 2* (Münster: LIT, 2005), 454–6.
⁵⁶Cf. Jean Calvin, *Institutes* (1559), III, 6–9. To that cf. Marco Hofheinz, *Ethik – reformiert! Studien zur reformierten Reformation und ihrer Rezeption im 20. Jahrhundert*. Forschungen zur Reformierten Theologie, vol. 8 (Göttingen: Vandenhoeck and Ruprecht, 2017), 64–113; and Pieter Vos, *Longing for the Good Life: Virtue Ethics after Protestantism* (London: T&T Clark, 2020), 63–108.
⁵⁷Jean Calvin, *Institutes* (1559), III, 11, 1.
⁵⁸Ibid., III, 3, 19.

staggering and limping, even crawling on the ground. So let us all, then, according to the measure of our little strength, do our walk and continue the way we have begun! No one's path will be so miserable that he will not be able to get a little bit behind him every day. But we do not want to stop striving to make constant progress in the way of the Lord, and we do not want to lose heart even when our progress is insignificant. Even if progress does not meet our desires, the effort is not lost if only today remains victorious over yesterday.[59]

Good works are now to be understood, as it were, as various steps in the process of sanctification. Governed and guided by the Spirit,[60] they may be smaller or larger. In this respect, a differentiation is possible here. There are such steps that correspond more to the coming kingdom of God and his Messiah and such steps that correspond less without degenerating into bad works.[61] This is exactly what a Protestant doctrine of the *opera supererogata* wants to point out. It wants to encourage instead of overburden. Therefore, it introduces the distinction between good and better works. As a standard, it is based on the teleological foundation of the *vita Christiana* (Christian life), according to which it is important to "reproduce in our lives" (*Christum [...] cuius formam in vita nostra exprimamus*) the form of Christ, the Messiah of God, "through whom we are again accepted in grace with God" (*per quem in gratiam cum Deo rediimus*).[62] In the sense of such a differentiation, the renunciation of meat or a vegetarian diet can now also be understood and considered.

If a vegetarian diet for Christians is viewed as supererogatory, one could emphasize three aspects:

1. It cannot be a rigorous or principled rejection of meat consumption. The danger of legalism, which poses a threat here, would not be completely avoided by the label supererogatory, but would be less severe.

---

[59]Ibid., III, 6, 5.
[60]Cf. Hans G. Ulrich, *Transfigured not Conformed: Christian Ethics in a Hermeneutical Key*, ed. Brian Brock (London: T&T Clark, 2022), 137–9.
[61]Or even cause an expulsion from the church. Cf. Jean Calvin, *Institutes* (1559), III, 6, 5.
[62]Ibid., III, 6, 3.

2. The question of a vegetarian diet, to quote Bonhoeffer, is not about the "ultimate" but about the "penultimate" because our salvation does not depend on it.[63]
3. Nevertheless, in the sense of testifying to the coming kingdom of God, abstaining or rather the vegetarian way of life remains quite desirable, provided that not all people live like this. A universal approach to this way of life would otherwise lead to the six problems outlined previously.

By keeping this in mind we make use of a universalistic theory. This, however, is theologically by no means inappropriate, since the perspective of the coming kingdom of God itself is quite a universalistic one, or more precisely: in its particularity it is at the same time universal: "So that God may be all in all" (1 Cor. 15:28; NRSV).[64]

# Bibliography

Aristotle. *Nicomachean Ethics*, translated by Terence Irwin. Indianapolis: Hackett, 1985.

Baranzke, Heike. "Auf der Suche nach dem Humanum in Ansehung des "animal turn" – die ethische Perspektive." In *Der Mensch, ein Tier? Das Tier, ein Mensch?* edited by P. Heusser and J. Weinzirl, 127–42. Würzburg: Königshausen and Neumann, 2017

Barth, Karl. *Church Dogmatics III/4, Doctrine of Creation*, edited by Geoffrey W. Bromiley and Thomas F. Torrance. Edinburgh: T&T Clark, 1961.

Black, C. Clifton. *Abingdon New Testament Commentaries: Mark*. Nashville: Abingdon, 2011.

Bonhoeffer, Dietrich. *Ethics, Dietrich Bonhoeffer Works 6*, edited by Clifford Green, translated by Reinhard Krauss, Charles West, and Douglas W. Scott. Minneapolis: Fortress Press, 2005.

Cadenbach, C. "Das Recht des Stärkeren." *Süddeutsche Zeitung Magazin*, no. 28 (July 3, 2018): 8–19.

---

[63]Cf. Dietrich Bonhoeffer, *Ethics, Dietrich Bonhoeffer Works 6*, ed. Clifford Green, trans. Reinhard Krauss, Charles West, and Douglas W. Scott (Minneapolis: Fortress Press, 2005), 145–61.

[64]Cf. Miroslav Volf and Matthew Croasmun, *For the Life of the World: Theology That Makes a Difference* (Grand Rapids: Brazos Press, 2019), 100.

Calvin, John. *Institutes of the Christian Religion*, edited by John T. McNeill, translated by Ford Lewis Battles. Philadelphia: The Westminster Press, 1960.

Clough, David L. *On Animals Volume 1: Systematic Theology*. London: T&T Clark, 2012.

Clough, David L. *On Animals Volume 2: Theological Ethics*. London: T&T Clark, 2018.

Delkurt, H. "Schöpfung – Aspekte der exegetischen Diskussion." *Zeitschrift für Pädagogik und Theologie* 55, no. 3 (2003): 236–53.

Ebach, J. "Bild Gottes und Schrecken der Tiere. Zur Anthropologie der priesterlichen Urgeschichte." In *Ursprung und Ziel. Erinnerte Zukunft und erhoffte Vergangenheit. Biblische Exegesen, Reflexionen, Geschichten*, 16–47. Neukirchen-Vluyn: Neukirchener, 1986.

Ebach, J. "Ende des Feindes oder Ende der Feindschaft? Der Tierfrieden bei Jesaja und Virgil." In *Ursprung und Ziel. Erinnerte Zukunft und erhoffte Vergangenheit. Biblische Exegesen, Reflexionen, Geschichten*, 75–89. Neukirchen-Vluyn: Neukirchener, 1986.

Eckey, W. *Das Markusevangelium. Orientierung am Weg Jesu*. Neukirchen-Vluyn: Neukirchener, 1998.

Engels, E.-M. "Art. Tier V. Ethisch." *Religion in Geschichte und Gegenwart* 8, no. 4 (2005): 406–8.

Grässer, E. "Das Seufzen der Kreatur (Röm 8:19-22). Auf der Suche nach einer 'biblischen Tierschutzethik.'" In *Jahrbuch für Biblische Theologie 5: Schöpfung und Neuschöpfung*, Ingo Baldermann, 93–117. Neukirchen-Vluyn: Neukirchener, 1990.

Grund, A. "Mitgeschöpflichkeit." *Religionsunterricht an höheren Schulen* 44, no. 6 (2002): 332–8.

Hauerwas, Stanley. *In Good Company: The Church as Polis*. Notre Dame: University of Notre Dame Press, 1995.

Hauerwas, Stanley. *The Peaceable Kingdom: A Primer in Christian Ethics*. Notre Dame: University of Notre Dame Press, 1983.

Hoch, J. "Die fröhlichen Veganer." *Süddeutsche Zeitung*, no. 111 (May 16, 2016): 51.

Hofheinz, M. *Ethik – reformiert! Studien zur reformierten Reformation und ihrer Rezeption im 20. Jahrhundert*. Forschungen zur Reformierten Theologie, vol. 8. Göttingen: Vandenhoeck & Ruprecht, 2017.

Hofheinz, M. *Gezeugt, nicht gemacht. In-vitro-Fertilisation. In theologischer Perspektive*, Ethik im Theologischen Diskurs, vol. 15. Münster: LIT, 2008.

Hofheinz, M. "Wahrnehmen – Urteilen – Prüfen. Explorative Annäherung an eine 'selbstdarstellende' theologische Identitäts- und Gemeindeethik." In *Was ist Theologische Ethik? Grundbestimmungen und Grundvorstellungen*, edited by M. Held and M. Roth, 62–80. Berlin: de Gruyter, 2018.

Hofheinz, M. "Whose Gift? Which Love? Das story-Konzept als Typ narrativer theologischer Ethik in der transplantationsmedizinisch-ethischen Debatte zur Lebendspende von Organen." In *Die Moral von der Geschicht'* …: *Ethik und Erzählung in Medizin und Pflege*, edited by M. Coors and M. Hofheinz, 149–84. Leipzig: Evangelische Verlagsanstalt, 2016.

Horkheimer, M. "Die Sehnsucht nach dem ganz Anderen. Ein Gespräch mit Helmut Gumnior (1970)." In *Max Horkheimer Gesammelte Schriften* vol. 7, edited by Alfred Schmidt and Gunzelin Schmid Noerr, 385–404. Frankfurt: Fischer Verlag, 1985.

Janowski, B. "Auch die Tiere gehören zum Gottesbund. Gott, Mensch und Tier im alten Israel." In *Die Zukunft der Tiere – Theologische, ethische und naturwissenschaftliche Perspektiven*, edited by B. Janowski and P. Riede, 31–60. Stuttgart: Calwer, 1999.

Janowski, B. "Der Wolf und das Lamm. Zum eschatologischen Tierfrieden in Jes 11:6-9." In *Der nahe und der ferne Gott. Beiträge zur Theologie des Alten Testaments* vol. 5, edited by B. Janowski, 55–70. Neukirchen-Vluyn: Neukirchener, 2014.

Janowski, B. "Die lebendige Statue Gottes. Zur Anthropologie der priesterlichen Urgeschichte." In *Die Welt als Schöpfung. Beiträge zur Theologie des Alten Testaments*, vol. 4, edited by B. Janowski, 140–71. Neukirchen-Vluyn: Neukirchener, 2008.

Janowski, B. "Herrschaft über die Tiere. Gen 1:26-28 und die Semantik des *rdh*." In *Die rettende Gerechtigkeit. Beiträge zur Theologie des Alten Testaments* vol. 2, edited by B. Janowski, 33–48. Neukirchen-Vluyn: Neukirchener, 1999.

Link, C. *Schöpfung. Ein theologischer Entwurf im Gegenüber von Naturwissenschaft und Ökologie*. Neukirchen-Vluyn: Neukirchener, 2012.

Lüpke, J. von. *Wege der Weisheit. Studien zu Lessings Theologiekritik*, Göttinger Theologische Arbeiten, vol. 41. Göttingen: Vandenhoeck & Ruprecht, 1989.

Mieth, D. "Narrative Ethik als in der literarischen Fiktion als Ermöglichung von 'ethischen Modellen.'" In *Die Moral von der Geschicht'*, edited by M. Coors and M. Hofheinz, 95–108. Leipzig: Evangelische Verlagsanstalt, 2016.

Neumann-Gorsolke, U. *Herrschen in den Grenzen der Schöpfung. Ein Beitrag zur alttestamentlichen Anthropologie am Beispiel von Psalm 8, Genesis 1 und verwandter Texte*. Neukirchen-Vluyn: Neukirchener, 2004.

Nussbaum, M.C. "Finely Aware and Richly Responsible: Moral Attention and the Moral Task of Literature." *Journal of Philosophy* 82 (1985): 516–29.

Oberdorfer, B. "'... ein jegliches nach seiner Art.' Tiere in der Schöpfung: Theologische Perspektiven." In *Von armen Schweinen und bunten Vögeln. Tierethik im kulturgeschichtlichen Kontext*, Ethik – Text – Kultur, vol. 10, edited by Stephanie Waldow, 53–70. Paderborn: Wilhelm Fink, 2015.

Ohly, L. *Ethische Begriffe in biblischer Perspektive*. Tübingen: Narr Francke Attempto, 2022.

Raedel, C. "Mahlzeit! Nachhaltiger Genuss aus christlich-ethischer-Perspektive." *Transparent* 20, no. 6 (2017): 3–6.

Rau, J. *Wer hofft, kann handeln. Gott und die Welt ins Gespräch bringen – Predigten*, edited by M. Schreiber. Holzgerlingen: Hänssler, 2006.

Rosenberg, M. *Der Traum zwischen Mensch und Tier. Eine christliche Tierethik*. Munich: Kösel, 2015.

Rosenberger, M. "Sich nähren wie ein Pelikan? Tierethische Überlegungen zur menschlichen Ernährung." *Loccumer Pelikan* 2 (2016): 70–3.

Rüterswörden, U. *Dominium terrae. Studien zur Genese einer alttestamentlichen Vorstellung*. Berlin: de Gruyter, 1993

Sauter, G. *Eschatological Rationality: Theological Issues in Focus*. Grand Rapids: Baker, 1996.

Sauter, G. *Gateway to Dogmatics: Reasoning Theologically for the Life of the Church*. Grand Rapids: Eerdmans, 2003.

Taureck, B.H.F. "Plädoyer für einen Veganen Humanismus. Was ist und was sein soll." *fiph. Forschungsinstitut für Philosophie Hannover* 29, no. 4 (2017): 27–34.

Ulrich, Hans G. "The Messianic Contours of Evangelical Ethics." In *The Freedom of a Christian Ethicist: The Future of a Reformation Legacy*, edited by Brian Brock and Michael G. Mawson, 39–63. London: T&T Clark, 2016.

Ulrich, Hans G. *Transfigured not Conformed: Christian Ethics in a Hermeneutical Key*, edited by Brian Brock. London: T&T Clark, 2022.

Ulrich, Hans G. *Wie Geschöpfe leben. Konturen evangelischer Ethik*, Ethik im Theologischen Diskurs vol. 2. Münster: LIT, 2005.

Volf, M. and M. Croasmun. *For the Life of the World: Theology That Makes a Difference*. Grand Rapids: Brazos Press, 2019.

Vos, P. *Longing for the Good Life: Virtue Ethics after Protestantism*. London: T&T Clark, 2020.

Wannenwetsch, B. "The Fourfold Pattern of Christian Moral Reasoning according to the New Testament." In *Scripture's Doctrine and Theology's Bible: How the New Testament Shapes Christian Dogmatics*, edited by M. Bockmuehl and A.J. Torrance, 177–90. Grand Rapids: Eerdmans, 2008.

Weippert, M. "Tier und Mensch in einer menschenarmen Welt. Zum sog. Dominium terrae in Gen 1." In *Ebenbild Gottes – Herrscher über die Welt*, edited by Hans-Peter Mathys, 35–55. Neukirchen-Vluyn: Neukirchener, 1998.

Witschen, D. *Mehr als die Pflicht. Studien zu supererogatorischen Handlungen und ethischen Idealen*, Studien zur Theologischen Ethik, vol. 114. Freiburg i.Ue. / Freiburg i.Br.: Universitätsverlag / Herder Verlag, 2006.

Wustmans, C. "Veganer essen ihre Freunde nicht? Anfragen an den Absolutheitsanspruch der Motive veganer Ernährung." *Ethik und Gesellschaft*, no. 2 (2016), https://doi.org/10.18156/eug-2-2016-art-7.

Zimmermann, R. "Von der Schönheit des Verzichts. Eine Ethik der Freiwilligkeit und Flexibilität kann die Welt verändern." *Zeitzeichen* 19, no. 8 (2018): 47–9.

# 8

# The Politics of Truth-Telling in the "Post-Truth" Age of "Fake News"

*Michael R. Laffin*

## Introduction

The election of Donald Trump to the US presidency in 2017 led many in the mainstream media to pin responsibility for his electoral success on "fake news" and its preferred channels of communication—the internet and social media.[1] Of course, as commentators on these events have argued, this assignment of blame is predicated on the mythology of journalism and its "liberal theory of the press," whereby the free press serves as a "fourth estate" that valiantly informs the public while calling power to account.[2] But Trump turned the tables on the mainstream media, and used his considerable skill as a master of the "image" and the "spectacle," to proclaim that it was actually they, and not his followers, who were

---

[1]Catherine Happer, Andrew Hoskins, and William Merrin, "Weaponizing Reality: An Introduction to Trump's War on the Media," in *Trump's Media War*, ed. Catherine Happer, Andrew Hoskins, and William Merrin (Cham, Switzerland: Palgrave Macmillan, 2019), 4.
[2]Ibid., 9.

the purveyors of "fake news." As a result, the public at large found themselves in a situation where:

> What began as a highly specific problem of deliberately written false stories designed to gain traction online in order to hurt a specific political cause or candidate soon mushroomed into a broader crisis of truth and trust, a question of validity and invalidity, and a recognition of the difficulty of dividing truth from opinion. Informational production suddenly underwent a very public crisis of legitimacy, with doubts raised over who had the right to lay claim to an audience or to truth.[3]

As important as the question concerning the place of the press and its relation to the citizenry in a democratic nation is, the current "crisis of truth and trust" also raises the more fundamental question about what is properly entailed in the practice of truth-telling, and what is the relation of such practice to the life of politics. How is truth-telling sensitive to the concrete contexts within which speech occurs, while not simply being a matter of opinion or *mere* context?

One of the basic "moral rules" that everyone knows is, "Thou shall not lie." This is enshrined in the Eighth Commandment and seems to be one of the obvious "principles" every decent person learns from early childhood. However, when we ask what it means to live faithfully to this commandment, what it means to tell the truth, to not lie, we quickly see that very different grammars can be applied to the commandment, and that the grammar of Christian ethics rooted in the theology of the living Word of God leads to a distinctive understanding of this otherwise commonplace command. This distinctive understanding proves especially important for one's understanding of politics.

However, some might argue that we have already made a category mistake at the very outset. What does the truth have to do with politics? The United States had a president who made a habit of lying. And do not all politicians lie, is it not simply what they do? This one is hardly the first. We all know that lying is wrong, but are we not being a bit naive or moralistic to require honesty of our politicians? And to request of politicians that they tell the truth, is

---

[3] Ibid., 7–8.

this not banal moralizing? What could Christian ethics possibly add to our sense that one should be truthful beyond simply repeating a cliched truism that is not worth much serious thought? Have we not irresponsibly entered the world of competing news outlets, social media culture wars, and the like? Surely there is nothing serious or worthwhile that Christian ethics could add to the discussion.

The argument of this chapter is that Christian ethics ought to enter this conversation, and that doing so is not merely an exercise in trite moralizing. Instead, Christian ethics, according to its distinctive grammar, has much to add to the conversation, not least in helping us come to terms with what it means to speak the truth. This distinctive grammar finds an especially potent form in Dietrich Bonhoeffer's famous essay, "What Does It Mean to Tell the Truth?"[4] His explication of truth-telling in the essay brings to the surface the performative nature of speech, and the web of relations within which speech occurs, a web of relations that is itself constituted by speech. We might call this web of relations the real, or reality. And Bonhoeffer provides profound insight concerning what it might mean to inhabit reality truthfully. These insights also help to bring to light the nature of our own political moment, a moment which we might call a moment of "flight from reality,"[5] a moment of deep untruthfulness.

## Dietrich Bonhoeffer's "What Is Meant by Telling the Truth"

In 1943, during a period of interrogation related to his involvement with conspirators against the Nazi government, Dietrich Bonhoeffer penned the essay fragment, "What Does It Mean to Tell the Truth?"[6]

---

[4]Dietrich Bonhoeffer, "What Does It Mean to Tell the Truth?" in *Conspiracy and Imprisonment, 1940–1945, Dietrich Bonhoeffer Works* 16, ed. Mark S. Brocker, trans. Lisa E. Dahill (Minneapolis: Fortress Press, 2004), 601–8.
[5]Cf. D.C. Shindler's recent book of a similar title, *Freedom from Reality: The Diabolical Character of Modern Liberty* (Notre Dame: Notre Dame University Press, 2017).
[6]Biographical details concerning the essay fragment's compositional setting can be found in Eberhard Bethge, *Dietrich Bonhoeffer: A Biography* (Minneapolis: Fortress Press, 2000), 814.

The fragment begins by making a distinction between concrete and principled speech, and insisting that truth-telling is a matter of concrete speech. As such, the inquiry regarding truthfulness begins by asking whether the one demanding truthful speech is justified in doing so. In other words, the question begins with the web of relations within which the speaker finds herself. The meaning of speaking the truth is dependent upon the relational context and what serves life within this context. And the first relation in which one stands is the relation to God. As such, Bonhoeffer writes, we can affirm that persons owe truthful speech to God, "as long as we do not thereby disregard that even God is not a general principle but is the Living One."[7] So, for Bonhoeffer, it is relationships and the service to life that is at the heart of what is required for speech to be true.[8] As he puts it, "This is precisely the point, namely, how I bring into effect in my concrete life, with its manifold relationships, the truthful speech I owe to God . . . Our word should be truthful not in principle but concretely."[9] We can see, then, that Bonhoeffer's emphasis on concrete rather than principled speech when considering the demands of truth-telling indicates a phenomenologically richer account of the Eighth Commandment than the simple imperative, "do not lie," might suggest.

The difference in Bonhoeffer's account from more common approaches is evident in the contrast to Immanuel Kant. Every student of ethics knows of Kant's famous argument that not lying is a categorical imperative, and therefore, one should not lie, even to a would be murderer who knocks on your door asking for the whereabouts of a person you are hiding in your house.[10]

---

[7]Bonhoeffer, "What Does It Mean to Tell the Truth?" 602. Cf. Dietrich Bonhoeffer, *Ethics, Dietrich Bonhoeffer Works 6*, ed. Clifford Green, trans. Reinhard Krauss, Charles C. West, and Douglas W. Stott (Minneapolis: Fortress Press, 2009), where Bonhoeffer uses this same formulation and argues that truth, "is not some kind of general concept from which one could deduce a corresponding system," 267.
[8]Perhaps Bonhoeffer learned this from Martin Luther. In his commentary on Luther's treatment of the Eighth Commandment in the *Large Catechism*, Albrecht Peters writes that Luther "clearly subordinates the duty of truthfulness to the basic commandment to love one's neighbor," Peters, *Commentary on Luther's Catechisms: Ten Commandments* (Saint Louis: Concordia Publishing House, 2009), 299.
[9]Bonhoeffer, "What Does It Mean to Tell the Truth?" 602–3.
[10]Immanuel Kant, "On a Supposed Right to lie from Philanthropy (1797)," in *Practical Philosophy, The Cambridge Edition of the Works of Immanuel Kant*, ed.

For Bonhoeffer, however, such a principled categorical imperative ignores the concrete situation in which true speech acts necessarily occur, such that the right of the would be murderer to ask the question and receive an answer in the first place is overlooked. True speech never occurs between abstract entities, but always between living persons placed in relations constituted by divine speech and human response to the always prior divine speech. Therefore, authorization for speech must be the starting point, something Kant ignores.[11] As Bonhoeffer writes in his *Ethics* in reply to Kant's imagined situation, "Since responsibility is the entire response, in accord with reality, to the claim of God and my neighbor, then this scenario glaringly illustrates the merely partial response of a conscience bound by principles."[12] It is this understanding that true speech is speech "in accord with reality" that is at the heart of Bonhoeffer's phenomenology of truth-telling, and reality is as variable as life itself, with persons rather than principles at its basis.

Contra Kant, then, intentionality is not the determining factor in truth-telling. It also requires "accurate perception and . . . serious consideration of the real circumstances. The more diverse the life circumstances of people are, the more responsibility they have and the more difficult it is 'to tell the truth.'"[13] To speak the truth, according to Bonhoeffer, is to find the "right word" for any given moment, a word that expresses the real. As such, true speech is dependent upon "the ever-greater capacity to perceive reality."[14] And this capacity is developed over time through experience and continual effort, and thus means that it is false to think that in matters of truth-telling "one's character alone must suffice."[15] It requires sensitive discernment that respects the mixed nature of a fallen world and therefore takes account of human weakness

---

and trans. Mary J. Gregor (Cambridge: Cambridge University Press, 1996), 605–15.
[11]Matthew Puffer argues, "Bonhoeffer's phenomenology is framed less by Kant's terms than by the Hebrew Bible's question about who authorizes one's speech such that it might be truthful." See his "Three Rival Versions of Moral Reasoning: Interpreting Bonhoeffer's Ethics of Lying, Guilt, and Responsibility," *Harvard Theological Review* 112, no. 2 (2019): 181.
[12]Bonhoeffer, *Ethics*, 280.
[13]Bonhoeffer, "What Does It Mean to Tell the Truth?" 603.
[14]Ibid.
[15]Ibid.

and shame, carefully ensuring the furtherance of life. In contrast, Bonhoeffer speaks of the "cynic" who is zealous for the "truth" and for "outing" the lie such that "He violates shame, destroys the mystery, breaks trust, betrays the community in which he lives, and smiles arrogantly over the havoc he has wrought and over the human weakness that 'can't bear the truth.'"[16] The cynic speaks an absolute word over an abstract and undifferentiated reality.

In a letter to Eberhard Bethge, Bonhoeffer spells out the problem of this cynical exposure further, writing,

> "Truthfulness" does not at all mean that whatever exists must be uncovered. God himself made clothing for human beings, that is, in *statu corruptionis* many aspects of the human being are to remain concealed . . . and even if cynics appear particularly honest in their own eyes or act like fanatics for the truth, they still miss the decisive truth, namely, that after the fall there is a need for covering [Verhüllling] and secrecy [Geheimnis].[17]

Bonhoeffer worries that this form of cynical exposing speech that overlooks the need for covering has come to characterize public communication in the modern media age. He writes:

> As a result of the increasing profligacy of public discourse in newspapers and the radio, the nature and limits of different

---

[16]Ibid., 604.
[17]Bonhoeffer, *Letters and Papers from Prison, Dietrich Bonhoeffer Works* 8, ed. John W. de Gruchy, trans. Isabel Best, Lisa E. Dahill, Reinhard Krauss, and Nancy Luken (Minneapolis: Fortress Press), 215. Here again we see the similarity in Bonhoeffer's account of truth-telling to that given by Luther in his explication of the Eighth Commandment. Luther says that our honor and reputation are an indispensable treasure to us, and the Eighth Commandment is meant to protect these. Luther argues, drawing on the image in 1 Corinthians 12 of the less honorable parts of the body being covered, that "we should use our tongue to speak only the best about all people, to cover the sins and infirmities of our neighbors, to justify their actions, and to cloak and veil them with our own honor," *Large Catechism*, 424. Luther puts this in terms of the difference between judging sin and having knowledge of sin. The latter does not necessarily give one right to the former. The danger with social media and its easy access to "public proclamation" of one's opinions is that the temptation arises to put oneself in the place of the judge without authorization to assume such place.

words are no longer clearly perceived: in fact, what is distinctive about a personal word, for example, is nearly destroyed. Chatter has replaced authentic words. Words no longer have any weight. There is too much talking. Yet when the limits of different words blur together, when words become rootless, homeless, then what is said loses hold of the truth; indeed, at that point lying almost inevitably emerges. When the various orders of life no longer respect one another, then words become untrue.[18]

Bonhoeffer illustrates his point about profligate, rootless speech that fails to respect the various orders of life with his famous example of the teacher who asks a child in front of the class whether it is true that the child's father is a drunk. In asking this question in this setting, the teacher encroaches on and violates the "order" of the family. As Bonhoeffer states, "The family has its own secret that it must keep."[19] In violating this order, the teacher disregards reality and thus is the one who lies, even if it is the child who denies that her father is a drunk (when, in fact, he is). The child's answer of "no," though not true in its content, is true in that "it expresses the truth that the family is an order sui generis where the teacher was not justified to intrude."[20] In so answering, the child's answer corresponds more closely to reality than if the child were to answer by telling the "truth."

Given this account of truth-telling and lying, where the context is so determinate, one may think that Bonhoeffer leaves us in a "situation" ethics whereby the danger of relativism looms large. However, this would be a gross misunderstanding of Bonhoeffer's treatment of truth. He does agree, "The usual definition, according to which the conscious contradiction between thought and speech is a lie, is completely inadequate."[21] But he does not take issue with the "usual definition" because he is a relativist or situationist, but rather precisely because he is concerned with speech that corresponds to reality and so recognizes that the essence of lying is found much deeper than in the contradiction between thought and speech. At

---

[18]Ibid., 605.
[19]Ibid.
[20]Ibid., 606.
[21]Ibid.

the center of reality is the living God. Therefore, "Lying is first of all the denial of God as God has been revealed to the world."[22] Lying is disregard for reality understood as the word of God spoken in Jesus Christ. Creation rests on this word and lying contradicts this word. As Bonhoeffer puts it, "lying is the negation, denial, and deliberate and willful destruction of reality as it is created by God and exists in God."[23] The true word, on the other hand, the word in union with the Word of God is authorized speech occurring within the boundaries of a concrete office that recognizes the place in which I stand as I speak and the context from which I speak. Accordingly, our word becomes true when we rightly recognize who it is that calls on us to speak and authorizes us to speak. Additionally, we must recognize the place in which we stand as we speak and put the subject about which we are speaking into this context.

To put all of this in more basic terms, Bonhoeffer reads truth-telling as about accurate perception and appropriate response to the concrete claim of God and the neighbor. This reading follows on from Luther, who, in his *Large Catechism,* explicates the Eighth Commandment regarding bearing false witness in terms of the preservation of God's "three-fold government"[24] which enables concrete obedience to the basic commandment to love God and neighbor. What Bonhoeffer here calls "concrete relationships," and what Luther in the *Catechism* refers to as authorized jurisdictions, provide a heuristic for perceiving reality faithful to the word of God in such way that the commandment to love the neighbor can be fulfilled. Much of the "public speech" occurring in the realm of the virtually real lacks this authorization as it is a word from a virtual no-place, addressed to no one concretely, without concern for preservation of the ordered relationships within which human life is necessarily situated if it is to be lived in accordance with the reality of God, which is to say, as concretely placed between God and neighbor. But speech must always be concretely related to these ordered relationships in which we live if it is to be justified and

---

[22]Ibid.
[23]Ibid., 607.
[24]This is Albrecht Peters's description of the three contexts (judicial-political, ecclesiastical, and household-economic) within which Luther situates his treatment of the commandment. See Peters, *Commentary on Luther's Catechisms*, 299.

true. In Bonhoeffer's words, "The justification for speech always lies within the boundaries of the concrete office that I fill."[25]

## Hannah Arendt on Truth and Politics

Having set out the structure of truth-telling as Bonhoeffer understands it, it now remains to show the connection to politics as a means of further uncovering the relation of speech to free action and faithful inhabitation of the real. But as noted at the outset, it seems we are making a category mistake at this point. Is not politics the one place where we should least expect to find insight on the practice of truth-telling? As Hannah Arendt notes, "Truthfulness has never been counted among the political virtues, and lies have always been regarded as justifiable tools in political dealing."[26] In fact, Arendt highlights the common suspicion that it is even "in the nature of the political realm to be at war with truth."[27] The suspicion arises given the nature of free human action that is not overdetermined by the given. Arendt goes so far as to say that the liar *is* "the man of action," the liar "is an actor by nature; he says what is not so because he wants things to be different than they are—that is, he wants to change the world."[28] That the liar lies would seem to be a sign of his freedom. As Arendt argues:

> our ability to lie—but not necessarily our ability to tell the truth—belongs among the few obvious, demonstrable data that confirm human freedom. That we can change the circumstances under which we lie at all is because we are relatively free from

---

[25] Bonhoeffer, "What Does It Mean to Tell the Truth," 608.
[26] Hannah Arendt, "Lying in Politics: Reflections on the Pentagon Papers," in *Crises of the Republic: Lying in Politics, Civil Disobedience, On Violence, and Thoughts on Politics and Revolution* (New York: Harcourt Brace & Company, 1972), 4; Cf. Arendt, "Truth and Politics," in *Between Past and Future* (New York: Penguin Books, 2006), where she claims, "no one, as far as I know, has ever counted truthfulness among the political virtues," 223.
[27] Arendt, "Truth and Politics," 235.
[28] Ibid., 245–6.

them, and it is this freedom that is abused and perverted through mendacity.[29]

From the viewpoint of politics, Arendt says, truth, particularly factual truth, is despotic, precluding the debate that is at the very essence of the life of politics.[30] The ability to lie and the ability to act are interconnected, and both arise out of our ability to imagine the world other than it is currently.[31] Perhaps this may go some way in explaining Arendt's observation,

> that, except for Zoroastrianism, none of the major religions included lying as such, as distinguished from "bearing false witness," in their catalogues of grave sins . . . Only with the rise of Puritan morality, coinciding with the rise of organized science, whose progress had to be assured on the firm ground of the absolute veracity and reliability of every scientist, were lies considered serious offenses.[32]

Is our instinct to insist that true speech should characterize the political realm a sign of our Kantian and puritanical moral impulses that would obey the law even to the detriment of life? Or an enlightened progress over the more pragmatic ancients who expected too little from their political leaders? Or, perhaps, can we understand truth-telling in politics in a manner consistent with Bonhoeffer's explication of the structure of true speech without thereby justifying the lie in the name of a political realism?

An answer to these questions can begin to be found in Arendt's further exploration of the relation between truth and politics. She argues that the conflict between the two originally arose in the context of two opposed ways of life: the philosophic life versus the life of the citizen. She points to the famous Platonic distinction between truth and opinion as an early elaboration of the conflict between the two forms of life. While the philosopher in her ascent from the cave can turn her attention to truth, the life of

---

[29]Ibid., 246.
[30]Ibid., 237.
[31]Arendt, "Lying in Politics," 5.
[32]Arendt, "Truth and Politics," 228.

the citizen, grounded in the need for agreement and cooperation, must be founded in opinion. From the standpoint of the city, the philosopher and her truth can only seem tyrannical, whereas, from the standpoint of the philosopher, the city and its opinions can only seem arbitrary and partial. The gap is bridged, at least by Plato, with the "noble lie," an opinion that is false but life-affirming in its making possible common life in the city, suggesting a compromise between philosophy and politics that leaves the philosopher in relative peace in relation to the city, without philosophy undermining the agreement making political life possible. However, Arendt is concerned that this ancient distinction has been lost in the modern era, such that "the last traces of this ancient antagonism between the philosopher's truth and the opinions in the marketplace have disappeared."[33] Her *political* concern, however, is not so much with the collapse of the distinction between the philosopher's truth (rational truth such as mathematical and philosophical/logical truths) and opinion, but that a similar collapse has occurred in terms of the distinction between factual truths (the example Arendt gives is the fact that Germany invaded Belgium at the outbreak of the First World War, and not the other way around) and opinion. As a result of this collapse, Arendt worries that the very possibility of politics itself is undermined.

Jacques Derrida helpfully spells out what is at stake in this transition from the philosophical truth/opinion distinction to the factual truth/opinion distinction and its eventual collapse. He says that the original lie (of which one might include the philosophical "noble lie") was about hiding or veiling, whereas the modern lie aims at the destruction of reality or of the original archive which bears witness to reality.[34] Remarkably, we see here in the distinction between the "Kantian lie" and "bearing false witness" the same grammar that Bonhoeffer is so sensitive to in his essay fragment, and which itself resonates powerfully with Luther's treatment in the *Catechism*. And it is at this point where Bonhoeffer's account becomes clearly distinguished from relativistic or situationalist accounts of "truth." For, as with Arendt, he is concerned with the

---

[33]Ibid., 231.
[34]Jacques Derrida, "History of the Lie: Prolegomena," in *Without Alibi*, Peggy Kamuf (Stanford: Stanford University Press, 2002), 42.

real, which is to say the shared and common world that gives human action, freedom, and response its meaning. Arendt argues that the danger in modernity's tendency to collapse the factual truth/opinion distinction is that the lie can become absolute, complete, and final. There is a danger that power will "maneuver" factual truth out of the world forever by destroying it. Unlike the axioms and discoveries of science and philosophy, the "facts" of history cannot be rediscovered when memory and the archives which bear witness to them have been destroyed. "What is at stake here," Arendt insists, "is [the] common and factual reality itself, and this is indeed a political problem of the first order."[35] And the reason it rises to a problem of the first order is because politics, although concerned primarily with the human capacity to begin something anew, is also dependent upon the awareness of human limit, such that while it exhibits natality, it is not thereby permitted "to start *ab novo*, to create *ex nihilo*."[36] It always begins something anew from the starting point of the given. And to be a true beginning, that starting point must be the common world, the shared, the real. The danger is that we mistakenly assume our position to be one between the Kantian absolute principle of truth and the relativist reduction of all truth to opinion. Instead, as Arendt notes, "The political attitude towards facts must . . . tread the very narrow path between the danger of taking them as the results of some necessary development which men could not prevent and about which they can therefore do nothing and the danger of denying them, of trying to manipulate them out of the world."[37] It is precisely acknowledgment of this situated givenness that is nonetheless not wholly determined, this acceptance of things as they are, acceptance of the shared and common reality, which Arendt calls truthfulness. And such truthfulness enables the faculty of judgment and therefore makes possible free action in response to reality.

---

[35] Arendt, "Truth and Politics," 232.
[36] Ibid., 258.
[37] Ibid., 254.

## The Real as the Common World

Arendt stresses that our ability to perceive reality, and therefore our ability to act politically, depend on sharing the world. She illustrates this point with a medieval anecdote according to which one night a sentry was on watch in a town watchtower, where he was responsible for alerting the people of the town to the approach of the enemy. The sentry thought that it would make for a good practical joke to sound the alarm and give the townspeople a scare. He proved successful, with the result that everyone rushed to the wall to take up positions of defense, and the sentry himself was the last to rush to his position too. Arendt explicates the tale as follows: "The tale suggests to what extent our apprehension of reality is dependent upon our sharing the world with our fellow-men, and what strength of character is required to stick to anything, truth or lie, that is unshared."[38] Arendt's point is not that truth is relative to our shared apprehension, but rather that our grasp on truth is tenuous without shared apprehension. And lies that contradict the "facts" or the archive of witness to the facts threaten to "maneuver" such facts out of the world.[39] Yet, as Arendt notes, reliable facts, which "constitute the very texture of the political realm," are necessary for the exercise of political judgment and action. She says that without the guarantee of factual information, where the facts are not in dispute, freedom of opinion is farcical. As she argues, "factual truth informs political thought just as rational truth informs philosophical speculation."[40] She does not deny that facts are not wholly independent of opinion and interpretation, but this does not justify a complete blurring of the fact/opinion distinction. For the distinction points to the distinction between the given and the changeable, a distinction that must always be explored and

---

[38] Ibid., 249.
[39] Arendt argues, "While probably no former time tolerated so many diverse opinions on religious or philosophical matters, factual truth, if it happens to oppose a given group's profit or pleasure, is greeted today with greater hostility than ever before" ("Truth and Politics," 231).
[40] Ibid., 234.

reconsidered, but never simply denied. The distinction reminds us of the limits of the political sphere. As she puts it, it is

> limited by those things which man cannot change at will. And it is only by respecting its own borders that this realm, where we are free to act and change, can remain intact, preserving its integrity and keeping its promises. Conceptually, we may call truth what we cannot change; metaphorically, it is the ground on which we stand and the sky that stretches above us.[41]

However, on the other hand, while the limit that truthfulness places upon the political is salutary, the "truthful" must be accounted for in a phenomenologically appropriate manner if it is not to be a tool of the overreach of the political. Without this limit, there is somewhat ironically a very real possibility of the totalization of the political, a totalization that Kant's "absolute" truthfulness actually funds, if telling the truth is read as putting everything under the light of exposure. Derrida reflects on those who insist that

> Everything must be made to appear in the transparency of the public space and its illumination. But I wonder if we do not see here signs of the inverse perversion of politicism, of an absolute hegemony of political reason, of a limitless extension of the region of the political. By refusing any right to secrecy, the political agency, most often in the figure of state sovereignty or even of reason of state, summons everyone to behave first of all and in every regard as a responsible citizen before the law of the *polis*. Is there not here, in the name of a certain type of objective and phenomenal truth, another germ of totalitarianism with a democratic face?[42]

In other words, this "certain type of objective and phenomenal truth" can be claimed for the sake of the unreal, of the claim of the political beyond the rightful limits that reality places upon it. The overreach occurs when the political loses sight of its situatedness within a larger whole, and when it seeks to overcome all conflict

---

[41]Ibid., 259.
[42]Derrida, "History of the Lie," 63.

by pronouncing the absolute, static, and final truth. Again, though, such pronouncement cuts short the judgment at the heart of genuine political action by assuming that the "law" or "principle" has already made the necessary decision. In refusing judgment, ironically, the absolutization of the political would mean the end of the political, of the free but bounded space in which human action is meaningful. As Martin Jay argues, we are in an "Arendtian world of agonistic political discourse in which opinions, rhetoric, and yes, the ability to lie are signs of a freedom that is—perhaps—inextinguishable so long as politics resist the domination of sacred imperatives of whatever kind."[43] To apply this to Bonhoeffer, we could say that his account of truthfulness is not one of "sacred imperatives," but rather one of discerning reality, which is to say, one of discerning the salutary limits which refuses the empty, rootless, cynical "truth." Too much talk, too much chatter, too much exposure. We might see this as the requirements of a Habermasian open society, but it might be more appropriately read as the totalization of politics, the totalitarianism of mass democracy that respects no authority, no order of life, but instead subjects all to the bright glare of the public light without respect for the salutary "coverings" necessary for life in a fallen world.[44]

But how do we come to discern these rightful and salutary limits without falling into a conservativism that quietistically bows its head to the status quo? It is at this point, again, that Bonhoeffer's phenomenology of truth-telling is instructive in that he sets it within the larger framing of ordered life. A full account would require detailed attention to Bonhoeffer's concepts of the mandates— work, government, marriage, and the church.[45] These constitute Bonhoeffer's reworking and reformulation of Luther's language of the three estates or institutions (the *ecclesia*, *oeconomia*, and

---

[43] Martin Jay, "Pseudology: Derrida on Arendt and Lying in Politics," in *Essays from the Edge: Parerga and Paralipomena* (Charlottesville: University of Virginia Press, 2011), 148.
[44] Jay suggests that the kind of proponent of "openness" that Derrida argues against here insists in a Habermasian manner "that secrecy of any kind is anathema to an open, transparent democratic polity, in which the public sphere is an arena for open discussion," ibid., 139.
[45] Bonhoeffer, *Ethics*, 68.

*politia*).⁴⁶ For now, however, we simply note that for Bonhoeffer and Luther these mandates or institutions serve as a heuristic indicating the shape of the promise of the divine provision for human life, such that creaturely life in both its potential and limits can be grasped in trust and freedom. One cannot be truthful if one violates these orders. Exposure that violates the family in the name of the public or the political is a lie. Exposure that undermines the *oeconomia* (economic life) in the name of politics is a lie, as is exposure that would absolutize the *oeconomia* and undermine the political (as is the case when elections become tied too closely to the "interests" of those with wealth). An absolutization of either the public or the private, a failure to distinguish between them (although certainly what constitutes the one or the other is constantly up for examination), fails to honor the various areas of human life and their respective integrity, an honoring that is required for human flourishing.⁴⁷ Democratic mass politics seeks to do away with all distinction, as evidenced in the chatter of "social media" and the twenty-four-hour news cycle that requires continual and indiscriminate exposure.⁴⁸ But such exposure is a betrayal of reality as willed by God and as revealed in Scripture's promises

---

⁴⁶For Luther on the "estates," see Oswald Bayer, "Nature and Institution: Luther's Doctrine of the Three Estates," in *Freedom in Response; Lutheran Ethics: Sources and Controversies*, trans. Jeffrey F. Cayzer (Oxford: Oxford University Press, 2007), 90–118.

⁴⁷Again, it is important that the boundaries between the public and private be left open to discernment, and that they remain fluid rather than static if the "mandates" are not to end up reinforcing a conservative status quo or a false dualism between the political and the non-political. For an argument reading the mandates in this revised direction, see Karen V. Guth, "To See from Below: Dietrich Bonhoeffer's Mandates and Feminist Ethics," *Journal of the Society of Christian Ethics* 33, no. 2 (2013): 131–50.

⁴⁸Bonhoeffer warns that, "mistrust and suspicion as the basic attitude toward other people is the rebellion of the inferior" (*Letters and Papers from Prison*, 456). However, the concept of "exposure" should not be overly simplified. Exposure that reveals police brutality or brings to public attention sexual abuse by those in positions of power or authority is surely to be applauded and encouraged. The exposure this chapter is concerned with is the exposure that would destroy the salutary "covering" and protection necessary for human relationships, particularly intimate or "private" relationships. The concern is that an *ethos* of exposure that fails to distinguish the differentiated contexts and boundaries that protect human flourishing will instead apply indiscriminately such that a uniform disciplinary apparatus, operating in the

concerning God's provision for human life. Trust in these promises is what allows for resistance to the temptation to absolutize and totalize, and which enables the acceptance of the healthy limits and boundaries which make visible the real. In the name of "truth-telling" and the supposed interests of the undifferentiated mass, such speech lies as it fails to perceive reality in its concrete richness.[49]

It has become a truism of our time to say that we live in a "post-truth" world, and nowhere is this claim said to apply more than in the realm of politics. But a post-truth world is an unreal world, a world that, by definition, cannot be shared, and hence is an unpolitical world (in the sense of being incapable of providing the medium for joint speech and action). Truth-telling is a way of inhabiting the "real" such that the world is shared, and such that human beings speak and act together in the freedom that is politics. Dietrich Bonhoeffer's reflections on truth-telling lend a fuller understanding to the meaning of the Eighth Commandment, and thus help us to see and inhabit reality in such a way that the world appears as a common world, a world fit for human habitation, a world in which politics is possible. Hannah Arendt's reflections on truth and politics demonstrate the necessity of the practice of true speech, which in Bonhoeffer is understood as inextricably linked to accurate perception of divine ordering for shared political life. The post-truth world of fake news and the speech which corresponds to a "post-truth" age threatens the human place in the world as a shared place determined by the ordering of divine speech and the free human response to the divine speech.

---

name of a "truth and openness" that fails to make distinctions, will seep down into all aspects of human life.

[49]In a similar vein, elsewhere, Bonhoeffer speaks of this in terms of leveling versus "quality": "Quality is the strongest foe of any form of bringing everything to the level of the masses. . . . Culturally the experience of quality signals a return from the newspaper and radio to the book, from haste to leisure and stillness, from distraction to composure, from the sensational to reflection . . ." (*Letters and Papers from Prison*, 48).

# Bibliography

Arendt, Hannah. "Lying in Politics: Reflections on the Pentagon Papers." In *Crises of the Republic: Crises of the Republic: Lying in Politics, Civil Disobedience, On Violence, and Thoughts on Politics and Revolution*, 1–47. New York: Harcourt Brace & Company, 1972.

Arendt, Hannah. "Truth and Politics." In *Between Past and Future*, 227–64. New York: Penguin Books, 2006.

Bayer, Oswald. "Nature and Institution: Luther's Doctrine of the Three Estates." In *Freedom in Response; Lutheran Ethics: Sources and Controversies*, translated by Jeffrey F. Cayzer, 90–118. Oxford: Oxford University Press, 2007.

Bethge, Eberhard. *Dietrich Bonhoeffer: A Biography*. Minneapolis: Fortress Press, 2000.

Bonhoeffer, Dietrich. *Ethics, Dietrich Bonhoeffer Works 6*, edited by Clifford Green, translated by Reinhard Krauss, Charles C. West, and Douglas W. Stott. Minneapolis: Fortress Press, 2009.

Bonhoeffer, Dietrich. *Letters and Papers from Prison, Dietrich Bonhoeffer Works 8*, edited by John W. de Gruchy, translated by Isabel Best, Lisa E. Dahill, Reinhard Krauss, and Nancy Luken. Minneapolis: Fortress Press, 2010.

Bonhoeffer, Dietrich. "What Does It Mean to Tell the Truth?" In *Conspiracy and Imprisonment, 1940-1945, Dietrich Bonhoeffer Works 16*, edited by Mark S. Brocker, translated by Lisa E. Dahill, 601–608. Minneapolis: Fortress Press, 2004.

Derrida, Jacques. "History of the Lie: Prolegomena." In *Without Alibi*, 28–70. Stanford: Stanford University Press, 2002.

Guth, Karen V. "To See from Below: Dietrich Bonhoeffer's Mandates and Feminist Ethics." *Journal of the Society of Christian Ethics* 33, no. 2 (2013): 131–50.

Happer, Cathrine, Andrew Hoskins, and William Merrin. "Weaponizing Reality: An Introduction to Trump's War on the Media." In *Trump's Media War*, edited by Catherine Happer, Andrew Hoskins, and William Merrin, 3–22. Cham, Switzerland: Palgrave Macmillan, 2019.

Jay, Martin. "Pseudology: Derrida on Arendt and Lying in Politics." In *Essays from the Edge: Parerga and Paralipomena*, 132–48. Charlottesville: University of Virginia Press, 2011.

Kant, Immanuel. "On a Supposed Right to lie from Philanthropy (1797)." In *Practical Philosophy*, The Cambridge Edition of the Works of Immanuel Kant, edited by translated by Mary J. Gregor, 605–16. Cambridge: Cambridge University Press, 1996.

Peters, Albrecht. *Commentary on Luther's Catechisms: Ten Commandments*. Saint Louis: Concordia Publishing House, 2009.
Puffer, Matthew. "Three Rival Versions of Moral Reasoning: Interpreting Bonhoeffer's Ethics of Lying, Guilt, and Responsibility." *Harvard Theological Review* 112, no. 2 (2019), 160–83.
Shindler, D.C. *Freedom from Reality: The Diabolical Character of Modern Liberty*. Notre Dame: Notre Dame University Press, 2017.

# 9

# Cancel Culture

# Mobilizing Christian Ethics at the Scene of Judgment

*Daniel R. Patterson*

## Introduction

In December 2013, Justine Sacco, a personal relations executive, posted a tweet before boarding a plane for Cape Town. It read: "Going to Africa. Hope I don't get AIDS. Just kidding. I'm white!" While on her long-haul flight and despite her relative obscurity and meagre 170 Twitter followers, Sacco's tweet, deemed highly racist, went viral attracting the hashtag #hasjustinelanded. The groundswell of outrage that swept across Twitter and other social media platforms awaited her arrival in South Africa. When Sacco finally landed and learned about the impact of her comment, she quickly deleted the tweet and her Twitter profile. But the damage was done. Sacco was *canceled*. She was publicly shamed, and she was fired from her job soon thereafter.[1]

---

[1] Ironically, Sacco's tweet was intended as joke to highlight the fact that AIDS is not a "black" problem. A full reflection on this scenario is found in Jon Ronson, *So You've Been Publicly Shamed* (New York: Riverhead Books, 2015), chap. 4.

Cancel culture events such as this were relatively rare in 2013. No longer. Hardly a day goes by without hearing that someone has stepped over a fatal line with a comment on sex, sexuality, gender, disability, race; an endlessly unstable set of tripwires. Teenagers find themselves snubbed by their peer groups, influencers are unfollowed on Twitter, a sportsperson's advertising contract is terminated, an author's books are thrown on a bonfire, a politician is called to resign, a church minister is defrocked, a local business is boycotted, a conference speaker is "no platformed," and professors become personae non gratae and their academic writings backlisted. Western culture has fallen in love with cancellation, which promises to extinguish involvement, eradicate impact, and destroy influence for social transgression.[2]

Cancel culture is not merely pervasive. It also appears to have structural significance for current society. In 2019 the *Macquarie Dictionary* chose it as their "Word of the Year," adding the commentary that it's "[a] term that captures an important aspect of the past year's Zeitgeist . . . an attitude which is so pervasive that it now has a name, society's *cancel culture* has become, for better or worse, a powerful force."[3] The spiritual nature of this analysis is hard to overlook, which should prick the Christian. Cancel culture, it seems, is a powerful force that indwells a person, taking over their mind and compelling them to act. If a person must be possessed by the spirit of the age before they can act in the power of that spirit, then cancel culture is just as concerned with possessing people as it is with cancelling people.

It is harder to name what this powerful spirit is which seizes and compels people to join into the group dynamics of cancellation. We must look for something which goes beyond the desire in the past to safeguard freedom of speech and religion, critical debate, experimentation, and robust engagement, aims that have long been

---

[2]Sarah Hagi, "Cancel Culture Is Not Real–At Least Not in the Way People Think," accessed December 27, 2023. http://time.com/5735403/cancel-culture-is-not-real/. Cf. Danielle Butler, "The Misplaced Hysteria About a 'Cancel Culture' That Doesn't Actually Exist," accessed December 27, 2023. http://www.theroot.com/the-misplaced-hysteria-about-a-cancel-culture-that-do-1829563238.
[3]Accessed January 25, 2023, https://www.macquariedictionary.com.au/resources/view/word/of/the/year/2019.

associated with academic, journalistic, and political speech.[4] Concern with free speech and its role in functioning liberal democracies is important on its own terms, but we have to ask broader questions about truth if we are to find sufficient grounds to justify or condemn cancel culture.[5] To ask this wider question takes us into the territory of the Pauline exhortation not to be conformed to potentially evil patterns, and so to look more closely at the patterns of behavior and thought that are characteristic of our own time and place.[6]

The argument I offer in this chapter is the Christian ethicist should be concerned with cancel culture because we are concerned with thinking about what it means to make good judgments based on the unique grammar of the gospel. Cancel culture has not yet been theologically analyzed as I do in this chapter in two movements: first, through an exploration of the critical, yet insufficient, philosophical reflections on judgment by Hannah Arendt and Judith Butler; and second, through the constructive theological reflections on the biblical theme of forgiveness by Jacques Derrida and Søren Kierkegaard. This critical and constructive engagement leads me to conclude that cancel culture is a stunted and therefore unethical mode of negotiating social justice characterized most problematically by an absence of forgiveness. My analysis does not propose replacing cancel culture with "forgiveness culture," but offers a more modest proposal that the *possibility* of forgiveness awakens judicial agency of a different, and more just kind. In the end, the possibility of offering forgiveness does not strip a person of the capacity to judge and punish yet does acknowledge and temper some of the characteristic injustices that have become familiar aspects of cancel culture.

---

[4]Alan Dershowitz, *Cancel Culture: The Latest Attack on Free Speech and Due Process* (New York: Skyhorse Publishing Company, Incorporated, 2020), 4. Dershowitz views cancel culture as the "new McCarthyism"; a new form of purging oppositional voices regardless of the other's political persuasion.
[5]*A Letter on Justice and Open Debate*, accessed January 25, 2023. https://harpers.org/a-letter-on-justice-and-open-debate/. See also Amina Srinivasan, "Cancelled," accessed January 25, 2023. https://www.lrb.co.uk/the-paper/v45/n13/amia-srinivasan/cancelled.
[6]Rom. 12:2. "[T]he means used to achieve political goals are more often than not of greater relevance to the future world than the intended goals." Hannah Arendt, *On Violence* (New York: Harcourt, 1979), 4. How much more so, we ask, must this be true for Christians and their desires for society?

# Exceptional Justice

## What Is Cancel Culture?

Cancel culture is a social movement of the self-elected that pursue justice by prosecuting transgression against a moral standard that is not codified by law. Cancel culture runs its course independent of a person's legal standing. It is an extrajudicial or exceptional mode of justice-seeking, a "democratisation of justice"[7] acting where law courts have limited or no jurisdiction, or where the punishment meted out by a court is deemed inadequate. The niche in which cancel culture thrives is the space where legal acts or words are deemed morally abhorrent or where legal sanctions are deemed to have punished insufficiently.

The professional basketballer Kyrie Irving's endorsement of the docuseries *Hebrews to Negroes: Wake Up Black America* provoked a familiar response.[8] Irving's endorsement of a media production already in the public domain was in no sense illegal, yet many saw it as antisemitic. Cancel culture offered a way to provide a socially recognizable response to an endorsement that was legally permissible and hitherto culturally unexceptional. He was lashed in the press and social media, suspended from playing, fined by his employer, stripped of lucrative apparel endorsements, and, in the end, forced to apologize publicly.[9] The popular author J. K. Rowling received very similar treatment after espousing second-wave feminist positions on trans-women which could not be classed as illegal but were deemed transgressive by many, especially on social media leading to widespread outrage on social media, her books being boycotted, banned, and burned.[10]

---

[7]Ronson, *So You've Been Publicly Shamed*, 9.
[8]See Glynn A. Hill and Ben Golliver, "Kyrie Irving Not Apologizing for Posting about Film Linked to Antisemitism," *Washington Post*, October 30, 2022, https://www.washingtonpost.com/sports/2022/10/29/kyrie-irving-accusations-antisemitism/.
[9]See Tania Ganguli and Sopan Deb, "What to Know about Irving's Antisemitic Movie Post and the Fallout," *The New York Times*, November 21, 2022, https://www.nytimes.com/article/kyrie-irving-antisemitic.html.
[10]For a summary of the ongoing saga see Ellie Muir, "A Timeline of JK Rowling's Comments About Women and Transgender Rights," *The Independent*, April 25,

These examples of cancellation, along with that suffered by Justine Sacco, show that cancel culture is a system of enforcing certain moral standards that pursues justice despite the absence of a recognizable and socially agreed-upon codified legal standard. In this sense, cancel culture is social action aiming to confront speech and action taken to be ethically unthinkable while being legally allowed.

## Naming the Transgression

There were no doubts in most people's minds that Irving's endorsement was morally beyond the pale, but if we include the cases of Rowling and Sacco, can we describe more precisely the crimes that led to their cancellation? What extrajudicial "law" did these people break such that they were liable for cancelling? Judith Butler's reading of Hannah Arendt's philosophical interpretation of the Eichmann trial sheds light on these questions.[11]

Adolf Eichmann was a Nazi commander who was tried in 1961 by an Israeli court in Jerusalem for his major administrative role in the genocide of Jews in the Second World War. Arendt's description of the trial is instructive: "the court here was confronted with a crime it could not find in the lawbooks and with a criminal whose like was unknown in any court."[12] Eichmann's actions were criminal in nature but did not initially fall under Israeli law.[13]

---

2023, https://www.independent.co.uk/arts-entertainment/books/news/jk-rowling-trans-twitter-timeline-b2326256.html.

[11] Arendt was commissioned by the *New Yorker* magazine to cover the event. She produced two articles which were later expanded and published in 1964 as *Eichmann in Jerusalem: A Report on the Banality of Evil*.

[12] Hannah Arendt, *Eichmann in Jerusalem: A Report on the Banality of Evil*, Penguin Classics (New York: Penguin Books, 2006), 298.

[13] Arendt describes the crimes for which he stood accused: "crimes against the Jewish people, crimes against humanity, and war crimes during the whole period of the Nazi regime and especially during the period of the Second World War" for which he was liable to receive the death penalty if found guilty (ibid., 21). Arendt's commentary in the "Epilogue" is a critical and at times conflicted or ambiguous technical and philosophical engagement with the trial process. While she does not disagree with the outcome, she wrestles with "the irregularities and or abnormalities of the trial" (ibid., 253) and pre-trial events like Eichmann's arrest on the streets of Buenos Aires by Israeli secret service (ibid., 261–7).

While Arendt narrates the trial and records the laws against which Eichmann would eventually be tried, found guilty, and sentenced to death by hanging, toward the end of the book,[14] she concludes her account with a more philosophical analysis and commentary on the trial which philosopher Judith Butler more recently examines.[15] According to Butler's interpretation of Arendt's commentary, the exceptional laws Eichmann transgressed were mundane moral laws—he failed to think and share—which chimes with Arendt's famous enigmatic subtitle of the book: "A Report on the Banality of Evil."

In the first place, Eichmann was deemed guilty of *not thinking*.[16] Arendt explains that Eichmann found himself in the dock because he found no fault with the Final Solution concerning the Jewish question. More specifically, he did not fault the laws imposed on him, and he found no good reason to disobey his superiors who regulated them. Eichmann argued that he was merely following orders like so many other German leaders. He complained that "he no longer 'was master of his own deeds,'" and "that he was unable 'to change anything.'"[17] But according to Arendt, the heavily conditioned context did not justify his lack of thinking.[18] In fact, it was precisely because he was subject to that kind of conditioning that Arendt believed thinking was imperative. In a context where evil had become terribly normal and even justified by the law, thinking was the key to accessing the universal principles—the moral law—that should have been grounding the laws governing Eichmann's context all along.[19]

---

[14]Ibid., 277–9.
[15]Judith Butler, "Hannah Arendt's Death Sentences," *Comparative Literature Studies* 48, no. 3 (2011): 280–95. This article is expanded in Judith Butler, *Parting Ways: Jewishness and the Critique of Zionism* (New York: Columbia University Press, 2014), 151–80.
[16]Butler, "Hannah Arendt's Death Sentences," 180–3; Arendt, *Eichmann in Jerusalem*, 278.
[17]Arendt, *Eichmann in Jerusalem*, 136, 278.
[18]Arendt narrates events that appear to show that Eichmann was not as conditioned as he made out. Late in the war Eichmann is shown to contradict Himmler's explicit orders because he was beginning to be lenient on the Jews. Eichmann did not agree with this softening approach and so disobeyed Himmler. Ibid., 137–8.
[19]Ibid., 136.

Butler's interpretation of Arendt's observations of the Eichmann trial is illuminating for our exploration of cancel culture. As we have already established, transgressing social morals might not always fall foul of the civil law, but this does not make one any less liable to a judgment of guilt and punishment against a moral law. As in the Eichmann case, an observed transgression raises the question: What is the law that has been transgressed? Eichmann transgressed the basic expectation that moral agents be self-reflective. A very similar logic and also banality seem characteristic of current justifications of cancel culture.

Consider the position taken by Kate Hudson, the actress who plays Birdie Jay in *The Glass Onion* (2023). In the movie, Birdie is herself subject to cancellation for various social *faux pas*. Reflecting on her character, Hudson observes: "People should just have a deeper awareness, right? . . . We *should* hold people accountable who do anything that's sexist, misogynistic, or racist . . . There are clear things that [warrant], you know, 'You're cancelled, bye!'"[20] Hudson justifies a person's guilt and punishment despite the absence of a civil law, instead appealing to an assumed moral expectation that "people should just have a deeper awareness" much like Sacco's critics who called her "ignorant" and "stupid." Hudson doesn't expand on what awareness means (i.e., of what and how), but she clearly thinks it makes the crucial difference when it comes to moral conduct. As Arendt expected of Eichmann, Hudson believes that even in the absence of a positive law establishing what good moral action is, and even if one lives in a culture that normalizes unjust action, like sexism, misogyny, or racism, it is important for people to be morally aware if they are to make good decisions. Hudson and Arendt appeal to the same expectation: we all have access to a universal moral law that instructs us on what is good and thus how we should act. Sacco's racist tweet, Irving's antisemitic endorsement, and Rowling's anti-trans comments may or may not be legal indiscretions according to Hudson's logic, but they are the

---

[20]Kate Hudson in Adam White, "'I've Not Led a Very Traditional Life': Kate Hudson on Glass Onion, Cancel Culture and Being a Nepo Baby," *The Independent*, December 24, 2022, https://www.independent.co.uk/arts-entertainment/films/features/kate-hudson-interview-glass-onion-knives-out-b2250000.html.

result of various levels of unthinking transgression of the accessible common moral sense of what is good.

Butler then notes that Arendt accuses Eichmann of failing to share.[21] Like his lack of thinking, this appears to be a minor indiscretion that lets Eichmann off lightly. On the contrary, this is the action for which Arendt demands he must hang. But she does not make this demand with her own words but as one of the judges in a hypothetical dramatization of what the judges would have said if they had addressed Eichmann. Speaking as and for the judges to Eichmann, she writes,

> And just as you supported and carried out a policy of not wanting to share the earth with the Jewish people and the people of a number of other nations—as though you and your superiors had any right to determine who should and who should not inhabit the world—we find that no one, that is, no member of the human race, can be expected to want to share the earth with you. This is the reason, and the only reason, you must hang.[22]

Butler identifies that the important detail of the judges' charge is that Eichmann's unthinking action amounted to a refusal to "share the earth" with the Jews. Arendt elaborates on the charge by identifying that he and his superiors had a mistaken sovereign claim on the earth that led to the lethal conclusion that they had the right to choose who was their neighbor. Arendt does not explicitly mention the famous biblical parable Jesus taught his disciples, but the question of "Who is my neighbor?" looms large.[23] If Eichmann and his superiors were the sovereign owners of the earth, they could decide rightfully who could inhabit the world with them. But for Arendt, speaking with the voice of one of Eichmann's judges, neither the Nazis in general nor Eichmann as an individual had the authority to set themselves up as the final arbiters of who could inhabit the world with them. The principal exceptional charge (philosophically conceived) for which Eichmann should be punished by execution

---

[21]Butler, "Hannah Arendt's Death Sentences," 287.
[22]Arendt, *Eichmann in Jerusalem*, 279.
[23]Lk. 10:25-37.

was his unthinking action to take in hand the decision of who will be counted as a neighbor. Applying Butler's analysis of Arendt's view of Eichmann to cancel culture, we find it preoccupied with judging those who assume to have the sovereign right to decide who can be part of society. Hudson's desire to root out speech and action that is sexist, misogynistic, and racist is one such sovereign claim to adjudicate political belonging. Speaking openly about who can inhabit a friendship group, school, business, toilet cubicle, university, or church, and so on, based on one's gender, race, physical ability, and so on, is precisely what Hudson and those who hold her position cannot accept.

Take another example where feminist writer and speaker Germain Greer was invited to a series of speaking events at Cardiff University in Wales in 2015. Greer is one of those second-wave feminist voices who have insisted that trans-women are not women but in fact undermine the fight for women's rights and equality.[24] The student union took umbrage that someone with these views was invited onto campus, prompting them to lobby the university administrators to revoke Greer's invitation because "hosting a speaker with such problematic and hateful views towards marginalized and vulnerable groups is dangerous."[25] In a BBC interview concerning the same event, Greer was asked to reflect on the possibility that her views were hurtful toward transgender women.[26] According to the student union and the angle of the BBC interviewer, Greer was not merely guilty of offending people by exercising her right to express her views, but was guilty of the much more serious moral failing of assuming the right to determine who could "share the earth" with her as a woman. Cancelling Greer was

---

[24]For example, the chapter called "Pantomime Dames," in Germaine Greer, *The Whole Woman* (New York: Knopf, 1999).
[25]Damien Gayle, "Caitlyn Jenner 'Wanted Limelight of Female Kardashians' – Germaine Greer," *The Guardian*, October 24, 2015, https://www.theguardian.com/books/2015/oct/24/caitlyn-jenner-wanted-limelight-of-female-kardashians-germaine-greer.
[26]Germaine Greer, "Germaine Greer: Transgender Women are 'Not Women,'" interviewed by Kirsty Wark, *Newsnight*, BBC, October 24, 2015, https://www.bbc.com/news/av/uk-34625512.

the exceptional response deemed necessary for her extrajudicial crime of not wanting to share the world with others.

Whether one takes the case of Sacco, Irving, Rowling, or Greer, each was found guilty of transgressing a *moral law* of racism, sexism, or misogynistic behavior, but the principal charge, philosophically conceived, for which they were punished by cancellation was their unthinking, immoral claim to engineer who counts as their neighbor.

## Pay It Forward

Cancel culture, like the Eichmann trial, is taken publicly to be beyond critique because of the serious nature of the moral charges it highlights, the indisputable reality of moral guilt, and the desirability of having harsh punishments available for people who are morally noxious. Yet Butler identifies the necessity for further reflection on this consensus by revealing the inconsistency (perhaps deliberate) in Arendt's philosophical commentary. Even though Eichmann was clearly guilty on both counts (not thinking and not sharing), Butler observes Arendt's unwitting (or unthinking) reiteration of the exceptional crime (of not sharing) she is prosecuting as part of the hypothetical judging panel.

After the charge is stated that Eichmann unthinkingly chose not to share the earth with the Jews, the judges (in whose voice Arendt ambiguously locates her own) do not immediately hand down the punishment—"you must hang"—but first justify the punishment by drawing down on another universal moral expectation: "we find that no one, that is, no member of the human race, can be expected to want to share the earth with you."[27] This is the second time "share the earth" is used in the explanation of the judgment. Throughout her book Arendt does not deny Eichmann's guilt and punishment but maintains that the trial was a troubled legal procedure. Having

---

[27] Arendt, *Eichmann in Jerusalem*, 279. These words of what the judges should have said reflect an earlier comment by Arendt who in her own words states that "Because he had been implicated and had played a central role in the enterprise whose open purpose was to eliminate certain 'races' from the surface of the earth, he had to be eliminated" (ibid., 277).

elsewhere outlined her reasons for this judgment,[28] her philosophical engagement demonstrates the problem more dramatically and subtly by pointing out that the judges too (of which she includes herself) lay claim to who will *not* share the earth with them and the rest of humanity, namely, the transgressor, Eichmann. In Arendt's dramatization, Butler observes the judges confessing to commit the same "crime" for which they are convicting and punishing Eichmann; that is, they will "determine who should and who should not inhabit the world"[29] with the rest of us.[30] Butler observes that rather than putting an end to the ethically unthinkable and legally inconceivable crime, "punishment invariably continues some part of the crime."[31] Justice is served to Eichmann but not without perpetuating some aspect of that which he is guilty of committing.

Butler's observation is important because it draws attention to the trouble that also characterizes cancel culture and its pursuit of those who are deemed to be wrongly laying claim to the right to adjudicate who can share in this world. This is true, for example, in the case involving Greer and the student union at Cardiff University. Insofar as Greer is deemed guilty and liable by some for determining what a woman is and thus who can share society with her according to that criterion, the student union reiterates some part of the crime by claiming that Greer cannot share the university campus with them based on criteria they determine. Is the student union's desire to cancel Greer not in some sense unthinkingly perpetuating the transgression of inhospitality that it seeks to remedy?

If cancel culture perpetuates some part of the crime that it seeks to prosecute, then the justice cancel culture claims to achieve invariably pays forward some part of the injustice it seeks to purge. The insightful question Butler is pressing is not only whether a person is guilty of transgressing the moral law and deserving of punishment but also how an exceptional judgment of guilt and punishment might avoid reiterating the crime being prosecuted.[32]

---

[28]Ibid., 274.
[29]Ibid., 279.
[30]Butler, "Hannah Arendt's Death Sentences," 291–2.
[31]Ibid., 295.
[32]A correlate is found in the Apostle Paul's unfolding argument in Rom. 2:1-4. Paul traces the same logic when justice is taken into one's own hands. He does not emphasize the error of the standard against which people are judged, but the nature

# The Impossibility of Forgiveness

## Looking beyond Mandatory Punishment

Exceptional moments of judgment call for a *thinking judge* because there is no precedent to which one can defer to determine a response. Where there is no precedent to guide one's judgment, all forms of punishment are in principle on the table in the event of a guilty verdict. Yet in exceptional cases such as the Eichmann trial and moments of current social transgression, the freedom of the judge is curtailed by the reality that forgiveness is not a possible option. This puts a person in a "predicament of irreversibility."[33] The gross evil of Eichmann's actions made forgiveness inconceivable. He deserved to be punished and so to avoid punishment would surely be unjust. Similarly, and for a comparatively lesser transgression, Hudson shows the same mandatory impulse when she justifies her judgment for social transgression: "There are clear things that [warrant], you know, 'You're cancelled, bye!'" Even though extralegal transgression demands thinking to determine right judgment, these two different scenarios reveal judges who are stripped of this prerogative as punishment was mandatory because forgiveness was impossible.

Butler's interpretation of Arendt's philosophical interpretation of the trial invokes further reflection on the Zeitgeist which is exposed as a conflicted and coerced judicial scene:

> the plurality enacted here . . . is unchosen, compelled, agonistic, and inconsistent. It is not the ideal of a group of people acting in concert, freely, and guided by a common goal. And yet it might be said that to cohabit the earth with those one never chose and

---

of human justice as reiterative. The same principle is the root of the biblical "eye for an eye" (Exod. 21:23-25): to disallow taking the law in one's one hand, which would be a case of vengeance as opposed to lawful retribution. The latter is to be in the hands of those appointed for the function, the former in the hands of the self-elected, the latter is a means to break the circle of violence, the former a means to perpetuate it. I'm grateful for Rory Shiner and Bernd Wannenwetsch for refining conversations on these biblical parallels.

[33]Hannah Arendt, *The Human Condition* (Chicago: University of Chicago Press, 1998), 237.

to develop an ethical and political obligation to preserve the lives of those one never chose is no easy task.[34]

Butler is not describing an undermined judgment but a troubled judicial process.[35] Whereas in exceptional moments of transgression the judge is called to think and judge, unfettered by precedent and mandatory stipulations, Butler believes Arendt and her fellow judges are caught up in an agonizing scene wherein judicial agency is hindered. Butler wonders whether the (hypothetical) judging panel's verdict represents a "theatrical vacillation between vengeance and some other version of justice."[36] Even when the verdict is given— "He must hang"—and we might add Hudson's—"You're cancelled, bye!"—we are sensitized to the possibility that these judgments are not the result of free thinking judges, but rather outcomes born of compulsion by a judging plurality or culture. Cancel culture is "mob justice" characterized more by the inertia of an unthinking mob than discerned judgment by individuals—"a vicious circle of mere reaction."[37] In the face of this problematic form of justice-seeking, Butler points to the need for a new ethical paradigm and vision that poses the *possibility* of the preservation of the unchosen lives of those who inhabit the world with us.

Butler, like Arendt, does not appeal against Eichmann's death penalty, but uses this moment to reveal that genuine, exceptional moments of transgression should enliven ethical discourse rather than curb it. This is "no easy task," Butler states, unlike judicial scenes where mandatory punishment makes judging easy once guilt is established.

This analysis sheds light on the trouble besetting cancel culture. It is likewise coercive, indwelling, and incorporating individuals into a stunted judicial plurality or unthinking mob. The mob rules, but the mob is no one or nobody in particular. Elsewhere, Arendt comments: "for the rule by Nobody is not no-rule, and where all are equally powerless we have a tyranny without a tyrant."[38]

---

[34]Butler, "Hannah Arendt's Death Sentences," 295.
[35]Dershowitz, *Cancel Culture*, 3.
[36]Butler, "Hannah Arendt's Death Sentences," 295.
[37]Bernd Wannenwetsch, *Political Worship*, Oxford Studies in Theological Ethics (Oxford: Oxford University Press, 2010), 307.
[38]Arendt, *On Violence*, 81.

This describes the mob that applies mandatory punishment to transgressive individuals instead of being provoked to engage in ethical discourse that invites individuals within the mob to wrestle with the *possibility* of preserving the transgressive lives of those with whom they would not choose to inhabit society or given community.

## Breaking the Cycle of Mandatory Cancellation

Butler's critique diagnoses the trouble with overconfident judicial agency and unthinking judging, and while this shows the need to reform ethical discourse, her critique provides no means by which this can happen.[39] Indeed, where unforgivable transgressors are subject to mandatory punishment, ethical dialogue and thinking judgment are unthinkable. What then can enliven the genuine *possibility* of the preservation of the unchosen, transgressive lives with whom we inhabit the world? Indeed, what can enliven the *desire* for the possibility of preserving the life of a transgressive person? The grammar of the gospel provides the answers to these questions, specifically, that the unforgivable can be forgiven. Where this is the case, the culture of judging transgression will not be qualified with cancel or forgiveness but free judgment. This means that a distinctly Christian contribution to this discussion is not seeking to replace cancel culture with forgiveness culture but to invite a mode of living with transgressive others that prizes genuinely free judgment made possible by (but without necessitating) forgiveness.

Nineteenth-century philosopher and theologian Søren Kierkegaard, under the pseudonym Anti-Climacus, offers a path for us to navigate Arendt's fear of a stunted trial which Butler later describes as problematic judicial agency. Kierkegaard's treatment of unforgivable sin reveals to us that what plagues cancel culture

---

[39]Butler claims that ethical prescriptions emerge from the fact we live in a context of unwilled cohabitation with others. While such an observation reveals the dynamics of political life, Butler derives an ethical ought from what is, which, on matters of the body for example, she derides. The question is begging: why should I desire to share the earth with another? Butler, *Parting Ways*, 125.

is not despair of justice but "despair of forgiveness."[40] Kierkegaard argues what is unforgivable is not in fact another's transgression but one's refusal to forgive.[41] This insight suggests that the spirit that possesses this age of cancel culture might in fact be the refusal to forgive grounded in a conviction that transgressors *can* be forgiven.

I am suggesting that cancel culture suffers from a despair of forgiveness, which includes being traumatized by its having been corrupted so often. Jacques Derrida has insightfully analyzed the secular globalization of Christianity's legacy of forgiveness in the face of grievous transgression—including the Shoah—in *On Cosmopolitanism and Forgiveness*. He laments the recent reduction of forgiveness to a sentimental process of normalizing international relations.[42] Derrida thinks the contradiction between unconditional and conditional forgiveness has gone missing in secular discourse, and that this represents a loss of the richer conceptuality carried in earlier Christian thought. Unconditional or pure forgiveness is given when it is not requested, sought, or even deserved like that "given by God, or inspired by divine prescript."[43] Conditional forgiveness, in contrast, is given to those who ask for it after they have recognized and repented of their transgression. The true value of forgiveness is lost when the contradiction between these two forms is resolved.

While unforgiveable crimes are indeed unforgiveable, Derrida calls on a Christian account of forgiveness to show that being unforgivable is in fact the condition for the possibility of any forgiveness at all. Speaking of unforgiveness, Derrida asks, "Is this not, in truth, the only thing to forgive?" which he distils when he

---

[40]Søren Kierkegaard, *The Sickness Unto Death: A Christian Psychological Exposition for Upbuilding and Awakening*, ed. and trans. Howard V. Hong and Edna H. Hong, Kierkegaard's Writings 19 (Princeton: Princeton University Press, 1983), 124.
[41]Ibid.
[42]This smoothing of relations so that day-to-day business can carry on as usual is how Amina Srinivasan concludes her investigation into cancel culture in the left/right divide in academia. She does not use the word "forgiveness" to describe this normalization of relations but "collegiality" which is not mere tolerance but a way of dwelling with others by reaching across the divide by listening to their needs with a view to meeting them. Amina Srinivasan, "Cancelled," *London Review of Books*, June 29, 2023, https://www.lrb.co.uk/the-paper/v45/n13/amia-srinivasan/cancelled.
[43]Jacques Derrida, *On Cosmopolitanism and Forgiveness* (London: Routledge, 2001), 44.

says that "forgiveness forgives only the unforgivable."[44] According to this reading of the Christian account of forgiveness, unforgivable transgression challenges mandatory punishment by providing the right conditions for forgiveness. If forgiveness is a *possibility*, then punishment cannot be *mandatory*. Instead, it must be thoughtfully *discerned*.

Where unforgiveable transgression is rightly identified as the condition for forgiveness, the temptation arises to mandate forgiveness. But when necessity replaces the impossibility of forgiveness, the conditions for pure forgiveness evaporate. The nature of the Christian notion of unconditional forgiveness refuses de-radicalization. Forgiveness, as such, "in order to have its own meaning, should have no 'meaning,' no finality, even no intelligibility."[45] This is why forgiveness, "surprises, like a revolution, the ordinary course of history, politics, and law."[46] Elsewhere, Derrida reinforces this when he says that "Forgiveness is not, it *should not be*, normal, normative, normalizing. It *should* remain exceptional and extraordinary, in the face of the impossible: as if it interrupted the ordinary course of historical temporality."[47] Unlike the mandatory judgment that cancel culture performs, pure forgiveness is scandalous and apocalyptic because it breaks into a scenario and reveals a previously unthought possibility: the unforgivable *can* be forgiven. Butler's desire for an ethical paradigm that can preserve life is realized by Derrida in the unique Christian grammar of forgiveness—particularly, forgiveness in the face of unforgivable crime. Where the conditions for forgiveness are found, judges cannot resort to mandatory punishment, but must freely determine not only who is guilty, but also whether forgiveness should be extended to those who are unforgiveable.

Cancel culture's despair of forgiveness is remedied where forgiveness is restored from its corrupt form where it is used as a facile tool to normalize relationships. The unique and radical Christian grammar of forgiveness offers no such thing, yet it still breaks into the stunted judicial scene, chastening the spirit of

---

[44]Ibid., 32.
[45]Ibid., 45.
[46]Ibid., 39.
[47]Ibid., 32.

mandatory punishment through cancellation, and thus demanding that one engage in the difficult task of thoughtful judgment. Hudson's comment "There are clear things that [warrant], you know, 'You're cancelled, bye!'"[48] reflects a stunted judicial scene that is ironically mobilized by her claim. Unforgivability is precisely the condition that provokes judgments about whether forgiveness *might* be possible here. The Christian grammar of forgiveness breaks into this moment, surprising us, and maybe the transgressor, displaying that the seemingly inexorable course of judgment and punishment can be disrupted.

## Agents of Forgiveness

The limitation of Derrida's account lies in the fact that while he observes the conditions for forgiveness, these conditions are superfluous if one is not able to forgive. The impossibility of forgiveness might mobilize stunted ethical discourse, but is this ethical discourse genuinely mobilized if I am not able to forgive? Derrida usefully highlights the importance of earlier notions of Christian forgiveness yet offers no alternative to our culture's despair of forgiveness. He must also account for one's incapacity to do so given the conditions.[49]

The grammar of the Christian faith diagnoses cancel culture as riddled with the malady of the despair of forgiveness. It also offers a remedy not reducible to a steady prescription-diet of the virtue of forgiveness. Returning to Kierkegaard, the impulsive turn to virtue reflects a faulty understanding of the spirit gripping the age. The logical remedy for despair of forgiveness is to forgive: if the sin is not forgiving, then beginning to forgive will deal with the sin. Kierkegaard observes, however, this logic fails because "opposites are constructed not as being sin/faith but as sin/virtue."[50] The Christian grammar that Kierkegaard is highlighting is the remedy for the sinful despair of forgiveness is not the virtue of forgiveness

---

[48]Kate Hudson in White, "I've Not Led a Very Traditional Life."
[49]Bernd Wannenwetsch makes a similar critique of Hannah Arendt's account of forgiveness in *The Human Condition*. Wannenwetsch, *Political Worship*, 307–11.
[50]Kierkegaard, *The Sickness Unto Death*, 124.

but *faith*. A distinct Christian intervention into the blight of cancel culture is not an announcement that people should develop more regular habits of forgiveness, but the proclamation and living out of faith.

According to Kierkegaard, the lack of faith in forgiveness is not an unfortunate lapse or something one suffers as an imposition. Indeed, despair can be construed as weakness but also defiance which, for Kierkegaard, is a demonstration of heightened sinfulness.[51] A culture that despairs of forgiveness has not retreated to a distance from God but has advanced toward God with a shaking fist at God's offer of forgiveness for their own transgression. Despair of forgiveness, therefore, manifests in society as a mob-refusal to forgive others, but only secondarily, having first individually refused (or forgotten) forgiveness for oneself. "Despair of the forgiveness of sins is a definite position over against an offer of God's mercy; sin is not solely retreat, not merely defensive action . . . now sin is attacking."[52] The denial of one's own need for forgiveness and thus the rejection of God's offer of forgiveness results in actively withholding forgiveness from others: "the despair to be oneself—a sinner—in such a way that there is no forgiveness."[53] Despair is therefore instructive. A person (and culture) despairs of forgiveness because they are not forgiven.

The remedy, Kierkegaard suggests, is a faithful embrace of God's forgiveness for our transgression. This, of course, first requires confession that one is a transgressor which Kierkegaard states "unconditionally splits up the 'the crowd'" or the mob.[54] Standing before God and confessing one's sinfulness, and in the next breath receiving by faith forgiveness through the atoning work of Jesus Christ, fractures the spirit that unifies the mob. As one not deserving forgiveness but having received it by faith, the spirit of the age that stunts one's imagination is broken, empowering one to hear and heed the Apostle Paul's exhortation: "Be kind to one another, tenderhearted, forgiving one another, as God in Christ has forgiven

---

[51] Ibid., 113.
[52] Ibid., 125.
[53] Ibid., 113.
[54] Ibid., 121.

you."⁵⁵ Rather than forcing people into being incorporated into an unthinking judicial body that coldly judges without the possibility of forgiveness, faith brings to life a new way of living by the Spirit in Christian community and the world with transgressive others. Believing in God's forgiveness for oneself leads to the realization that with God all things are possible, including forgiveness for those who are unforgiveable.⁵⁶

The trouble wracking those possessed by cancel culture is not remedied by Butler's critical and Derrida's constructive ethical reflections, however promising. Whereas Butler rightly observes the poverty of an ethics that does not desire the life of transgressive others, and Derrida identifies the apocalyptic and life-giving nature of pure forgiveness, both efforts fail to break the bind of unthinking mass judgment. In his commentary on Kierkegaard and forgiveness, Hugh Pyper states: "Not to believe, however, gives victory to the despair which is not only the reaction to evil but its cause in the first place."⁵⁷ Belief that God forgives through the death and resurrection of Jesus Christ does more than redeem a person from despair of forgiveness, it also defeats evil, the spirit that possesses minds, lives, and relationships in *this* age. One can forgive a person who has transgressed because one has received forgiveness for their own transgression.⁵⁸ Where one does not despair of forgiveness because they have received it, offering forgiveness is not only possible but something one can genuinely offer.

## Conclusion

Arendt and Hudson's expectation that a person can simply access what is good and right via thinking despite the spirit of the age that grips a person is shown to be somewhat mistaken for both the perpetrator and judge. The perpetrator's incapacity to simply know *and* act on what is good is matched in part by judges who assumptively believe that in contrast to the perpetrator they know

---

⁵⁵Eph. 4:32. (NRSVUE)
⁵⁶Mt. 19:26.
⁵⁷Kierkegaard, *The Sickness Unto Death*, 121.
⁵⁸Eph. 4:32.

and act well. Our inquiry has revealed that acting and judging are both stations of life that are susceptible to the same spirit that grips the age. The irony is laid bare: mere thinking undermines judicious judgment and action on all sides.

A cautious approach to one's susceptibility to the spirit of the age, here cancel culture, is necessary to avoid taking part in stunted modes of acting and judging. This does not result in abandoning thinking and thinking-guided action. It takes seriously the view that thinking and acting that are not grounded first in the Christian grammar of God's desire to share the earth with us through forgiveness will likely succumb to lives and action that do not seek to share the world with innocent and transgressive others. Butler is right to highlight the need for new ethical discourse that entertains the possibility of living with others we do not choose, and Derrida's resurrection of a Christian notion of pure forgiveness is shown to be vital for realizing Butler's vision. However promising, their views do not offer a treatment for the malady besetting cancel culture, that of despair of forgiveness or one's inability to forgive. Kierkegaard rightly diagnoses that culture's *symptom* of a lack of forgiveness is not remedied by acting out the virtue of forgiveness but by realizing first that a lack of forgiveness is merely symptomatic of the more problematic *malady* of a sinful lack of faith. When we faithfully embrace God's forgiveness for our sin, we do not find ourselves in a coercive culture or mob that demands that I withhold *or* offer forgiveness. As a part of Christ's body, judging the action of others becomes a difficult task because forgiveness is a genuine possibility.

Encouraging outcomes begin to emerge from mobilizing a judicial scene that induces thinking by virtue of the genuine possibility of forgiveness. For example, regarding the Sacco incident, it was later learned that her tweet was written ironically and intended to provoke people to think critically about the very things she was charged with transgressing. Where judgment is not mandatory but rigorously discerned, the judicial process is slowed, demanding more thorough consideration of Sacco's context and thus her intent. Her innocence would no doubt have been realized and this would have been reflected in the final judgment. This example ought to chasten unthinking, coerced mob judgment on social media platforms wherein we are usually not privy to the details behind the levelling of accusations. The possibility of the offer of forgiveness breaks the stranglehold of cancel culture as it unfolds in virtual settings by mobilizing judicious agency under the weighty realization of the need to discern a just judgment.

But even in cases in which we encounter neighbors with whom we have legitimate disagreement or reservations about propriety of engagement, say within an academic, political, or media context that involves verified transgression of moral standards and/or law, the genuine possibility of forgiveness does not mandate the offering of forgiveness, but enlivens the potential for inquiry, interrogation, and dialogue which includes active listening and careful responding. Far from condoning the other's transgressive views or actions, drawing close with the possibility of forgiveness sets one free from mandatory judgment. Space is freed for thinking, writing, and speaking with transgressive others on a range of matters. For those who enjoy God's forgiveness, the impossibility of forgiveness no longer underwrites stunted ethical academic, political, and media discourse and community but undermines it, offering the conditions to engage in robust ethical dialogue and community despite its demand to encounter those with whom we might not choose to live or interact.

These ends do not exhaust the productive value of this theological assessment of cancel culture, nor do they provide the reason or means to mobilize Christian ethics at the scene of social transgression. Whatever the upshot of a Christian engagement with cancel culture, this chapter has shown that cancel culture is a stunted mode of justice-seeking that the Christian should utterly repudiate. The Christian does not callously mandate forgiveness in its place but enjoys the mobilization of a just mode of justice-seeking by holding to the genuine possibility of forgiveness having been forgiven first by God.

# Bibliography

Arendt, Hannah. *Eichmann in Jerusalem: A Report on the Banality of Evil*. New York: Penguin Books, 2006.
Arendt, Hannah. *On Violence*. New York: Harcourt, 1979.
Arendt, Hannah. *The Human Condition*. Chicago: University of Chicago Press, 1998.
Butler, Judith. "Hannah Arendt's Death Sentences." *Comparative Literature Studies* 48, no. 3 (2011): 280–95.
Butler, Judith. *Parting Ways: Jewishness and the Critique of Zionism*. New York: Columbia University Press, 2014.

Derrida, Jacques. *On Cosmopolitanism and Forgiveness*. London: Routledge, 2001.

Dershowitz, Alan. *Cancel Culture: The Latest Attack on Free Speech and Due Process*. New York: Skyhorse Publishing Company, 2020.

Ganguli, Tania, and Sopan Deb. "What to Know about Irving's Antisemitic Movie Post and the Fallout." *The New York Times*, November 21, 2022. https://www.nytimes.com/article/kyrie-irving-antisemitic.html.

Gayle, Damien "Caitlyn Jenner 'wanted limelight of female Kardashians' – Germaine Greer." *The* Guardian, October 24, 2015. https://www.theguardian.com/books/2015/oct/24/caitlyn-jenner-wanted-limelight-of-female-kardashians-germaine-greer.

Greer, Germaine. "Germaine Greer: Transgender women are 'not women.'" Interviewed by Kirsty Wark. *Newsnight*, BBC, October 24, 2015. https://www.bbc.com/news/av/uk-34625512.

Greer, Germaine. *The Whole Woman*. New York: Knopf, 1999.

Hill, Glynn A. and Ben Golliver. "Kyrie Irving Not Apologizing for Posting about Film Linked to Antisemitism." *Washington Post*, October 30, 2022. https://www.washingtonpost.com/sports/2022/10/29/kyrie-irving-accusations-antisemitism/.

Kierkegaard, Søren. *The Sickness Unto Death: A Christian Psychological Exposition for Upbuilding and Awakening*, edited and translated by Howard V. Hong and Edna H. Hong. Kierkegaard's Writings 19. Princeton: Princeton University Press, 1983.

Muir, Ellie. "A Timeline of JK Rowling's Comments About Women and Transgender Rights." *The Independent*, April 25, 2023. https://www.independent.co.uk/arts-entertainment/books/news/jk-rowling-trans-twitter-timeline-b2326256.html.

Pyper, Hugh, S. "Forgiving the Unforgivable: Kierkegaard, Derrida and the Scandal of Forgiveness." *Kierkegaardiana* 22 (2002): 7–22.

Ronson, Jon. *So You've Been Publicly Shamed*. New York: Riverhead Books, 2015.

Srinivasan, Amina. "Cancelled." *London Review of Books*, June 29, 2023. https://www.lrb.co.uk/the-paper/v45/n13/amia-srinivasan/cancelled.

Wannenwetsch, Bernd. *Political Worship*. Oxford Studies in Theological Ethics. Oxford: Oxford University Press, 2010.

White, Adam. "'I've Not Led a Very Traditional Life': Kate Hudson on Glass Onion, Cancel Culture and Being a Nepo Baby." *The Independent*, December 24, 2022. The Saturday Interview. https://www.independent.co.uk/arts-entertainment/films/features/kate-hudson-interview-glass-onion-knives-out-b2250000.html.

# 10

# Family as Mystery

# Theological Ethics beyond Polarization[1]

*Petruschka Schaafsma*

## Introduction

Finding an inner logic or grammar in Christian ethics on the subject of family is, of course, quite a challenge. Family seems to be the area par excellence where, appealing to Christian traditions, the most divergent and mutually condemning views are held. In my teaching of graduate students, I often begin explorations of the family as a moral issue with the following question: Imagine being asked to prepare an ethics workshop or discussion evening in your student club, your local church congregation, district or village, or to write a small brochure on "family" for your national church or political party. What should it be about? How would you design it? The most common responses roughly boil down to two perspectives.

---

[1] I cover many elements of this chapter in more detail in my book *Family and Christian Ethics* (Cambridge: Cambridge University Press, 2023).

They both stem from worry, but are completely opposite. There is agreement that family is an endangered good in our time, which must be defended. For the one group, however, this means the designed workshop should discuss issues like the widespread crumbling of fidelity in marriage. Fidelity is often related to a notion of givenness. This givenness is mixed up with biology, genetics, and gender. A respect for "how things are by nature" is said to be missing. The other group, on the contrary, objects that such views place too much emphasis on a so-called traditional family, which does not do justice to the existing diversity of forms. The workshop they propose should discuss how the exclusion of nonmainstream forms of family can be countered.

Both workshops imply a view of ethics that starts from worry or concern. Something threatens to go wrong. Something good needs protection from this threat. A completely opposite worry is sometimes expressed by a third, smaller group of students. They are worried about the high, idealized status of the family. Are not families places of abuse as well? Is not poverty transferred via family lines? A focus on family leads to a focus on happiness for "your own" and thus hinders coexistence as a whole. This third group might provocatively name their workshop "abolish the family."

Thus, already at first glance, three quite different basic ethical approaches to family are noticeable. Does it make sense, then, to look for a unifying grammar or inner logic? Perhaps such a grammar could be formulated in very general terms, for instance as "an ethical critique of the status quo in view of how life is meant to be." But what is the use of naming this grammar if it can lead to such different substantive outcomes on an issue like family?

What do we aim for if we are looking in this volume for the grammar of Christian ethical thought? The volume started from the idea that a focus on grammar in relation to concrete phenomena differs from an approach focused on ethical theories like deontology, utilitarianism, or virtue ethics. In my view, such a search for grammar means two things in particular. First and negatively, it is a critique of the suggestion that theories can solve our moral problems and that ethics is a matter of different theories fighting each other with rational arguments. Second and constructively, it is an attempt to let ethical reflection emerge from the issue itself, from how it is lived or alive, imagined and being discussed in academic circles and beyond. Such reflection could foster conversation between different approaches and convictions so that polarization is avoided, even if one ends up taking different positions. I think such a conversation is sorely needed in our times of pluralism and polarization. The risk, however, is the suggestion that starting from the issues or phenomena themselves rather than theories would somehow be neutral, and would avoid positions that have already been taken. Reflection is never neutral. We will try to remain aware of this risk when we start developing an ethical reflection on family that distances itself from a highly polarized field and explore how bridges can be built between seemingly different ethical views. I will find an opportunity to do so by locating the specificity of a theological-ethical perspective vis-à-vis secular ones in the way reality is approached. This will be further qualified as an approach to reality that is attuned to let itself be *interrupted by mystery*. Finally, I will outline the constructively illuminating power of that approach in relation to polemical tendencies in talking about family that we also find outside theology.

## Theological Approaches to the Family

With the aim of letting reflection emerge from the subject itself rather than from theory, let us begin by looking at how the family is discussed in theological ethics. The current state of research reflects our first impression of a division into a primarily suspicious, family-relativizing tendency and a primarily trusting and family-encouraging tendency, resulting in so-called "pro-family" views and in completely opposite defenses of family diversity.

For the suspicious approach, reference can be made to New Testament views in particular. In the gospels, family is clearly not just a good thing. Infamous are Jesus's statements in the synoptics declaring his fellow believers to be family as distinct from what we often refer to today as one's "natural" mother and brothers.[2] The story of how, even at the age of twelve, Jesus's call to be in God's house outweighing the obvious company of his parents also contributes to this image.[3] On the other hand, those and other

---

[2] Mt. 12:46-50; Mk 3:31-35; and Lk. 8:19-21.
[3] Luke 2.

passages do mention that Jesus has a family.⁴ Again, not much emphasis is placed on this family life. Only in John do we read how Jesus, of the three Marys at the cross, addresses his mother when he is about to die. He assigns her a new son—and this son a new mother. This ad hoc constructed adoption-like relationship reinforces the special position of "the disciple whom he loved."⁵ It is also reminiscent of Joseph's adoptive relationship with Jesus according to Matthew, prompted by a divine vision in a dream. In the New Testament letters, we also find family language primarily with metaphorical meaning, especially in the general address of the community as "brethren."⁶

In the Old Testament as well, metaphorical family imagery is abundant, especially to name the believer's relationship to God. Israel is often painted as either a child or a spouse, in both cases frequently and precisely denouncing Israel's failure to do what is appropriate to that relationship (e.g., Hosea). In addition, the numerous family histories in the narrative writings from Genesis to Kings offer insight into how difficult it is when kindred or brothers dwell together (Ps. 133:1): fratricide is a fact from the first pair of brothers, Cain and Abel. Human beings are instructed to procreate (Gen. 1:28) but have the greatest difficulty in managing this, it seems.

When we look at the place of family in concrete Christian practices throughout history, the ambiguity of the Scripture passages recurs. Thus, both biblical and historical examples can be used to relativize the importance of family. Some contemporary theologians emphasize how, in Christian practices, the community of believers, the church, takes precedence over that of the family. With the earliest forms of Christian community, room emerged to distance oneself from the emphatically procreative Roman culture.⁷

---

⁴Mt. 13:55; Mk 6:3; Jn 7:3, 5; Acts 1:14; and 1 Cor. 9:5.
⁵Jn 19:26-27.
⁶In the Pauline epistles *adelphoi* (brothers) is a common, unspecified address of the entire congregation, sisters included. A more extended family metaphor can only be found in 1 Timothy 5 where the congregation is called upon to treat each other as if they were family.
⁷For example: Michael Banner, *The Ethics of Everyday Life: Moral Theology, Social Anthropology, and the Imagination of the Human* (Oxford: Oxford University Press, 2014), chaps. 2 and 3; Lisa Sowle Cahill, *Sex, Gender and Christian Ethics*

It became possible to live holy lives without procreation, even in marriage. The monastic communities function as a new family for their members. Celibacy eventually became the highest state of holy living. The Reformation represents a movement in the other direction, although marriage as a "weltliches Ding" (worldly thing) as we find it with Luther shows well that family life as such is not yet simply spiritual life.[8]

This ambiguity is not consistent with the obviousness found among the designers of the first two workshops. They represent the widely held view today that from a Christian perspective family is a good to be fostered and, in our times, actively protected against fragmenting forces. This view is part of a much longer line of history. In the Roman Catholic Church of the late nineteenth and early twentieth centuries, numerous societies with the Holy Family as their patron saint emerged and the Roman Catholic Feast of the Holy Family (1893 and 1921) was created.[9] To this day, the Holy Family is held up by the Pope as an example to believers to strengthen their own family life.[10] Also on the Protestant side it is not uncommon to see family as something to fight for precisely from a Christian perspective, especially in evangelical circles.[11] In recent theological ethics, we often find the view of family as a self-evident Christian good underpinned by references to an order of creation,

---

(Cambridge: Cambridge University Press, 1996); Stanley Hauerwas, "Sex in Public: How Adventurous Christians Are Doing It," (1978), and "The Radical Hope in the Annunciation: Why Both Single and Married Christians Welcome Children" (1998), in *The Hauerwas Reader*, ed. John Berkman and Michael Cartwright (Durham: Duke University Press, 2001), 481–518.

[8]M. Darrol Bryant, "Celibacy and the Protestant Traditions: From Celibacy to the Freedom of the Christian," in *Celibacy and Religious Traditions*, ed. Carl Olson (New York: Oxford University Press, 2007), 109–32.

[9]Hildegard Erlemann, *Die Heilige Familie. Ein Tugendvorbild der Gegenreformation im Wandel der Zeit. Kult und Ideologie* (Münster: Ardey-Verlag, 1993), e.g., 15, 19, 167ff.

[10]"For the Church was born of a family, the Holy Family of Nazareth, and is made up mostly of families." Homily Pope Francis 25/06/2022, Tenth World Meeting of Families, https://sites.google.com/view/popefrancishomilies/family?pli=1 .

[11]For an analysis of the rise of "family values" in the politics of the United States, see, for example, Seth Dowland, *Family Values and the Rise of the Christian Right: Politics and Culture in Modern America* (Philadelphia: University of Pennsylvania Press, 2015).

that is, to "nature" as revealing divine purpose.[12] The permanence of the community of husband, wife, and children is seen as best living up to this purpose. Authors that oppose this "naturalist" view need not be suspicious of family as such. Their concern is rather that currently family is being claimed by conservative, heteronormative voices that disregard or even actively marginalize the good they see embodied in the variety of possible family forms.[13] In theological ethics, the suspicious or family-relativizing views are rather inspired by a strong focus on the importance of community in Christian character formation, as highlighted in virtue ethics.[14] Thus, our first attempt to let ethical reflection emerge from the issue itself rather than theory reveals a divided field. On the basis of shared sources, like the Bible and tradition, people criticize any glorification of family relations but also stand up for family, either the "traditional" or the "modern" one.

# Implicit Assumptions of What Family Might Mean

In a second attempt of beginning from the issue itself, we broaden our focus beyond academic theological discussions to find out how family is discussed more broadly, and what is at stake in these discussions. I limit myself to discussions in Western settings. It is not difficult to discern the aforementioned tripartite division there. What is striking, however, is that the fundamental question of what family might mean is rarely addressed in any of the discussions. If

---

[12]Apt examples can be found in, for example, the work of Don Browning who directed the "Religion, Culture, and Family Project" in the 1990s until his death in 2010. Representative of his referring to nature is his article "World Family Trends," in *The Cambridge Companion to Christian Ethics*, ed. Robin Gill (Cambridge: Cambridge University Press, 2006), 243–60. A different way of referring to nature, inspired by, among others, Dooyeweerd's orders of creation is found in Brent Waters, *The Family in Christian Social and Political Thought* (Oxford: Oxford University Press, 2007).
[13]See, for example, Susannah Cornwall, *Un/familiar Theology: Reconceiving Sex, Reproduction and Generativity.* (London: T&T Clark, 2017).
[14]For examples, see in particular Hauerwas and Banner mentioned above.

family is primarily relativized in favor of the broader community, the focus is on the latter not on what family might mean. If, on the contrary, family counts as something good, then it seems to be something that needs no clarification. It needs to be fought for, as it is threatened. In particular, this is true when family is defended as something natural. The good is closely related to what is called the "natural" fact that offspring requires husband and wife. This core should be protected to create good family relations. But even if, on the other hand, not nature but love or justice are propagated as the defining values for good family life, attention goes to these values and not to what is specific to family relationships compared to other relationships.[15] Yet this seems an important question to answer, precisely when trying to bring the different views into conversation. Are they actually talking about the same thing when discussing family? Let us try to discern the implicit images of family in each of the three approaches.

The suspicious tendency mainly warns against family. Apparently, it embodies certain risks. What might these be? It is not difficult to imagine that family may be suspected due to a certain closedness that may hinder connecting with people outside one's own circle. Many people regard it as perfectly natural to spend most of their leisure time with family and only a small part with others. The human tendency to favor relatives with attention but especially in material terms seems widespread, at least in many Western societies.[16] Inheritances do not go to needy people but to one's children, even if they are well off. Family can also impede connectedness with others because of the specific values or customs lived and transmitted there. A classic question in moral philosophy

---

[15]A good example of this emphasis on justice is the German church document of the Evangelische Kirche in Deutschland (EKD), *Zwischen Autonomie und Angewiesenheit. Familie als verlässliche Gemeinschaft stärken* (München, 2013), https://www.ekd.de/325.htm, which evoked quite some controversy.
[16]Plato's *Republic* is cited as the classic example of the criticism of the family because of this prejudice, which was also a controversial view in his day. See Penelope Murray, "Tragedy, Women and the Family in Plato's Republic," in *Plato and the Poets*, ed. Pierre Destrée and Fritz-Gregor Herrmann (Leiden: Brill, 2011), 177. The preference for the well-being of family members, also in a material sense, threatens the community at large, and is the reason why the class of guardian rulers are not allowed to have wives of their own or care for their own children.

is whether those customs and ideals serve the interests of the child on the one hand and society on the other. There is also closedness in the sense that the reach of state control is limited and stops at the front door of people's homes. Doesn't most abuse take place within the family circle?

Another mistrust concerns the conservative nature that family seems to have. Families are characterized by certain traditions that, among other things, take shape in role patterns. Think of the tasks assigned to men or women in particular, but also of certain professions seen as characteristic of a family. Likewise, poverty is often passed down through family. So are related aspects of education level and lifestyle-related health problems. In short, the closed nature of family combined with its prominence in parenting gives reason to distrust family and advocate its opening up in favor of the individual and the wider community and their values.

While this suspicion is widespread and far from recent, it is not necessarily the dominant or even primary attitude toward family in many Western countries. That attitude is just as much a positive one, as evidenced by the other tendencies. Family is valued precisely because of its part in bringing up children, caring in practical and financial terms during illness and old age or, more generally, because of the enduring and unconditional nature of its connection. For many people, caring for a child with a disability, a partner with a life-threatening illness, or elderly parents is self-evident. Nieces and nephews arrange financial affairs for an elderly aunt or uncle who have no children of their own. The government also counts on this, even more today than when the welfare state was in full bloom. This side of family is seen by ethicists as much as wider society as a reason to support families, including financially. For a healthy society, healthy families seem important.

However, as divorce has increased exponentially in many Western countries since the 1970s and care has mostly been outsourced to professionals, many people worry whether these aspects of family are losing momentum. It is in these circles of concerned people that we find the pleas for protection of family and of values like permanence and natural care often claimed as "traditional." This often implicitly or explicitly echoes heteronormativity. Others, while agreeing that sustained involvement with and care for each other is of great importance, do not see this as something that necessarily has to take place in the family circle, nor as something that family guarantees. Commitment and care should be undertaken consciously, with reciprocity playing an important role. Moreover, the heteronormativity associated with the appeal to traditional family values is seen as undermining the wide variety of family forms that have emerged as a result of the emancipation of divorced people entering into new relationships as well as same-sex relationships.

The characteristics of family implicit in these opposed contemporary tendencies can be well illustrated by everyday sayings. The closed nature of the family community, for example, is evident from phrases like "being one of us" or being "among us." What the "us" means you only know if you belong to it. The fact that habits, customs, and traditions belong to this closed community is echoed in phrases such as "this is how we do things in our family." And the unconditional commitment to and care for each other can be heard in expressions like "it is still family after all, isn't it" or "surely you have that to spare for your family." What is striking about these expressions is that they do not name what family exactly means, but that it means something, something you have a feeling for if you are part of that group. That implies a certain kind of responsibility and action you can hold another family member accountable for. There is normally no need to point this out to the other: the responsibilities and actions are undertaken self-evidently. And if it does need to be, the above expressions show that this need not always encourage specification but rather the statement that one is family. Family is mundane, everyone knows what it means but words are rarely given to it. It may even be quite difficult to formulate or underpin explicitly what family means, and the moral responsibilities and acting that goes with it. For families are different in this, and again, one only has a feeling for it if one belongs to it. This unnamed and perhaps unnameable meaning also seems to be characteristic of family.

Thus, these two attempts to let reflection emerge from the issue of family itself do not directly seem very fruitful. Analyzing the explicit level of very different views of family and the implicit one of what is at stake in these views reveals a diversity of meanings and evaluations of these meanings. Moreover, what family might mean turns out to be difficult to name. How then do we arrive at the level of a grammar in Christian ethics which may open the way to conversation beyond polarized oppositions?

## Ethics as Making Aware through Interruption

This disappointing conclusion seems to be arrived at a bit too fast, however. The variety of views and implicitness or even unnameability of meanings should also be addressed at a different level. They reveal something important about the nature of moral reflection. All kinds of everyday issues such as housing, work, health, or, more in the relational sphere, friendship or parenthood can be said to have unnamed moral meanings. When life takes its course, these are obvious and mundane. Only when the ordinary course is interrupted, fortunately or as a result of a crisis, we can no longer cope with the existing patterns of how we are supposed to live. We need to rethink what is right to do or find a new orientation. Ethics is about rethinking which results from an interruption of life, one's own or that of others. In the latter case, the ethical rethinking may be more artificial. It does not so much start from an actually experienced desire to find a new moral orientation, because one's life seems obvious. Thus, many people may experience family as something obvious and do not feel the need to reflect on its moral meaning. Ethics is then experienced as artificial. Suddenly, one's moral convictions are questioned by confrontation with unknown moral situations or different views of the good life.

The interruptive character of ethics is a delicate matter, however, as it implies a paradox. This interruption is necessary to create awareness of a moral issue. But this awareness seems to destroy the very heart of morality, that is, its obviousness. And this obviousness is not something that can be easily recreated.[17] One may wonder whether that is possible at all. To find moral direction, ethics usually relies on rational reflection, coherent, consistent argumentation based on shared premises. Or, referring to the central metaphor of this volume, ethics aims to create a grammar. But is that possible

---

[17] This is called the "paradox of ethics." For a recent discussion of this, see the special issue edited by Ariën Voogt and Petruschka Schaafsma, "Should Moral Commitments be Articulated?" *International Journal of Philosophy and Theology* 84, no. 5 (2023): 303–8. The Special issue is based on an article by Nicholas Adams, "Obstacles to Moral Articulation in Interreligious Engagement," *International Journal of Philosophy and Theology* 84, no. 5 (2023): 309–25.

independent of a living language? This question expresses once more the skepticism toward theorization that was the very reason to look for a grammar emerging from the moral issue itself.

In trying to answer this question and finding a way out of the paradox of ethics, I think it is important to consider the specific character of theological ethics, because here interruption-based awareness and reflection is of a specific kind. Theology brings transcendence into play. One could see the reckoning with transcendence, in an ultimate sense with God, as regarding interruption as fundamental to human life. Fundamental in the sense that human beings depend on something from outside. The immanent world, the earthly that can be observed is not the only or true reality. There is another higher or deeper dimension that fundamentally eludes our human grasp and yet is also the meaning of our existence. If God is in play, human existence is not to be understood as something that exists by itself or in isolation, nor as embedded in an order of cause and effect. It depends on something else for its existence. Taking this into account implies a "fundamental interruption" of the self-evidence of one's existence, perhaps we may say also of being full of oneself. Then, "interruption in the moment" by some event, or artificially by questioning makes ethics come into a different light. It recalls the fundamental, the deeper meaning that human beings cannot simply grasp but on which they depend.

This has consequences for what is expected of ethics. Human reflection is limited. From a Christian perspective, this limitation is particularly signified as sin, as being focused on immanence, on oneself, one's own ego.[18] To discover true meaning, to find the good, human beings must be liberated from that limitation. This is not something ethics can arrange by thoughtful analyzing of explicit moral views or implicit ones of what is at stake in these views. The path to goodness cannot be outlined by reflection. Insight into the good is a gift. In this sense, it is also transcendent: it cannot be controlled. Reality does not simply reveal its meanings. They must be sought with no guarantee that they will be found, and never in

---

[18]For a separate reflection on the central meaning of interruption for Christian perspectives on human life see Petruschka Schaafsma, "Interruption that Liberates to Love. On the Positive Potential of the 'Paradox of Ethics'," *International Journal of Philosophy and Theology* 84, no. 5 (2023): 326–32.

a clearly fixed form. This relativizes the status of ethical reflection. On the other hand, it confirms its importance as an interruption grafted onto that fundamental interruption of the liberating gift of the good. It views ethics as starting from a trust that there is a meaning, and that it can be sought, and at times found. A moral reflection rooted in transcendence, in a fundamental interruption, is not a "wallowing in the arcane."

This tension between being dependent on the gift of insight from outside and trusting that such insight is possible, and also actions that are grafted on to it, is well expressed in the figure of the incarnation. That God takes on flesh and blood in Christ, a human being, reveals that what is created matters, and in it God can be served. The way Jesus lived, giving flesh and blood to God's will among human beings, did interrupt the ordinary course of creation, its own laws. Human logic was interrupted in numerous ways: healings, miraculous feedings, picking heads of grain on the Sabbath or the message to the rich man to sell everything he owned. The disciples accepted Jesus's invitation to follow him along the path of this other life, which at the same time they could not carry out. Their limitation was that of all people who ultimately try to save their own skin. This becomes ultimately clear in the suffering Jesus endured because of how he lived. Those who serve God on earth evoke resistance; following Jesus costs them their heads. And at the same time, the Christ event makes it clear that death is not the last thing: the human being who serves God in the most ultimate sense is the resurrected, the risen one. Trust in this salvation from ruin extends beyond Christ. It liberates all those who devote themselves to it, to a life in the footsteps of Jesus. At the same time, the incarnation makes clear how much people depend for this good life on something from outside, which interrupts, appeals, liberates, and gives direction. It is here that we may trace something of a grammar, an inner logic of Christian ethics: in the inseparable intertwining of relativization and trust in a reflection grafted onto the fundamental interruption of the gift of the good.

In my view, this inner logic is first of all about an attitude toward reality. The possibility of interruption, of being addressed, of an experience of a surplus of meaning is eminently something people characterize as happening to them. But it can still mean something in ethics because we can be alert to it, or sensitive or open to it. Interruption may happen when we approach reality in an attitude of gratitude, awe, or piety. I find that approach very pithily expressed in French philosopher Gabriel Marcel's distinction between "problem" and "mystery." When we approach reality as a problem, we focus on clearly defined, fact-based issues that require resolution. That approach is often appropriate, but not always. In my words (giving my own elaboration of Marcel's distinction): problems often presuppose a difficulty that cannot itself be so clearly defined or delineated, which, moreover, is rather caused by a glimpse of the nature of life itself in its deepest sense. It is here that we return to the theme of the family. Remarkably, Marcel emphasizes the importance of such a mystery approach in relation to the theme of family. For Marcel, the difficulty of living with family in our times has precisely to do with a lack of attention to the experiences of awe and gratitude. This is due to the current dominance of more factual, historical, or technological approaches. According to Marcel, it is precisely in the family context that many people "catch a glimpse of the meaning of the sacred bond which it is man's lot to form with life."[19] But sensitivity to this "glimpse of meaning," this surplus of meaning, is not nurtured in a climate geared toward conscious, autonomous choosing in life. For Marcel, it is up to philosophy, and I would say theology, to reflect in such a way that people are nonetheless drawn into this different approach to reality as mystery.

## A Mystery Approach to Family

Let us consider what this notion of mystery at the heart of a theological ethics of interruption might concretely mean in ethical reflection on family, given the very different and polarized views with which we started. We probe this in two current academic family discussions that are related to the three basic ethical approaches to family identified above. First, in a polemic that has many variants: that between advocates of the importance of the "natural family" and those of the family as a "social construct." Authors who argue

---

[19] Gabriel Marcel, "The Mystery of the Family," in *Homo Viator: Introduction to the Metaphysic of Hope*, trans. Emma Craufurd and Paul Seaton (South Bend: Graham, 2010), 82.

for anchoring family in "nature" do so to counterbalance the idea of family as "made," "chosen," or as being the consequence of certain practices like care. The right thing to do is what fits human nature, whether it is seen as creation or not: living in sustainable connection with biological kin. On the other hand, these thinkers also sometimes indicate that "nature" in itself does not simply contain the good, but has yet to be cultivated along the yardstick of the rational or rather Christian values.[20] Yet speaking in terms of nature usually does not lead to an elucidation of what exactly it is about this cultivation that is still needed.

This appeal to nature is strongly criticized by others who argue that the idea of family as "natural" involves a Western, conceptually confused characterization. Social scientists, and social anthropologists in particular, argue that in all cultures, kinship is understood differently. The focal point of kinship is by no means always the nuclear family, nor is responsibility for raising and caring for old and young approached along "genetic" lines. On the other hand, anthropologists in particular note that in contemporary settings like the fertility clinic, where "nature" seems to have completely given way to human construction in the sense of technology, speaking in terms of nature remains in vogue. Such technology counts as "giving nature a helping hand" or "meeting the 'natural need' of having a 'child of one's own.'"[21] Apparently, this language of the natural expresses something of what family means, even though "nature" here is in fact far from it.

A mystery approach could draw attention to the ambiguities in such apparently very unambiguous, opposing positions. Those ambiguous moments could be clarified as resulting from the mystery character of what may be called the "givenness,"

---

[20] For example, Don Browning argues that the function in general of religious symbols or narratives is that of "stabilizing and deepening" natural inclinations, and "giving them a more permanent ethical form" which really means a "transformation" ("World Family Trends," 254).

[21] The characterization of the desire behind reproductive technology by this phrase stems from anthropologist Marylin Strathern, *Reproducing the Future* (Manchester: Manchester University Press, 1992), 20. For recent anthropological studies of new reproductive technologies and the new understandings of the biological or natural to which they give rise see, for example, Sarah Franklin, *Biological Relatives: IVF, Stem Cells, and the Future of Kinship* (Durham: Duke University Press, 2013).

"inevitability," and "unconditionality" of family. To approach those aspects as mystery would emphasize that they can never be taken as unambiguous references to anything factual, as is suggested in the language of "naturalness." At the same time, these aspects express widely recognizable experiences that we indicated above with the established sayings like "it's still family after all." We already explained the character of these sayings as hinting toward the difficulty of specifying what family might mean. Thus, acknowledging these experiences of givenness does not simply lead to their being directional, for example, by recommending lasting, unconditional commitment, or being faithful, or a so-called "natural form." But such commandments and the language of the "natural" can be understood as attempts to express the mystery of enduring, unconditional commitment, without being limited to the form of man-woman with own child. Following this analysis of the language of the natural as rooted in an experience of mystery, ethics could constructively search for other expressions to do justice to the experiences of givenness without reifying it into a particular form.

Another debate in which family also appears in relation to the unconditional takes place in care ethics. Care ethicists call attention to relationality and dependence as a fundamental feature of being human. They miss this view in much bioethics in which independence and autonomy are central values. They argue that it is precisely the phases of childhood and old age or the situations of (chronic) illness and disability that show that a human being never exists in isolation but can only live in dependence on others, although this takes many different forms. This criticism of basic patterns of modern thinking is often linked to a plea to recognize care as fundamental to human existence. This should also be given political expression in the recognition of informal care that is provided in family contexts, often by women and alongside other, paid work.[22] The unbalanced distribution of that care should be countered, as should the lack of appreciation for it, including in a financial sense. In these views, dependence and unconditional commitment are on the one hand seen as characteristic of the sphere of family. But, on the other hand, they are taken away from there and assigned to society as a whole.

---

[22] For example, Martha Albertson Fineman, *The Autonomy Myth: A Theory of Dependency* (New York: The New Press, 2004).

For the closed nature of the family encourages such care to remain invisible, and thus undervalued and unpaid. Thus, dependence is recognized as fundamental to being human, but family as the place where this proves preeminent is seen as a problematic sphere. As a result, dependence ultimately remains, in spite of its fundamental nature, primarily something incidental: something of the moments of care as a child, elder, sick, or disabled person.[23]

A mystery approach would suggest that this aspect of dependence should not be approached as a problem requiring a solution. What matters here is the aspect of the closed nature of family. This colors relationships and dependence. It extends beyond care or parenting. Dependent relationships in family are rooted in the aforementioned "being one of us," in being so connected to each other that individual identity cannot be thought of without the connection to the other. That connection is thus neither good nor bad, it is an aspect of being family apart from the question of how this takes concrete shape. The answer to the problematic effects of this dependence, which result from the specific closed nature of this family community, cannot then merely be that it should be opened up to the wider community, that care and upbringing should be partly outsourced to professionals or at least financially compensated. Even then, the closed nature of family remains; it is something we have to deal with. After all, it may also mean a strength. It is precisely when the specific nature of dependence in that closed community is recognized as a mystery that cannot simply be grasped that its impact, opportunities, and risks come to light.

What a mystery approach can bring to the polarized field of family discussions is a different attitude to reality that reveals the inadequacy of the existing conceptual dichotomies of "given" versus "made," and "autonomous" versus "dependent." As important as it is to think through each of those poles, if this is done polemically in relation to the other, no deepening understanding of the distinct character of family emerges, and the difficulty of that in our time.

---

[23]In her theological study on dependency, Sandra Sullivan-Dunbar makes a similar observation and critique, but ultimately she herself remains suspicious of the family as a context for living dependency in *Human Dependency and Christian Ethics* (Cambridge: Cambridge University Press, 2017), 222–7.

So far, we elaborated the possible contribution of mystery in general terms, but it can also be elaborated in more explicitly theological language. For it is not by chance that the notions of givenness and dependence have become central to the reflection above on the family as a mystery. They testify to the theological character a mystery approach might have. Regarding givenness, theology may refer to its understanding of reality as creation. Theology's rich reflections on creation may offer different language for what is otherwise called the "given" and often directly flattened to the actual or natural. Interpersonal dependence, on the other hand, also takes on a different color when human beings are understood to be in a dependent relationship with God that is essential to identity. Then, dependence is not primarily seen as something potentially conflicting with individuality, choice, or self-development. Acknowledging oneself as a child of God means being connected to others and all of creation in such a way that one can only flourish together, because the other is just as much a child. One of those places where that connection is lived at the cutting edge is family.

## How to Discuss Family?

Let us return to our opening question of how you would design a workshop or brochure on family. Could we imagine the mystery approach being part of it? This might be elaborated in the sense that one first invites people to discover their basic feelings and assumptions in relation to family and morality. If this leads to a great diversity of views and perhaps even a polemical atmosphere, a next step might be to become aware of the strong feelings and convictions associated with the issue: to become aware that what is being discussed here touches one deeply. This becoming aware would already hint at the mystery that is experienced in the family: the glimpse of life's depth that is seen here. In the attempt to put a name to this depth, one might discover that there is a lack of language for its expression. People might discover that the family's value is never covered by defining it as "biological" or rather "chosen." But because of the depth of existence at stake, people still long for and use such seemingly clear language. Discovering this impasse may help explain why many views of family are so firm and therefore prone to one-sidedness—that which makes them not recognizable to the other party. This need not be a sad observation, but a reason to look for alternatives to the impasses. This might be done in the workshop by offering a choice of pieces of art or brief literary fragments that can be associated with the mystery character of family. A conversation on why one has chosen a certain piece might entail a shift from general defining characteristics or polarizing observations about "the others," to talking about personal experiences of family, in all their variety of sadness and joy. One might discuss what characterizes these experiences in comparison to other relationships: the great, almost inescapable intensity of the appeal of the other to us.

A mystery approach may thus help to critically analyze the language we use to make sense of our lives, and seek the space to provide new language. It does so by an attentiveness to the moment of being interrupted, to something that claims you, appeals to you, makes you become aware of life's depth. This inquiry is pre-moral in the sense that it is not yet about whether this is a good thing. We must first become aware of what is at stake for us. If we undertake this awareness together, it may prevent moral polarization. We create a common starting point from which to explore how each of us, in our own way, can respond to the depths of existence. In a time of pluralism and polarization, this seems much needed.

# Bibliography

Adams, Nicholas. "Obstacles to Moral Articulation in Interreligious Engagement." *International Journal of Philosophy and Theology* 84, no. 5 (2023): 309–25. https://doi.org/10.1080/21692327.2024.2308123.

Banner, Michael. *The Ethics of Everyday Life: Moral Theology, Social Anthropology, and the Imagination of the Human.* Oxford: Oxford University Press, 2014.

Browning, Don S. "World Family Trends." In *The Cambridge Companion to Christian Ethics*, edited by Robin Gill, 243–60. Cambridge: Cambridge University Press, 2006.

Bryant, M. Darrol. "Celibacy and the Protestant Traditions: From Celibacy to the Freedom of the Christian." In *Celibacy and Religious Traditions*, edited by Carl Olson, 109–32. New York:

Oxford University Press, 2007. https://doi.org/10.1093/acprof:oso/9780195306316.003.0006.

Cahill, Lisa Sowle. *Sex, Gender and Christian Ethics*. Cambridge: Cambridge University Press, 1996.

Cornwall, Susannah. *Un/familiar Theology: Reconceiving Sex, Reproduction and Generativity*. London: T&T Clark, 2017.

Dowland, Seth. *Family Values and the Rise of the Christian Right. Politics and Culture in Modern America*. Philadelphia: University of Pennsylvania Press, 2015.

Erlemann, Hildegard. *Die Heilige Familie. Ein Tugendvorbild der Gegenreformation im Wandel der Zeit. Kult und Ideologie*. Muenster: Ardey, 1993.

Evangelische Kirche in Deutschland (EKD). *Zwischen Autonomie und Angewiesenheit. Familie als verlässliche Gemeinschaft stärken*. München, 2013. https://www.ekd.de/325.htm.

Fineman, Martha Albertson. *The Autonomy Myth: A Theory of Dependency*. New York: New Press, 2004.

Franklin, Sarah. *Biological Relatives: IVF, Stem Cells, and the Future of Kinship*. Durham: Duke University Press, 2013.

Hauerwas, Stanley. "Sex in Public: How Adventurous Christians Are Doing It (1978)." In *The Hauerwas Reader*, edited by John Berkman and Michael Cartwright, 481–504. Durham: Duke University Press, 2001.

Hauerwas, Stanley. "The Radical Hope in the Annunciation: Why Both Single and Married Christians Welcome Children (1998)." In *The Hauerwas Reader*, edited by John Berkman and Michael Cartwright, 505–18. Durham: Duke University Press, 2001.

Marcel, Gabriel. "The Mystery of the Family." In *Homo Viator: Introduction to the Metaphysic of Hope*, translated by Emma Craufurd and Paul Seaton, 62–90. South Bend: Graham, 2010.

Murray, Penelope. "Tragedy, Women and the Family in Plato's Republic." In *Plato and the Poets*, edited by Pierre Destrée and Fritz-Gregor Herrmann, 175–93. Leiden: Brill, 2011.

Pope Francis. Homily 25/06/2022, Tenth World Meeting of Families. https://sites.google.com/view/popefrancishomilies/family?pli=1.

Schaafsma, Petruschka. *Family and Christian Ethics*. Cambridge: Cambridge University Press, 2023.

Schaafsma, Petruschka. "Interruption that Liberates to Love. On the Positive Potential of the 'Paradox of Ethics.'" *International Journal of Philosophy and Theology* 84, no. 5 (2023): 326–32. https://doi.org/10.1080/21692327.2024.2302094.

Strathern, Marilyn. *Reproducing the Future*. Manchester: Manchester University Press, 1992.

Sullivan-Dunbar, Sandra. *Human Dependency and Christian Ethics*. Cambridge: Cambridge University Press, 2017.
Voogt, Ariën and Petruschka Schaafsma. "Should Moral Commitments be Articulated? An Introduction." *International Journal of Philosophy and Theology* 84, no. 5 (2023): 303–8. https://doi.org/10.1080/21692327.2024.2310028.
Waters, Brent. *The Family in Christian Social and Political Thought*. Oxford: Oxford University Press, 2007.

# 11

# The Grammar of Christian Ethics in Human Rights

## Christine Schliesser

### Introduction

Bucha. The name of this small town near Kyiv has become synonymous with gross human rights violations and Russian atrocities in the Ukraine war. Yet Bucha is only one brick in the endless wall of human right violations, sitting side by side with the Hongkong umbrella movement, Lesbos, and #MeToo, among countless others. As human rights are on everyone's lips, human rights violations are all around. Ever since the proclamation of the Universal Declaration of Human Rights (UDHR) by the United Nations General Assembly on December 10, 1948, there has been hardly a political vision whose increase in significance can be compared to the postulation of universal human rights, that is, the "idea, then, that all human beings—by virtue of their title as human beings alone, and regardless of their biological, social, and individual differences—are entitled to morally grounded rights that any legitimate legal order must recognize and guarantee."[1] While

---

[1] Hans-Richard Reuter, *Ethik der Menschrechte. Zum Streit um die Universalität einer Idee*, part 1 (Tübingen: Mohr Siebeck, 1999), vii. All translations mine if not indicated otherwise.

the relevance of human rights is hardly questioned, current debates center on their concrete interpretation and, in turn, their foundations. Situated within the tension between a universal claim of validity on the one hand and particular moralities on the other, human rights are both *dependent on* and *open for* different foundations.[2] Both aspects are fundamentally important here. "Human rights cannot truly go global unless it goes deeply local," as a report by Human Rights Watch points out.[3] The idea of universal human rights needs to find a home in every context and tradition, religious or not. Otherwise there is a danger that human rights are being perceived as something foreign, secular and/or Western.

For Christian ethics, this entails the task of deciphering its own, particular grammar in human rights. Christian ethics is called to show how it contributes to human rights, not as a foreign concept, but as a concern intrinsically related to its own core beliefs. The following four steps serve to guide this endeavor. In a first step, I will delineate the (for a long time problematic) relationship between Christian ethics and human rights. This brief historical overview will be followed by an exploration into the theological foundations of human rights. Here, I will draw in particular on Dietrich Bonhoeffer and his differentiation between the ultimate and the penultimate. A third part then employs a Christological perspective for deciphering the grammar of Christian ethics in human rights. The three traditional Christological *topoi* of incarnation, crucifixion, and resurrection are useful for this task. I will conclude with a summary of the benefits of this approach for both Christian ethics and human rights.[4]

---

[2]Michael Bünker, "Gesetz und Evangelium – die Evangelische Kirche und die Menschenrechte," in *Weltethos und Recht*, ed. Anton Pelinka (Berlin: Lit, 2011), 207–16.
[3]Jean-Paul Marthoz and Joseph Saunders, "Religion and the Human Rights Movement," *Human Rights Watch World Report 2005*, accessed August 10, 2022, https://www.hrw.org/legacy/wr2k5/religion/1.htm.
[4]In my arguments, I draw on thoughts I developed in Christine Schliesser, "Menschenrechte – Zum Beitrag theologischer Ethik im aktuellen Menschenrechtsdiskurs," *Zeitschrift für evangelische Ethik* 65 (2021): 261–72.

# Christian Ethics and Human Rights: Tales from a Troubled Relationship

Human rights are grounded in human dignity—the "root of human rights"[5]—that every human being shares simply by virtue of being a member of the human family. In European history of thought, the understanding of human dignity was influenced by Greek-Roman Stoa on the one hand and by the Christian tradition on the other.[6] For Cicero, for example, reason is the main indicator for human dignity.[7] From the perspective of Christian ethics, it is the biblical account of creation (Gen. 1:26f.), emphasizing that all human beings are created in the image of God, which is made fruitful for the conviction of a dignity common to all human beings. The creation-theological foundation of human dignity is often linked to the Pauline concept of human beings as children of God (Gal. 3:26-28). This decisive commonality that binds together all members of the human race makes individual differences between people secondary. In the history of theology, the idea of human dignity based on the image of God has been expressed to varying degrees. It found special acceptance in Italian humanism, such as in the work of Pico della Mirandola, as well as in the Spanish scholasticism of Francisco de Vitoria and Francisco Suárez.

The Reformation then proved to be a further milestone for the Christian understanding of human dignity. In the Lutheran doctrine of justification, human beings are not defined by their achievements, but solely by their relationship to God. Accordingly, human dignity is understood solely in terms of God's justifying grace (*sola gratia*) which is beyond any human achievement. This understanding of justification is intrinsically connected with the freedom of conscience and religious belief according to Wolfgang Huber: in "this principal sense . . . freedom of faith and with it freedom of religious belief

---

[5]Jürgen Moltmann, *Menschenwürde, Recht und Freiheit* (Stuttgart: Kreuz-Verlag, 1971).
[6]For a more detailed overview of the history of thought and theology cf. Wolfgang Huber, "Art. Menschenrechte/Menschenwürde," in *Theologische Realenzyklopädie*, vol 22, ed. Gerhard Müller (Berlin: De Gruyter, 1992), 577–602.
[7]Marcus Cicero, *De officiis* I 30, ed. Heinz Gunermann (Hamberg: Buchner, 1996).

form the core of human rights for an understanding trained on the Reformation."[8]

In spite of these strong resources within Christian theology, both the church and theology have long kept their distance from the ideas of human dignity and human rights. Reasons for this distance included both theological and social-political motives.[9] In terms of theology, three factors were particularly problematic. For one, the doctrine of original sin proved to be harmful for the development of an independent theological conception of human dignity and human rights. The doctrine of original sin, which held that human beings were marred by the power of evil from birth onward, was combined with the assumption that human beings had thereby forfeited the dignity bestowed upon them by God. Furthermore, the distinction between Christians and non-Christians or heretics had severe consequences. From this perspective, human dignity was understood as the privilege of Christians only, which then served to justify the horrors of the witch hunts, the inquisition, or the pogroms against the Jews. And, third, Christian anthropology was influenced by a hierarchical conception of society and church. Rather than the unifying meaning of dignity (*dignitas*), which belongs equally to all human beings, it was the understanding of dignity as *honor* that was dominating. Dignity as *honor*, however, implied that people were entitled to dignity in varying degrees which was determined by birth or by achievement. The close connection between human dignity and the image of God, as we see in Mirandola or Vitoria, constituted the exception to the rule. In addition to these inner theological obstacles against a constructive relationship with the ideas of human dignity and human rights, other problems arose from social and political developments. The connection of human rights with the French Revolution, for instance, and its explicitly anti-church agenda and its terror regime served to discredit these concepts for a long time to come.

Eventually, it was the experiences of the horrors of two world wars that helped to form the conviction also in the context of theology and the church that at times national law does not suffice

---

[8] Huber, "Menschenrechte/Menschenwürde," 579.
[9] Cf. Wolfgang Huber and Eduard Tödt Heinz, *Menschenrechte. Perspektiven einer menschlichen Welt* (Stuttgart: Kreuz, 1977).

and that an ultimate appellate body is required beyond regional and national civil rights. In the postwar period, it was particularly the ecumenical movement that became formative for the theological discussion on human rights, not least by means of its ongoing ecumenical conciliar process on "Justice, Peace and Integrity of Creation."
Despite the fact that the historical development of human rights is connected to a specific context that includes the influences of Greek and Roman philosophy, Christianity, the Renaissance, and Enlightenment, it would be shortsighted to conclude that human rights are only understandable or applicable in this specific context.

> The identification of such historical and philosophical references must . . . not lead to the short-circuit conclusion that the idea of human rights is, as it were, grounded in the cultural-genetic potential of the occidental tradition from the very beginning and is therefore substantially and exclusively bound to the horizon of Western culture.[10]

Even these cursory glimpses into the historical development of the idea of universal human rights have revealed that the relationship between Christian ethics and human rights was not love at first sight. Rather, the development of human rights took place over long periods of time without or even against theology and the church. From this it follows that any contribution from Christian ethics to the discussion of human rights needs to take place from a perspective of humility and self-critical awareness of one's own troubled past.

---

[10]Heiner Bielefeldt, "'Westliche' vs. 'islamische' Menschenrechte? Zur Kritik an kulturalistischen Vereinnahmungen der Menschenrechtsidee," in *Facetten islamischer Welten. Geschlechterordnungen, Frauen- und Menschenrechte in der Diskussion*, ed. Rumpf Mechthild, Gerhard Ute, and Mechtild M. Jansen (Bielefeld: transcript Verlag, 2003), 123–42.

## On What Grounds? Human Rights and the Quest for Foundation

It must be said up front that there is not one single foundation of human rights that is plausible for each and everyone. This does not mean, however, that we need to discard any attempt to find a foundation of human rights, as Richard Rorty prominently called for.[11] Nor is it convincing to renounce the quest for a foundation in favor of a pragmatic consensus as some constructivist positions proclaim.[12] The argumentative aporias are too obvious when contingent social attributions are to be criteriologically grasped with the help of norms that themselves stem from contingent social attributions. Much more convincing is Friedrich Lohmann's proposal to accept the necessity of "referring back to what is non-arbitrarily prior to any social convention" rather "than throwing the baby out with the bathwater (de-) constructivistically."[13] Against any skepticism regarding foundations, I contend: the acceptance of human rights by each and every one of us as global citizens depends fundamentally on our respective particular perspectives along with their different foundations. In other words: polyphony of foundations rather than foundational abstinence.

Yet there are different perspectives also within Christian ethics regarding the question of foundations. Some argue strictly against a theological foundation of human rights in order to "keep the secular, worldly character of human rights" (Martin Honecker).[14] Others seek to uncover the "Christian roots" (Konrad Hilpert) of

---

[11]Richard Rorty, *Contingency, Irony, and Solidarity* (Cambridge: Cambridge University Press, 1989).

[12]Thorsten Bonacker and André Brodocz, "Im Namen der Menschenrechte. Zur symbolischen Integration der internationalen Gemeinschaft durch Normen," *Zeitschrift für Internationale Beziehungen* 8 (2001): 179–208.

[13]Friedrich Lohmann, "Gerechter Frieden und Menschenrechte. Entwurf einer Theologie der Menschenrechte in friedensethischer Absicht," in *Eine Theologie der Menschenrechte. Frieden und Recht*, vol 2, ed. Sarah Jäger and Friedrich Lohmann (Wiesbaden: Springer 2019), 47–120.

[14]Martin Honecker, "Menschenrechte/Menschenwürde (ethisch)," in *Evangelisches Soziallexikon*, 9th edn., ed. Jörg Hübner et al. (Stuttgart: Kohlhammer, 2016), 1009.

human rights.¹⁵ In the following, I will take a middle route. Against Honecker I argue that the historical genesis of human rights without or even against theology and church does not inevitably necessitate the rejection of a theological foundation of human rights. Rather, we need to subject the history of theology itself to a critical scrutiny in terms of problematic hermeneutics (as was done, for example, with regard to theological justifications of slavery or Apartheid). Hilpert's position, on the other hand, seems prone to the danger of a particularistic usurpation of human rights.

Christian ethics contains potent resources for a particular foundation of human rights that need to be uncovered and embraced. Recently, Friedrich Lohmann explored these resources in his theology of human rights. He points to the following four prerequisites that my contribution builds on as well.¹⁶ First, human rights as we encounter them in society and politics are not static. Rather, perceptions of human rights mirror images of human beings. A specifically Christian understanding of human rights is therefore always connected to a specific anthropology. Second, a theological contribution to human rights does not come with a claim to exclusivity. The claim made here is equality, not special treatment, as one voice within the choir of other religious and nonreligious voices. Third, even though the primary target audience of a Christian perspective on human rights is other Christians, the target audience also goes beyond a mere inner-Christian conversation. By means of translation and bilinguality,¹⁷ the particular Christian perspective

---

¹⁵Konrad Hilpert, *Menschenrechte und Theologie. Forschungsbeiträge zur ethischen Dimension der Menschenrechte*, vol 1. (Freiburg: Herder, 2001), 255.
¹⁶Lohmann, "Menschenrechte," 65ff.
¹⁷While the metaphor of translation, prominently endorsed by Jürgen Habermas, aims to translate religious concepts into secular understandable language games, the concept of bilinguality goes further. For translation comes with the danger of becoming invisible as a theologian in public discourse as one's theological identity recedes behind the translated "product." Bilinguality in turn calls for speaking in two or more "languages" simultaneously. As a theologian, this means speaking one's own theological language while at the same time seeking to make this "inner circle language" understandable to others. Public theology is a theological paradigm that explicitly seeks to foster the competencies of religious literacy and bilinguality. Cf. Christine Schliesser, "Theologie im öffentlichen Ethikdiskurs. Studien zur Rolle der Theologie in den nationalen Ethikgremien Deutschlands und der Schweiz, Leipzig" (Zurich: University of Zurich, 2019), 348–54, https://doi.org/10.5167/uzh-168983.

becomes comprehensible to non-Christian audiences as well. And, fourth, to endorse a specific Christian perspective on human rights does not mean that there are no overlaps with other approaches. At the same time, however, Christian theology orients itself toward the witness of Jesus Christ, which accounts for the specificity of this approach and which will be explored below in terms of the *trias* incarnation, crucifixion, and resurrection.

Dietrich Bonhoeffer developed "the first theological-ethical doctrine of basic human rights"[18] in German-speaking Protestant theology. His approach to the topic of human rights is somewhat unusual in the sense that he does not start with the individual or an individualistically understood right to freedom. He rather begins by making a fundamental distinction. And instead of employing the problematic spatial distinctions of the so-called "Two-Realms Doctrine" in the Lutheran tradition, Bonhoeffer introduces dimensions of time in order to relate the worldly and the spiritual, namely, the ultimate and the penultimate. The premise from which Bonhoeffer works is this: "The origin and essence of all Christian life are consummated in the one event that the Reformation has called the justification of the sinner by grace alone."[19] This is what he calls the "ultimate." It is ultimate in two ways: qualitative and temporal: The *qualitative* aspect refers to the fact that there is no word of God that goes beyond God's grace; it is the ultimate reality. Its *temporal* dimension means that there is always something penultimate preceding the ultimate, such as "some action, suffering, movement."[20]

In trying to establish their mutual relationship, Bonhoeffer first points to two misapprehensions: The *radical solution* emphasizes the ultimate to the utter neglect of the penultimate, while in the *compromise solution* the penultimate becomes something in its

---

[18]Dietrich Bonhoeffer, *Ethics, Dietrich Bonhoeffer Works 6*, ed. Clifford Green, trans. Reinhard Krauss, Charles C. West, and Douglas W. Stott (Minneapolis: Fortress Press, 2009), 218.
[19]Ibid., 146.
[20]Ibid., 150.

own right. Bonhoeffer gives a succinct characterization of both radicalism and compromise:

Radicalism hates time. Compromise hates eternity. Radicalism hates patience. Compromise hates decision. Radicalism hates wisdom. Compromise hates simplicity. Radicalism hates measure. Compromise hates the immeasurable. Radicalism hates the real. Compromise hates the word.[21]

To Bonhoeffer, the only solution which avoids both pitfalls is Jesus Christ. We encounter here a theme that runs through Bonhoeffer's theology, his Christocentricity. "In Jesus Christ God's reality and human reality take the place of radicalism and compromise."[22] The penultimate depends on the ultimate for its existence; there is no penultimate as such.

As Jürgen Moltmann puts it: "It is the ultimate that gives meaning to the penultimate."[23] Yet to surmise from this a disregard for the penultimate on Bonhoeffer's part would be misconceived. Quite the contrary is the case. For the sake of the ultimate the penultimate is endowed with a rather high standing: For if the penultimate is wounded, so is the ultimate: "Arbitrary destruction of the penultimate seriously harms the ultimate."[24] And: "When, for example, a human life is deprived of the conditions that are part of being human, the justification of such a life by grace and faith is at least seriously hindered, if not made impossible."[25] The penultimate must be understood, therefore, as a preparing of the way ("Wegbereitung") for the word.[26]

---

[21] Ibid., 156.
[22] Ibid., 155.
[23] Jürgen Moltmann, "Das Letzte gibt dem Vorletzten seinen Sinn," in *Ethik der Hoffnung* (Gütersloh: Gütersloher Verlagshaus, 2010), 20.
[24] Bonhoeffer, *Ethics*, 160.
[25] Ibid.
[26] In a similar vein, Karl Barth writes that the state "could administer justice and protect the law. . . . In so doing, voluntarily or involuntarily, very indirectly yet none the less certainly, it would be granting the gospel of justification free and assured course." Karl Barth, "Church and State," in *Community, State, and Church*, ed. W. Herberg, trans. R. Smith (Gloucester: Peter Smith, 1968), 101–48; Bonhoeffer, understanding "justification" as ultimate and "justice" as penultimate, agreed with Barth. Cf. the discussion by Andreas Pangritz on Bonhoeffer and Barth's essay in:

Bonhoeffer makes it clear that hunger, poverty, slavery, injustice, and so on are concrete obstacles to the ultimate, while bringing "bread to the hungry is preparing the way for the coming of grace."[27] This, one could say, contains *in nuce* the foundation of Bonhoeffer's social ethics. Preparing the way is not only understood as an inner activity, but takes place as a clearly visible and concrete action.[28] "The hungry person needs bread, the homeless person needs shelter, the one deprived of rights needs justice, the lonely person needs community, the undisciplined one needs order, and the slave needs freedom."[29] Against this background, human rights can be understood as intrinsic to the Christian faith rather than secondary or foreign. In other words: engagement in human rights is participation in the kingdom of God.

## Deciphering the Christian Grammar in Human Rights: A Christological Perspective

The innate relationship between the ultimate and the penultimate becomes even more explicit as Bonhoeffer seeks to apply the traditional Christological *topoi* of incarnation, crucifixion, and resurrection to Christian existence. "Christian life means being human [Menschsein] in the power of Christ's becoming human, being judged and pardoned in the power of the cross, living a new life in the power of the resurrection. No one of these is without the others."[30] The following deliberations spell out what this Christological perspective means for human rights.

---

Andreas Pangritz, *Karl Barth in the Theology of Dietrich Bonhoeffer: A Clarification Whose Time Has Come* (Grand Rapids: Eerdmans, 1999), 63ff.
[27] Bonhoeffer, *Ethics*, 163.
[28] Bonhoeffer bases his ideas on a socio-ethical interpretation of biblical scripture speaking of the coming of the Lord: When it says in Isaiah 40:4 that "Every valley shall be lifted up," Bonhoeffer understands the valley to mean the "depth of human misery . . . of human bondage, of human poverty" (Bonhoeffer, *Ethics*, 161).
[29] Bonhoeffer, *Ethics*, 163.
[30] Ibid., 159.

With the *incarnation*, theology has at its disposal an immensely powerful image for the discourse on human rights. God incarnate refers us first of all to the bodily dimension of human rights. Human rights necessitate embodiment. As human beings, we are not "brains on a stick," but bodies. The UDHR draws attention to precisely this fact by means of the inconspicuous little word "born" in Article 1. With philosopher Anne Reichold, we can link our reflection on the normative relevance of the body to its vulnerability: "That the idea of a person worthy of ethical protection is intelligible at all rests on the premise that we understand ourselves as vulnerable beings."[31] From a theological perspective, then, the incarnation as the ultimate expression of vulnerability points at the same time to the power and the normative claim that arise from this vulnerability. It raises awareness to the blind spots within human rights discourse, for example, when it is still narrowly focused on civil and political human rights in the Western context. With the bodily dimension of human rights, the so-called ESC rights (economic, social, and cultural rights) increasingly come into view. Moreover, the incarnation is linked to the idea of the sacredness of the person. A God who becomes human? What a statement of the dignity and worth of every human being! Beyond the internal theological discourse, this thought can be explicated, for example, in the sense of a genealogical progression, as Hans Joas has exemplarily shown.[32]

The *crucifixion* then first and foremost points to the powerlessness of God. In the Son of God, tortured to death, God's compassion for the suffering of this world becomes apparent. It is at the cross where the "biblical option for the weak"[33] is shown in an unsurpassable way. In the victims of human rights violations, we also encounter the Man of Sorrows today. "Vietnam is Golgotha," claimed Dorothee Sölle, as she voiced her protest against the Vietnam War. From

---

[31]Anne Reichold, "Ethik und die vergessene Leiblichkeit. Zum Personbegriff in der gegenwärtigen Philosophie," in *Körper-Kulte. Wahrnehmungen von Leiblichkeit in Theologie, Religions- und Kulturwissenschaften*, ed. Christina Aus der Au and David Plüss (Zürich: TVZ, 2007), 113.
[32]Hans Joas, *Die Sakralität der Person. Eine neue Genealogie der Menschenrechte* (Berlin: Suhrkamp, 2011).
[33]Heinrich Bedford-Strohm, "Menschenrechte und Menschenwürde in der Perspektive Öffentlicher Theologie," *International Journal of Orthodox Theology* 2, no. 3 (2011): 14.

God's radical desire for the weak arises human solidarity with the disenfranchised.

The judicial murder that was committed two millennia ago further draws attention not only to the limits of any legal system, but at the same time to the ways in which power functions. Against the unlimited belief in the power of even liberal law, Ulrike Auga points to the "paradox of law" which becomes apparent in the fact that the marginalized, that is, those whose rights are being violated, usually have no access to legal discourse. In this way, law serves the power of the powerful. Human rights discourse, theological or otherwise, must also be critically and self-critically scrutinized for such implicit exclusionary mechanisms. This is especially true when their protective function is sidelined and they are misused as an instrument of empowerment.

> In Western postmodern societies, the phrase "I have a right to X" is used interchangeably with the expressions "I desire or want X" or "X should be given to me". This linguistic inflation weakens the association of human right claims with significant human goods and undermines their position as central principles of political and legal organisation.[34]

Finally, the crucifixion points our attention to human failure and shortcomings—in theological terminology: sin. Failure and injury are taken seriously here, yet at the same time constructive ways of overcoming them are being opened up. Forgiveness and reconciliation come into view as powerful resources that enable a new beginning for victims and perpetrators alike. Contexts such as post-genocide Rwanda illustrate the importance of reconciliation processes following experiences of massive human rights violations that reach far beyond the religious sphere. This already echoes the motif of the *resurrection*.

The Christian conviction that violence, injustice, and death do not have the last word reflects a radical hope. Against despair and cynicism, the Christian perspective of hope opens a broad horizon that embraces and at the same time transcends one's own

---

[34]Costas Douzinas, *Human Rights and Empire: The Political Philosophy of Cosmopolitanism* (Abingdon: Routledge, 2007), 12.

individual life. This connects not only with consolation in the face of unspeakable suffering, but also with the drive to stand up against injustice. Against this background, human rights can be seen as criteria for concrete action on state, institution, and individual levels. By providing orientation toward the good of the neighbor, human rights thus become a guide to a better, more just world.

And yet another aspect is connected with the resurrection, namely the insight into the *extra nos* of grace and thus of the unavailability of faith. Knowing that one's faith is never one's own doing leads to an openness to other religious and nonreligious traditions. Human rights both as discourse and as engagement thus present themselves as fundamentally cooperative affairs that involve and connect people with different roots and backgrounds. In view of current global challenges, cooperation with Islam is particularly important, not least in order to counter prejudices and misunderstandings that portray human rights as a purely Western affair.

A Christological perspective on human rights thus brings together the *incarnational* reference to human embodiment and vulnerability as essential points of reference for human rights, the compassion for the suffering, and advocacy for their rights as pointed to by the *cross* as well as a perspective of hope radiated by the *resurrection* that is also reflected in the joint engagement for human rights across different traditions. What then are the benefits of this approach for both Christian ethics and human rights? There are (at least) four dimensions along which the added value of this approach can be explicated.

# Conclusion: Benefits (and Some Limitations) of Deciphering the Christian Grammar in Human Rights

## Benefits for Human Rights

It became clear that human rights are not only open for different foundations but are also in need of them. Human rights depend on different justifications in order to anchor them firmly both in our collective consciousness as world citizens and within our respective particular contexts. It is therefore an urgent task of the various traditions and religions to work out their own points of contact with human rights. For only by developing local roots will the idea of universal human rights be protected from erosion. In this vein, Christian ethics can contribute—side by side with other religious as well as nonreligious approaches—to strengthen and nurture the foundation of human rights.

## Benefits for One's Christian Self-Understanding

While in Europe the shadows of the French Revolution are still long, in the African context, for example, the perceived link between human rights and secularism can be problematic. Human rights are often seen as something Western and are placed in the vicinity of colonialism, exploitation, rampant individualism, and the destruction of traditional values. Viewed from this perspective, human rights appear as something foreign, as an imported discourse that is to be met with mistrust, if not rejection. It is evident that this point of view makes a constructive incorporation of human rights into indigenous theology and church more difficult. Against this background, it is particularly important to identify human rights as something inherent to the Christian faith and to emphasize their common concerns. A theological grounding of human rights is therefore paramount in order to identify with them as a genuine Christian concern.

## Benefits for the Diagnosis of Human Rights Violations

Christian theology's comprehensive understanding of human fallibility—theologically conceived as sin—as act and being as well as an individual and supra-individual phenomenon makes Christian ethics particularly sensitive to human rights violations not only at the individual but also at the structural and institutional levels. In this way, entire social systems can also be viewed as unjust. This dimension becomes apparent when former US president Barack Obama describes slavery as "America's original sin," the problematic effects of which are still visible today in this country's social and political structures.

## Limitations of a Christian Espousal of Human Rights

Dietrich Bonhoeffer is adamant in emphasizing that there are times and places when any conceptuality and language can be subverted. Speaking of the "huge masquerade of evil"[35] he shows how all ethical concepts can be thrown into confusion, including reason, conscience, duty, freedom, and virtuousness. Human rights are no exception when it comes to the danger of being perverted. So while Christian ethics can contribute to strengthening and nurturing the foundations of human rights, history shows that there have also been times when the exact opposite has been the case. Christian support and justification of slavery or the theological legitimation of apartheid well into the second half of the twentieth century are distressing examples of the subversion and perversion of Christian conceptuality and language. Here, the limitations of a Christian espousal of human rights come clearly into focus. In order to not be reduced to functioning as a justification mechanism for political expediency, Bonhoeffer reminds his fellow Christians to remain sober and vigilant. And he points, as was shown above, to the Christological triad of incarnation, crucifixion, and resurrection to be taking shape in Christian life.[36] These dimensions both empower and limit each other, and in both their mutual empowerment and limitation, they can serve as guidelines for a life that is genuinely human and for rights that truly serve humanity. "Christian life means being human [Menschsein] in the power of Christ's becoming human, being judged and pardoned in the power of the cross, living a new life in the power of the resurrection. No one of these is without the others."[37]

---

[35]Dietrich Bonhoeffer, *Letters and Papers from Prison, Dietrich Bonhoeffer Works* 8, ed. John W. de Gruchy, trans. Isabel Best, Lisa E. Dahill, Reinhard Krauss, and Nancy Lukens (Minneapolis: Fortress Press 2010), 38.
[36]Bonhoeffer, *Ethics*, 159.
[37]Ibid.

# Bibliography

Barth, Karl. "Church and State." In *Community, State, and Church*, edited by W. Herberg, translated, R. Smith, 101–48. Gloucester: Peter Smith, 1968.

Bedford-Strohm, Heinrich. "Menschenrechte und Menschenwürde in der Perspektive Öffentlicher Theologie." *International Journal of Orthodox Theology* 2, no. 3 (2011): 5–20.

Bielefeldt, Heiner. ""Westliche" vs. "islamische" Menschenrechte? Zur Kritik an kulturalistischen Vereinnahmungen der Menschenrechtsidee." In *Facetten islamischer Welten. Geschlechterordnungen, Frauen- und Menschenrechte in der Diskussion*, edited by Rumpf Mechthild, Gerhard Ute, and Mechtild M. Jansen, 123–42. Bielefeld: transcript Verlag, 2003.

Bonacker, Thorsten and André Brodocz. "Im Namen der Menschenrechte. Zur symbolischen Integration der internationalen Gemeinschaft durch Normen." *Zeitschrift für Internationale Beziehungen* 8 (2001): 179–208.

Bonhoeffer, Dietrich. *Ethics, Dietrich Bonhoeffer Works 6*, edited by Clifford Green and translated by Reinhard Krauss, Charles West, and Douglas W. Stott. Minneapolis: Fortress Press, 2006.

Bonhoeffer, Dietrich. *Letters and Papers from Prison, Dietrich Bonhoeffer Works 8*, edited by John W. de Gruchy, trans. Isabel Best, Lisa E. Dahill, Reinhard Krauss, and Nancy Lukens. Minneapolis: Fortress Press, 2010.

Bünker, Michael. "Gesetz und Evangelium – die Evangelische Kirche und die Menschenrechte." In *Weltethos und Recht*, edited by Anton Pelinka, 207–16. Berlin: Lit, 2011.

Cicero, Marcus. *De officiis* I 30, edited by Heinz Gunermann. Hamberg: Buchner, 1996.

Douzinas, Costas. *Human Rights and Empire: The Political Philosophy of Cosmopolitanism*. Abingdon: Routledge, 2007.

Hilpert, Konrad. *Menschenrechte und Theologie. Forschungsbeiträge zur ethischen Dimension der Menschenrechte*, vol 1. Freiburg: Herder, 2001.

Honecker, Martin. "Menschenrechte/Menschenwürde (ethisch)." In *Evangelisches Soziallexikon*, 9th ed., edited by Jörg Hübner et al., 1001–13. Stuttgart: Kohlhammer, 2016.

Huber, Wolfgang. "Art. Menschenrechte/Menschenwürde." In volume 22 of *Theologische Realenzyklopädie*, edited by Gerhard Müller, 577–602. Berlin: De Gruyter, 1992.

Huber, Wolfgang and Heinz-Eduard Tödt. *Menschenrechte. Perspektiven einer menschlichen Welt*. Stuttgart: Kreuz, 1977.

Joas, Hans. *Die Sakralität der Person. Eine neue Genealogie der Menschenrechte.* Berlin: Suhrkamp, 2011.
Lohmann, Friedrich. "Gerechter Frieden und Menschenrechte. Entwurf einer Theologie der Menschenrechte in friedensethischer Absicht." In *Eine Theologie der Menschenrechte. Frieden und Recht,* volume 2, edited by Sarah Jäger and Friedrich Lohmann, 47–120. Wiesbaden: Springer, 2019.
Marthoz, Jean-Paul and Joseph Saunders. "Religion and the Human Rights Movement." *Human Rights Watch World Report,* 2005. Accessed August 10, 2022. https://www.hrw.org/legacy/wr2k5/religion/1.htm.
Moltmann, Jürgen. *Ethik der Hoffnung.* Gütersloh: Gütersloher Verlagshaus, 2010.
Moltmann, Jürgen. *Menschenwürde, Recht und Freiheit.* Stuttgart: Kreuz-Verlag, 1971.
Pangritz, A. *Karl Barth in the Theology of Dietrich Bonhoeffer: A Clarification Whose Time Has Come.* Grand Rapids: Eerdmans, 1999.
Reichold, Anne. "Ethik und die vergessene Leiblichkeit. Zum Personbegriff in der gegenwärtigen Philosophie." In *Körper-Kulte. Wahrnehmungen von Leiblichkeit in Theologie, Religions- und Kulturwissenschaften,* edited by Christina Aus der Au and David Plüss, 95–116. Zürich: TVZ, 2007.
Reuter, Hans-Richard. *Ethik der Menschrechte. Zum Streit um die Universalität einer Idee,* Part 1. Tübingen: Mohr Siebeck, 1999.
Rorty, Richard. *Contingency, Irony, and Solidarity.* Cambridge: Cambridge University Press, 1989.
Schliesser, Christine. "Menschenrechte – Zum Beitrag theologischer Ethik im aktuellen Menschenrechtsdiskurs." *Zeitschrift für evangelische Ethik* 65 (2021): 261–72.
Schliesser, Christine. "Theologie im öffentlichen Ethikdiskurs. Studien zur Rolle der Theologie in den nationalen Ethikgremien Deutschlands und der Schweiz, Leipzig." 348–54. Zurich: University of Zurich, 2019. https://doi.org/10.5167/uzh-168983.

# 12

# Preserved in God's History

# On the Ethics of Dying with Some Regard to the Discussion about Assisted Suicide

## *Hans G. Ulrich*

### A Challenge or Place for Reflection

All creatures die, but human beings die in a very special way. We need to discuss this today because we are faced with questions about whether (or how) we should shape, determine, and design our own deaths. This inquiry sits alongside other questions we constantly ask about how humanity should be shaped: what is human labor, how should we produce offspring, how ought we to die, and even end the lives of others. Every element of the form of life we call "human" can be questioned.

This is what is special about human life and death. Each element of our existence can be questioned, and is seemingly totally undetermined and so able to be guided in many different directions under the control of impulses that come from many different directions. The question of human dying has become acute today due to the heightened control over life that we have gained through medical knowledge and technique. But it also presses us today because something has changed in our culture's understanding of humanity that is very difficult to grasp. What seems easy to grasp are the growing problems and uncertainties that arise from the technological mediation of death. People do not necessarily die when bodily exhaustion or illness would seem to naturally dictate. Life can now be extended or shortened according to decisions made by medical professionals that have a range of aims, such as to keep a body alive longer in order to save its working organs for transplantation into someone else. Alternatively, many today actively work to prolong life, even seeking a total liberation from dying. In the meantime there are increasingly sophisticated techniques and tools available to ease the dying process as it occurs. Whatever the impact of technology on the human experience of death, dying is part of human life, which is always also "vita passiva"—one of the dimensions of human life that is passively experienced and suffered.

To speak about what human beings do not choose but suffer replaces a key emphasis of contemporary discussion that persistently emphasizes the question of action. Beginning with the passive aspects of human existence immediately changes the *place* where we think about dying. Where in the general public debate can we ask about the passive aspects of dying without provoking suspicion about our agenda? The contemporary discussion seems settled. The roles played by discussions of medical ethical and legal considerations shape our understanding of medical care and practice. But these settled decisions about what counts as a reasonable discussion about dying are brought into question by approaching these questions from the totally different angle of the passive reality of human life. It is vital that we find a place where dying with all its meaning and reality to which it belongs comes into view. Dying happens to us, it comes on us, and until this passive reality of dying is brought into view and discussed, we have not truly begun to talk about it. Where is the place we can talk about what human dying really means and probe how is it constitutive of our essential being? And where can we talk about the implications of being people who die not only as individuals, but also as self-aware humans who do not just "switch off" and cease functioning? These questions press beyond narrow ethical questions about good and bad ways to die.

In Ps. 90:12 the psalmist prays: "teach us to count our days that we may gain a wise heart." This plea is found in a psalm that presents the whole history of human death and dying and therefore its meaning and purpose as the faithful Israelites experienced it. This prayer furthermore introduces us to their worship in its real liturgy, which means that it does not stand on its own but is part of a tradition of faith, embedded in the whole context of praying and listening. The worshipper is presented therefore with the context of worship in which we humans appear as we are and allowed to be within the whole context of the reality and history of which we are a part. Definitions of human dying and what it means are revealed to be not beholden to finitude or mortality, nor any philosophical account of the phenomenon of human existence in its orientation toward death. Death here gains an aspect of being a boundary to be crossed or as a gate to be passed through in holding to a promise or question that looks beyond death. When we look across the boundary of death, it appears in a new way. Where a person does not possess this horizon of "beyond death," their death becomes something they must make, somehow expressing everything that is important to them, and so taking its meaning from whatever they can grasp of themselves. Such a death is lonesome which can be called placeless when compared to the prayer of the psalmist whose death has a place with God and among the saints. Those who pray with the psalmist are not thrown back on themselves, but are preserved in history, in which human death exclusively has a meaning that is explicitly assigned to it and linked to our destiny. It is assigned by God who has chosen us as partners, who wants to live together with us in his time, in his eternity. According to the biblical message, God has put an end to the death that entered the world when human beings turned away from God's will and which continues to rule in the world outside of paradise. God has put an end to this curse-death by raising Jesus Christ and promising that he wants to live with us as new people for eternity.

## "Vita Passiva" and What Happens from God

This perception of human existence within God's history is overlaid with questions and thoughts by which we seek to orient ourselves. For example, what is a good process of dying that is bearable?

In many ethical problems the question arises: how does human thinking, speech, and acting remain distinct from what humans experience and suffer? And how can both be present at the same time: a "vita activa" and an associated "vita passiva."[1] This distinction is important to delineate the aspects of a situation that can be affected by human action and what remains, or should remain, unaffected by it. This distinction, in any case, is crucial to keep in mind when we question the limits of human intervention in the life and death of another human being. It must also take into account the given (and shifting) limits of human action in a given time and place, prompting reflection on the capabilities of our action and what they entail for a justified meaningful practice. We should not, for instance, attempt open heart surgery if we do not have the ability to properly anesthetize a patient. The problem of distinguishing between the "vita passiva" and the "vita activa" should not only shape our intervention into the lives of others, but also our own understanding of, and shaping of our own lives. The act of self-shaping is what we typically call self-determination. It is not always easy for an individual to know where the appropriate limits of self-determination should be. Discussions of "do not resuscitate" orders in hospital are just one example of how we may choose (actively) to not have someone act to revive our heart once it has stopped and so actively choosing to accede to the passive aspect of our failing body. Yet such decisions are difficult, and sometimes reversed by the patient, pointing again to the difficulty of self-determination.

It has always been clear that in the context of aid in dying and end-of-life care, the distinction between its passive and active parts is not one that in practice can be clearly maintained. There are too many overlaps and transitions between what is experienced passively and what is actively brought about or determined. Nevertheless, the constant interweaving of the "vita passiva" and active intervention still describes an important reality of human life and so should not be discarded. Our thinking is far too abstract if we understand dying solely as a passive letting happen. It is equally abstract to believe that we can take dying completely

---

[1] For the broader conceptual field see Philipp Stoellger, *Passivität aus Passion. Zur Problemgeschichte einer "categoria non grata"* (Tübingen: Mohr Siebeck, 2010). See also Reinhard Hütter, *Suffering Divine Things* (Grand Rapids: Eerdmans, 2000).

under our own control, not least because this would almost always require the supporting acts of others. Holding together the "vita activa" and "vita passiva" as human beings die helps us not to forget that the person is supported in dying in a human way. This is the task of a practice in which a dying person can experience aid and relief from others within a context that is characterized by understanding and communication that does not leave the dying person alone. There will be experiences that the dying person lives and works through or processes on their own, but people should not die alone. The active-passive distinction helps us to see the importance of the distinction between a lonely death and the accompanied death that preserves human death as the sort of reality that is true to our humanity. It is particularly important for truly human dying to be accompanied, which means that in this truly personal moment no one is absolutely isolated and thrown back on themselves.

These observations usefully illuminate more narrowly conceived questions about the ethics of dying and helping to die. It is important as we ask these more familiar questions that we remain attentive to, and critical in understanding what it means that we have to die and what this means for us. This question is clearly evident despite all the focus on dying well or dying in a humane way, and it is also present in the distinction between a "vita passiva" and "vita activa." The meaning of "vita passiva" is not one that is grounded in our experience, such as that of suffering, whether it be bodily, internal, or spiritual. Rather, a distinction must be made between what we encounter in the context of our world of experiences and what happens to us in our humanity that breaks through our world of experiences. Dying is one such "breakthrough" experience since death and dying are so alien and strange to us despite being something we share with other living beings. We humans are mortal, that is, we will end, but something more than this bare assertion needs to be said.

We only begin to speak of death with its proper depth when we set it within the realization that there is something alien and threatening about death that is more than saying it is just another part of life. Death invades our lives as displayed in the death under the curse, to which Jesus was also subjected. The biblical story of the crucifixion of Jesus shows that there is a different way of dying apart from the cessation of the bodily life that all mortal humans will experience. It matters that Jesus did not die of old age as a wise teacher of religious truths. Jesus was instead subjected to a specific and horrifying death, which was the type of death that God wanted to end in order to open up for us a new existence as God's human creatures. The rule of this strange and threatening form of curse-death only becomes a part of God's story through the death of Jesus and God's raising him from this death. In Jesus's resurrection the alien nature of this kind of death is revealed, in that it is this death that God has determined to overcome. Outside of this story, we would be able to speak of life and death, of transience and mortality, of the strength of life against death, but not of the curse-death that God himself has ended.[2] Understanding this message and keeping it present in ethical discussions of humane dying prevents us from grasping death as something that belongs to us, however strange death may seem to us, or from wanting to take control of death by shaping and ethical molding in order to resist its strangeness and menace.

Jesus's revelation of the threatening aspect of human death allows Christians to gain a critical perspective on our own ethical practices that must recognize, open up, and test the reality to which we belong and which determines us.[3] A critical understanding follows the specific distinctions that are given and granted with God's story in which we find ourselves when we ask what and who we are. These distinctions differ from the ones we come up with when we imagine the lives we would like to have, that is, manufactured grounds to which we might appeal for this self-determined life. From a theological perspective, a critical understanding is one that explores our lives within the distinctions that are constitutive of God's history, which allow it to become vivid and determinate.[4] The liberation from the curse-death that is preserved through the promise given to us, that we will also rise with Jesus, is the guarantee of the vividness of our story with God.

---

[2] See Eberhard Jüngel, *Tod* (Stuttgart, Berlin: Kreuz-Verlag, 1971).
[3] On the theological reflection on "reality" see Wolf Krötke, *Was ist wirklich? Der notwendige Beitrag der Theologie zum Wirklichkeitsverständnis unserer Zeit* (Berlin: Humboldt-Universität zu Berlin, 1996).
[4] For this interpretation of Romans 6 see Karl Barth, *The Epistle to the Romans*, 6th edition, trans. Edwyn C. Hoskyns (Oxford: Oxford University Press, 1968).

I have already suggested that some of the key distinctions of this explorative work of understanding what belongs to humanity are found within God's story. In the story of Jesus the "vita passiva" is given a specific configuration which overlaps with aspects of the "vita activa." As we focus on the simultaneity of "vita activa" and "vita passiva," the question of how dying and death are to be understood—as in the prayer of Psalm 90, which takes place where there is access to this understanding—remain beyond what one must ethically reflect on and balance. The whole story appears in Psalm 90 where people find what they are and may be, but also what dying and death mean for them. This stands in contrast to the description of human existence in which humanity holds death in its presence while running headlong into death, in the belief that it is only in death that human beings are provided with a view of the whole of human life. In Martin Heidegger's influential philosophy, death reveals the actual reality of human beings. In his philosophy, only fixing a human in place by death allows them to become aware of their true reality.[5]

I have been suggesting that the biblical traditions locate our deaths in a different place, where we find ourselves as human beings who are not thrown back on our own attitudes, ideas, and thinking, but are allowed to experience—from the outside—what dying and death mean. Against the background of the biblical traditions (and parallelling some philosophical voices), it seems that the critical point is not in humans seeing their reality in death, but in being addressed by another person. Without the address from another person (without this extra *nos*) and the response to it, self-definition is nothing more than a conversation with the self. Self-given identity can only speak from within the limits of what the individual intends, grasps, or has appropriated. In such a self-given identity there remains a multiplicity of options if the individual is never encountered or claimed personally by another. Only an address that reaches us as a message, as a proclamation that applies to us as the unique addressee of this message, allows us to become the aware selves that we are. When the address

---

[5] See Alberto Rosales, "Das Vorlaufen in den Tod als Seinsverständnis," in *Transzendenz und Differenz. Ein Beitrag zum Problem der Ontologischen Differenz beim frühen Heidegger*, ed. Alberto Rosales (Dordrecht: Springer, 1970), 173–9.

of another person reaches us, the nature of human beings as relational beings is confirmed. In addition, our own address to another person, insofar as it is not determined by this other person as the addressee, but is in turn a response to an address, is also a way of being taken out of our self-centeredness. We see this in prayer to God who allows himself to be asked for what he has already promised, allowing us to experience liberation from our intentions, desires, and wills that bind us. This is explicitly stated in the petition "Thy will be done!"

Being addressed becomes real when I hear something that applies to me as an individual; a message, an address to me specifically. Where else does this happen than in Christian worship? Where else but exclusively in worship, where the word can be heard, like God's word of forgiveness or the word of the promise: "Receive the Holy Spirit" (Jn 20:22)? This is how the Risen One speaks to the disciples. With this address, the whole story to which God's word belongs, and to which we may belong, becomes present. Within this whole story, what constitutes dying and death also now appears in a new and ethically revealing context. The significance of death is not found when we understand ourselves as transient, as all living things are, but only when it is understood within the specific story to which it belongs. This story reaches beyond death because God has realized his promise through the resurrection of Jesus. In this resurrection God reveals God's desire to continue to live with us; that we be God's people existing in God's presence eternally. We humans are allowed to participate in this story beyond death—in the story that God has been pursuing with us since creation and which he has reinstated through the resurrection of Jesus. Otherwise, we would be relegated to what we are able to think, hope, or long for beyond death, which is somehow there and beyond the death of Jesus. This hope is a mere human longing, a groundless and history-less hope. It is different from the hope that has a reason, which we see in Jesus's prayer on the cross in which God is asked: "Why have you forsaken me?" Such a prayer expresses a hope that Jesus will not fall out of the history that God is pursuing. This is the form of hope that has a logic rooted in this story, one that cannot be grasped without knowing this story, since it is not accessible to reason alone.

## Job's Freedom and Liberation

This reversal in a person's disposition, as in the entire story of Jesus, has been captured by biblical-theological language in God's address to us as our human prayer to God. Only when a person encounters an other, this extra *nos*, does she no longer find herself trapped in her own horizon or story that includes dying and death. This is what happens to Jesus, who prays in Gethsemane: "Your will be done." It also happens in a paradigmatic way in the story of Job, who, reaching the limits of bearable suffering and abandonment, comes to the point of wishing for death. Job finds himself lonely and abandoned even though he is surrounded by friends who are constantly counselling him. They give him advice on how to get out of his situation, and they believe that he is indeed responsible to find his way out of it. Job's refusal to accept his suffering is a problem for them because they think it can be explained or categorized somehow. They believe that since Job too lives within a given order of things, he can and must submit to it by following it, especially since God is responsible for it. But Job, infuriatingly, refuses to submit to this logic. He sees himself close to death as he knows it—as belonging to the order of things—but at the same time falling out of the story in which he knows himself connected to God. His friends talk past him by talking about a different reality which does not in fact address his central concern, thereby conveying no message that fits with Job's view of death as being lost to God's story. When they insist that Job admit that his suffering is due to his deviation from the just order of things, and therefore really his own fault, they also foist on him an understanding of death and dying. But Job refuses to follow such a logic. He insists on remaining within the specific story he has known with God, the only reality from which his unique identity as Job makes any sense. To do otherwise would be to throw himself back onto a self-constructed identity in which he is alone. Job wants to remain connected to God. No disposition, however realistically conceived, can replace the destiny (*destinatio*, not *determinatio*) of a person in God's history. Therefore Job waits and hopes for a message that really applies to him. This is the reality of his hope in the face of a reality that is oppressive to him. Job insists that the particular story that God has begun with him will continue. Job cannot see in death an exit that liberates him, but only one in which he is finally lost. In his hope, he reaches toward the continuation of the life and story God has started with him by addressing him personally rather than falling into the form of death that dies forgotten by God, and so lost.

In this insistence and persistence, which is not the insistence of a sovereign subject, but the insistence of a human being who is not thrown back on himself, Job receives the confirming message from God: "You have not fallen out of my story. You have rightly kept hope and not exchanged it for all the well-meaning theories of your friends. You can continue to live in my story." Job hears this in his "vita passiva" and the message reaches him. Job's friends may have been attentive counsellors, but they have not managed to relieve him from the loneliness and abandonment in which he finds himself. Who would call this loneliness freedom? Is Job really a person who determines himself? And what human dignity does Job possess? Job knows that his dignity is in the face of God, in his pleading and complaining speech to God, dignity that he does not want to lose by making a deal with a God who would be denoted to the status of a distant lawgiver or world-orderer. It is the dignity of which Job literally says: "What are humans, that you make so much of them" (Job 7:17, see also Ps. 8:1). Job expresses very precisely the dignity of any human being, that God has included them in his story. Job changes radically the *imago Dei* logic, as it is often understood, when he says: "For he is not a mortal, as I am, that I might answer him, that we should come to trial together" (Job 9:32). No, I, this poor human being, am worthy of God turning to me and I to God. In turning to God in this way the *imago Dei* is fulfilled, God's election of human beings as God's counterparts. Job insists on this, and this is his dignity. This does not make Job a model or example to be imitated, but reveals that the dignity of his prayer is in fact the dignity given to all people, who each have their own story with God. This story, according to the message Job is trying to convey, also encompasses death. God does not allow anyone to fall into nothingness and so Job could have prayed with the psalmist: "If I ascend to heaven, you are there; if I make my bed in Sheol, you are there" (Ps. 139:8).

## "Vita Passiva": In the Challenge

This understanding of a "vita passiva" within God's history becomes even clearer in the recurring question of the possibility for humans to kill themselves. Suicide is a human act intended to end a passive suffering, whatever the nature of the suffering, and thus leaving the "vita passiva" behind. Every suicide is caught up in an abysmal drama that faces the horror of being thrown back on oneself and one's "vita activa" and passiva, and on the loss of the "vita passiva" with God. Recognizing this theological description means rejecting all models of suicide conceived as acts of self-preservation, self-assertion, self-determination, or sovereign exercise of freedom. It is logically problematic to find a way to define self-determination in a manner that imagines that the notion of choice here could be defined as universally valid. The real significance of suicide cannot be conceived in any such model. The model that legal doctrine fixes has no validity beyond the limited definition the law must set in order to fulfil its specific protective function—in this case to ensure the protection of people from being exposed to conditions that promote suicide as they are confronted with their own death or desire to die, or from being overly influenced by people they depend on in their struggle with dying and death.

Definitions or models are, of course, already implied outside of legal theory when we talk about suicide based on a reasoned decision, judgment, or even self-determination. It is always insinuated that the subject is sovereign to the extent that it can and may decide on the continuation of its life and act accordingly; that is, it can balance the "vita activa" and passiva on its own. Suicide is thus identified as belonging to the human being, anthropologically, as an always given possibility, as an always available, not closed exit. It should nevertheless not become a normal option but remain a possibility beyond comprehending rationally.[6]

Concerning the idea of the sovereign human being, the story of Job displays the exercise of human sovereignty in the form of not

---

[6]This is currently the subject of a new political debate in Germany after the Constitutional Court of the Federal Republic of Germany invoked this model in order to justify the impunity of suicide and at the same time the impunity of assisted suicide.

being bound to human images and morals. Because his story is in God's hands, Job is allowed to remain in God's story by refusing to admit that death is an appropriate way of escaping from his story with God. He is empowered to hope for an outcome other than choosing to escape in death because of his certainty that he owes his existence exclusively to God's destiny. He has admitted that he is at the mercy of this destiny and is preserved in it. The book of Job, therefore, suggests that Job's freedom is in fact passively received that is found in being preserved and at the mercy of God.

Of this special kind of human sovereignty Karl Barth has commented: "The suicide seems to act with final sovereignty and with a view to asserting it. But he does so paradoxically by throwing it away, by refusing to go on living, by effectively securing that he need exist no longer."[7] This is the reason why Christians must conclude that there is no theoretical model of suicide that can be justified without become self-contradictory. And what is more, suicide cannot be located anywhere, not even as a borderline case (as Barth discusses), because this understanding localizes suicide precisely where a border runs, is set, or is given, which means that at least the outermost part of our human life still encompasses it. When a person, therefore, finds herself in a state of emergency, she emerges as a de facto sovereign who no longer has anything or anyone above her and thus can freely act (at least violently). The situation in which we see Job, of being challenged and suffering, is depicted quite differently from a state of emergency which a sovereign actor has the right to resolve as they choose. Yet, Karl Barth comments:

> Consider that the person who is contemplating suicide is in any case in the darkness of temptation. But the temptation consists in the fact that God is hidden from him as his God, that he is in danger and about to sink into the abyss of divine rejection or—which amounts to the same thing—into the abyss of atheism, to see himself alone, himself as sovereign, above himself—and now for some reason also around him, behind him and before him—a dreadful emptiness. There he stands as a sovereign who

---

[7] Karl Barth, *Church Dogmatics* III/4, *Doctrine of Creation*, ed. Geoffrey W. Bromiley and Thomas F. Torrance (Edinburgh: T&T Clark, 1961), 406.

no longer knows what to do with his sovereignty, who no longer sees a future ahead of him in all his sovereignty! . . . Only one light shines into that darkness, but this light is penetrating and victorious—not a "You shall live", but the "You may live", which no human being can say to another and no one can say to himself, but which God himself has spoken and continues to speak. The reason for temptation always consists in the fact that man no longer hears God speak, that he no longer hears him say it.[8]

In the situation of temptation human beings always find themselves left alone, precisely where they see themselves falling out of all reality in which even death still has its meaning, and yet they cannot see themselves at the mercy of this falling out. This is also where the demand is made to maintain the concrete conditions so that the affected person can still remain in hope, fear, and waiting—waiting for the support that people themselves cannot give, and waiting for the word, the promise that people cannot give nor fulfil.

## Without History: Preserved in the Other Story beyond Death

Job was one such figure captured in temptation. Job is challenged in the absolute, unwavering dependence on the fact that he can entrust himself to the only one who preserves his life. This challenge is still a sign of his dignity, that of being the addressee of this message that he, however, is no longer able to hear. Much less can he receive the well-meant and even correct admonition that he should stay alive. He continues to insist that the saving message that God will continue the story that he started with him is still valid. In the situation of temptation he is not able to hear God's personal address nor is he able to simply decide that he will affirm his life. In this situation of temptation the questions "What will happen to me?" and "Where do I find myself?" still remain, as does the question "When will the suffering end—when will the suffering end?" and the cry "Make an end, O Lord, make an end!"

---

[8]Ibid., 408–10.

This situation of temptation does not exclude accepting help and support that can alleviate the suffering. Yet it cannot be dissolved into a surrender that is inverted humility that feigns relief before it has received real support.

Job's pain and suffering remain a provocation from God. Job's *ars moriendi* (art of dying) is to bring his suffering and aloneness plaintively before God. He stays in a state of temptation and remains at the same time in a hopeful abiding, which nevertheless does not exclude human help and assistance. Job, the challenged man, wants to hear God speak here and now, whatever God has to say. The talk of his friends is no substitute for this divine presence, and this is precisely why their presence makes him lonely. Job's loneliness is that of someone who cannot be comforted, despite the human comforters around him. In biblical language, consolation is something resistant and protective, just as the shepherd's crook comforts in the psalm: "Your rod and your staff, they comfort me" (Ps. 23:4). Job waits, hoping for another word, a resistant word, the word of the one who can and does stand up for his word. Anything else would simply be a pledge made by people who are not authorized to promise real help or rescue.

Now we can grasp the understanding behind the declaration of the Constitutional Court and those who agree with it that a person possesses a certain dignity which is to be protected by law. It is the dignity of the human being in whose life no one may interfere in such a way that his or her decision, which belongs to him or her alone, is affected. This sovereign being remains alone. Everything that concerns him substantially (existentially) and must be decided remains his business alone—he has to bear this burden. So the question may arise, as with Job's friends, as to what provides human beings with relief? What could they appeal to if not the order of things that Job's friends take for granted? This appeal is definitely not enough for Job. It points him in the wrong direction, away from the truth that God is responsible for continuing the story that he started with him. He attributes to God the dignity that God has shared with him. He does not excuse God and he does not engage in theodicy. He holds God responsible for the fact that he must decide and direct and cannot blame Job for this. The message that Job finally is able to hear, directly from God because his friends are unable to bear witness to it, is: "Job, you have the right to disagree with what is happening to you. That is your dignity and your freedom here and now."

## The Other Freedom: In the Other Story

This is the freedom of the one who does not have to bear the burden of directing his life and who does not have to come to terms with the strange threat of death. It is the freedom to take God at God's word. It is the freedom of lament and provocation, the freedom to cast your abysmal worries on God: "Cast all your anxiety on him, because he cares for you" (1 Pet. 5:7). This change of jurisdiction and responsibility for our life in all its reality is decisive for the biblical grammar. The fact that God has taken us into God's story is the message of liberation that can be heard here. My own story, the story that God has started with me, does not come to an end with death, but remains part of the larger story God is committed to continue. The message God addresses to me tells another story in which death is not the border or the threshold that delineates this world from the hereafter, which like every threshold must be crossed one way or another. But over which bridge and to where? Death is an end imposed on each human being, but death itself also has an end in God's story, specifically, the death that leads to nothingness. This death is conquered in the other history that God has started anew with the resurrection of Jesus Christ.

The audacity of the message and its resistance to death results in the certainty of human witnesses within this other story. Those who are baptized are baptized into this other story, into the story of this Jesus whom God raised from the dead (Rom. 6:3). This is the beginning of the new life in the midst of life, the new life that does not end with the death of the mortal body. This other story also includes another death, the death of death, which is no longer the curse-death. God has cancelled this death through the resurrection of Jesus.[9]

---

[9]For this focus see Dietrich Bonhoeffer, especially: Burmeister Luise, "Auferstehung in die Nachfolge. Dietrich Bonhoeffers nicht-religiöse Interpretation der Auferstehung," in Die Wirklichkeit der Auferstehung, ed. Hans-Joachim Eckstein and Michael Welker (Neukirchen-Vluyn: Neukirchener, 2002), 111–19.

Paul, in particular, put this story in his own fresh manner: We are "always carrying around in the body the death of Jesus, so that the life of Jesus may also be made visible in our bodies" (2 Cor. 4:10). We can have certainty that we have been transferred to this other history that does not end with the death that leads to nothingness. Our human death now is embedded into this other history: "If we live, we live to the Lord; if we die, we die to the Lord. Therefore, whether we live or die, we are the Lord's" (Rom. 14:8). No attitude or stance is required here. Everything depends on this other story and its reality remaining present in our listening, praying, and doing.

## Pastoral Practice

Between the dying that comes to us and the dying that we take into our own hands, or even the death that we bring about ourselves, there appears to be an unbridgeable difference between two completely different stories, indeed different realities that cannot be cancelled out. What a deception to think of death as an exit that is to be taken into the unknown, seeing this self-determination as the ultimate freedom of human beings! What an illusion to see the prospect of a new possible, real life in running ahead into death, which remains nothing but a mere possibility. In contrast, what impossible things must be achieved from an accompaniment in dying that would help direct the dying instead of resisting the trust to participate in God's story in which death is overcome in Jesus Christ? The dying we are offered in Jesus Christ is one shaped by a promise that God wishes to reach beyond death and to end our old humanity and its death. Because of this hope that reaches into our lives Christians can live in the grounded hope that God will continue his story with us, human beings, his creatures.

Why is dying, as it belongs to the human being, not recognized in many discourses as uniquely human, as something that belongs to and is granted to the human with all the help and assistance that can be provided, but above all with everything that is present in dying within that other story? Remaining in the "Anfechtung" (temptation), just as we remain in the story that God has created and maintains, frees us from having to take control of dying and come to terms with death. This freedom is what constitutes the *ars moriendi*, if this is how we should speak of it (because "ars" also suggests direction by active choice). Such a hope will fund a pastoral practice based on the message that we humans are worthy of belonging to this other story that God has begun with us, God's creatures, and that God has promised to continue for eternity. Pastoral practice should focus on strengthening this very precisely configured trust and in a manner that allows its liberating force to offer this divine story to reach all people.

## Bibliography

Barth, Karl. *Church Dogmatics* III/4, *Doctrine of Creation*, edited by Geoffrey W. Bromiley and Thomas F. Torrance. Edinburgh: T&T Clark, 1961.
Barth, Karl. *The Epistle to the Romans*, 6th ed., translated by Edwyn C. Hoskyns. Oxford: Oxford University Press, 1968.
Burmeister, Luise. "Auferstehung in die Nachfolge. Dietrich Bonhoeffers nicht-religiöse Interpretation der Auferstehung." In *Die Wirklichkeit der Auferstehung*, edited by Hans-Joachim Eckstein and Michael Welker, 93–100. Neukirchen-Vluyn: Neukirchener, 2002.
Hütter, Reinhard. *Suffering Divine Things*. Grand Rapids: Eerdmans, 2000.
Jüngel, Eberhard. *Tod*. Berlin: Kreuz Verlag, 1971.
Krötke, Wolf. *Was ist wirklich? Der notwendige Beitrag der Theologie zum Wirklichkeitsverständnis unserer Zeit*. Berlin: Humboldt-Universität zu Berlin, 1996.
Rosales, Alberto. "Das Vorlaufen in den Tod als Seinsverständnis." In *Transzendenz und Differenz. Ein Beitrag zum Problem der Ontologischen Differenz beim Frühen Heidegger*, edited by Alberto Rosales, 173–79. Dordrecht: Springer, 1970.
Stoellger, Philipp. *Passivität aus Passion. Zur Problemgeschichte einer 'categoria non grata.'* Tübingen: Mohr Siebeck, 2010.

# 13

# What Belongs to Whom? Property and Sustainability in Theological Light

## *Cornelis van der Kooi*

### Introduction

The water in the sea, the air we breathe, the oil in the seabed, the gas in the earth, the metals in our mobile phones, the airspace above us, the interstellar space, the flight of geese passing in formation: Whose is all that? This is the underlying and fundamental question in connection with the need for sustainable habitation of the shared house that we inhabit, the *oikos* of this world. What belongs to whom?

The examples mentioned in the first lines show how easily a claim to property and the right to use goods can lead to discussion and how elusive the concept of property is.[1] While history already shows a picture of continuous legal and political struggles over property, today the social debate has broadened and sharpened. The demand for property becomes urgent when it comes to goods that

---

[1] Kevin Gray and Susan Francis Gray, *Elements of Land Law* (Oxford: Oxford University Press, 2009), 86.

are important for life, prosperity or well-being. We have become aware, in contradiction to what for a long time was assumed, that natural resources are limited. In this contribution I will restrict myself to two examples: property of precious metals for batteries and intellectual ownership of lifesaving medicines.

1. When it comes to the metals in our mobile telephones or the production of batteries for electric cars, the picture is clear. The question of property, access to resources, and the necessity not to damage the ecosystem has become urgent. In such cases, the limited availability of a good has not only a technical, legal, and economic component, but also a moral dimension. Property then has to do with availability, accessibility, and occupation.

2. The COVID-19 era has brought the moral dimension of property to light more sharply than ever. Who owns the knowledge with which a vaccine can be produced? Where is intellectual property located? Certainly, with the manufacturer who has invested in it and acquired the patent on it. Or should the accessibility of the acquired knowledge be broadened in the case of something as important as a lifesaving vaccine? Is there abundance that must be shared on moral grounds?

An essential characteristic of the concept of property can be derived from these two examples that have been mentioned. It is a functional concept. Property itself is not a thing, it is control over something. To a greater or lesser extent, it is power over a good and thus stands in function of a good.

In order to find an answer to the question, at least the beginning of an answer, I will discuss a number of fundamental notions about property and sustainability from the perspective of Christian theology. The contribution is divided into three parts. In the first part, I introduce a classical theological view of property and outline the French Revolution as a defining moment of the break with that tradition. In this context, some notions of property rights in the Bible and its possible application to the use of raw materials and waste are also discussed. In the second part, four theological notions that are important in connection with property and sustainability are briefly discussed: vulnerability, cooperation, voluntary self-withdrawal on behalf of others, and gratitude. In the third and final part, I will draw some conclusions regarding our use of some examples we started with, particularly our use of resources.

## Property: The Decisive Perspective

What belongs to humankind? What belongs to animals? And what part does God as Creator of this strange and wonderful universe play in it? We are used to thinking and feeling from the perspective of people and their needs, anthropocentrically. The role of humans in the use and depletion of resources has been unequivocally demonstrated in reports such as that of the Intergovernmental Panel on Climate Change. Reports on raw materials indicate that there will be scarcity in the foreseeable or even short term, such as cobalt and coltan for our cell phones, zinc, antimony, molybdenum, and, more fundamentally, there will be scarcity of water, and in some places temperatures in which it is almost impossible to live. The use of the word "scarcity" is significant: it is based on human need which is an anthropocentric perspective. It is we who look for raw materials to meet human needs. This is a movement of taking in and putting into use in which the human being as the acting subject takes precedence, or more precisely, those who have the financial and technical possibilities to gain access to those things. A correction of the direction of gaze is needed here, or even stronger, a reversal of perspective. Perhaps the order should no longer be the *people, planet, profit*, launched by John Elkington,[2] but *planet, people, profit*. This means a thorough critique of the concept of private property as it has developed from the early modern period.

On this point, however, Christian theology still has its own contribution and its own perspective, which also puts this newly proposed triad in its own light. The first and fundamental theological notion is that the world belongs to God. It follows that human beings have no absolute right of ownership and that they are God's recipients and participants in the whole of God's work. Humans have a special place in this whole and bear a responsibility, which

---

[2]John Elkington, "People, Planet, Profit," *John Elkington* (blog). June 4, 2008, https://johnelkington.com/2008/06/people-planet-profit.

can be described with the concept of stewardship. The theological notion of God as owner is at odds with the anthropocentric view of property which appeared in the centuries before the French Revolution and was enacted in legislation from 1789 onward.

## Property as a Sacred and Inviolable Right

The emphasis on and self-evidence of private property is relatively new. To understand how this concept came to be, we must return to the French Revolution which caused a definitive break with the way previous generations and thinkers thought about property. The assumption that formed the philosophical and cultural starting point well into the early modern period was that the world as a whole was given to humanity. Within that communal framework, private property is more likely to be regarded as a regulation or concession that is not self-evident and therefore requires separate argumentation. At most, there is a right of use and not an absolute right.

Since the French Revolution established the right to property in the *Déclaration des droits de l'homme et du citoyen* of 1789 and labelled this right a "droit inviolable et sacré" (inviolable and sacred right), the notion of private property has been defined from the point of view of the individual. While in the motto *liberté, égalité et fraternité* (liberty, equality, and fraternity) the distaste for any form of divinely sanctioned power relationship became audible, private property took on the radiance of the sacred and inviolable. From then on, the right to property could only be limited by government legislation and regulations. The latter is, of course, a powerful and limiting precondition, and it could be argued that what was first given with one hand is taken back with the other. Nevertheless, its tone and direction are set: property is unassailable and sacred. Any restriction on property will henceforth be regarded as infringement. The *Déclaration* of 1789 is the prelude to what Piketty calls an ownership society.[3]

---

[3] Thomas Piketty, "The Invention of Ownership Societies," chap. 3 in *Capital and Ideology* (Cambridge, MA: Harvard University Press 2020).

The abolition of the feudal system with its estate society, in France and wherever implemented, meant a thorough rearrangement of social structures and relationships. Private property and public power were henceforth separated from each other, at least ideally.[4] Jurisdiction and political rights thus came to lie elsewhere, but property was regarded as indivisible and inviolable. This was new. Under the old system it was possible to borrow and use, in addition to acquiring use for rent or part of the proceeds. The idea of absolute private property, however, was never conceived in this system. What individuals could acquire was a kind of right of use and nothing more. In the new situation this was radically different. The weight was shifting to private property. According to Cambacérès, one of the ardent champions of the new legislation, ownership implied complete dominance over the goods one had acquired,[5] up to and including the right of destruction.[6] It is these assumptions of dominance and their effect on our use of the Earth that are now in need of revision.

## The Tradition on Property: Thomas Aquinas, Hugo Grotius, and John Locke

The realization that the earth has been given collectively to people for use has long been part of the collective consciousness. It was the starting point in the *Decretum Gratiani*, which would form part of the

---

[4]Rutger Claassen, *Privaat eigendom, publieke macht. Op weg naar een nieuw feodalisme?* (Meppel: Boom 2020), 11–12 and Rafe Blaufarb, *The Great Demarcation: The French Revolution and the Invention of Modern Property*. (Oxford: Oxford University Press 2016), 136–7. In the system under the Old Régime, property, political power, and jurisdiction were intertwined. An earl or lord also had jurisdiction over the persons in his jurisdiction. Enjoyment of a good was part of a large hierarchical whole in which at the top of the pyramid stood the Crown or a monarch who granted rights and favors. The notion of royal domain as codified in the *Edict of Moulins* (1566) contained the notion of inalienability as the most important element.
[5]Article 544 of the Civil Code: "Property is the right to enjoy and dispose of things in the most absolute manner, provided that they are not used in a manner prohibited by laws or regulations." See Blaufarb, *The Great Demarcation*, 209.
[6]Ibid., 213.

*corpus iuris canonici*.[7] We find it also in Thomas Aquinas's *Summa Theologica* where he asks the question whether it is permissible for humans to have property.[8] After all, everything belongs to God, so it is not natural for humans to have property. On the other hand (*sed contra*), humans are allowed to make use of things. Thomas puts forward two grounds for this: first, an argument based on an assumed hierarchy of things, the great chain of being. That is, the lesser or lower is made for the greater or higher. The human being as the higher may therefore make use of animals as the lower. Thomas grounds this view both on natural law and on the Bible, specifically on Aristotle and on Gen. 1:26, namely, that the human being as a rational being is the image of God and that he will rule over the fish of the sea. Thus, God has decreed: for their sustenance humans may make use of external lower things. In this way Thomas concludes that personal possession is possible. It is, however, a favor granted—the starting point remains the communal. In short, this means a relativization of private property rights from a theological perspective. The world and those who inhabit it belong to God.

The relativization of the right to property is apparent in questions that arise in times of need and lack. Can a hungry or needy person use goods that belong to another in times of need? Thomas considers that this is justified in times of excessive need. Then the principle that all things are given to humanity as a whole comes into effect: *In necessitate sunt omnia communia* (In need all things are common).[9]

Earlier, in Article 2 of question 66, Thomas has already put forward an additional argument as to why allowing private property is wise and meaningful. Humans are more careful in dealing with things that they own than with things that are in common. If it is not clear who is responsible for what, the care for the good is left behind. In short, Thomas recognizes a right to property as an addition to the natural law principle of the commonality of

---

[7] See for an overview Marc de Wilde, "'God Hath Given the World to Men in Common.' Limits to Private Property in Case of Emergency and Waste in Medieval and Early Modern Natural Law," *Netherlands Journal of Legal Philosophy* 42, no. 1 (2013): 8–28.
[8] Thomas Aquinas, *Summa Theologica*, trans. Fathers of the English Dominican Province (New York: Benziger Brothers, 1911–1925), II.2.66.
[9] Ibid., II.2.66. Art. 7.

all things, but with the condition that this right may not conflict with social duties toward one's fellow human being. There is an obligation on abundance of "property."

## Hugo de Groot

We find the same realization in Hugo de Groot.[10] In *De iure belli ac pacis* (1625) De Groot founded the right to property in the proposition that it is part of the law of nature that humans are social beings, aimed at a community with a certain order of connections. In that order, the distinction between mine and thine, what is mine and that of the other, is an essential element.[11] Civil law, still referred to by De Groot as city law (*lex municipalis*), had been developed based on that principle in the way of experience. And, as is well known, he defended the evidence of this right to property with the famous sentence that this right would remain even if God did not exist (*etsi deus non daretur*), which is an impossible thought for De Groot.[12] The right to property therefore lies in our nature, or more precisely in our instinctive nature that we share with all animals, namely the need and drive to survive and to maintain our bodies with food.[13] What is naturally of ourselves (*suum*) is our life, our limbs, and our freedom.[14] These give people a right of use. It is precisely in this recognition of a right of use for our own conservation that the justification for private property lies. When I take food, segregate it, and consume it myself, it is no longer available to others. What is mine (*suum*) takes on a form of exclusivity: the food is on my plate, and, once consumed, takes on the form of intangibility. In *Mare liberum*, his treatise on the free sea, he calls this *occupatio* (taking into possession). Goods that were once common are used in such a way that they are withdrawn from the common.[15] Property

---

[10]I base my discussion of De Groot and Locke largely on Stephen Buckle, *Natural Law and the Theory of Property. Grotius to Hume* (Oxford: Oxford University Press, 1991).
[11]Ibid., 29.
[12]Ibid., 23.
[13]Ibid., 25.
[14]Ibid., 29.
[15]Ibid., 42.

rights in a society are built up and founded on this primary fact.[16] De Groot might be seen as a forerunner on the way to an ownership society, but in the background is still the biblical notion of property as concession.

## John Locke

Another thinker who played a major role in thinking about property is John Locke. He is often referred to as the one who pioneered the modern right to private property. He would even defend a "possessive individualism," a view in which the individual should defend his own interests without concern for wider society.[17] It fits the image of Locke as a pioneer and champion of free-market thinking. That image has since been thoroughly revised.[18] According to Locke, private property finds a limit in situations of necessity or of excess and waste. The foundation he gives to private property is still very rewarding. In the second treatise of his *Two Treatises of Government*,[19] he argues in chapter four that humans are free. He thus contests the idea (against Robert Filmer) that every human being as a slave or property is subject to a lord or prince. In his own way he picks up on the centuries-old tradition of the dignity of each human being as an image of God. The natural state is that each is free and not subject to any other power. In society everyone is free insofar as he is not subject to a legislature established by agreement or consent. In the next and famous chapter 5, Locke then talks about property. He quotes Ps. 115:16 right at the beginning: "The earth he has given to the children of man." In the following lines he states that once a person is born, he has the right to survive and thus has the right to food and drink. The right to take food and drink for the maintenance of one's own life is a right that arises from existence itself: the urge to preserve one's own life. Typical of the tradition in which Locke and the aforementioned thinkers

---

[16]Ibid., 30–2.
[17]Thus C.B. Macpherson, *The Political Theory of Possessive Individualism* (Oxford: Clarendon Press, 1962), 263–4.
[18]Buckle, *Natural Law*, 74.
[19]John Locke, "The First Treatise of Government," in *John Locke: Political Writings*, ed. David Wooton (Indianapolis: Hackett Publishing, 2003), 261–386.

stand is the double appeal they make, namely, to natural law and to Scripture. These two work together.

The right to property therefore concerns first and foremost one's own person and physicality. The necessity of preserving one's own life means that one may take what the world offers. Ownership then also means with Locke that the work of our hands, our labor, is ours. Property arises as a result of productive labor. If someone digs up a piece of land in a desolate area and tills it to reap its fruits, this person may regard that land as his or her own. Property is thus the mixing of productive labor with raw material.

We must dwell on this for a moment because in Locke we encounter an essential mark of property which we mentioned previously in all clarity. Ownership never stands alone. It is always a function of something else. The basis is that property is a function of self-preservation, maintenance, and progress of life.

## Property Rights in the Bible

Together with natural law, biblical notions still preserved in these voices provide a comprehensive framework for thinking about property. The world and its goods are collectively given to humanity on loan. There is no absolute property right for humans. Everything there is, from land to fruit and animals, offers space at the most for a right of temporary use. Creation, the trees, the animals, the mountains, have their own subjectivity in the Bible. Who owns it is not a question. In Psalm 24, this is cause for praise: "The earth is the Lord's, and all that is in it, the world, and those who live in it, for he has founded it on the seas, and established it on the rivers." Humans are a small element in a world full of dynamism and life, who marvel and praise the Creator. Nor can Psalm 8 be said to give rise to anthropocentrism. On the contrary, predominant is the wonder and gratitude for what humankind has been entrusted in this mighty universe, which determines our position. The human being is called to fulfill the role of steward, manager, and caretaker of the house. That is a serving role. The world is evidence of God's care, of his love. In view of the God-established relationship with his creation, it is therefore indefensible to say that creation revolves around the human being. This thought is much too anthropocentric, and, moreover, it ignores the fact that in Scripture all kinds of elements in creation are assigned their own subjectivity.

The notion of gratitude for our living world as a gift and as a token of God's love can be found in many ways, not only in the use of the world in a spatial sense, but, for example, also in the division of time. A week has seven days, in which the seventh day is a day where what has been received may be celebrated in a special way. God is not only the owner of the earth, of space, he is also the Lord of time. Significantly, the French revolutionaries also banned this division of time, in a conscious effort to get rid of this structure inherited from Israel and return to what was customary in Egypt, a ten-day division. The seventh day is associated with the notion of restoration and liberation.[20] This also concerned property relations. The relationship to God as owner is sharpened in the arrangement of a sabbatical year: "The land shall not be sold in perpetuity, for the land is mine; with me you are but aliens and tenants" (Lev. 25:23). Every seventh year the land had to lie fallow so the soil was not exhausted. Forms of soil depletion were already known then. Moreover, during the sabbatical year, the poor were allowed to harvest freely from what grew spontaneously on the land in a fallow year. There is even mention of an institution that designated every fiftieth year, after seven cycles of seven, as a year of release, the so-called *yobel* or jubilee, which was to provide for a complete restoration of property relations. While it is historically highly uncertain whether such a Jubilee ever took place, the ideological significance in a situation where the economy is entirely dependent on land is perfectly clear. The Jubilee provided the ransom or release of fellow citizens who had fallen into poverty—a social and economic reset. For a substantiation of the Sabbath, the Sabbath year, and the Yobel year, reference is made in various places in the First Testament to the liberation from slavery in Egypt (e.g., Exod. 23:15; Deut. 5:15, 15:1-18).

It is these notions of release and restoration that are also found in the New Testament. Around Jesus Christ, as the bringer of the Kingdom of God, the contours of a new world with new relationships become visible. An example is Acts 2, where verse

---

[20]Rolf Rendtorff, *Theologie des Alten Testaments. Ein kanonischer Entwurf. Bd. 2: Thematische Entfaltung* (Neukirchen: Neukirchener Verlag, 2001), 48–50.

44 mentions that all who had accepted the faith stayed together and had everything in common. The great commandment in the words of Jesus, "You shall love the Lord your God with all your heart, and with all your soul, and with all your mind" (Mt. 22:37), is constitutive of all that is in our existence and can be obtained. Paul can therefore call the believers in Corinth to an apparently paradoxical attitude to life, namely, to treat acquired property as if it were not property (1 Cor. 7:30).

These notions cannot be immediately applied to the present day and the world economy, but they do provide a framework for reviewing ownership relationships and obligations associated with the use of goods. In any case, we will have to get rid of the anthropocentric perspective. In its one-sided application, this has obscured the awareness of fief and of the obligation to care. The Bible offers an inclusive world view in which people are part of a greater whole and must take responsibility.

## Four Theological Notions

In the foregoing, some theological reconsiderations were given for the concept of property. Theologically, the world belongs to God, and in that whole we have the place of receivers and participants. In line with this primary notion, we will now briefly elaborate four theological notions that are directly related to the realization that we do not own this world, but that it is a gift and that we have no more than a limited right to use it. There would certainly be more notions to be mentioned, such as justice, but I limit myself to vulnerability, cooperation, voluntary self-limitation, and gratitude.

### Vulnerability

Vulnerability is a theological notion that I mention as the first of the four because it says something essential about what has been entrusted to humanity. We live in a fragile world where things can break. That is how God made the world. The world, our common house or *oikos*, is good, in the sense of useful and good for the covenant of God and humanity. It proceeds from his love and benevolence. At the same time, it is finite, fragile, transient, and vulnerable. We know of cosmological disasters, meteorite impacts, of the extinction of the dinosaur, and of threatening possibilities. The world created by God was not perfect in the sense of what the Platonists thought: untouchable and imperishable. The Genesis 1 recurring formula "and God saw that it was good" (*tóf*) (Gen. 1:3, 10, 12, 18, 21, 25, 31) is not an independently observable quality, it is God's own assessment. What he created is good for someone or something and thereby functional.[21] The myth of an "aurea aetas" (a golden era) has no basis in the Bible. This creation is characterized by an ingrained vulnerability. There are systemic imperfections or risks: vulnerability linked to supply, vulnerability related to gravity, and vulnerability because raw materials are not infinitely available. It is in and with this vulnerability that God must be served and praised. And this vulnerability becomes a curse when a strange voice incites distrust and the desire to escape from the dependency to the Creator (Gen. 3:1-7).

There is something else to add. This world is made in such a way that we live at the expense of other life. Even vegans cannot escape it. Again, that is how the Creator willed and made it. He created a world marked by impermanence which was not the result of the Fall. Creation was the habitat in which God wanted to dwell and walk in the garden (Gen. 3:8). But there was also a porous openness, an opportunity to comprehend another voice, that of the serpent. So not a sweet dream about a perfect creation. No holistic mirages about living with nature where all sharp edges have been polished away. No, the Creator chose a cosmos that moves through a history, that is porous, perishable, and therefore not yet imperishable. A creation where pain is suffered as well as death. The imperishable is yet to come (1 Cor. 15:42). This is the hope that comes from Easter. Christ is ahead of us.

## Cooperation

The second concept, which is at odds with an absolute conception of property, and which is elementary in our world, is cooperation. We find forms of interplay, mutual influence, and cooperation at

---

[21]Cf. Claus Westermann, *Genesis 1. Teilband Genesis 1–11* (Neukirchen: Neukirchener Verlag, 1983), 228.

a fundamental level in all forms of life, and it is also a theological notion. There are more actors who are incited to activity by the Creator than just humans. We find it already in the beginning of Genesis 1: "And God said, Let the earth bring forth vegetation: plants yielding seed, and trees of every kind bearing fruit with the seed in it" (Gen. 1:11). In short, cooperation. We already find cooperation before there are humans in the natural world, in everything that cooperates according to its nature. Trees, fields, mountains, birds, and fish are actors who participate in Scripture. Biology provides countless examples. We know about fungi in the soil that communicate with each other from a distance. We know that soil is fertile by virtue of an incredible complexity of life and cooperation. There are a multiplicity and diversity of actors. In the poetry of the psalms, we find it again: mountains clap their hands and the trees and fields rejoice.[22]

What can be observed in cooperation in the natural world can be confirmed theologically: God uses plants and animals according to their nature. This too comes from God's love and favor. The concept of cooperation might evoke the idea of cooperation between equal partners, but this notion of equality is not implied here. It is precisely unequal and disparate partners who in our creation are actors in a complex interplay. The inequality of partners also appears to be the case in the covenant between God and humans. There is, in an expression made famous by Karl Barth, an infinite qualitative difference between God and the human being. The story of the Bible is the story of God seeking a relationship, seeking reciprocity. We call that covenant. In the words of the covenant formula, "I will be your God, and you shall be my people."[23] Humans are engaged by God's Spirit in a project of life, which can only be referred to here very briefly: the Spirit works in creation, engages people, overshadows

---

[22] A question that arises from the recognition of actors other than humans is how this should be recognized in a legal sense. Can a river be given legal personality? In New Zealand, a river was granted legal personality in 2012 with a Maori tribe also designated as an advocate. Rivers and Natural Ecosystems as Rights Bearing Subjects—Global Alliance for the Rights of Nature (GARN). This opens a field of questions that fall within private law, but which certainly require interdisciplinary collaboration. How can plants, rivers, animals, and mountains be protected?

[23] E.g., Gen. 17:7; Exod. 6:2-8. For an overview see Rendtorff, *Theologie des Alten Testaments*, 29–33.

Mary, and is the driving force in the life of her son. It is this Spirit who is poured out by the exalted Lord and who is pursuing life, progressing, flowering, and completing. When that Spirit affects people, then they are activated with their faculties, made creative, old boundaries are crossed, and new policies are made—all aimed at the future for the world as a common home for God's creatures. With this view one can consider climate activists, pray for students in various domains, but particularly in the domain of chemistry and technology, and invest in promising initiatives.

## Creative Self-withdrawal

Living together in the house of creation on the way to the consummation also means creative self-limitation on behalf of the other. This self-withdrawal is a distinguishing feature of the Spirit of Christ, the Spirit of life. This Spirit is opposed to a spirit of usurpation and confiscation in which self-preservation at the expense of another is the guiding principle. It is the justice welling up where the Spirit of Christ reigns. The Holy Spirit implements the elements we find in the life of Jesus, including what I now call with brevity cruciformity. So voluntary and creative self-withdrawal costs something.[24] One does not need to look far to see it. We observe it in young parents when they get out of bed before their young children and are sometimes chronically tired themselves. We see it between generations when it is especially the younger generation that insists on a different diet. We see it when economists push for absolute reductions in emissions. Voluntary self-withdrawal with a view to livability for humans, animals, and biodiversity requires courage: personal courage, political courage, and community initiative. It is behavior that can be theologically affirmed that befits the way Psalm 24 speaks of the world: "The earth is the Lord's and all that is in it, the world and those who live in it."

---

[24]The term is from Michael Welker, *God the Revealed: Christology* (Grand Rapids: Eerdmans 2012), 223–6.

## Gratitude

Finally, the concept of gratitude should be mentioned here. Humans have not created the world and its possibilities, but have been placed in it and are primarily recipients. The appropriate response to that gift is not suspicion—as the serpent's suggestion is to the woman in Gen. 3:5—but that of thanks. Peace offerings therefore occupy an important place in the liturgy of Israel, as does the praise to God for the life, harvest, flowering, beauty, and happiness given (cf. e.g., Psalms 65, 67, 103, 136, 148, 150). In the prayer for blessing that is said before and after the meal, thanks for what has been received signifies the fundamental attitude to life. It is the attitude that we find in the accounts of the last supper (Lk. 22:17) and in the Pauline epistles (e.g., Phil. 4:4-8; Col. 3:12-17). Praise and thanks are the attitude to life, that is, the answer to life given, to salvation and coming redemption, and which can be expected to seep through in our dealings with each other and the world.

# Applications

What do the notions of vulnerability, cooperation, self-withdrawal, and gratitude mean with regard to the concept of property and our use of resources? In this last part I will apply some of the insights gained from our exploration to the two examples we mentioned at the start. When our world is theologically a gift, and gratitude should be a basic attitude, then we must rethink our use of God-given resources. We become increasingly aware of the reality of the limitations of raw and precious materials, and the need for access to lifesaving medicine.

## Precious Metals

An appealing example of the facts that our planet is finite and important resources are not unlimited can be applied to the moral question of the use of the raw material cobalt. It is mined in Congo and sold to companies that process it for use in our mobile phones. Raw material is mixed with labor and becomes part of a product that is sold. But whose is it? There are different owners and actors in the chain from extraction to sale. In fact, there is a chain of cooperation. What does this mean for our view of property with its rights and obligations? First, the question must be asked about a *fair share* in the chain of mining, transportation, processing, sale, and consumption. What about the people who go in search of the metal at the risk of their own lives? Here we immediately encounter the fact that access to rare raw material is mainly in the hands of those who can afford and organize it. We are, therefore, confronted with the unequal distribution of wealth and power, and thus, the quest for justice.

Moreover, the pricing does not usually take into account the hidden and external costs of the product in the final phase of use. What are the consequences if I throw away the cell phone I bought? Am I free then of my property and obligations? Before I bought it, there had already been a chain of parties and hands through which the raw material, semi-finished product, and end product has passed. What is the calculation in this chain of cooperation with the principle that the raw materials of our world are in principle given to people in common? From that principle one should argue that nowhere in this chain is there absolute property and absolute right, but that at every moment in this chain of cooperation the realization must be given concrete form that what one uses from the earth has been received and that responsibility is transferred. A basic theological consideration is the gratitude mentioned earlier. No human created the precious materials. The only human effort consists in one of the steps in the whole chain of mining and production. An absolute claim of property is not at stake. Every human being participating in this chain may receive some profit, but at every step of this chain the owner's restricted and relative position must be taken seriously. Gratitude may open the possibility and willingness for sharing and self-withdrawal.

When focusing on precious metals the problem of waste becomes unavoidable. Ownership and use do not go without responsibility and with that the question of justice and the necessity of circularity is on the table.[25] For a long, long time, waste was not a problem. Creation itself is circular with forests and oceans that absorb $CO_2$. However, under the influence of humans, waste has become a problem—there is too much of it. Gone are the days when we can

---

[25]See also the contribution of Brian Brock in this volume.

think of waste as property that we want to get rid of as soon as possible and for which we do not want to take responsibility. The need for recovery will have to be taken into account from the very start of a chain in the design phase. *Waste is a design failure.* Here, too, the question of justice is unavoidable. The use that modern Western people make of raw materials, precious metals and $CO_2$ emissions produced, is disproportionately high compared to countless other inhabitants of the world who live in less developed areas.[26] It is not just a matter of using property that has been given to us together, it is a form of confiscation which is final and limits its accessibility to others.

A well-known shortcut to combat the problem of waste can be found in the threefold: *reduce, reuse, recycle.* The first two are already major steps with their own consequences and will probably initially lead to a reduction in production. However, it is of great importance that the last element of this triad, recycling or total recovery of the raw material, must also be taken into account. It has to do with the responsibility that is taken as soon as there is use, or as per Hugo de Groot's concept: *occupatio*, taking possession.

## Lifesaving Medicine

The second example is the intellectual ownership of knowledge to produce lifesaving medicine. The field of discussion on intellectual ownership has become a vast field of claims, considerations, and restrictions. Everybody understands that the development of medicine takes a huge effort of investment, research, experiment, time, and entrepreneurial creativity. It is known that only a small percentage of the ideas that have been elaborated and have gone through the phases of development and control are successful. The question of a fair price (*iustum pretium*) is an old but pressing question[27] and it has turned out to be wise not to interfere too quickly in the market by governmental coercion or restricting measures.

---

[26]See e.g., R. Daniel Bressler, "The Mortality Cost of Carbon," *Nature Communications* 12, no. 4467 (2021): 1–12. See also Matthias Olthaar and Paul Schenderling, *How Do I Act Honestly* (Middelburg: Skandalon, 2021).
[27]Fabio Monsalve, "Scholasti Just Price versus Current Market Price: Is it Merely a Matter of Labelling?" *European Journal of the History of Economic Thought* 21,

But having said this, here also the aforementioned theological considerations might be brought to the table. In remembrance of the vulnerability of the human condition it might be said that medicine is usually not a luxury we can do without. The development of new medicines has built on all possible forms of cooperation in the past and continues to build in the present. And here, too, the notion of gratitude is a fundamental theological notion that might motivate for taking a step back and making the claims of profit reasonable and not maximized.

## Conclusion

Rethinking the notion of property in the light of biblical notions may fuel our creativity and readiness to take responsibility.

## Bibliography

Aquinas, Thomas. *Summa Theologica*, translated by Fathers of the English Dominican Province. New York: Benziger Brothers, 1911–1925.

Blaufarb, Rafe. *The Great Demarcation. The French Revolution and the Invention of Modern Property*. Oxford: Oxford University Press, 2016.

Bressler, R. Daniel. "The Mortality Cost of Carbon." *Nature Communications* 12, no. 4467 (2021): 1–12.

Buckle, Stephen. *Natural Law and the Theory of Property. Grotius to Hume*. Oxford: Oxford University Press, 1991.

Claassen, Rutger. *Privaat eigendom, publieke macht. Op weg naar een nieuw feodalisme?* Meppel: Boom, 2020.

De Wilde, Marc. "'God Hath Given the World to Men in Common': Limits to Private Property in Case of Emergency and Waste in Medieval and Early Modern Natural Law." *Netherlands Journal of Legal Philosophy* 42, no. 1(2013): 8–28.

Elkington, John. "People, Planet, Profit." *John Elkington* (blog), June 4, 2008. https://johnelkington.com/2008/06/people-planet-profit.

---

no. 1 (2012): 1–17. *Report Medicine Pricing and Access in Europe and Beyond* (published by the Health Action International Amsterdam 2021).

Gray, Kevin and Susan Francis Gray. *Elements of Land Law*. Oxford: Oxford University Press, 2009.
Locke, John. "The First Treatise of Government." In *John Locke: Political Writings*, edited by David Wooton, 242–58. Indianapolis: Hackett Publishing, 2003.
Macpherson, Crawford Brough. *The Political Theory of Possessive Individualism*. Oxford: Clarendon Press, 1962.
Monsalve, Fabio. "Scholastic Just Price versus Current Market Price: Is it Merely a Matter of Labelling?" *European Journal of the History of Economic Thought* 21, no. 1 (2012): 1–17.
Olthaar, Matthias and Paul Schenderling. *Hoe handel ik eerlijk*. Middelburg: Skandalon, 2021.
Piketty, Thomas. *Capital and Ideology*. Cambridge, MA: Harvard University Press, 2020.
Rendtorff, Rolf. *Theologie des Alten Testaments. Ein kanonischer Entwurf. Bd.2: Thematische Entfaltung*. Neukirchen: Neukirchener Verlag, 2001.
Welker, Michael. *God the Revealed: Christology*. Grand Rapids: Eerdmans, 2012.
Westermann, Claus. *Genesis 1: Teilband Genesis 1–11*. Neukirchen: Neukirchener Verlag, 1983.

# 14

## Stress or Vocation

## Ethics and/in Work

*Edward van 't Slot*

### Introduction

To look at work and labor from a biblical perspective is to consider it in entirely different ways than one is commonly inclined to do.

Psalm 104 is a good starting point to illustrate this. It is a jubilant hymn about the richness of creation. All elements one can think of, in their immeasurable abundance of colors and shades, of sounds and smells, of ingenuity and simplicity, in their various positions in the immense broadness of the heavens, waters, and earth, have their own modest ways of reflecting different aspects of the greatness of their Creator. Human beings, rising from their beds early in the morning to fulfill their daily jobs and returning home after a day's work, only represent a small feature of this vast and detailed picture, as in a Brueghel painting. In the world of this psalm, it seems hardly imaginable that one would spend too much thought on the issue of human labor. Regarding one's own place in the picture, it seems worthwhile to be a working human being, growing one's food, to earn one's daily wage swiftly and earnestly (Lev. 19:13), if only in order to have the energy and opportunity to sing the praise of the

Lord. One of the greatest virtues for human beings, so it seems in the Psalms, is that they know about their consigned and limited place in creation: they are not God, perhaps a little more than the animals, that is: a little more conscious about their role in manifesting God's praise. It is the work of God which demands praise and attention; human labor serves only to this praise. Therefore, our work ought to be executed with a calm and deep attentiveness for the larger picture in which we are operating, and with a deep openness for the possibility of joy.

To a twenty-first-century reader it might almost seem an affront to be so lighthearted about one of the most important phenomena of human life: work. Working life explores our ability to add to the richness of creation, to contribute to the value of our own lives and to those of others. It is of great interest, no doubt, to consider "work" in this volume. Work plays such a determining role in our lives that it would be strange not to pay any attention to it. But the role of work, and our estimation of it, may very soon become far *too* determining for what it means to live as a human being. It may be ever since the nineteenth century, which gave rise to idealist and romantic ideas about individuals and their talents (and, if possible, their geniality), that people in Western societies tend to feel that the meaning of one's life is decided by the extent to which one has succeeded in living according to these talents. When considering the issue of human labor, its value, its ethical dimensions and dilemmas, it is important to bear in mind the psalm quoted above. If we tend to regard our lives as fulfilled and meaningful almost *only* to the degree that we are or have been able to do the work(s) we want(ed) to do, then one of the main perspectives of the entire Holy Scripture seems to relax our expectations on this point. There is more to life than work (Lk. 10:42).

These and similar nuancing lines about the importance of labor may be more than welcome in an era in which over-worked-ness seems one of the most common plagues in many societies. Due attention to the issue of *stress* will be offered in this chapter. During the nineteenth and twentieth centuries, labor has, alongside its idealistic and romantic image, played its positive role as one of the most emancipating powers for those classes whose work had been undervalued for ages. But emancipation and individualization seem also to have led to a great many individuals whose identities seem unhealthily related, almost exclusively, to their responsibilities in work, be it in their own self-view or in the way they feel addressed by society.[1] From a theological perspective, it is tempting, and not wholly unjustly so, to remind all these hard workers about the scandalous, counterintuitive, *and* liberating doctrine of salvation *without* any of one's own works. After all, the Bible seems quite straightforwardly dismissive of all human ideas about "works" which would "justify" our lives (cf. Eph. 2:9). For a Christian drowning in work and being busy may even be seen as a firm testimony of stubborn unbelief.[2]

But it is important not to oversimplify the difficulty. Work, after all, needs to be done, and it is not immediately clear how those theological truths can be helpful in finding an attitude in what needs to be done anyway. A more positive and appreciative biblical story about work can be told as well, and it is this story which will help in finding a theologically more profound (and relaxed) understanding of what it means to be a working being.

## Ethics in Work/Ethics and Work

A person who reads (sings and prays) Psalm 104 may get the impression of the wholesome *limits* which are given to human beings and human work. There is a natural and self-evident space assigned to human labor: in the vastness of creation and in the ever-ongoing rhythm of night and day, there is this relative and modest thing to which people are called—to do their jobs, mostly during the day-time, as long as the sun serves with its light (an idea which may provoke some thoughts in an age of electricity and 24/7 economics). Within their jobs, of course, they confront issues about how to practice their trade, how to do their work well, and with issues that call for ethical decisions in instances like conflict or conflicting values. This is what I will call, rather simplified for the sake of clarity: ethics *in* work.

---

[1] Cf. Oliver O'Donovan, "The Communication of Work," in *Entering into Rest: Ethics as Theology* (Grand Rapids: Eerdmans, 2017), 121–7.
[2] This is accentuated emphatically with regard to busy *pastoral* workers by Eugene Peterson, "The Unbusy Pastor," in *The Contemplative Pastor: Returning to the Art of Spiritual Direction* (Grand Rapids: Eerdmans, 1993), 17–25.

Psalm 104 also makes us aware of the *goals* of our work. The psalm locates the picture of working people within the greater theatre of creation praising the Lord and asking him for its sustenance: our works, and more importantly *we* as the work*ers*, are assigned to deliver our parts in sustaining ourselves and our surroundings, and, above all, in the praise of our Creator. That is to say that our work serves, and has to serve, goals which go beyond the working sphere itself. This means that work is not only (and not in the first place) a means to self-fulfillment, nor to fulfilling the targets of our working context, but to relating to creation in a more general sense. We will draw our attention to this issue of work regarding these broader goals of life, or of ethics *and* work, in the largest section of this chapter, and we will return to the issue of ethics *in* work only at the end. By then, the insights gained about ethics-and can provide us with some evident conclusions about ethics-in.

This distinction between ethics-and and ethics-in is reflected in a remark by Dietrich Bonhoeffer in his *Ethics*. In this passage, Bonhoeffer reflects on *Beruf*, which might be best translated as "profession-as-vocation," which must be

> understood simultaneously in all its dimensions. The call of Jesus Christ is the call to belong to Christ completely; it is Christ's address and claim at the place at which this call encounters me; vocation comprises work with things and issues [sachliche Arbeit] as well as personal relations; it requires "a definite field of activity," though never as a value in itself but only in responsibility to Jesus Christ.[3]

Bonhoeffer seems to distinguish between *sachliche Arbeit* ("things and issues") on the one hand and "personal relations" on the other, between the "definite field" connected with one's working sphere and one's broader "responsibility to Christ." Of course, it is important to pay attention to the ethics involved in exercising, for

---

[3]Dietrich Bonhoeffer, *Ethics, Dietrich Bonhoeffer Works* 6, ed. Clifford Green, trans. Reinhard Krauss et al. (Minneapolis: Fortress Press, 2009), 292–3; cf. Bonhoeffer's essay on "Personal- and Objective Ethics," in *Conspiracy and Imprisonment, 1940–1945, Dietrich Bonhoeffer Works* 16, ed. Mark S. Brocker, trans. Lisa E. Dahill (Minneapolis: Fortress Press, 2004), 550–62.

instance, the job of a medical doctor,[4] or in whatever profession one practices (ethics-in); but this kind of ethics ought never to be regarded in isolation from the person one is in relation to Christ and to fellow humans, nor from the broader field of society in which we exercise our professional tasks (ethics-and). As persons, as *called* ("vocated") persons, we are far more than the professionals doing our jobs, even in professional circumstances. It is important to bear in mind this interconnectedness of "professionality" and "personality," and of profession in a narrow sense and of vocation in a wide sense, when dealing with "professional ethics." More importantly, although less self-evidently, in this quote, Bonhoeffer stresses that no professional issue has its own substance *apart* from the seemingly more personal call of Christ. (For this reason, we will explore the issues of "ethics-and" in the first place, and "ethics-in" only in the second instance.)

Another important point made by Bonhoeffer in this connection is (again) about the limits of work. When he introduces his ideas about divine "mandates" for the very first time, "work" is the first sphere of life he sees in this light,[5] besides the spheres of marriage, government, and church. He sketches these as interconnected, but nevertheless, they serve their own issues of life in their own right, and it would be unjust to make one of them absolute as opposed to the other spheres. Neither government nor work should rule out the course and way of life of marriage or church. So, it is important to bear in mind the *limited* field of each of the mandates.[6] If work pervades all spheres of one's life, it is clear that one has lost the right view of the *relative* claim work may have over one's life.[7] This is another reason to think about ethics and work from the broader perspective of life as a whole.

---

[4]Bonhoeffer, *Ethics*, 293.
[5]Ibid., 68–71.
[6]Ibid., 72.
[7]Ibid., 69–70.

## Ethics and Work: Profession and Vocation

In Protestant theology, traditionally *and* paradoxically, the issues of profession (or of profession-as-vocation) are dealt with in connection with the highly eschatological phrases Paul utters about one's calling (i.e., vocation) in 1 Cor. 7:17-31. In these verses, one's professional status (and even the whole of one's living conditions) is clearly not identical with the call to live as a loving Christian,[8] but these are connected paradoxically. In Luther's translation, and likewise in the King James Version, there is an ambivalence which has had its consequences in the theological reception of the idea of "profession-as-vocation":

> Luther's Translation: "20 Ein jeglicher bleibe in dem Beruf, darinnen er berufen ist. 21 Bist du ein Knecht berufen?"
>
> KJV: "20 Let every man abide in the same calling wherein he was called. 21 Art thou called (being) a servant?"
>
> NRSVUE: "20 Let each of you remain in the condition in which you were called. 21 Were you a slave when called?..."

In the older versions, Paul's words about the "vocational condition" (ἐν τῇ κλήσει, v. 20) in which one can be "called as a slave" (δοῦλος ἐκλήθης, v. 21) could be read as if one could be called *to be* a slave, or to the profession of slavery. Such a reading could, if applied to professions in general, give rise even to the idealist or romantic ideas about one's vocation *and* profession which we have seen before, in which the ultimate sense of one's self-fulfillment becomes closely tied to one's work and its fortune. In order to rule "out ... disastrous misunderstandings"[9] like these, Dietrich Bonhoeffer takes quite some trouble to disconnect the ideas of vocation and profession, or at least, to qualify the connection between both. From a careful re-examination of Paul, Bonhoeffer redefines "vocation" (*Beruf*) as

---

[8]Cf. Brian Brock and Bernd Wannenwetsch, *The Malady of the Christian Body: A Theological Exposition of Paul's First Letter to the Corinthians*, vol. 1 (Eugene: Cascade, 2016), 150.

[9]Bonhoeffer, *Ethics*, 290.

"the *place* at which one responds to the call of Christ"[10] ("this *life* is now my vocation [*Beruf*]"),[11] which sets us "limited task[s]" in a *professional* sense, but mainly calls us to a *responsibility* in a broader sense.[12]

This does not mean, however, that there is no connection at all between vocation and profession. The New Testament's attention, especially for slaves as being free in Christ (cf. 1 Pet. 2:15-20), brings Oliver O'Donovan to the observation that the Bible witnesses to a

> Christian revaluation of work, which allowed the socially neglected to find themselves recipients of a high vocation that passed through and transformed the menial tasks they confronted on a daily basis . . . menial work was a royal road to dignity of the highest order.[13]

Whatever professions Christians practice, since their jobs are only part of a contingent worldly "scheme" (σχῆμα) which is in the process of passing away (1 Cor. 7:31), these can and should be performed in an unshakable consciousness of freedom. It is the Christians' vocation to freedom (cf. 1 Cor. 7:24) which accounts for the ultimate justification or fulfillment of their life, and which, as such, determines the worth they attach to their provisional, penultimate situation in a practical and professional sense.[14] "[And] yet," Giorgio Agamben notes in his explanation of 1 Corinthians 7:29, "it is precisely, and above all, in these penultimate realities that an ultimate reality bears witness and is put to the test."[15] It is in (among other things) our professions, that our vocation can find its proper expression. And in this revaluation of professional vocation, the scope of work-as-vocation expands extensively.[16] Vocation can

---

[10] Ibid., 291. (My emphasis.)
[11] Ibid., 290. (My emphasis.)
[12] Ibid., 291.
[13] Cf. O'Donovan, "The Communication of Work," 130.
[14] For the distinction between "ultimate" and "penultimate" see Bonhoeffer, *Ethics*, 146–70.
[15] Giorgio Agamben, *The Church and the Kingdom*, trans. Leland de la Durantaye (London: Seagull Books, 2012), 19.
[16] Cf. O'Donovan, "The Communication of Work," 133.

be expressed in a great range of professions and in many working spheres, albeit relatively and provisionally.

In these working spheres, many professionals have been blessed with *colleagues*. Colleagues *are* a blessing, though often, admittedly, a puzzling one. It is not always easy to appreciate differences in professional style, but part of the "vocation" perspective may be, that professionals are called (not only by God, but also by their managers) to (be willing to) learn from one another, and not to be ashamed of some of one's own lesser professional qualifications: those were, after all, to be expected. Nobody starts as the perfect professional; no one ever acquires utmost perfection if only because a person's character, so basic in one's performance even as a professional, will never stop to evolve. Again, it may be helpful to realize, that all these different colleagues are *called* professionals: called by *one* vocation, in different guises. This insight may help one to commit oneself to stable and cooperative working relations, in which, together, people will continue to discover new proper expressions of their common vocation.

## Profession, Character, and Vocation

Although, ideally, vocation is distinctive for how one understands their life and, thus, for their formation as a person and while, ideally, vocation is also decisive for the way in which one practices one's profession, it is also true that, conversely, the other person's identity will often be formed to a large extent by the professional skills and virtues one has learned in one's professional formation. If I need to work very precisely as a craftworker, the habit of working and expressing myself very precisely is quite likely to become an integral part of who I am as a person, in my personal sphere as much as in my professional working place. Moreover, the way in which both vocation and profession are exercised is, of course, to a large extent dominated by the personal style, or character, of the one who performs the job. One pastor, or medical doctor, or bus driver, differs from another in the performance of one's job in many ways, although both may share the same professional education and values. As O'Donovan expresses:

> with what we are equipped to give, [we can] mold [our work] creatively and return it to the world as a cultural contribution...

[We can] bring the resources of [our] gifts and personalities to bear on them.[17]

If we picture this interconnectedness of one's professional life *as* a professional, *as* a distinctive person, and *as* a called person, then it can be presented as a triangle, in which, ideally, the three angles of professional skills, personal character, and vocation are balanced in such a way that all three perspectives play their own, appropriate part in one's professional life. The professional-vocational axis can "bear" the person in a stable professional life.[18]

This model can be used to reframe and elucidate some of the problems professional workers meet, in which, often, the vocational perspective is the promising factor which may add new vistas in working situations. In the practice of supervising pastors, for instance, this triangle may offer insights to a young minister, who, being trained in the professional skills of church ministry (the perspective of profession), may nevertheless feel very restrained in taking the lead or in exercising her authority ("what authority?") in her first congregation. "Who am I after all," she says, "that I should exercise any authority at all?" She may feel too young or too inexperienced for the situation (the personal perspective, of character and personal development). For her it is helpful to be advised that she is focusing on only one angle, or, rather, on one side of the triangle. Yes, she *is* a starting professional and a young person, but because of her education and how she is expected to perform by her bishop or by her congregation to fulfill her role as a professional, she is also a person *called into the ministry*, called by the church, and/or by God (the perspective of vocation in this case: the vocation of ordained ministry, *Amt* in German). This lends her an authority, and raises expectations from her congregation in a way that is unaffected by her personal and professional hesitations. This perspective will help the young pastor to view her own work in a new light, and to take up this role, to answer her calling, more freely.

---

[17]Ibid., 119–20.
[18]Cf. Gerben Heitink, *Biografie van de dominee* (Baarn: Ten Have, 2001), 266–70; Frans Siegers, *Handboek supervisiekunde* (Houten/Mechelen: Bohn Stafleu Van Loghum, 2002), 249–50.

We may note in passing that this example makes immediately clear that these three perspectives of person, profession, and vocation are embedded in the broader professional context, and are dependent on interactions, expectations, relations, and the normative frames of this context (in this example: the context of congregation and church).[19] Practicing one's profession in a well-balanced way will mean exactly this: responding to the call of this context in a communicative way, engaging those present in this professional context freely, professionally, and personally. Vocation, moreover, and "authority" will often be connected precisely by this "call from a context": *in* one's vocation, the one who is calling is always implied, granting the proper authority to the professional. Thus, a professional can often be regarded as a representative of the calling instance, which may even explain the sometimes-archetypal tinge of some of those representative jobs, and also some of the hesitations to apply this "authority" to oneself.

But it is not only the young pastor from our example who has received a vocation. Something very similar may apply to, for instance, an experienced drug store employee, who is confronted unexpectedly with a homeless person who needs some aspirin, but who has no money. The professional drugstore rules are very likely to forbid its employees to give away aspirin for free. The employee herself may, as a person, feel very reluctant to let this client have some aspirin or she may, on the contrary, feel inclined to be kind and indulgent toward homeless people. In any case, she is, by the power ascribed to her, simply by her being-the-employee-in-service, called to make a decision. In this call very different values play distinguished roles (what actions would serve the client, society, the drugstore, the employee's own rest, etc. the best?). The perspective of vocation may, at first, only seem capable of complicating the issue at stake, and of making the employee suspicious of her first inclinations. But it could also be the case that the perspective of vocation, or of freedom, is given to us to do exactly that: to set us free from self-evident rules, and to offer a space to give our full attention to the situation (e.g., in the professional sphere) in its robust concreteness.

---

[19]Cf. O'Donovan, "The Communication of Work," 114, 124–6.

So, while in many cases the vocational point of view adds new perspectives to the professional way of dealing with ethical issues in work, and to personal inclinations, ideally these three points of view are in balance in one's motions in one's professional life. The vocational point of view, particularly, seems capable of connecting person and profession (ethics and work) in a rich and fertile way. It sets the called person *free* and gives one the authority to execute one's profession in a professional but also in one's distinctive personal way.

## Profession, Goals, and Limits (on Stress and Career-making)

One of the greatest worries in many professional lives, in "Christian" professional lives as much as in any other, concerns avoiding "burn-out." Work often exceeds its limits and extends into the personal sphere; often, working pressure rises to unhealthy levels. Stress and burn-out are one of the evident flip sides of the working ethos of which so many people boast. While it would not be wise to simplify this enormous issue, still, some of the following remarks, all connected to what we up to this point have found about ethics and work, may offer a few helpful perspectives on this tendency.

First, there is the motive found in Psalm 104. Our jobs, of course, must be done, but if our jobs hinder us in the goal of praising the Creator, this indicates that work has passed beyond its limits, and we have to ask ourselves what our own role in this respect has been? Are we still working toward the goal of praising our Creator, or are we "making ourselves important" by aiming at other goals which have silently become more important than this one?[20]

Second, closely connected to the eschatological motives referred to above, there is the Easter perspective. To refer to another significant passage in Paul's first letter to the Corinthians, the resurrection of Christ means that everything "belongs to" those who are in Christ (1 Cor. 3:22-23). Work will never add to that. So

---

[20]Søren Kierkegaard, "Christian Discourses: The Cares of the Pagans," in *Kierkegaard's Writings*, ed. and trans. Howard V. Hong and Edna H. Hong (Princeton: Princeton University Press, 2009), 21-2.

our jobs do not make us any richer in an essential sense. There is nothing essential that life cannot give us unless we would overwork ourselves. As Bonhoeffer puts it, Christ's resurrection prevents us from "the idolization of *death*" (my italics):

> Where death is final, earthly life is all or nothing . . . Where, however, it is recognized that the power of death has been broken, where the miracle of the resurrection and the new life shines right into the world of death, there one demands no eternities from life. One takes from life what it offers, not all or nothing, but good things and bad, important things and unimportant, joy and pain. One doesn't cling anxiously to life, but neither does one throw it lightly away. One is content with measured time and does not attribute eternity to earthly things.[21]

"Not demanding any eternities from life," nor from work (and expecting new life and fulfillment only from "the new human being," from Easter) is promising in many ways. There is no need to think of our work as erecting monuments for eternity (Ps. 119:96).[22] Nor is there need for the idealized or romanticized misunderstandings of vocation in which we demand that all work needs to be meaningful and fulfilling. We can relax and even be grateful in the sight of the provisionality of the things we wrought.

This Easter-belief even offers new perspectives on one of the important phenomena of post-modern societies: the issue of our *careers*. In Western society, one of the greatest virtues one can think of, is effectiveness in pursuing one's career. Our working life has to be squeezed until it has given its last drop, otherwise everything will be counted as loss, as nothing. Clearly, and certainly, the Bible would offer another view of "career." Easter nuances all expectations from a working life that do not follow from "the power that has conquered death." If work is being done in the belief that our penultimate jobs can express, but do not conincide with,

---

[21] Bonhoeffer, *Ethics*, 91–2. Quotations in the next two paragraphs have been taken from these pages.
[22] Cf. O'Donovan, "The Communication of Work," 114: "we celebrate the value God has set upon what is impermanent."

our ultimate vocation, then it will thrive, doubtlessly, but it will do so in different ways and with even greater satisfaction.

This means, a third perspective, that every part of our daily work can become a vehicle of praise: the tiny odd jobs should not be scorned as, at best, remotely connected, as unimportant means, to the one great productivity goal. Instead, they are *directly* connected to the one great task of God's praise. This insight from Benedictine spirituality can easily be applied in all work: God can be glorified in every job. So when I am dedicating myself to a particular professional task, then I may do so attentively. But when the time has come to turn to something different, then *that* is the thing to which I direct my attention. It is better not to let my mind roam to all the jobs I am *not* wielding at the moment.[23] And when the time for rest has come, unexpected works, and fruits, may accompany us—eschatologically and beyond control (cf. Rev. 14:13).[24]

In the fourth place, therefore, there is every reason to keep the sabbath, the resting day, or the festive day from which our working life springs. The sabbath is a crucial training school, not only to make time and space for rest and joy and praise, but even to celebrate the limits of our professional practice, and to learn to start only and always from this starting point.[25] As Robert van Putten puts it:

> The sabbath totally reverses the order of the three ways in which we [tend to] experience time. The sabbath is primarily emptied time (putting down our work and doing nothing), which leads

---

[23]See, for instance, Wil Derkse, "Gezegend werk: een benedictijnse kijk op ons dagelijks werk," in *Gezegend leven: Benedictijnse richtlijnen voor wie naar goede dagen verlangt* (Tielt: Lannoo, 2007), 81–98. The Benedictine motto, *Ut in omnibus glorificetur Deus* (Benedictine Rule, chap. 57), refers to 1 Pt. 4, 11.

[24]Cf. O'Donovan, "The Communication of Work," 128.

[25]Cf. Dietrich Bonhoeffer, "Meditation on Psalm 119," in *Theological Education Underground, 1937–1940, Dietrich Bonhoeffer Works* 15, ed. and trans. Victoria J. Barnett et al. (Minneapolis: Fortress Press, 2012), 496–7 ("... the beginning has already occurred ... the life with God consists not only and not essentially of ever-new beginnings."); Karl Barth, "The Holy Day," in *Church Dogmatics, Doctrine of Creation:* III/4, ed. Geoffrey W. Bromiley and Thomas F. Torrance (Edinburgh: T&T Clark, 1961), 50–76; O'Donovan, "The Communication of Work," 120–1, 134.

into fulfilled time (encountering the Eternal), after which the passage to productive time takes place again.[26]

In all of these motives, it is again the perspective of *vocation* which offers relaxation: nobody is ever called to exceed the limits of a life which can offer praise, to lead a life of squeezing one's time until the last drop, to work from another starting point than the remembrance and joy of the finished work of Christ. To be sure, these considerations may not liberate one from the plague of stress immediately, but if one allows oneself, hopefully, while being helped by benevolent colleagues, supervisors, and/or friends and family members, to deepen one's consciousness of these motives, they will, no doubt, offer new space to develop (and to relax) one's working attitude. These will, ultimately, change one's work itself.

## Professional Ethics (Ethics in Work)

Up to this point, our reflections about the goals of labor have also directed our attention to its limits. There is, as Bonhoeffer put it, no need to expect "eternities" from our work, and though the divine command to have dominion over the earth (e.g., Gen. 1:28; 2:15) may sound as an invitation to work hard to transform creation in permanent ways, the one really clear thing is that "dominion over" certainly does not mean dominion *against*, but rather dominion *for* the earth.[27]

This again calls our attention to the limits of what human labor may achieve beneficially. The idea that labor might be the expression of a "cultural mandate" without limits, can itself be seen as an expression of the optimistic, idealistic, and romantic ideas about

---

[26]Robert van Putten, *Een kwestie van tijd: Bezieling en professionaliteit in een verontruste wereld*, Lectorale rede (Ede: Christelijke Hogeschool Ede, 2023), 35. (My translation.)
[27]Cf. Dietrich Bonhoeffer, *Creation and Fall: A Theological Exposition of Genesis 1–3*, *Dietrich Bonhoeffer Works* 3, ed. John W. de Gruchy, trans. Douglas S. Bax (Minneapolis: Fortress Press, 1996), 61–7.

human vocation which, as we have seen before, tend to overstate the range of fulfillment that our works may produce.[28]

To be aware of the limits of work does not preclude our sight of the broad impact of work, including on our personal lives. Work issues can easily influence one's feelings about one's life as a whole, and one's happiness and sense of fulfillment beyond the working sphere. This is precisely *because* work has to do with vocation, with meaning, with relations, with one's formation and with being seen and valued as a person with one's own specific personal skills and characteristics. That is one of the reasons why "ethics in work" is still an important issue. It would be an unhelpful reduction to consider work only as a means toward an end: labor-in-itself is a phenomenon to consider ethically as well.[29] The Benedictine notion, mentioned in the section above, of attentiveness for every detail within work—because any detail-in-itself can serve to God's praise—is sufficient reason to give any working situation its due attention and also in an ethical sense.

Of course, it is easy to think of circumstances in which it is not so evident how work (in general, or in detail) could serve the great goal of the Creator's praise. As Bonhoeffer makes clear, it is exactly in those situations, in which things have become not straightforward and complicated, that ethical considerations are required.[30] If all available options seem to have unfavorable sides or consequences, can our works then still be proper expressions of our vocation? But it is exactly the perspective of vocation—as the eschatological call to be free and to act freely—which can help in making decisions and undertaking actions in situations like these, in which most of the time, *not* to act would be the worst decision. The perspective of vocation provides the *framework* in which one may feel free to

---

[28]Cf. Jan J. Boersema and Anthonia Boersema-Bremmer, "'The Wilderness has been Made to Blossom': Nineteenth-Century Dutch Immigrants and the Natural World," in *Sharing Pasts: Dutch Americans through Four Centuries*, ed. Henk Aay, et al. (Holland: Van Raalte Press, 2017), 25–50.

[29]Cf. Søren Kierkegaard, "Purity of Heart Is to Will One Thing," in *Upbuilding Discourses in Various Spirits, Kierkegaard's Writings*, ed. and trans. Howard V. Hong and Edna H. Hong (Princeton: Princeton University Press, 1993), 15: III; Bonhoeffer, *Ethics*, 88–9.

[30]Bonhoeffer, *Ethics*, 274, 366–70.

ponder, to decide, and to act: exactly as is shown for many cases in this volume.

This freedom can be understood as the divine permission,[31] to make use, for instance, of the concrete tools our professional context provides us with, such as the professional codes available, even if these feel too generic, too straightforward for the situation in which the professional may find oneself. To use this tool in decision-making, without hiding behind the tool, that is, to use it freely and to take responsibility for one's own decision, is exactly what a free and called professional has been called to.

Likewise, other tools and ethical points of view may be considered, when the professional situation is complex and a decision must be made. The call to survey any situation freely, in the light of the divine permission to make decisions, means that the professional is not exclusively bound to one ethical approach; one can think over the pros and cons of different points of view, the clashing values, and the different interests of the various persons involved, one's duties and the virtues called for, the goals and the measures of happiness involved—and decide. Karl Barth mentions the fundamental eclectic attitude toward philosophy which follows from one's call to freedom,[32] and the same can be said about one's attitude toward ethical models. Because of the provisional character of all human models, *and* because one's vocation may find room for expressing itself within this provisional sphere, one can freely, maybe even pragmatically, consider the different points of view, and be honestly open to their insights—and dare to make distinct decisions.[33] Considerations like these will train the professional's ear and sense for God's commandments, always in unique circumstances.

Again, it is the sober, non-romantic perspective of vocation which proves to be helpful: not to get stuck in all kinds of troubled considerations, but to reflect, to decide, and to act—to act freely.

---

[31]Ibid., 382–3.
[32]Cf. Eberhard Busch, *Karl Barth: His Life from Letters and Autobiographical Texts*, trans. J. Bowden (London: SCM Press, 1976), 387; cf., e.g., Karl Barth, "Philosophy and Theology," in *The Way of Theology in Karl Barth: Essays and Comments*, ed. H. Martin Rumscheidt (Eugene: Pickwick, 1986), 80–1, 93.
[33]See, for instance, Loy D. Watley, "Training in Ethical Judgment with a Modified Potter Box," *Business Ethics: A European Review* 23, no. 1 (2014): 1–14.

# Bibliography

Agamben, Giorgio. *The Church and the Kingdom*, translated by Leland de la Durantaye. London: Seagull Books, 2012.
Barth, Karl. *Church Dogmatics* III/4, *Doctrine of Creation*, edited by Geoffrey W. Bromiley and Thomas F. Torrance. Edinburgh: T&T Clark, 1961.
Barth, Karl. "Philosophy and Theology." In *The Way of Theology in Karl Barth: Essays and Comments*, edited by H. Martin Rumscheidt, 79–95. Eugene: Pickwick, 1986.
Boersema, Jan J. and Anthonia Boersema-Bremmer. "'The Wilderness has been Made to Blossom': Nineteenth-Century Dutch Immigrants and the Natural World." In *Sharing Pasts: Dutch Americans through Four Centuries*, edited by Henk Aay, et al., 25–50. Holland: Van Raalte Press, 2017.
Bonhoeffer, Dietrich. *Creation and Fall*, *Dietrich Bonhoeffer Works* 3, edited by John W. de Gruchy, translated by Douglas S. Bax. Minneapolis: Fortress Press, 1996.
Bonhoeffer, Dietrich. *Ethics*, *Dietrich Bonhoeffer Works* 6, edited by Clifford Green, translated by Reinhard Krauss, Charles West, and Douglas W. Stott. Minneapolis: Fortress Press, 2006.
Bonhoeffer, Dietrich. "Meditation on Psalm 119." In *Theological Education Underground, 1937–1940*, *Dietrich Bonhoeffer Works* 15, edited and translated by Victoria J. Barnett et al., 496–526. Minneapolis: Fortress Press, 2012.
Bonhoeffer, Dietrich. "Personal- and Objective Ethics." In *Conspiracy and Imprisonment, 1940–1945*, *Dietrich Bonhoeffer Works* 16, edited by Mark S. Brocker, translated by Lisa E. Dahill, 550–62. Minneapolis: Fortress Press, 2004.
Brock, Brian and Bernd Wannenwetsch. *The Malady of the Christian Body: A Theological Exposition of Paul's First Letter to the Corinthians*, vol. 1. Eugene: Cascade Books, 2016.
Busch, Eberhard. *Karl Barth: His Life from Letters and Autobiographical Texts,* translated by J. Bowden. London: SCM Press, 1976.
Derkse, Will. "Gezegend werk: een benedictijnse kijk op ons dagelijks werk." In *Gezegend leven: Benedictijnse richtlijnen voor wie naar goede dagen verlangt*, 81–98. Tielt: Lannoo, 2007.
Heitink, Gerben. *Biografie van de dominee*. Baarn: Ten Have, 2001.
Kierkegaard, Søren. *Christian Discourses: The Cares of the Pagans*, vol. 17 of *Kierkegaard's Writings*, edited and translated by Howard V. Hong and Edna H. Hong. Princeton: Princeton University Press, 2009.
Kierkegaard, Søren. "Purity of Heart Is to Will One Thing." In *Upbuilding Discourses in Various Spirits*, vol. 15 of *Kierkegaard's Writings*, edited

and translated by Howard V. Hong and Edna H. Hong. Princeton: Princeton University Press, 1993.

O'Donovan, Oliver. *Entering into Rest*, vol. 3 of Ethics as Theology. Grand Rapids: Eerdmans, 2017.

Peterson, Eugene. "The Unbusy Pastor." In *The Contemplative Pastor: Returning to the Art of Spiritual Direction*, 17–25. Grand Rapids: Eerdmans, 1993.

Putten, Robert van. *Een kwestie van tijd: Bezieling en professionaliteit in een verontruste wereld, Lectorale rede*. Ede: Christelijke Hogeschool Ede, 2023.

Siegers, Frans. *Handboek supervisiekunde*. Houten/Mechelen: Bohn Stafleu Van Loghum, 2002.

Watley, Loy D. "Training in ethical judgment with a modified Potter Box." *Business Ethics: A European Review* 23, no. 1 (2014): 1–14.

# 15

# The "Risk of Faith" and the Desire for Safety in a Security Society[1]

*Pieter Vos*

## Introduction

Safety can be regarded as a basic human need. Life is dependent on safe consumption of food, having the shelter of a home, and having the confidence that one is protected against violence and terror by legal authorities. In our time, we seem to fulfill our need for safety to a high extent through security-oriented measures and control systems. We no longer observe the condition of the fruit and vegetables we eat, but simply check the expiration date. We not only lock the door of our homes and offices but also secure them with alarm systems. Government regulations, risk management in companies and organizations, scientific calculations, and technical security systems must protect us against all sorts of possible

---

[1] This chapter is partly based on my former reflections on this topic in Pieter Vos, "Zonder garanties: Religie en de morele ambivalenties van een veiligheidscultuur," in *In vertrouwen leven: Tegendraadse beschouwingen over veiligheid*, ed. Ronald van Steden and Jan Hoogland (Amsterdam: Buijten & Schipperheijn, 2013), 68–80.

calamities. With all these measures we try to combat and, if possible, eliminate the uncertainty and insecurity that life confronts us with. However, security is not the same as safety.

The unprecedented health crisis that the COVID-19 virus caused worldwide demonstrated that our security systems cannot fully guarantee our safety. A virus could emerge in our high-tech controlled world that precisely should have protected us against such a virus. At the same time, we responded to this crisis mainly with the help of our high-tech handling of risks and diseases. In principle, there is nothing wrong with this. During the pandemic, newly developed adequate vaccines turned out to be a blessing. The ability to estimate the infection rate was of great importance. And taking measures that limited the number of infections was crucial for the sake of public health. The point that I want to make from a Christian ethical approach is not to criticize particular measures, but to open up a different perspective. Although there may be good reasons for criticism, such criticism often remains trapped in the same limited logic of a security-oriented approach, for example, when antivaxxers claimed that the vaccines are unsafe or that the government was deliberately robbing citizens of their civil freedoms. Christian ethics starts from the belief that the gospel addresses us on a deeper existential level and opens a different perspective on our safety needs.

## Ambivalence in the Desire for Safety

The German sociologist Ulrich Beck famously characterized late modern society as a *Risikogesellschaft* (risk society).[2] This characterization does not mean that we live in a time in which the threats have increased substantially, but that we deal with those threats in a different way. We organize and control our lives and activities in terms of risk. Living in a risk society means that we have a calculating attitude toward the open possibilities of our lives, which can turn out both positively and negatively and therefore asks for an ongoing anticipatory calculation. The Dutch

---

[2]Ulrich Beck, *Risk Society: Towards a New Modernity* (London: Sage Publications, 1992).

social psychologist Hans Boutellier explains well how the openness toward life is related to our desire for safety. Our preoccupation with safety through security control and risk management must be seen as the flipside of what he calls "the vitality of postmodern society."[3] The desire for safety is part of the social context of an unprecedented experience of freedom. This experience of freedom is expressed in the desire for fast, expressive, and emotion-oriented activities in areas such as consumption, entertainment, media, sports, and travel. In the risk society it is primarily our vitalist freedom that must be protected. This desire for risk-free freedom has a utopian character. According to Boutellier, maximum freedom and optimal protection are mutually related in this utopian dream. He characterizes this with the metaphor of bungee jumping: an ecstatic experience of freedom, yet danger-free.[4] We expect, for instance, that the apparatus has been tested thoroughly. If something goes wrong with bungee jumping, it is not those who jump who are responsible but the organization or "the authorities." In turn, the bungee jump organization takes out legal clauses and insurances in order to limit the risks and liability.

The desire for risk-free freedom is not only utopian in nature. It is also a constant source of new uncertainty and insecurity. Therefore, it generates a great need for new security. This creates a paradoxical situation: in order to lavishly celebrate freedom, it must be limited. According to Boutellier, living in a risk society means that we surrender freedom, whereby we expect the government to protect us as well as possible against all kinds of dangers.[5] This may explain why citizens were initially very eager to follow COVID-19 measures implemented by the government. After all, the vast majority of people understood that they were necessary to protect them. However, the paradox of strict measures to guarantee protection and precaution is not only that it limits our freedom and may even bring us close to a control state, but also that it increases our fears. This explains the increasing protest from people who considered such government measures as curtailing their freedom

---

[3] Hans Boutellier, *The Safety Utopia: Contemporary Discontent and Desire as to Crime and Punishment* (Dordrecht: Kluwer, 2004), 2.
[4] Ibid., xi.
[5] Ibid., 2.

or even as part of a conspiracy. The discomfort often arises when the government cannot meet our safety needs or when we have to surrender too much freedom for security reasons. For, despite the strict measures at that time, infections with the COVID-19 virus initially continued to increase. The experienced uncertainty and vulnerability are projected on the government, which at the same time is the institution that is expected to protect us against threats, which illustrates the inherent ambivalences of the safety needs in a risk society.

Note that the increased unsafety that people experience is subjective in nature. For instance, researchers point out that perceived unsafety does not correspond to the objective figures of a significant crime drop in past years. The felt unsafety is much higher than what crime and terror people actually face, especially in safe and prosperous countries like the Netherlands. Yet, particularly young Dutch people express their fear in terms of fear of war, migration, refugees, and terrorism.[6] The longing for safety seems to be more than objective unsafety due to the actual threat of viral infections, nuclear disasters, terrorist attacks, climate disasters, or financial crises. Rather, diffuse feelings of powerlessness and vulnerability seem to be hidden behind the need for objective security. These feelings are projected on visible phenomena such as crime and terrorism and express a strong need to protect ourselves against external risks. This is not to say that we don't need to take these subjective experiences seriously, on the contrary. But it would be misleading if we reduce the desire for safety to a question of more control and better security systems. The point is that by organizing safety as systematically as possible with security measures, we are not yet able to respond to the underlying existentially experienced uncertainty.

We can understand this existential dimension from the underlying idea of freedom in a security society. The vitalist concept of freedom seems primarily to be a form of negative freedom (being free from) that lacks a positive interpretation (being free to). After all, security only ensures that we are free from dangers and threats, but has nothing to offer when it comes to how we can best live our lives

---

[6]See, e.g., Beatrice de Graaf, *Heilige strijd: Het verlangen naar veiligheid en het einde van het kwaad* (Utrecht: Boekencentrum, 2017), 25–34.

freely. It is still an open question how to live in a world full of options that can be chosen. Boutellier remarks that many perceive this great freedom of choice precisely as threatening: "I can be anyone at all so who should I be?"[7] In this sense, vitalism itself is a source of fear and uncertainty. This raises the question whether the vitalist idea of freedom and the utopian desire for safety are really adequate to cope with the perceived threats and fears that accompany it.

## Existential Uncertainty: Anxiety and Freedom

All of this brings us to the more existential layers of our desire for safety. The longing for safety that is so characteristic of late modernity does not diminish our fears. On the contrary, there are all kinds of experimental indications that taking protection and security measures does not reduce fear but rather increases it. For example, those who always wash their hands due to the risk of contamination see this danger as increasingly real. Why else would you always wash your hands? The paradox of such behavior focused on protection and security is that it reinforces the perception of insecurity rather than offering safety.

This observation leads me to an interpretation of the obsession with safety that points to our underlying fears and anxieties. Risks are less manageable than we think. We wrongly believe that we have control over risks in the way insurance companies calculate risks. Many risks cannot be controlled because they are constantly related to changing circumstances and what we know about them. Ultimately, fear of potential dangers and threats cannot be overcome by making risk calculations and taking security measures based on them. Our time is no more frightening than earlier times. Only the nature and form of our fears have changed.

Our fears are related, among other things, to the fact that the self has become a "reflexive project," in Anthony Giddens's terms.[8]

---

[7]Boutellier, *Safety Utopia*, 20.
[8]Anthony Giddens, *Modernity and Self-Identity: Self and Society in the Late Modern Age* (Stanford: Stanford University Press, 1991), 32–4.

Whereas, traditionally, the process of becoming an adult and the development of an identity followed fixed patterns and the respective *rites de passages* (rites of passage), nowadays the self must develop in a reflexive process, in which personal and social changes must be constantly aligned. Late modern life is characterized by existential uncertainty about the lifestyle that one must choose from a large number of options. The individual cannot fall back on the safe haven of a tradition and community. People stand on their own and can only rely on abstract systems or "experts" that are supposed to provide what one lacks.

However, existential questions cannot be answered by systems or experts. These questions mainly arise during periods of crisis, both at the level of personal identity and at the level of society. Giddens points to the domain of intimate relationships. On the one hand, this domain offers great opportunities for self-expression. On the other hand, intimate relationships are risky because they are changeable, not settled and "open." This makes them a potential source of pain and anxiety. Or rather: in crises that people experience in life (a relationship that ends) a fundamental "existential anxiety" manifests itself. According to Giddens, this anxiety must be understood in relation to "the overall security system that the individual develops, rather than only as a situationally specific phenomenon connected to particular risks or dangers."[9]

In bringing existential anxiety to the fore, Giddens is a good student of both Sigmund Freud and Søren Kierkegaard. Both distinguish anxiety from object-concerned fear. While fear has a specific object, anxiety does not relate to anything in particular. We fear "something" such as spiders, getting on the airplane, a crisis, terrorist attack, hostile invasion, dangerous infection or whatever else there is to fear. In contrast, anxiety is not focused on something specific. In Kierkegaard's analysis (in fact, it is his pseudonymous author Vigilius Haufniensis) anxiety is related to "nothing."[10] That anxiety relates to "nothing" does not mean that it has no object at all. Rather, anxiety relates to something that is indefinite and

---

[9]Ibid., 43.
[10]Søren Kierkegaard, *The Concept of Anxiety: A Simple Psychologically Orienting Deliberation on the Dogmatic Issue of Hereditary Sin*, ed. and trans. Reidar Thomte and Albert B. Anderson (Princeton: Princeton University Press, 1980), 41.

undetermined. The indefinite is pre-eminently that which lies in the future and is therefore pure "possibility." This indefinite "something" evokes existential anxiety, that is, fear of the empty future, which is nevertheless one's own future. Anxiety is the fear that affects our lives *as such* and thus the "overall security system" that Giddens mentions.

In his analysis, Giddens mainly follows the psychological interpretations along the lines of Freud. However, I think that Kierkegaard's analysis enables us to better understand the *moral* ambivalences of security and vitality in late modernity. According to Kierkegaard, anxiety is closely linked to freedom. Anxiety is essentially fear of oneself, fear of being confronted with being a free being. However, anxiety is an ambiguous concept. It directs our attention to the possibility of our own freedom, but at the same time freedom is exactly what frightens us, which means that we lose freedom. In that sense, anxiety makes us unfree.

At the same time, according to Kierkegaard, anxiety marks the transition from an unconscious, immediate existence to an awareness of "the self." It is not without reason that Kierkegaard locates anxiety precisely where a person experiences maturing. Because freedom is not available without anxiety, anxiety is "an adventure that every human being must go through."[11] In this sense, anxiety has a positive meaning. In anxiety one becomes aware of oneself and of one's possibilities. Kierkegaard calls this "freedom's possibility."[12] The task is to relate this possibility to what is given as necessity, that is, as this particular person with all the limitations that one simply is.

According to Kierkegaard, human beings tend to avoid existential anxiety and as a consequence do not face freedom as one's own particular freedom. As a result, we end up in a situation where we lose our freedom. We do this, for example, by turning anxiety into fear. In doing so, we detect an object as the source of our anxiety and make it manageable. For where we have fear "for something," there is something to do: we can eliminate or make manageable what evokes fear. This is precisely what happens frequently in the dynamics of a security society in which we are

---

[11] Ibid., 155.
[12] Ibid.

continuously protecting ourselves against the risks that we fear. Kierkegaard shows us that we thereby avoid the actual challenge of our existential anxiety: becoming aware of ourselves as free persons. The freedom involved in Kierkegaard's concept of anxiety is not a negative freedom, as if it is a state in which there are simply no limitations, as in the vitalist concept of freedom. Freedom is related to givenness and this is precisely what makes it *my* freedom. According to Kierkegaard the self is constituted by two opposed elements. On the one hand, we are determined by what is given (in Kierkegaard's terms: necessity, the physical, the finite, the temporal): our own history, upbringing, body, our talents, and cultural background, and so on, in short: the entire contingency of being this person and not someone else. On the other hand, as a person one is free possibility (in Kierkegaard's terms: potentiality, the psychical, the infinite, the eternal). Because the self is as much possibility as it is necessity, freedom is not an unbound, indefinite freedom.[13] It is limited by the contingent givenness of our lives. Only if I acknowledge my limitations am I free to become this particular person, a self, a "single individual." This concept of freedom can serve as a correction to the vitalist concept of freedom in which maximal, expressive freedom without limitations is paramount.

Kierkegaard's existential interpretation of anxiety and freedom shifts our gaze from the external to the internal. The "safety problem" does not primarily concern external risks that threaten us and ask for security, but first and foremost the "self." This is in contrast to contemporary tendencies in which feelings of uncertainty, insecurity, and discontent mainly focus on the external world as the cause of our fear: "the politics" that do not take care of our concerns, "the banks" and their grazing culture, and "the strangers" who are the cause of crime and nuisance on the street. These concerns may or may not be justified for a wide variety of reasons—that is not the point, but on a deeper level, they often appear to be externalizations that conceal underlying "existential anxiety" given with human existence as fundamentally marked by uncertainty. The question is how we can relate to this fundamental

---

[13]Søren Kierkegaard, *The Sickness unto Death: A Christian Psychological Exposition for Upbringing and Awakening*, ed. and trans. Howard V. Hong and Edna H. Hong (Princeton: Princeton University Press, 1980), 35–42.

uncertainty. What might a Christian "grammar" of certainty and faith derived from the gospel reveal with regard to this existential (un)certainty?

## The "Risk of Faith" and Its Dialectical "Grammar"

Theologically speaking we can say that in trying to secure ourselves against uncertainty, we want to save our lives and enforce salvation. The gospel, however, reads: "For those who want to save their life will lose it, and those who lose their life for my sake, and for the sake of the gospel, will save it" (Mk 8:35, NRSV). If we want to save our life ourselves, we will precisely lose it. It is, as Kierkegaard writes in one of his upbuilding discourses, referring to this text, "an upside-downness that wants to reap before it sows."[14] Life is fragile, full of uncertainty, but we cannot save ourselves from that by establishing our safety by what Kierkegaard calls "finite certainty."[15] The word of the gospel interrupts such attempts: "those who want to save their life will lose it." The soteriology that is hidden behind any safety utopia is exposed as inadequate.

In addition to a focus on security, which can be legitimate in all sorts of ways (security checks before boarding the aircraft, strengthening NATO given the Russian aggression against Ukraine, testing for COVID-19 in case we have symptoms, etc.), we should acknowledge that our existential uncertainty requires a different approach, an approach that meets a deeper desire for safety and salvation.

Various theologians and Christian scholars have pointed out that we should talk not only about *securitas* (security) but also about *certitudo* (certainty or certitude).[16] We can learn something from this distinction that is not honored in current security thinking: that we cannot achieve safety only through external means in

---

[14]Søren Kierkegaard, *Eighteen Upbuilding Discourses*, ed. and trans. Howard V. Hong and Edna H. Hong (Princeton: Princeton University Press, 1990), 381.
[15]Ibid.
[16]Van Steden and Hoogland, *In vertrouwen leven: Tegendraadse beschouwingen over veiligheid* (Amsterdam: Buijten & Schipperheijn, 2013).

systems that are focused on *security*, but that we are in need of inner *certainty* that is religious in nature. Security can be regarded as a relative, finite good, but becomes problematic if its hidden but false promise is to provide us with "infinite certainty" as something that is in our own reach. According to Luther, who uses the pair of concepts illuminatingly, this path is an illusion: people do not have salvation in their own hands (by doing good works). On the path of salvation through Christ, where one can find *certitudo*, on the other hand, one receives salvation as a gift from God. This is not illusory, but the only certainty that really safeguards. At least, this applies to those who are prepared not to organize their salvation themselves and to take the risk to build on a certainty that they cannot control.[17]

How promising this perspective may be, yet it cannot end here. Because in this way it seems that the gospel offers an alternative solution to our safety desires. The path of salvation and *certitudo* in faith will then act as a solution, the only true solution that cannot be offered by security measurements. *Certitudo* then would offer a guarantee that *securitas* cannot offer. This would fall prey to the temptation to introduce faith and God as a final "troubleshooting" offered at the moment we as human beings can no longer manage things.

I don't think that the Christian faith aims to offer safety in this sense. In the gospel narratives "the path of salvation" fundamentally entails uncertainty, unrest, and risk. Time and again it is emphasized that those who want to follow Jesus must be willing to give up the safety of their home and hearth as Christ "has nowhere to lay his head" (Mt. 8:20; Lk. 9:58, NRSV). Apparently, believing means giving up the certainties of this world, even more: "If any wish to come after me, let them deny themselves and take up their cross and follow me" (Mk 8:34, NRSV). As Dietrich Bonhoeffer explains this text: "Those who enter into discipleship enter into Jesus' death. They turn their living into dying."[18] Being a Christian is not a safe but a rather risky affair. If faith has to do with *certitudo*, then this

---

[17]Cf. Niels Gregersen, "Risk and Religious Certainty: Conflict or Coalition?" *Tidsskriftet Politik* 8, no. 1 (2005): 22–32.
[18]Dietrich Bonhoeffer, *Discipleship, Dietrich Bonhoeffer Works* 4, ed. Geoffrey Kelly and John D. Godsey (Minneapolis: Fortress Press, 2001), 87.

"certainty" expresses itself at least paradoxically in a life that is marked by the uncertainty and insecurity of risking and even losing one's life at the same time.

Therefore, we cannot limit ourselves to just offering religious *certitudo* as an alternative to *securitas*. The nature of this *certitudo* must be deepened. The text of Mk 8:35 (and similar texts, such as Mt. 10:38-39, Lk. 17:33, and Jn 12:25) has a deeper meaning than just offering an alternative safety as a solution. Its "grammar" contains a dynamic that cannot be captured in a solution-oriented approach. The dynamic exists in a dialectic that does not dissolve and does not secure. We ignore this dynamic if we see the text as a methodical path that we can follow step by step: first we shed our illusory urge for self-organized security (because whoever wants to save his life will lose it), then we seek our salvation and our redemption where they can actually be found (we lose our lives for the sake of Christ and the gospel), and finally we find true safety (we "save our lives"). This would give the path of *certitudo* a new probability, which is essentially not different in structure to that of *securitas*.

But "what would it avail a person," Kierkegaard continues in the same upbuilding discourse, "if, double-minded and fork-tongued, he wanted to dupe God, trap him in probability, but refused to understand the improbable, that one must lose everything in order to gain everything, and understand it so honestly that, in the most crucial moment, when his soul is already shuddering at the risk, he does not again leap to his own aid with the explanation that he has not yet fully made a resolution but merely wanted to feel his way."[19] Then, according to Kierkegaard, you would force a "figurative victory" and convert the actual task into worldly calculation "changing God's gift of grace to the venturer into temporal small change for the timorous."[20] In our terms: the task of going the uncertain road of *certitudo* would be reduced again to the calculation of *securitas* if we see *certitudo* as a "solution" that has a new probability. The dynamics of the gospel word is diffused when it is made into a middle-purpose structure: I lose my life *in order to* save it.

---

[19] Kierkegaard, *Eighteen Upbuilding Discourses*, 381.
[20] Ibid.

The surprising thing about the dialectical inversions in the gospel text is that they make the dynamics continue. As soon as you think you can secure your life by following the gospel word, the same gospel word ironically strikes you in the back. It comes again into effect: "who want to save their life will lose it"! The text therefore contains a dialectic that is not canceled out. If there is a path of certification, it remains risky. Threat and risk in life are not eliminated by the certainty of faith, but rather acknowledged. The vulnerability of existence is not solved. Those who want to save their life by losing it for Christ's sake must always dare to lose it. For, salvation is really expected from elsewhere, completely beyond my own abilities and expectations. This becomes clear from the wider context of Mark 8. The words about the disciples who lose and save their lives follow after Jesus's announcement that he "must undergo great suffering and be rejected . . . and be killed" (Mk 8:31, NRSV). The risky road of discipleship is connected not only with Jesus's suffering, but also with the grace and joy that is contained in this suffering, as Bonhoeffer explains: "Discipleship is being bound to the suffering Christ. That is why Christian suffering is not disconcerting. Instead, it is nothing but grace and joy."[21] For it is *Christ himself* "whom disciples find when they take up their cross."[22]

## Implications for Living in a Security Society

What does this mean for how we should deal ethically with experiences of uncertainty and our desire for safety? Rather than providing a solution, the grammar of faith as "dialectical inversion" opens up a different space, which expresses the irreducible nature of faith. It opposes our thinking in terms of risk and security and provides an alternative to this language as a whole. This has two implications.

---

[21]Bonhoeffer, *Discipleship*, 89.
[22]Ibid, 91.

In the first place, the developed Christian perspective responds to what I referred to as "existential uncertainty." Behind our fear of all kinds of threats in a security society lies a deeper existential anxiety. This anxiety relates to our basic freedom that we cannot deal with adequately. One of our strategies is to replace anxiety with object-concerned fear. We try to protect ourselves against these dangers we fear by security measures. By focusing on the objects of our fear through security measures, however, we do not have to recognize the deeper existential anxiety. Faith is preeminently the "space" where we can face and overcome this anxiety. In the Christian faith, anxiety can be overcome by entrusting oneself to God. Such a belief is neither a solution to our security problems, nor an escape from society with its dynamics of risk and security problems, but does lead back to a deeper dimension of existence in which the ultimate ground, meaning, and purpose of our existence are at stake. The believer finds this ground, meaning, and purpose in a life *coram Deo* (before God), in which one no longer falls back on any self-established ground. In faith we acknowledge that life cannot be made but is received as a divine gift.

Second, faith conceived as letting go of securing the certainties of what is given and finding one's certitude in God, defines the basic Christian ethic from which security issues can be dealt with. It is precisely this ethic of letting go that makes it possible to relate to the dynamics of the security society in a different way. Being able to let go of certainties allows one to break the spiral of more and more security measures and control mechanisms. Rather, we acknowledge that every attempt to guarantee safety brings us new risks. New and more fundamental insecurities emerge at the end of every path to security. Take, for instance, the modern hospital that focuses on hygiene, health, and combating diseases. Precisely because everything is geared toward that, the hospital ironically becomes the place par excellence where people get infections that are extremely difficult to combat.[23] This example shows that every attempt to protect ourselves by security systems entails unexpected new dangers and risks. Instead of securing ourselves more and more,

---

[23]Erik Borgman, *Metamorfosen: Over religie en moderne cultuur* (Kampen: Klement, 2008), 50, referring to Zygmunt Bauman, *Modernity and Ambivalence* (Cambridge: Polity Press, 1993).

accepting existential uncertainty and finding the ultimate ground in faith provides us with an underlying trust that goes beyond what we can secure and is not based on pre-given guarantees. In faith, in which we entrust ourselves to God, we are able to accept at a basic level the insecurities and uncertainties of our late modern life.

In this respect it is interesting how Giddens links the concept of "risk" with "trust," which he describes in Kierkegaardian religious terms: "Trust presumes a leap to commitment, a quality of 'faith' which is irreducible."[24] According to Giddens, trust mainly concerns a basic sense of safety amid potential dangers inherent in daily life. Basic trust allows us to deal with the abstract and uprooted systems that are characteristic of late modernity. Trust in this sense must be distinguished from a form of trust based on prior knowledge. This applies, for example, to air travel. Knowledge and experience from the past provide a certain basis for whether or not to travel with a particular airline. In contrast, basic trust refers to what is absent in time and space. People cannot get direct certainty about this on the basis of expert knowledge or calculating considerations. Basic trust lies under the many choices we make in everyday life, since we do not fully know the exact functioning and intentions of people and systems that surround us. Our handling of risk and danger is therefore to be supported by a more basic trust.[25]

Entrusting ourselves to God does not mean that we can completely escape the moral ambivalences of a security society. Even those who put their trust in God and experience certainty in Christ live in a risk society. Both nonbelievers and believers have to deal with the inescapable problems of our time in their daily lives. Yet, there are better or worse ways to deal with those problems. The dominant narrative reveals an obsession with security, which in the end falls back on a modern belief in manageability that is untenable. We must therefore recognize that there are no final solutions. The "Christian grammar" as explained from Mark 8 teaches us that there are no guarantees for a safe and risk-free life. Rather, it makes us, late modern people, acknowledge that there are limits to the

---

[24] Giddens, *Modernity and Self-Identity*, 19.
[25] Ibid., 22.

manageability of our lives.[26] Also, it makes it possible to entrust the ultimate fulfillment of our lives and our life projects to God and thereby to a source that is beyond our own reach.

# Bibliography

Bauman, Zygmunt. *Modernity and Ambivalence*. Cambridge: Polity Press, 1993.

Beck, Ulrich. *Risk Society: Towards a New Modernity*. London: Sage Publications, 1992.

Bonhoeffer, Dietrich. *Discipleship, Dietrich Bonhoeffer Works* 4, edited by Geoffrey Kelly and John D. Godsey, translated by Barbara Green and Reinhard Krauss. Minneapolis: Fortress Press, 2001.

Borgman, Erik. *Metamorfosen: Over religie en moderne cultuur*. Kampen: Klement, 2008.

Boutellier, Hans. *The Safety Utopia: Contemporary Discontent and Desire as to Crime and Punishment*. Dordrecht: Kluwer, 2004.

De Graaf, Beatrice. *Heilige strijd: Het verlangen naar veiligheid en het einde van het kwaad*. Utrecht: Boekencentrum, 2017.

Giddens, Anthony. *Modernity and Self-Identity: Self and Society in the Late Modern Age*. Stanford: Stanford University Press, 1991.

Gregersen, Niels. "Risk and Religious Certainty: Conflict or Coalition?" *Tidsskriftet Politik* 8, no. 1 (2005): 22–32.

Kierkegaard, Søren. *Concluding Unscientific Postscript*, edited and translated by Howard V. Hong and Edna H. Hong. Princeton: Princeton University Press, 1992

Kierkegaard, Søren. *Eighteen Upbuilding Discourses*, edited and translated by Howard V. Hong and Edna H. Hong. Princeton: Princeton University Press, 1990.

Kierkegaard, Søren. *Søren Kierkegaards Skrifter*, vols. 1–28, K1–K28, edited by Niels Jørgen Cappelørn, Joakim Garff, Jette Knudsen, Johnny Kondrup, Alastair McKinnon, and Finn Hauberg Mortensen. Copenhagen: Gads Forlag, 1997–2013.

Kierkegaard, Søren. *The Concept of Anxiety: A Simple Psychologically Orienting Deliberation on the Dogmatic Issue of Hereditary Sin,*

---

[26] For an analysis of the manageability of life in late modern accounts of the philosophy of the art of living, see Pieter Vos, *Longing for the Good Life: Virtue Ethics after Protestantism* (London: T&T Clark, 2020), chap. 1.

edited and translated by Reidar Thomte and Albert B. Anderson. Princeton: Princeton University Press, 1980.

Kierkegaard, Søren. *The Sickness unto Death: A Christian Psychological Exposition for Upbuilding and Awakening*, edited and translated by Howard V. Hong and Edna H. Hong. Princeton: Princeton University Press, 1980.

Van Steden, Ronald and Jan Hoogland. *In vertrouwen leven: Tegendraadse beschouwingen over veiligheid*. Amsterdam: Buijten & Schipperheijn, 2013.

Vos, Pieter. *Longing for the Good Life: Virtue Ethics after Protestantism*. London: T&T Clark, 2020.

Vos, Pieter. "Zonder garanties: Religie en de morele ambivalenties van een veiligheidscultuur." In *In vertrouwen leven: Tegendraadse beschouwingen over veiligheid*, edited by Ronald van Steden and Jan Hoogland, 68–80. Amsterdam: Buijten & Schipperheijn, 2013.

# INDEX

Note: page numbers followed by 'n' indicates the note number(s).

Agamben, Giorgio 289
animals 141–3
  in the Bible 145–51
anxiety 306–9, 313
Aquinas, Thomas 268–9
Arendt, Hannah 173–9, 181, 187, 189–97, 203
Aristotle 26, 143, 268
artificial intelligence 57–73, 120
Ashworth, Andrew 21–3
Augustine 15–17, 24, 27–30, 65–6, 71

Barker, James 125
Barth, Karl 5, 143, 155, 235 n.26, 250 n.4, 256–7, 275, 298
Baudrillard, Jean 45
Bayer, Oswald 132
Beck, Ulrich 302
Benjamin, Walter 44–5
Berry, Wendell 43
Bethge, Eberhard 170
Bolcher, Henry 35 n.3
Bonhoeffer, Dietrich 3, 5, 63–4, 66, 69, 83–92, 109, 112, 159, 167–73, 175, 179–81, 234–6, 241, 286–8, 294, 296, 297, 310
Boulay, Juliet 53
Boutellier, Hans 302–3

Brock, Brian 76, 89, 93, 94, 136
Browning, Don 212 n.12, 220 n.20
Butler, Judith 187, 189–97, 200, 203, 204

Calvin, John 157–8
capitalism 37, 41, 42, 46, 49–50
care 42, 125, 214–15, 221–2
  caring communities 104–6
  crisis 100–3
  health care 100
  institutions of 113–14
  as life form 107–9, 111, 113
  participation in God's 112
  as witness 111, 113
Church 210–11
  ministry 291
  and surveillance 123–5
Clough, David 143
commodification 37–40
creation 37, 49, 53
  christocentric view 83, 85–6
  as eschatological notion 144–5
  fragility 87–9, 91, 93, 273–4
  (im)perfection 86–8, 274
  mandates 69, 109, 112–13, 179, 287, 296–7
  narratives 35–6, 68, 85 n.36
  stewardship 271–2

de Groot, Hugo 269–70, 279
de Lange, Frits 107
death 245, 294
  as curse 247, 249–50, 259
democracy 93–4
Derrida, Jacques 175, 178, 187, 199–201, 203, 204
disability
  impairment 78
  Jesus Christ 84, 87
  modernity 77–8
  ontology 82, 92
  social model 81
Douzinas, Costas 238

ecology
  ecological crisis 34–5, 49, 71
  environmental ethics 52–3
  nature 36–7
Eiesland, Nancy 84, 87
Ellul, Jacques 63
Enlightenment 24, 27, 47, 76, 93
eschatology
  new creation 68
  post-Christian 73
ethical deliberation 69, 70, 217–18
ethics
  categorical imperative 168–9
  consequentialism 60, 70
  deontology 60, 70
  eschatology and 150–1
  ethical theories 208
  and gospel 3–4, 7
  interruption and 216–19
  Reformation 9
  scripture 6
  situation 9, 171
  and the university 8, 10–11
  virtue 61, 70, 201–2, 212
Eucharist, *see* Lord's Supper
evil 65, 70, 203
  demons 65, 66
  transhuman powers 64–5

faith 128–9, 181, 202–3, 310, 312–14
Fall 47, 64, 91–2, 272
feasting 45–6
forgiveness 187, 196, 198–205
freedom 173–4, 259–61
  autonomy 76–7, 79, 90, 92–3, 107
  choice 24–5, 70
  Christian 289, 298
  existential 307–8
  for others 91
  risk-free 303–5
  of speech 187
Freud, Sigmund 306–7

Giddens, Anthony 305–8, 314
Globalization 3
God
  as Creator 88–9, 274
  divine care 48–9
  divine knowledge 131–2
  divine promise 180–1, 260
  divine provision 180–1
  kingdom of 155–6, 159
  *pro me* 126–30
  Word of 132–3, 137, 258
gratitude 46, 53, 272, 277
Greer, Germain 193–4

Habermas, Jürgen 102, 108
Hauerwas, Stanley 75, 81, 82, 144, 149–52
Heidegger, Martin 63, 251
Heikkilä, Melissa 120
heteronormativity 214–15
Hilpert, Konrad 232–3
Holy Spirit 89, 135–8, 275–6
Honecker, Martin 232–3
Hope 238–9, 252–3, 260–1
Horkheimer, Max 150–1
Hough, Mike 19–20
Huber, Wolfgang 229
humanity

# INDEX

as creature 48–52, 283–4
as dependent 92–4
dignity of 229, 230, 254, 258–9
fragility of 83, 87–8, 312
as prisoner 15
self-determination 76–7, 92–3, 248
*theosis* 67
will 15, 25, 26

idolatry 135
image of God 89–92, 229, 254, 268, 270
*analogia relationis* 90
impurity 68–9
intellectual property 279–80
Iwand, Hans Joachim 114, 128–9

Jacobson, Jessica 19–20
Jay, Martin 179
Jesus Christ 65
   cross 85–7, 89, 128, 203, 237–8, 249–50
   for us 127–8, 133, 138
   incarnation 218, 237
   mediator of creation 88–9
   prisoner 14–15, 30
   raising the dead 28
   as reality 83–8
   resurrection 87, 89, 93, 128, 203, 238–9, 250, 252, 259, 293–4
just war 71
justice 188–9, 197, 205
justification 229

Kant, Immanuel 27, 76, 128, 134, 168–70, 178
Kennedy, Greg 39–40, 52
Kierkegaard, Søren 5–6, 187, 198–9, 201–4, 306–9, 311

lament 259
Laube, Martin 77
Locke, John 46, 270–1
Lohmann, Friedrich 232, 233
Lord's Supper 34, 47–8, 50–1, 53–4
Luther, Martin 3, 5, 27, 47–9, 111, 126–35, 168 n.8, 170 n.17, 172, 175, 179–80

McEwan, Ian 64
McIntyre, Alasdair 62
Mâle, Emile 15
Marcel, Gabriel 219
medicine 246, 279–80
modern humanism 75–6, 93
Moltmann, Jürgen 88 n.44, 235
monasticism 16, 211
natural law 268–71
neurobiology 61
Nussbaum, Martha 144

O'Donovan, Oliver 63, 64, 289–91
Orwell, George 120

Pelagius 15–17, 27
personal mitigation 19–21
Peters, Albrecht 172 n.24
Piketty, Thomas 266
Plato 174–5, 213 n.16
politics 173–81
poverty 43–4
praise 271, 277, 283–4, 293, 295, 297
preaching 129–30, 133
Priestly, Joseph 27
private property 266–7, 270
Puffer, Matthew 169 n.11
Pyper, Hugh 203

Raedel, Christoph 154–5
reality 171–2, 176–81
reason 76–7, 92–3

recycling 41–2, 50
Reichold, Anne 237
Reinders, Hans 94
Reiner, Robert 24 n.31
Repentance 50
Ricoeur, Paul 25, 110–11, 113
rights
 of AI 71–2
 and Christian ethics 220–2, 241
 and Christology 236–9
 property 266–73
 and sin 240
 theological foundation 232–6
risk society 302–3, 314
Ritschl, Dietrich 79–81, 86
Rorty, Richard 232
Rosenberger, Michael 152–4

sabbath 272, 295–6
St Benedict 16
sanctification 157–8
Schoberth, Wolfgang 81
Schuurman, Egbert 65
secularism 26, 35
Sewell, Graham 125
sin 24, 25, 28–9, 52, 133–4, 238
 bondage of the will 24, 26, 27
 original 230
 unforgiveable 198–200
Sölle, Dorothee 237
Solnit, Rebecca 120
Song, Felicia 137
spiritual discernment 135–6
Srinivasan, Amina 199 n.42
Stoddart, Eric 131 n.49
suicide 255–7

Sullivan-Dunbar, Sandra 222 n.23
supererogatory work 156–8
Swinton, John 78, 82 n.28, 87 n.43, 94

technology 63–5, 119–20, 131–2, 137
 and death 246
 temptation 256–8, 260
Tett, Gillian 123
theological anthropology 79
 christological 81–3, 87, 90–1
transhumanism 62, 67–8
Tronto, Joan 108–9

Ulrich, Hans 145

van Putten, Robert 295
veganism 142, 150, 154–6
vegetarianism 142, 149, 151–2, 154–6, 158–9
Virgil 149
virtual reality 57, 72–3
*vita passiva* 246–52, 254–6
vocation 286–93, 296–8
Von Hirsch, Andrew 21–3

waste 33–54, 278–9
Waters, Brent 66–7
Weber, Max 102
West, Cornell 52
Witschen, Dieter 156 n.53
Wittgenstein, Ludwig 107
Wolf, Ernst 109
worship 46–54, 247, 252

Žižek, Slavoj 34–6, 52
Zuboff, Shoshana 131